'I have named it the Bay of Islands...'

'I have named it the Bay of Islands...'

Jack Lee

HODDER AND STOUGHTON
AUCKLAND LONDON SYDNEY TORONTO

Copyright © 1983 Jack Lee
First published 1983
ISBN 0 340 338784

Typeset by Computype Services Ltd, Wellington.
Printed and bound in Hong Kong for Hodder & Stoughton Ltd
44-46 View Road, Glenfield, Auckland, New Zealand.

Contents

Author's Note 9

Introduction 11

1. Lieutenant James Cook 15
2. Marion du Fresne 19
3. Early Contacts 26
4. Tribal Movements at 1800 31
5. Maori Adventurers 37
6. Prelude to the *Boyd* Massacre 45
7. The *Boyd* and its Aftermath 52
8. Mission Settlement at Oihi 59
9. Southseamen and Missionaries 70
10. The Tribal Wars and the Missionaries 78
11. Inland Exploration 87
12. Troubles and Changes in the Mission 102
13. Kororareka 117
14. The Last Years of Hongi Hika
    and Their Aftermath 134
15. The Transition Period 150
16. The Pace Quickens 171
17. Disorder and Confusion 189
18. Chaos 203
19. Climax 221
20. Stagnation 240
21. War 252

Appendices 275

Bibliography 309
Index 314

ROSALEEN MERLE LEE

Dedication

He tohu maharatanga tenei mo taku wahine kua mate,
ko ROSALEEN MERLE
who was born at Okiato (old Russell) in 1922 and
died in 1977
Our grandchildren are the sixth generation from
WILLIAM COOK,
a shipwright who settled at Kororareka *circa* 1823,
and
TIRAHA,
daughter of the Ngapuhi chief
PAPA HARAKEKE,
and his wife
KOPU,
a Kapotai woman
of the Bay of Islands,
and are descended from
RAHIRI,
the great ancestor of Ngapuhi,
through both the wives
AHUA-ITI and WHAKARURU

The publishers gratefully acknowledge a grant from the Maori Purposes Fund Board to assist the publication of this book.

Author's Note

THOSE WHO ARE genuinely interested in the history of the north have little literature available to them which is authoritative and at the same time easily digestible. Such books that do exist on the Bay of Islands tend to emphasise the activities of missionaries there, almost to the exclusion and often to the derogation, of the commercial ascendancy which the Bay achieved in the Pacific in the early nineteenth century. Similarly, the role of the Maori, and the way in which his underlying political situations influenced events there have usually been only lightly touched on. The popular conception of the Bay of Islands is therefore dominated by legends of the missionaries and their animosity to the inhabitants of Kororareka, now Russell — the 'Alsatia of the Pacific'.

This has led me to offer to the general reader a wider view of the subject. My old friend Gilbert Mair, a grandson of a settler at the Bay in 1824, referred me to a letter written to him about 1914 by the late Dr Robert McNab, New Zealand's great shipping historian: '. . . when Dr McNab was writing up New Zealand . . . he said, "the mission records are all right as far as they go, but only tell the one side of things & that from the Missionary point of view . . ." ' Mr Mair continued, 'I have seen in print myself such statements as, "beyond the Missionaries & a few traders all the others at the Bay of Is . . . were either escaped convicts or runaway sailors".' Here it is hoped to demonstrate the enormity of such statements.

While sorting through the mass of evidence necessary to compile such a work, I have frequently profited from the willing assistance of many kind and helpful people. I do not name these here because of their great number and the inordinately long period this work has endured, making it impossible to recall and do justice to every individual involved. But now, whoever and wherever these kind people are, I here gratefully acknowledge their generous assistance.

Groups who come readily to mind, however, are the staffs of the Auckland Institute and Auckland Public Libraries, the Turnbull Library, the Department of Internal Affairs, the Auckland Land Registry, and the Lands and Survey Department. To these, past and present, I offer my sincere thanks.

For research students, a more comprehensive copy of the original manuscript has been deposited in the library of the Auckland Institute and Museum.

To the Maori people who for over 40 years have been my friends — Ngapuhi from Mangakahia to the Bay of Islands, and from there to Hokianga — I am especially grateful, for they have been a source of information that few in these times are privileged to draw upon.

For inspiration I had my late wife Merle and her father, Leonard Schmidt. Their family owned Okiato — Old Russell — where they lived. Len was a man to whom the traditions of his home were living and real, since he was a descendant of William Cook, a shipwright who settled near Kororareka *circa* 1823. Cook's wife, Tiraha, was a distinguished woman of the Popoto *hapu* of Hokianga, and Kapotai of the Bay of Islands, descended from a long line of chiefs. My wife's family were surrounded by their relatives, five generations of whom have been born and have died at the Bay of Islands since the 1820s.

J.R. Lee
Kaikohe, 1983.

Introduction

I have named it the Bay of Islands, on account of the Great Number which line its shores, and these help to form several safe and Commodious Harbours, wherein is room and Depth of Water for any number of Shipping.

On 7 DECEMBER 1769 Lieutenant James Cook sailed away from this bay, having duly recorded its newly acquired name on the chart he had made during the preceding week. Nowhere had his talent for place-naming nor his appraisal of a harbour been better demonstrated. Within 75 years, the Bay of Islands had become a focal point in the Pacific for trade and industry, as well as for every sort of commercial chicanery, land-jobbing and general lawlessness. Subject to a curious experiment in civil government and intensive missionary enterprise, within a short time these events would lead to open war, eventually eroding and destroying the ancient pattern of life of the proud people Cook had originally found there.

These 75 years may be conveniently divided into five periods, the first beginning with Cook and ending at the turn of the nineteenth century. Marion du Fresne's visit, and his death at the hands of Maoris at Orokawa Bay, occurred during this time. It was, however, a time of tentative and increasing contacts, when useful communication between seamen and the Maori people began.

During the second period, between 1800 and 1814, the relationship developed to the benefit of both Maori and Southseaman. Wood, water, fresh food, and the company of women were available in return for iron, iron tools and some firearms. Despite the taking of the *Boyd* in 1809 at Whangaroa, and the subsequent rough handling by whalers of the chief Te

Pahi's people at the Bay of Islands, this traffic continued so that when the Rev. Samuel Marsden established the Church Missionary Society's artisan-missionaries at Oihi in 1814, relations had been entirely restored.

The third period ended about 1830, and during it the impact of European contact and trade on the Maori was immense. The most significant outcome was the arming of the northern tribes with firearms, with which Ngapuhi war expeditions ranged far south, with appalling slaughter. At the Bay, the trade which had contributed to these events had also established the reputation of the port. It was now a widely used rendezvous for whalers, and as time passed, petty shore-based traders and a sprinkling of Pakeha-Maori settlers appeared. Whaleships refitted there, and some officers set up households ashore, presided over by Maori women. At the close of the period, the Anglican mission had little to show for 16 years of work, apart from its comfortable village at Paihia, and its outposts at Te Puna and Kerikeri. Influential chiefs had not been persuaded to embrace Christianity, or even display any serious interest in it, preoccupied as they were with their local and southern wars.

In the years between 1830 and 1840, tribal warfare declined, due largely to the deaths of the leading fighting chiefs, particularly Hongi Hika, the most active and successful of the protagonists. The missions were in full array, and Catholic, Anglican and Methodist denominations were represented. The Maori people, demoralised by war and disoriented by the influence of European culture, now turned to the God of the missions, who, it must have appeared to them, favoured the Pakeha in every way. Whatever motives inspired those converted to Christianity, they frequently put to shame the nominal Christians around them in the practice of their new faith. Commercial enterprise, now firmly established ashore, had become centred on Kororareka, where an undisciplined complex of tradesmen, merchants, grog-sellers and brothel-keepers catered for the needs of the Pacific whale-fleet. The citizens comprised deserted or paid-off seamen, escaped or released convicts from Australia, the ubiquitous trader, the occasional minor capitalist and professional, and often the half-caste children of these people. In the late 1830s, they were

12

joined by itinerant land speculators, who operated so intensively that in later years, the Old Land Claims Commissioner, Mr Dillon Bell, found that most of the 10 million acres of land then claimed throughout New Zealand, were purchased between 1837 and 1839. A significant body of 'respectable' settlers also existed by this time, some away from Kororareka, on their newly acquired estates along the shores of the inner harbour. Ship-chandlers, merchant traders and similar people were at the forefront of the rising clamour for British rule, and their rallying-point was the British Residency at Waitangi, where the luckless James Busby had been established since 1833.

In 1840 Captain William Hobson arrived at the Bay, and having proclaimed his Commission as Lieutenant-Governor, was successful over the next few months in inducing some 500 New Zealand chiefs to execute the instrument of cession known as the Treaty of Waitangi. This event, although it was not apparent at the time, marked the highest point in political and commercial achievement at the Bay of Islands. Hobson's eventual selection of Auckland as his capital struck a blow at the economy of the Bay from which it did not recover. Commercially it declined to the point where its European settlers were impoverished, and its Maori people no longer enjoyed the material things which had in part compensated them for the loss of their land and their authority. Unrest grew, encouraged by disgruntled Europeans, and in 1845 culminated in war with the embittered Maori element, led by Hone Heke and Te Ruki Kawiti, which inevitably ended in their defeat in the next year at Ruapekapeka.

The years have flowed over the Bay of Islands and have left a grossly commercialised playground where vigorous industry once thrived. But its beauty remains. Enclosed as it is between the two bold capes, Wiwiki and Rakaumangamanga (Brett), some 12 miles distant from each other, it contains many long and devious inlets which drain the country far inland, and converge to form a great, roughly semi-circular tidal basin wherein are sandy beaches, reefs and rocky points, and the many islands which inspired the name inscribed by Cook on his

13

chart in December 1769.

Kororareka itself, now Russell, lies with its back to the Pacific Ocean, on the inside of a peninsula which forms one shore of the largest tidal arm of the Bay. Opposite, on the western mainland, are Paihia and Waitangi, and a few miles upstream from these is the unpretentious Port of Opua. On this tidal river, and in the area described, occurred many of the events to be told here.

This is the story of the Bay of Islands. Although swiftly moving events overtook and destroyed it as a South Sea metropolis, it was here that New Zealand as a nation was born.

1

Lieutenant James Cook

THE PRESENCE OF Cook on the coast of New Zealand in the barque *Endeavour* during the last months of 1769 was incidental to an expedition to the South Seas placed under his command by the British Government, and equipped firstly to observe the transit of Venus at Tahiti, and thereafter to navigate from there to the south and west to determine the presence or otherwise of the 'great southern continent', a question which had caused much speculation among geographers since the early circumnavigations of the world. The first objective was achieved in August, and Cook sailed south to 40 degrees, then west on a course which, according to a prominent school of thought, should have brought him into contact with the continent. Instead, in October, he reached the east coast of New Zealand, just as Tasman, on a similar mission, had come upon the west coast 127 years earlier.

Having explored a little to the south, *Endeavour* returned and passed up the coast, and on 27 November 1769, came abreast of a great cape. On that day Cook wrote in his journal: 'At 3 passed the point of land aforementioned, which I have named Cape Brett in honour of Sir Piercy . . . Near one mile from this is a small high Island or rock with a hole pierced thro' it like the Arch of a Bridge, and this is one reason why I gave the Cape the above name, because Piercy seemed proper for that island. This cape, or at least some part of it, is called by the natives Motugogooo.'[1] Motukokako is in fact the pierced rock, which retains the name of Piercy Island perpetuating Cook's geographical pun. Cape Brett was then known by the Maori as Rakaumangamanga, a name suggesting the presence of a conspicuous leaning tree, now, with the name, long gone.

On the west of the cape, Cook found 'a large and pretty deep bay, in which there appeared to be several small Islands. The point which forms the N.W. I have named Point Pocock.' The Maori knew this as Wiwiki, a name that has generally prevailed over Cook's. Many fortified villages were observed, both on the mainland and on the islands themselves, and soon several canoes boldly approached *Endeavour*. Cook did not intend to linger here, and continued on his course, but near the Cavalli Islands, contrary winds prevented further progress north and the ship drifted back to Cape Brett.

During the next week, Cook met the local Maori people. Among these was the Hokianga chief Tapua, father of Patuone and Nene, who 75 years later was to form a contentious alliance with British forces. Patuone, whose reputed age was well over 100 years on his death in 1872, claimed that he was present as a child, when his father, Tapua boarded Cook's vessel from his canoe, *Te Tumuaki*.

Patuone later described [2] the appearance of *Endeavour* off Cape Brett when his father and others were fishing from canoes off Matauri Bay, some 10 miles away. 'I saw Cook's vessel. To meet it went the people in four large canoes. No. 1 was named *Te Tumuaki*, commanded by my father, Tapua, manned by 80 men; No. 2, *Te Harotu*, commanded by Tuwhera, with 40 men; No. 3, *Te Homai*, commanded by Tahapirau, with 40 men; and No. 4 named *Te Tikitiki*, commanded by Ne, with 60 men. The canoes were paddled to the vessel, the chiefs went on board, and my father received presents of garments, . . .'

The encounter was described by Cook in his journal: 'Between 300 and 400 Natives Assembled in their Canoes about the Ship, and to one of the Chiefs I gave a piece of Broad Cloth and distributed a few Nails, etc. among some of the others.' [3]

According to tradition, [4] the Whangaroa and Bay of Islands coastal areas were then in the hands of various *hapu* whose genealogies indicate that they may have been remnants of the Ngatiawa people, dominant in the north until the beginning of tee sixteenth century. But at about that time, due to pressure by the emergent Ngapuhi, many of them began to disperse, some migrating to the Bay of Plenty and to Taranaki, and others along both northern coasts.

Between 1700 and 1750, Ngapuhi from Hokianga gained

possession of land from these people at Kerikeri and the Mangonui Inlet, apparently by conquest. The fighting which had led to this was in reprisal for a war in which a Hokianga chief Taura-tumara, had been killed at Whirinaki, and his eyes plucked out and taken back to the Bay for ceremonial purposes.[5] This accounts for the presence of the Hokianga people and canoes that met Cook at Matauri Bay. But by the beginning of the nineteenth century, the whole of the Bay coast had fallen by marriage, default or war, to Ngapuhi Hokianga or to Ngapuhi Taumarere, as the inland division of that tribe was sometimes known.

Since progress to the north was prevented by wind conditions, Cook returned to the Bay after this encounter, and anchored his ship at 11 o'clock on 30 November, 'under the S.W. side of one of the many Islands which line the S.E. side of the Bay, in 4½ fathoms'. [6] Here, inside Motu Arohia, or Roberton Island, hundreds of Maoris gathered around the *Endeavour* in canoes, and at this stage the ship went aground at her anchor on a sandspit. While she was being moved into deeper water, the pinnace went off to take soundings, and an attempt was made by Maoris to board her by force. Later they tried to steal an anchor, whereupon Cook ordered a 'Great Gun' to be fired, and this restored order. At three o'clock Cook, Banks and Solander went ashore with two armed boats at a cove on Motu Arohia, where extensive cultivations had been observed, but further hostile manouevres occurred there, and since musket fire did not seriously discourage an attempt to seize the boats, the ship's guns were again discharged, whereupon, as Cook observed, the Maoris became 'as meek as lambs'. No more trouble occurred during the remainder of the stay here — a tribute no doubt, to the chastening influence of 'Great Guns'. De Surville's experience at Doubtless Bay a few weeks later was curiously similar. Here, in the same way, the Maoris evinced little fear of musketry, but were dismayed by heavy gunfire.

The *Endeavour* examined the adjacent shores during the next few days, and considering the time available, a reasonably good survey was made of the general outline of the nearer parts of the inner harbour and the immediate surroundings of the anchorage. At Manawaora Bay, Cook was particularly impressed by the size and quality of the fishing nets, one of which measured 2000ft in length. Of the 375 acres of Moturua Island, some 50 acres were under cultivation. The inhabitants of the Bay were clearly a brave, industrious and ingenious people.

On Wednesday, 6 December at 4 a.m., *Endeavour* stood out of the Bay, but the wind dropped, and as she drifted towards the eastern islands, the ship struck a reef, but freed herself, and resumed her north-westerly course at midnight.

So Cook sailed away, having inscribed on his chart names which we still use — Cape Brett, Piercy Island, Point Pocock, and Whale Rock, the reef on which *Endeavour* so nearly came to grief. 'I thought it quite sufficient ,' he wrote, 'to be able to Affirm with Certainty that it affords a good Anchorage and every kind of refreshment for Shipping.'[7] Later, he wrote that the Thames and the Bay appeared to him to be the most suitable parts of the country for settlement.

Although the explorer de Surville, in *St. Jean Baptiste*, was on the north-east coast some 10 days after Cook's departure from the Bay of Islands, and although their vessels passed each other near North Cape without either knowing of the other's presence, the French expedition came no further south than Doubtless Bay, which was named Lauriston Bay. Between Cook and the arrival of Marion du Fresne, some two years later, there is no record of European contact at the Bay.

---

1. Cook, James. *Captain Cook's Journal,* ed. W.J.L. Wharton.
2. Davis, C.O. *The Life and Times of Patuone*, p.7.
3. Cook.
4. Maori tradition transmitted to the author.
5. The Taonui Manuscript, p.41. Interesting confirmation of this is to be found in the deed of sale of 3000 acres of Kerikeri land to Mission families in 1831. This Deed was signed by Hokianga chiefs, or those having a strong Hokianga background or connections. (Turton, H.H. 'Turtons' Deeds of Old Private Land Purchases, No. 91.)
6. Cook.
7. Ibid.

2

Marion du Fresne

In MAY 1772, two and a half years after Cook's departure, the Maori people at the Bay observed two great ships cruising off the coast near Cape Brett. They were the *Mascarin,* commanded by Marion du Fresne, and his storeship, *Marquis de Castries,* under M. du Clesmeur.

Du Fresne's visit, like Cook's, was incidental to another objective. He was returning Ahu-toru, a native of Tahiti, to his home, from where he had been taken by Bougainville to France in 1769, and from there sent to Ile de France, or Mauritius, to await a passage back to the Society Islands. Du Fresne, a resident of Mauritius, a wealthy man and a competent seaman, offered to finance an expedition to undertake the voyage, and for this purpose, and in the interests of exploration generally, two government vessels were placed at his disposal. The expedition sailed from the island in October 1771, proceeding to the Cape of Good Hope, and from there the journey to the east commenced at the end of December. [1]

The two ships kept to the south of the 40th parallel, with the same objective as Tasman and Cook, and with as little success. No great southern continent appeared, but on 22 March 1772 Mount Egmont rose out of the sea. The ships, now distressed for want of water and supplies, battled their way up the barren west coast and round North Cape in severe storms, but the weather improved on the east side of the island, and on 1 May, they lay a little to the north-east of Cape Brett. They had come at last to the place which Cook had so recently declared to be suitable for their needs.

For three days *Mascarin* and *Marquis de Castries* cruised in this area, du Fresne noting Cook's Cape Brett, which he named Cap Quarre (Square Cape). On 4 May both ships approached the land and anchored on the outside of the islands Moturua and Motukiekie. On the way in, *Marquis de Castries* narrowly avoided striking on another of Cook's discoveries, Whale Rock, which du Clesmeur named Razeline Reef.

Du Fresne was unaware that Cook had been here, since he had left Mauritius before news of this had reached the island, but it seemed, on observing the reaction of the Maoris to firearms, that they were not unfamiliar with them. Two chiefs and their attendants who had boarded *Mascarin* at sea from canoes, became alarmed when the ships tacked away from the land, and this may have been due to their knowledge of de Surville's abduction of a chief from Doubtless Bay two and a half years earlier. However, the ships anchored and a lively trade quickly commenced, the French obtaining the fresh vegetables and other supplies they needed at bargain prices. As Lieutenant Roux of *Mascarin* remarked: 'For an old nail they would give any thing we asked for.'[2]

Since it was now clear to du Fresne that he had come to a place suitable to his needs, he went with Roux to explore inside the islands for a permanent anchorage, and found a harbour '...as safe as it is beautiful'. This they named Port Marion, after du Fresne, and on 11 May the vessels entered between Moturua and Motu Arohia, anchoring in the channel south of Urupu-kapuka, two miles east of Moturua, which was also named for Marion.

The expedition had several objectives here, the first of these being the care of the sick. A camp was immediately set up in a bay on the south-west side of Moturua at a place called Waipao[3], near a little stream. Here a hospital tent was erected, a small tent for the officers, and quarters for the guard. Supplies were now not a problem, and preparations for refitting the ships were therefore initiated at once. The ships were lightened and half-heeled for cleaning and repairs, and on 18 May a party went to the west in search of timber for spars. The *Mascarin's* longboat rounded Tapeka Point, which was named the Point of Currents, and crossed to the south-west side of the Bay. In a little cove, probably at or near Waitangi, excellent oysters were found, but no timber, and the party returned to the ships.

On the mainland due south of Moturua, the principal chief

20

of this locality, 'Tacoury' (Te Kuri) had his village, and the visitors quickly established a good relationship with the people here, and with those at Pikiorei's *pa* to the west, called Tangitu. Various opinions have been expressed as to the tribal name of these Maoris. White [4] knew them as Ngatiwai, Maioha [5] as Ngare Raumati, while S.P. Smith [6] states that they were Ngatiuru, and connected with the Whangaroa people. But Ngare Raumati is the name they were subsequently known by. There is no doubt, however, that the cordiality of their early relations with du Fresne contributed to the subsequent unguarded behaviour, which led to his death.

As work on the vessels continued, minor incidents occurred, none by themselves alarming, although it does appear that Lieutenant Roux, at least, was not entirely satisfied that the expedition was in no danger. One curious incident involved a negro servant of one of the ships, who, apparently intending to desert to the Maoris, stole a small canoe from Moturua, and, with two negresses, made for the mainland. About half-way across, and in danger of swamping, the man killed one of the women, apparently to lighten the canoe. The other very prudently leapt overboard at once and swam ashore.

But nothing had taken place that indicated that a dangerous situation might arise. Therefore, when the officers were informed of a fine stand of timber at the head of the tidal inlet now known at Clendon Cove, in Manawaora Bay, a camp was established there and preparations were put in hand for mast-making. The work began on 29 May, and on 6 June the spars were ready for transportation. During this operation a considerable number of Maoris had assembled near the hauling-party, and a greatcoat, a musket and a 300-pound anchor had been stolen. Alarmed, the officer in charge sent two men back to the mast camp for help, and du Clesmeur, who was in charge there, immediately despatched 12 armed sailors. Early next morning, a local chief, Rawhi[7], was captured and held for questioning. He accused Pikiorei of Tangitu of the theft and was released. The White paper, which is an account of the du Fresne incident, apparently by Hakiro, son of Kemara Kaiteke Tareha, a subsequent conqueror of this territory, states that the capture of the chief 'exasperated the natives, who collected from Ngapuhi, Waimate and Hokianga to avenge the insult thus given, and dividing into parties each numbering 100 they waited a proper opportunity to carry into effect their revenge'. Clearly Rawhi was a Ngapuhi. Kelly [8] confirms that the presence of the ships had attracted Ngapuhi, including Ngatihine, from inland, and that these people were acquainted with du Fresne and had visited him. Ngapuhi, who were related to the Ngare Raumati by marriage, may therefore have influenced Te Kuri and Pikiorei to participate in the tragic events which followed.

Lieutenant Roux later visited the mast camp and was told of the anchor incident and its consequences. This, and other incidents he had witnessed on his shooting expeditions, disturbed him. Du Fresne, confident of his prestige with the Maoris, had entertained no fear for the safety of his people until he heard Roux's views. Even then he did not appear to have been seriously alarmed, but instructed Roux to go to the hospital camp on Moturua and to take charge there. By this time, Roux had few illusions left, and during the next few days kept a close watch on the Maori people on the island, whose actions and demeanour did nothing to restore his confidence. At the mast camp where further suspicious behaviour had occurred, Marion du Fresne reinforced the guard, but his confidence was apparently unshaken. A few days earlier he had, by his own account, been made a chief at Te Kuri's village, and there seems no doubt that he had personally been shown every consideration by the people there. But on 12 June, on Moturua, Roux considered the situation to have deteriorated to the extent that he felt obliged to inform the chief Kotahi, of Paeroa *pa*, that if his people continued to come around the camp at night he would have them shot. On the *Mascarin*, Crozet, du Fresne's 'second captain', had observed a curious state of affairs on 11 June. On that day, the people who had been visiting the ship in great numbers for a month, failed to appear at all.

But on the next day at two o'clock, du Fresne, confident as ever despite these disquieting incidents, decided to go netting and oyster-gathering at Orokawa Bay. Te Kuri and half a dozen other Maoris who were on the ship accompanied him in the gig

22

with two young officers and ten crew. That night they did not return, but on the ships it was assumed that the party had spent the night at the mast camp. In fact, so little alarm was felt that next morning the longboat from *Marquis de Castries* was sent to Orokawa Bay with a dozen seamen, for firewood. Two hours later, only one of these men remained alive, and he had escaped a deliberate massacre of the boat's crew by fleeing across the isthmus separating Orokawa from the outer Bay, and swimming to the ship.

The survivor, Yves Thomas, had been chopping wood with a companion when they were suddenly attacked by several Maoris. Thomas fled, but before he escaped, he witnessed the slaughter of the remainder of his party at the hands of the several hundred Maoris who had assembled there.

It was now apparent that Marion du Fresne and his crew, if not dead, were in great danger, and the crisis was aggravated by signs of an impending attack on Roux's hospital camp. Du Clesmeur at once sent armed assistance there, and a boat was despatched to the mast camp. This went by Orokawa Bay, where du Fresne's cutter was seen still hauled up on the beach of the little cove Te Hue. The relief boat continued without delay to the camp, and found it surrounded by some 500 armed Maoris, who retired on the approach of the boat, shouting that Marion was dead. Crozet, who was then in charge of the camp, was some distance away supervising the hauling of spars. Having been advised by the relief party of the gravity of the position, he assembled the 60-odd men and marched them to where the boat had been left, some miles away. The Maoris made no attempt to attack the party, but followed them, reiterating the dismal tidings that du Fresne was dead and eaten.

Upon arriving at the boat, Crozet appears to have displayed considerable courage and resource, announcing to a chief that he would shoot the first man who advanced beyond a certain mark. He also instructed the chief to tell the people, who by this time numbered about a thousand, to sit down, which, according to his account, they did. The embarkation was achieved without incident, but when the boat, grossly overloaded, left the beach, all restraint departed and many Maoris attempted to follow it into the water. These were driven back by musket-fire without loss to the French, and the boat returned to the anchorage.

In the meantime, on Moturua, Roux had been told by a much distressed chief, that Marion was dead, and at about that time a boat arrived from the ships with the unhappy news of the recent events. Now fully informed, Roux decided that insufficient firm action was being taken, and since his own position was threatened by the *pa* at Paeroa, he prepared to attack it. He armed 26 men with muskets, pistols and cutlasses, and with great resolution carried the *pa*, burned it, and drove the people out, killing some 250. About 200 escaped in canoes, having witnessed the demoralisation of a brave people by the devastating effect of the firearms used by determined men against a massed enemy.

For the French there now remained only the task of preparing for their departure from a land now as hostile as it had previously appeared hospitable. More than three weeks after du Fresne's death, Te Kuri's *pa* on the mainland was entered and burned, the inhabitants having previously departed. Evidence was found there of the fate of the expedition's leader and his boat's crew, who were obviously all dead, and many eaten. On 12 July the ships were ready for their departure from Cook's Bay of Islands, but to these saddened people this place was the Bay of Treachery, and so it was named. On the day they sailed, a ceremony was enacted on Moturua at which Crozet proclaimed New Zealand to be a possession of France. A bottle containing the Arms of the kingdom and a formal document claiming the land, was buried four feet down at Waipao, on the island, 57 paces from the mark of high spring tides and 10 paces from the left bank of the little stream there. On 14 July 1772 *Mascarin* and *Marquis de Castries* sailed away, leaving behind their leader, two of his officers and 24 seamen. As to the bottle, it may well have been dug up within days, or even hours of their departure.

Few events in New Zealand history have aroused more conjecture, both as to exactly how and why du Fresne and his men died. But it appears certain that, in some way, French action had seriously offended the people. Kelly, from whom much of the foregoing account has been taken, has dealt fully with the various possibilities, but the local politics leading to the tragedy are considerably clearer than the causes of the event itself. However White is more specific in this respect, but such sources that were available to him were Ngapuhi, and we have no version from the indigenous people at that time, who, in the years after the incident were driven out by Ngapuhi.

The east coast Maoris were not Ngapuhi, and there was a tribal relationship between them and some of the Whangaroa people. Te Pahi, the leading coastal chief at the western side of the Bay at the beginning of the nineteenth century, was also related to the Whangaroa Maoris. In fact, he was married to the daughter of Te Puhi, a leading figure in the *Boyd* massacre some 37 years after du Fresne.[9]

Traditional accounts indicate that in the time of Auha, Hongi Hika's grandfather, who flourished in the mid-eighteenth century, Ngapuhi had not completely subjugated their inland neighbours in and around Waimate, and were engaged in sporadic skirmishing with them. Ngapuhi power was at that time centred around Hokianga and the Kaikohe district. Pakinga was their main *pa*.[10] Kelly suggests that by the late 1700s they were peacefully infiltrating the east coast and certainly their final armed conquest of the people there was made some time after the du Fresne incident, and was perhaps related to it.

---

1. McNab, R. *Historical Records of New Zealand*, v.2, pp.348 et seq.
2. Ibid.
3. Kelly, L. *Marion du Fresne at the Bay of Islands*.
4. White, J. White Papers, Auckland Public Library, No 30.
5. Kelly, L. 'Fragments of Ngapuhi History' *JPS*, v.47.
6. Smith, S.P. 'The Peopling of the North', *JPS*, supp. to v.5.
7. White.
8. Kelly.
9. Maori tradition transmitted to the author.
10. Ibid.

3

Early Contacts

Before embarking on an account of the events which occurred subsequent to the early European contacts at the Bay of
Islands, a description is necessary of the attractions of the area
from Whangarei northwards, which for hundreds of years had
made it the most sought-after and fought-over territory in New
Zealand. For climatic reasons alone, the area was probably the
earliest settled, and would certainly have been the first choice of
migrant Polynesians from the tropical islands of the Pacific.
Only in the North would the kumara survive the winter in the
ground, and only there could it have been propagated until the
techniques for its survival were evolved, making its cultivation
possible further south. Thus, many of the people now located
further to the south may have migrated or have been expelled
from the North, and many canoes said to have come from
'Hawaiki' may well have arrived from elsewhere in New
Zealand, particularly from the North.

Cook, having visited a good deal of the east coast, confirmed
the desirability of the Bay of Islands, and in evidence of this
observed that it was the most populous district he had encountered. After his visit, and those of de Surville and du
Fresne, which occurred within two and a half years of one
another, a period of about 30 years elapsed during which there
is no reliable record of European visitors to the Bay of Islands.
Nor, in fact, for some 15 years after Cook's last visit to Queen
Charlotte Sound in 1777, do we know of a ship reaching New
Zealand, unless we accept insubstantial accounts such as that
by Te Taniwha,[1] of a French visitor to the Hauraki Gulf shortly
after Cook.

The authorities responsible for financing these expeditions
were only interested in the commercial and scientific benefits

26

which might accrue from such voyages. At that time there were no great overseas empires other than that in the Americas, which was even then collapsing after nearly 300 years of Spanish rule. Indeed, the British Government, due to the separation of the American colonies, had little enthusiasm for further such adventures. India was in no sense a colony, but rather a feudal conglomeration of principalities suffering gross exploitation by the Honourable East India Company. This organisation, and the French and Dutch companies, were alone in their interest in the South Seas at that time, and none were apparently impressed by the commercial potential of Australia and New Zealand. On Cook's authority, dressed flax and spars were the only valuable merchandise obtainable at New Zealand, and, as the du Fresne expedition had demonstrated, these could not be secured except at the risk of bloody encounters with a cannibal people. The chartered companies were unaccustomed to embarking on such chancy adventures. Nevertheless the British Company's charter granted it an absolute monopoly in industrial enterprise in the southern oceans, which was supported by an authority occasionally invoked with some success.

Thus, although Cook and du Fresne had both claimed New Zealand for their respective monarchs, neither government had evinced any further interest, and commercial enterprise came no closer than the Americas, the East Indies and the Philippines. These places, with the exception of the Spanish American cities of the west coast, were mere trading outposts of the old world. However the founding of the English convict settlement in New South Wales in 1778, and the consequent concentration of shipping at Port Jackson, brought this phase to a close. Vessels arrived as convict transports and supply ships, and remained here, opening up the Pacific and New Zealand waters to sealers and whalers. These operated under licence to the Company, or perhaps in defiance of it, and later independently.[2]

In January 1778 the 11 ships of the First Fleet arrived at Port Jackson, and Governor and Captain-General Arthur Phillip established the convict settlement there with a population of about 1000. A month later, Philip Gidley King was appointed

Lieutenant-Governor of Norfolk Island, where a base was established to process the flax growing there. New Zealand had no place in Governor Phillip's plans, although he apparently toyed with the idea of sending particularly vicious criminals there and leaving them to the mercy of the cannibals. [3] However, in 1791 King visited London, where he saw a sample of prepared flax fibre which Sir Joseph Banks had obtained at the Bay of Islands. Since difficulty was being experienced in processing Norfolk Island flax, he decided that on his return he would 'procure' some New Zealanders so that they could demonstrate their methods. As a result, the Admiralty was persuaded to instruct HMS *Daedelus*, a storeship with Vancouver's expedition, '... to take "a flax dresser or two" from New Zealand to Sydney.'[4] But two years elapsed between King's visit to London and the arrival of the *Daedelus* off the New Zealand coast, and in the meantime he had approached Captain Eber Bunker, of the *William and Ann,* with the same request. Bunker did, in fact, make the attempt. He left Norfolk Island in December 1791 on the first recorded whaling venture into New Zealand waters, and called at Doubtless Bay, but was unsuccessful in inducing any Maoris there to return with him.[5]

HMS *Daedelus* did in due course accomplish its mission. Where Bunker was content with persuasion, Lieutenant Hanson, untroubled by tiresome scruples, 'procured' his New Zealanders in his bluff, direct Royal Naval way, simply by kidnapping them. They were duly delivered to Sydney (Port Jackson), and from there transferred to the convict transport *Shah Hormuzear*, reaching Norfolk in April 1793. However, all the useful information they could impart was obtained from them in one day. Among the Maoris, flax-dressing was essentially a woman's activity, although the contribution the men were able to make does seem to have been of some value.[6]

The names of these Maoris were, according to Lieutenant Governor King, Hoo-doo Co-co-ty To-wa-ma-how-ey, who said he came from Teer-a-witte, and Too-gee Te-ter-re-nu-e Warri-pe-do, who lived about two days walk by land and one day by sea from Teer-a-witte. Let them be called Huru and Tuki. It can be justifiably assumed that Huru's home was Te Rawhiti, and that Tuki came from Doubtless Bay, which would

28

be about the right distance, as described, from Te Rawhiti where, some 20 years earlier, du Fresne had met his death.

There is no doubt that the *Daedelus* picked the men up near the Cavalli Islands, since, in their narrative they stated that they went aboard the ship while it was cruising off the islands called Ko-mootu-kawa and Opanaki, which are clearly the large and small Cavallis, Motukawa and Panaki.

Interestingly, although Huru came from Te Rawhiti, he was at that time living with his wife's father, the chief of Motukawa, and was closely related to Povoreek (Pohoriki?), another chief of the district — further evidence of the relationship between the people of the outer Bay of Islands and those of the Whangaroa district.

King kept Huru and Tuki at Norfolk for about six months, and, having entertained them generously in his own home, decided to repatriate them. His relationship with the New Zealanders was apparently a sincere one, and his interest extended to compiling a vocabulary of 257 words of their language. In November 1793 he accompanied them to New Zealand in the *Britannia* whaler, delivering them to North Cape, from where they returned home.[7] Undistinguished personalities, they re-appeared briefly in later years, but with little impact. King later became Governor of New South Wales, and his early experience of New Zealand and its people no doubt influenced him in his subsequent sympathetic attitude to them.

But it was the adventurers such as Eb. Bunker who, in pioneering the whaling industry in New Zealand waters, established the Bay of Islands as a major South Seas port. Inevitably they brought in their wake other adventurers — settlers and traders, missionaries and soldiers — all of whom contributed to the achievements and failures that followed. The whalers rested and refitted here, trading for pork, fresh vegetables, fish, spars and the favours of the Maori women. In return they gave iron, European clothes, manufactured goods, and later muskets and powder, as the demand for these became clamorous. It is doubtful whether the Maori people derived any substantial immediate benefit from this traffic, since the early results were the prostitution of slaves and single women, and internecine warfare on a greatly more sophisticated basis than hitherto. But what they did was of their own free will, and unlike less fortunate indigenous peoples who were quickly brought under control and subdued, they retained their pride and their dignity.

Undoubtedly the whalers made peaceful settlement at the Bay possible, even for the missionaries who came after them. Commerce grew and prospered greatly despite the disapproval of the missionaries, who had little influence on the course of events there during the first 20 years of their residence. So astute did the Maori become in these circumstances, that in 1837 J.S. Polack remarked that they knew the value of their land to such an extent that every unpurchased part of the Bay would be found fully as expensive as in any populous city in Europe.[8] An extravagant statement in the Polack style, this no doubt contained a nucleus of truth.

1. Thomson, A.S. *Story of New Zealand*, v.1, p.238.
2. McNab, R. *From Tasman to Marsden*, p.96.
3. McNab, *Historical Records*, v.1, p.69.
4. McNab, *From Tasman to Marsden*, p.78.
5. Ibid, p79.
6. Collins, D. *An Account of the English Colony in New South Wales*, v.1, p.282-3.
7. Ibid, p.519.
8. Polack, J.S. *A Narrative of Travels and Adventures in New Zealand*, v.2, p.215.

4

Tribal Movements at 1800

THE TRIBES INVOLVED in events in the North at the turn of the century were Aupouri, Rarawa, Ngatikahu, Ngatipou, Ngatiuru, Ngapuhi, Ngatiwai, Ngatimanu, Kapotai, Ngaitahuhu, and Ngatiwhatua. Of these, Ngatipou and Ngatiuru of Whangaroa were perhaps rather sub-tribes of Ngatikahu, whose people inhabited the east coast from the Bay to Mangonui. Ngatirehia, of the western Bay of Islands, could also be so classified, but all other groups encountered in this narrative, with the exception of Ngare Raumati, a division of Ngatiwai, are *hapu* of Ngapuhi. Ngatiawa was the ancient tribe preceding the others in time, and from which many of them sprang, but it had ceased to exist as a corporate entity during our period.

Maori society was divided into *iwi,* or tribes, as described above, and *hapu,* which would be described as sub-tribes of the *iwi*. The *hapu* would usually have originated from families in the *iwi* which due to their exploits or the fame of their head, established a clear identity of their own. In Ngapuhi, there are, or have been, in excess of 150 *hapu,* some so powerful and influential as to be, in later years, almost *iwi* themselves. Although it has been argued that Ngapuhi is a loose confederation of different tribes, there is no doubt that it is a single tribal group. It is essential that all Ngapuhi of consequence must descend from their great progenitor, Rahiri, and from his grandfather, Puhi-moana-ariki, the tribe derives its name.[1]

For many years Ngapuhi had been infiltrating into the eastern coastal areas by marriage or by warlike means, so that early in the nineteenth century those coastal people who had not been subdued by war were dominated politically, with the exception of Ngatirehia, on the north-west of the Bay of Islands. Until his death, about 1810, Te Pahi, the chief, was

31

sufficiently in command of the situation to maintain his authority unchallenged in the Rangihoua and Te Puna districts. He was the first New Zealand chief of such standing to be entertained by the Governor of New South Wales in his own home, and through this relationship European plants and animals were introduced into the Bay, to the benefit of trade with the whale-fleet. But on Te Pahi's death in the turmoil following the *Boyd* massacre, Ngapuhi took advantage of the political vacuum this caused, and soon had a firm hold on his territory.

In earlier times, the newly emergent Ngapuhi were responsible for the departure of large sections of the old Ngatiawa from the North, following conquests by Rahiri's Hokianga descendants. Although they still are present in the North under other names, such as Ngatikahu, after Kahu-unuunu, a chief of ancient times,[2] large numbers migrated down both coasts, where, in Taranaki they are now known as Atiawa, and in the Bay of Plenty as Ngatiawa.

As a result of the skirmish at Whirinaki, and the reprisal raid through Kerikeri by Hokianga people following the death of Taura-tumara, the invaders, a group of Hikutu, a Ngapuhi *hapu*, settled at Kaihiki, in the Mangonui Inlet. Ngapuhi tribal interests were also served by the marriage of Auha's son, Te Hotete, of Kaikohe, to Tuhikura, daughter of the Ngatiuru chief Tahapango. Then, Te Hotete's brother-in-law, Te Koki, married Mutunga of Ngatirehia, and produced two girls, Turikatuku and Tangiwhare, both of whom married Te Hotete's son, Hongi Hika.[3] At about the same time, Ruatara, a Ngatirehia chief related by marriage to Hone Heke, an inland chief of the Ngatirahiri *hapu* of Ngapuhi,[4] married the daughter of Waraki, a coastal chief domiciled at Waitangi.[5] Turi-o-kana, a son of Moka, of Hokianga,[6] appears to have married an important Te Puna woman, and Makoare Taonui, also of Hokianga, married Hinuata of Ngatirehia. Thus, by the turn of the century, Ngapuhi were in a strong position on the coast, against which, on Te Pahi's death, his sons could not prevail.

Another military advance by Ngapuhi occurred possibly at about the time of Cook's visit. The chiefs involved in this, Auha, Hongi Hika's grandfather, and Auha's half-brother, Whakaaria, overcame the Ngatipou *hapu* Ngatimiru and Wahineiti at Waimate, many of whom fled to Kerikeri and the Mangonui Inlet. Then, in order to forestall any retaliation, the brothers descended on these places, drove the people out, and took possession of the *pa* Kororipo at Kerikeri. The defeated people again retreated, this time to Whangaroa and the coast north of the Bay. Thus, in early European times at Kerikeri and Te Tii Mangonui, the Ngapuhi chiefs Tareha and Kaingaroa, Hongi Hika's half-brother, were in authority.[7] On the eastern side of the Bay further inroads were soon to be made by Ngapuhi.

Possibly about 1800 or a little after, a Ngatiwai party, probably Ngare Raumati,[8] took a party inland from the Te Rawhiti district and raided Waimate, only recently taken from the Ngatimiru. The immediate cause of the invasion was the death of two of the coast people's kinsmen near Taipa, in the north, at the hands of Te Hotete. At the time of the Waimate raid, Te Hotete was away on a skirmish at Hokianga, and returned to find his *pa*, Okuratope, sacked and his people killed. Auporo, the mother of the chief Rewa (Maanu),[9] and his sister were among the victims, and Te Hotete at once led a reprisal attack to Rawhiti by way of Kerikeri, and destroyed two *pa*. He then returned to Kerikeri and sent word to Hokianga and other Ngapuhi. These rallied under Tapua, Tamati Waaka Nene's father,[10] and another attack was launched from Kerikeri by canoe. This developed into a naval battle with Ngare Raumati off Tapeka Point from which Ngapuhi again emerged victorious and returned to Kerikeri. Further indecisive skirmishing occurred until finally Rewa (Maanu) gave notice to Ngare Raumati that he intended to make war on them in earnest. Three Ngapuhi *hapu* were those mainly involved in this expedition. These were Ngaitawake, whose territory was at Mataraua and Waimate, Ngatitautahi of Kaikohe, and Ngatirahiri, who were at that time in the Puketona district. People from Oihi, Takou and other places also seem to have taken part, but the chiefs concerned in this campaign who were well known in European times were the Ngapuhi Titore Takiri,[11] Wharerahi, Rewa and Moka,[12] and Kaiteke (or Tareha or Kemara).[13] The Ngatimanu, Whareumu[14] and the Whangaroa chief Ururoa (Rewharewha)[15] were also involved. By this time Te Hotete had died at Tapuaeharuru, the *pa* at Lake Omapere, from puhipuhi, or dropsy.

This concerted attack by Ngapuhi was decisive, and the power of the Ngare Raumati (or Ngatiwai) of Te Rawhiti, the last of the ancient tribes in the area from Kororareka to Cape Brett, was finally broken. Although they were driven out and fled to Whangaroa, it is unlikely that the whole population departed *en masse,* but at some time later, the district was occupied by the invaders. However, Korokoro,[16] who was part Ngapuhi and part Ngare Raumati was permitted to retain Paroa due to this relationship. Eventually, Kaiteke appropriated Moturua, Whareumu Kororareka, and Titore, Rewa and others settled on the coast and the islands. Also, Titore retained an interest in Kororareka.

Of the invaders, Ngaitawake appear to have been a particularly adventurous *hapu,* since their ancestral lands at Mataraua were some 12 miles south-west of Kaikohe, and they were now extended through Waimate and to the coast.

As is the case with most Maori accounts of events, their chronology is not very clear, and these could have occurred over a period of 40 years or so following the du Fresne incident. The occupations mentioned were clearly not simultaneous, or even immediately following the conquests. Butler [17] noted the presence of the Ngatimanu Whareumu and Titore Takiri as chiefs of Kororareka about 1820. Titore appears to have been a Ngapuhi 'caretaker' of the conquered Te Rawhiti lands, and clearly spent much time at Kororareka, but there is little evidence that the other chiefs occupied their coastal lands in force until the death of Hongi Hika, in the late 1820s. From about 1815 until this time, these Ngapuhi chiefs were preoccupied with war expeditions to the south, and their gathering-place was Kororipo *pa* at Kerikeri. The omens decreed that no other place was suitable. In the meantime Titore exercised some authority over the conquered territory, with Whareumu in residence at Kororareka and Korokoro at Paroa. These uneasy Ngatimanu and Ngare Raumati tenures survived only until Korokoro's death in 1823 and the Girl's War at Kororareka in 1830.

The Ngapuhi advance to Waitangi from the Ngatirahiri land at Puketona, some six miles west on the road from Paihia, appears to have taken place after the above events. Te Hotete's father, Auha and his allies had previously expelled the Ngatimiru and Wahineiti from the Waimate and Kerikeri districts. Following this, the Waimate district was given in charge of one Toko, a cousin, and later to Te Hotete. Ngapuhi were thus in a position to descend through the Puketona district to Waitangi. An advance as far as Puketona had been made before about 1793, when the Ngatimaru of Waitemata attacked the Ngapuhi *pa* here.[18] Although all the country to the north, south and west of this *pa* was Ngapuhi stronghold, the Ngatimaru could still use the river valley from Waitangi as their attack route. This, of course, could not have been achieved had this place been in Ngapuhi hands at the time. They were clearly not in control of it during the attacks on Ngare Raumati, since these operations had to be routed through Kerikeri, involving a sea journey of some 16 miles, or twice the distance from Waitangi to the Ngare Raumati stronghold at Rawhiti. From missionary sources we know that even in their time Waitangi was occupied by Waraki, Ruatara's wife's father,[19] from whom the catechist Hall acquired 50 acres of land in 1815. Waraki was a Ngatipou or Ngatirehia, and even then was not in firm control at Waitangi, as Hall's problems there demonstrated.[20] It seems likely that at the time Waitangi was under heavy pressure from inland, and soon capitulated.

---

1. See Appendix 1 and 2.
2. Smith, 'The Peopling of the North', p.38.
3. See Appendix 1.2.
4. See Appendix 1.3.
5. Elder, J.R. *Marsden's Lieutenants*, p.22.
6. Smith, S.P. *Maori Wars of the Nineteenth Century,* p.84.
7. Te Rawhiti Block Committee's Minute-books.
8. Kelly, 'Fragments of Ngapuhi History'.
9. See Appendix 1.5.
10. Appendix 1.6.
11. Appendix 1.7.
12. Appendix 1.8.

13. Appendix 1.5.
14. Appendix 1.9.
15. Appendix 1.2.
16. Appendix 1.10.
17. Barton, J. *Earliest New Zealand*, p.358.
18. Smith, 'The Peopling of the North'.
19. Elder, *Marsden's Lieutenants,* pp.22 and 83.
20. Ibid, p.127 et seq.

5

Maori Adventurers

Since the whaling industry had become well established in
New Zealand waters by the beginning of the nineteenth century, it might be expected that some settlement had occurred
ashore. However, except for a few isolated cases at the Bay of
Islands, there is no evidence of this. Nevertheless in 1805, the
Ferret whaler reported that the Maoris there were growing
immense quantities of potatoes to supply the whalers.[1]
Catching whales and trying out the blubber was done at sea,
and 'bay-whaling', which involved shore stations, was not
undertaken until many years later. But the whalers used the Bay
and its people at their convenience, with apparently little effort
to establish any other sort of relationship. There is evidence that
some visiting whalers dealt barbarously with the people,[2] and
that when lying at anchor they kept their boarding-nets rigged
out to prevent surprise attacks. But serious attacks by Maoris on
shipping at the Bay were confined to the du Fresne incident and
the *Parramatta* in 1808 (see Chapter 6).

These conditions were seemingly acceptable to both parties.
In 1805, King, then Governor of New South Wales, observed in
a letter to Lord Camden that whaleship crews now included
New Zealanders, who 'are found a very tractable people in this
situation. The many vessels that have put into the Bay of Islands
and other parts of that coast have never, as far as I have learned,
had any altercation with the natives.'[3]

Among Maoris who joined ships in this way was Ruatara, a
relation by marriage of Hone Heke, of later fame.[4] He lived on
the coast and was related to the people of the local chief Te Pahi.
In 1805, he came aboard the *Argo* at the Bay, and eventually
became acquainted with the Rev. Samuel Marsden. The
influence of both Ruatara and Te Pahi on the Rev. Samuel

Marsden seems to have affected his decision to found a Christian mission in New Zealand. Realising the benefit that would accrue to shipping if satisfactory relationships were established with the Maori people, Governor King instructed the *Coromandel*, at Norfolk Island, to send livestock to one of the principal chiefs at the Bay. Thus 26 sows, 4 boars and 2 goats were brought by the *Venus*, and the *Adonis* and *Argo* whalers, later in 1805, and delivered to Te Pahi at Te Puna near the mouth of the Mangonui River.

Te Pahi's son, Matara, had already visited Sydney, and upon receiving the stock, the chief resolved to visit the man who had sent it to him. He therefore got a passage for himself and his sons to Norfolk Island on the *Venus,* completing the journey to Port Jackson (Sydney) on HMS *Buffalo*. Here Te Pahi and one son were housed and entertained at Government House for some three months, and the chief made a very favourable impression on all who met him. To quote King:

Tip-a-he is 5 feet 11 inches high, stout, and extremely well made. His age appears about 46 or 48. His face is completely tattooed with the spiral marks shown in 'Hawkesworth's and Cook's Second Voyage,' . . . To say that he was nearly civilized falls far short of his character, as every action and observation shows an uncommon attention to the rules of decency and propriety in his every action, and has much of the airs and manners of a man conversant with the world he lives in. In conversation he is extremely facetious and jocose, and, as he never reflected on any person, so Tip-a-he was alive to the least appearance of slight or inattention in others.[5]

The chief was greatly upset during this visit, upon attending the trial of two soldiers and a convict accused of stealing pork from the Government store. When he heard that one of the prisoners was to be sentenced to death, he voiced his disgust so effectively that the sentences were reconsidered. The idea of execution as a punishment for stealing food was quite unacceptable to his people.

While Te Pahi was at Port Jackson, the *Ferret* called at the Bay, and out of this visit came the first published work devoted entirely to the Bay of Islands.[6] John Savage, the erstwhile Assistant Surgeon at Parramatta, New South Wales, had been suspended for refusing to attend a woman in child-birth, and since he had been court-martialed, and the evidence had been sent to England for consideration, he was on his way there to plead his case. His visit to the Bay was in the course of this voyage.

The *Ferret* entered the harbour on 20 September 1805, only a few weeks after Te Pahi's departure, and anchored near Te Puna. Here Savage had two months in which to observe the place and people. Savage described Te Puna (during Te Pahi's absence, his brother 'Tiarrah' was in charge) as the 'capital' of the Bay, built 'partly on the mainland and partly on a small island, . . . and consists in the whole of about an hundred dwellings.'

On the mainland the people lived and had their cultivations, but the island was devoted entirely to the household of Te Pahi, who, according to Savage, had four sisters as wives and 'several concubines'. What distinguished the wives from the concubines he does not explain. One of Te Pahi's wives is known to have been Ngaraa, the daughter of Te Puhi of Whangaroa.[7] Te Pahi himself told King that he had '. . . several wives . . . [and] . . . fifty-two children living, but that he now attaches himself to only one young woman.'[8]

The places Oihi, Te Puna and Rangihoua may be confused, particularly since contemporary writers often did not distinguish between them. They all lie within Rangihoua Bay, Oihi being a desolate little cove at the north of the bay, and Te Puna the steep pebbly beach, backed by low rolling country to the south. Te Pahi's Island, still so named, is a little south of the southern end of the bay. The old *pa* of Rangihoua, a precipitous terraced hill rising abruptly from the shore, is between Oihi and Te Puna.

Although Te Puna is frequently mentioned as an anchorage, the name included the sheltered waters in the mouth of the Mangonui Inlet. Any part of Rangihoua Bay is not a safe anchorage in any strong wind conditions other than north or west. Duperrey's 1824 chart of the Bay does, in fact, show the lower reaches of the Mangonui River as 'Port Te Pouna'.

At the time of Savage's visit, the Maoris there were growing great quantities of potatoes, keeping most of them for trade and consuming few themselves. The canoes which transported this provender to the ships were partitioned off in sections, so that each family kept its individual wares separated. Incidents inevitably arose from this traffic, and Savage observed, 'I am inclined to believe, in many instances where disagreement takes place between Europeans and savages, the former are the aggressors'. This view was consistent with other responsible comment, and the few instances of violence that occurred here in later years confirmed Savage's opinion.

A half-caste child was seen at the Bay and described by Savage. He was the first of mixed blood known to have been observed in New Zealand, and according to the writer was timid and bashful, comparing unfavourably in demeanour with those of full Maori parentage. The father was not seen, since he was said to retire inland when ships came to anchor. He may well have been the first European to make his home with the Maoris, apparently settling there about 1800, and was no doubt a deserter from a whaleship. The child was perhaps the half-caste slave seen by Marsden at the Waitemata some 20 years later. His age, and the description of his home at the Bay and his early life, as related to Marsden by his master, suggest this probability.[9]

Savage is most coy in his description of the dances that the girls performed (haka waiata). While he refrained from describing them in detail, it is plain from his prim innuendoes that they were quite uninhibited.

Savage departed in October 1805, and took with him to England Moehanga, a man belonging to the Bay. Although Savage judged Moehanga to be intelligent, and hoped that his experiences would benefit his people, he appears to have profited little from his visit to England. He is mentioned by contemporary writers after his return, who have nothing to say to his credit. But he was the first Maori to visit England, and while there, stayed for a time with Lord Fitzwilliam. Savage purchased three bill-hooks for him in the Strand, which pleased

Moehanga, who announced that on his return he intended to use one to slay one Urutuki — a comment which suggests a limited capacity for influencing his people to their advantage on his return.

In February 1806 Te Pahi started on his return journey, King having ordered the Government vessel *Lady Nelson* to return him and his sons to their home. With them they brought a prefabricated house, tools and gifts from many donors. Included was a silver medal and chain, especially made by the Governor for the occasion of Te Pahi's visit, and inscribed 'Presented by Governor King to Tip-a-he, a chief of New Zealand, during his visit at Port Jackson in January, 1806.' The medal and chain were last seen at Oihi in 1815, in the possession of Te Pahi's daughter, by J.L. Nicholas, who accompanied Marsden to New Zealand.[10]

On the 25 April, after a protracted voyage, the *Lady Nelson* dropped anchor under the island of Motuapo, the nearest of the Te Pahi Islands to the mainland, and on Te Pahi's home island carpenters erected the house. In a week the job was finished, and on 2 May the ship left the Bay, taking with her as presents from Te Pahi seven spars, seed potatoes, fishing lines and weapons.[11]

This was the *Lady Nelson*'s second visit to New Zealand. An armed tender of 60 tons, she had been at the Thames in 1804 and had been given a very cordial reception by the people at their anchorage, where provisions and water were freely supplied. But it was on this 1806 visit that a convict employed on the vessel named George Bruce deserted, perhaps with the complicity of Te Pahi.[12] Either way, he obtained the chief's protection and married his daughter, to her ultimate sorrow.

King had intended to send a party of suitable men to live under the care of Te Pahi for a few months, to observe the place and its people. However he was prevented from doing so by the appointment, as Governor in his place, of the unlucky Bligh, of *Bounty* fame. But the retiring Governor had done much service, on a personal basis, in establishing communications with the New Zealanders, and by his efforts had encouraged the introduction and cultivation of European plants and animals at

41

the Bay.

Only a month or so after the departure of the *Lady Nelson*, trouble at Port Dalrymple, Tasmania, led to the arrival at the Bay in December, of the ship *Venus*. This vessel had lately been in the sealing trade at the Penantipodes Islands, under Captain S.R. Chace, and had been manned, due to a shortage of labour, partly by convicts. This was perhaps the reason for the considerable cargo pillaging that had been taking place, and further trouble developed when the first mate, Kelly, joined with 10 others in evicting non-sympathisers from the ship. They took possession of the ship and put to sea.[13]

On its arrival at the Bay of Islands, the *Venus* had on board 11 people. Four of these and an infant remained there, and the rest took the vessel down the coast. Its fate and that of the crew was never determined, although it was later reported on the east coast. It is unlikely that the *Venus* left New Zealand, since she had no navigator on board. The crew took to abducting Maori women, and at the Bay and Whangarei made unfortunate selections, taking both the sister and the niece of Te Morenga, one of the most prestigious chiefs north of Auckland.[14] This led to two war expeditions, one to the east coast with Hongi Hika in 1818 to avenge the death of Te Morenga's sister, who had apparently been taken from the *Venus,* and killed and eaten by the Ngati-porou there, and another to punish the Ngai-te-Rangi for the death of his niece under similar circumstances. This Te Morenga led himself, in 1820.

Those of the *Venus* who remained at the Bay were Kelly, a man named Lancashire and two women convicts, Catherine Hagerty and Charlotte Edgar and her infant child. They apparently lived in Te Pahi's territory, where Kelly and Lancashire built huts for themselves. But they enjoyed little freedom, both being retaken in 1807, Lancashire by the ship *Brothers* and Kelly by the *Britannia*, in accordance with the Proclamation of 1806 by the Governor of New South Wales requiring their arrest.

About March 1807, the brig *Commerce*, called at Te Puna on its way to Port Jackson from the Penantipodes sealing-grounds, and Captain Birnie offered to take Charlotte Edgar aboard, but she refused. Of Catherine Hagerty, Captain Bunker of the

Elizabeth reported that she had died ashore not long after her arrival. These were the first two European women known to have lived in New Zealand, but of the subsequent life of Edgar and her child nothing is known. Apparently neither were there in 1814, when the Mission was established, as their presence was not reported.

The *Commerce* reported on her return to Port Jackson that Te Pahi had treated her crew with all consideration, and had supplied all their needs, and that maize sent over by King had been successfully grown and harvested at Te Puna.

For some years until the *Boyd* massacre, Te Pahi was to continue to honour his pact of friendship with the ex-Governor, to the benefit of the sealing and whaling industries, and their ships, under his protection, used the port freely and in safety. Evidence of this is the reported presence shortly after the *Venus* incident of the vessels *Commerce, Brothers, Elizabeth, Britannia, Inspector, Albion* and *Indispensible.* Unfortunately, however, this friendly and profitable relationship was soon to be overtaken by tragic events.

---

1. McNab, *From Tasman to Marsden*, p.102.
2. Ibid, p.151.
3. McNab, *Historical Records of New Zealand*, v.1, p.255.
4. See Appendix 1.3.
5. McNab, *Historical Records of New Zealand*, v.1, p.264.
6. Savage, J. *Some Account of New Zealand.*
7. Maori genealogies in the possession of the author.
8. McNab, *Historical Records*, p.267.
9. Elder, J.R. *Letters and Journals of Samuel Marsden*, p.273.
10. Nicholas, J.L. *Narrative of a Voyage to New Zealand*, p.179.
11. Lee, Ida. *The log-books of the Lady Nelson*, p.285.
12. Evidence of the desertion of Bruce, *alias* Druce, appears in the Lady Nelson's log-book under the date 22 April 1806, when the ship lay at anchor at a place, which, by its recorded latitude, has to be Karikari Bay, in Rangaunu Bay. The log entry reads, 'Run from the ship Joseph Druce'. Karikari is some 60 miles from the

Bay of Islands, and it was no doubt the influence of Te Pahi in the intervening country that allowed Bruce to later find his way to Te Puna unharmed.

13. McNab, *From Tasman to Marsden,* p.110 et seq.
14. See Appendix 1.7.

6

Prelude to the *Boyd* Massacre

THE SATISFACTORY RELATIONSHIP existing between the Maoris and the shipping developed during what appears to have been a time of comparative freedom from intertribal conflict, but this equilibrium was soon to be upset.

The demands made by these vessels on the resources of Te Pahi's district were apparently more than it could tolerate, particularly since, fighting was then occurring between the Ngatikorokoro, a Ngapuhi Hokianga tribe, and the coastal Maoris at the Bay.[1] In this period mention is first made of shipping resorting to the eastern side of the Bay, that is, the Kororareka (Russell) peninsula and the Kawakawa River. There, good and perhaps better shelter was to be found, ample provisions, and more importantly, spar timber, of which there was none available at the western or Te Puna side.

The period 1807 to 1814 is not a happy one in the history of the Bay of Islands. King, who, of all the Governors of New South Wales, had the interests of New Zealand and its people most at heart, was gone, and was succeeded by the unfortunate Bligh, and he, prone to calamity, found enough trouble to keep him occupied at Sydney.

The Bay and the Maoris were therefore left to their own devices, visited only by whalers and sealers, who took what they wanted and sailed away, often without paying for it other than in abuse and barbarous ill-treatment. That such ill-treatment of Maoris by ships' crews was prevalent is well substantiated. In 1810 William Leith, who commanded a trading expedition to New Zealand for Australian businessmen, wrote in a report to his employers, 'I am . . . of opinion that the masters of the different ships have to thank themselves for all the evils they have brought on by their injustice and ill-treatment of the

45

natives.'²

The seriousness of the situation was such that the ill-treatment and injustice Leith mentions were the subject of a proclamation dated 1 December 1813, by Bligh's successor at New South Wales, Governor Lachlan Macquarie.³ The proclamation made it mandatory for masters of ships clearing Australian ports to execute a Deed binding them to a rigid code of behaviour toward the native people of New Zealand and other Pacific islands. Breaches of this code were punishable by a fine of £1000 and other penalties, to be imposed on offenders in New South Wales courts. Every aspect of relations with the natives was dealt with in detail, and they were declared to be under the protection of the King of England. Offences were to be punished 'with the utmost rigour of the law,' but since there was no way of policing, and thus enforcing this laudable directive, it was largely ineffective.

Victims of this callous behaviour were George Bruce and his wife, Te Pahi's daughter, who were mentioned in the last chapter. Conflicting opinions on Bruce, sometimes called Druce, are to be found, but that of Governor Macquarie, in a report to the Under-Secretary of State is perhaps the most reliable. Macquarie describes Bruce as an ex-convict, '... a man of no principle whatever, of desperate fortune, much given to drunkenness and every kind of dissipation, and of most profligate manners in all other respects.'⁴ He also confirms Bruce's desertion at New Zealand from the *Lady Nelson,* and his marriage to Te Pahi's daughter.

Bruce and his wife had been married only 18 months when the *General Wellesley* called at Te Puna, and as the captain, Dalrymple, had business up the coast that required a guide, he persuaded Bruce and his wife to assist him. The matter completed, their services were no longer required, and an attempt was made to land them, but this was unsuccessful, and the captain, apparently unconcerned, continued on his voyage with the unfortunate pair aboard. After a protracted passage the ship reached Malacca, where Bruce went ashore to complain to the Governor of his treatment, but in his absence, the *General Wellesley* put to sea with his wife still aboard. After three months and much travelling, Bruce was re-united with her, but over a year had elapsed since their departure from New Zealand before they managed to get as far as Sydney, having made a voyage through the East Indies to India, and thence to Tasmania. A child was born to the chief's daughter during the latter stage of the journey, but the unfortunate woman never returned to her home. She arrived at Sydney a little after her father, who had lately made another visit there, had left for New Zealand. Cruelly and shamefully neglected by her husband, she survived only a short time in Sydney, and died on 25 February 1810. Her child was taken in by the orphan school at Sydney, and Bruce himself, after an unsuccessful attempt to return to New Zealand with Leith, in the employ of the newly formed New South Wales New Zealand Company, left the country in May 1810 for England, and never returned.[5]

In the middle of 1808, shortly after the departure of Bruce and his wife, there occurred at the Bay the first recorded attack by Maoris on shipping since du Fresne. The schooner *Parramatta* left Port Jackson on 14 April and failed to return. She was presumed lost, and no definite information as to her fate was forthcoming until the return to Sydney (Port Jackson) of one John Besent, who had lived with the Maoris at the Bay for a year, from March 1812.[6] In a statement sworn before Samuel Marsden, Besent stated that during his residence in New Zealand he had received from the Maoris an account of the *Parramatta*'s destruction. The vessel, he stated, had arrived at the Bay in distress, needing provisions and water. These were freely given, but when payment was demanded, the Maori people on the ship were fired upon and thrown overboard. The anchor was weighed and the vessel put to sea. But she had not gone far when she was driven ashore, where the injured parties awaited and slaughtered all survivors. That was the Maori version, and its truth cannot be verified. Besent deposed that he had seen three people who had been wounded with small shot during this incident. The site of the wreck was described by Besent as 'between Cape Brett and Terra's district' — Terra (or Tara), a Ngatimanu, being a Kororareka chief. This being the case, the schooner went ashore between Cape Brett and Paroa Bay, and its remains were still there in 1813.

Besent did not mention which of the Maori people were involved, but they were presumably Tara's or Korokoro's people. Remarkable features of the incident, however, are that ships would no doubt have been at the Bay within a short time of the tragedy, and yet saw or heard nothing of it, and that no news concerning it was forthcoming for some five years. This could have been due to the understandable reticence of the people on that side of the Bay, who were then in the opening stages of their profitable commercial contacts with the shipping.

In May 1808 another vessel, the brig *Harrington*, was seized at Port Jackson and taken to sea by its pirate crew.[7] As soon as this became known, the Government sent the *Pegasus* to the Bay of Islands on the assumption that the brig's crew would make for there in the hope of plundering the American brig *Eliza*, which was thought to be at the Bay. But on arrival, the *Pegasus* found the *Commerce* sealer, and the *Inspector* and *Grand Sachem* whalers anchored near Te Puna. The *Harrington* had not been there, but two days after the Government ship left, a brig stood into the Bay, but came about and sailed away to the east. It was assumed that this was the missing vessel, whose crew were alarmed at the presence of the three ships. The *Harrington* was finally captured on its way to the Philippines by the frigate *Phoenix*.

As we know, supplies were now scarce at the Bay, or at least at the Te Puna side, and when, in the middle of 1808, Captain Ceroni of the *Commerce* sought to revictual there, he was advised by Te Pahi to go to Whangaroa, where his needs would be supplied by his kinsman Kaitoke.[8] It is remarkable that this harbour had been unknown to Europeans before 1807, when Captain Wilkinson of the *Star* sealer had chanced upon it. Whangaroa lies only 30 miles to the north-west of the Bay of Islands, but had remained undiscovered because the peculiar geographical features of the coast at its entrance make it difficult to pick up from the sea. Although the *Star* lay under the island Ririwha (Stephenson's Island) for a night, directly off the entrance, Wilkinson was unaware that such a commodious harbour was so close until informed of it by the local Maoris next day.[9]

Ceroni, acting on Te Pahi's advice, took the *Commerce* around to Whangaroa, taking with him Te Pahi and three of his sons, who, learning that the ship was bound for Port Jackson, took this opportunity of paying another visit there. The ship being well provided for, Ceroni sailed for Norfolk Island, and thence to Port Jackson. At Norfolk, Te Pahi met Alexander Berry, whose path he was shortly to cross again in bitter circumstances. Berry described him, noting that he was 'lame of one leg'. He was very ill on the voyage. At Sydney, the unhappy Governor Bligh had been illegally arrested following the 'Rum Rebellion', and as his successor, Lachlan Macquarie, had not yet arrived, Te Pahi was accommodated by Lieutenant Governor Foveaux in his own house.

After a short stay Te Pahi returned to New Zealand a little before the return of his son Matara, who had been to England with ex-Governor King, on HMS *Buffalo*. From Sydney, in January 1809, Matara took a passage back to his home on *The City of Edinburgh*, too soon, as we have seen, to rescue his sister.

On board *The City of Edinburgh* were Alexander Berry and Ceroni, formerly of the *Commerce*. Pattison, the captain, intended to refit her with new spars and sheathing while in New Zealand, but Berry, anxious to try Whangaroa, was vigorously dissuaded from doing so by Ceroni. However, the wind dictated the course and the ship was taken to Te Puna, where Matara was put ashore and assistance was sought from Te Pahi. As with the *Commerce* a year before, Te Pahi refused, this time because he and his people were going over to Whangaroa to attend the ceremony following the death of the chief Kaitoke, who had died as the result of an epidemic.

An event at Whangaroa during Ceroni's 1808 visit may have accounted for Te Pahi's refusal and the hostility which he seems to have displayed at this stage. On his previous visit, Ceroni had discovered that his watch was a source of awe and wonder to the Whangaroa Maoris, and much gratified by this, he had exhibited it on every possible occasion. However, during one of his performances he had dropped it into the sea. This apparently terrified the Maoris, who considered it to contain an *atua*, or god, which would now remain with them. The epidemic which occurred later was attributed to this watch, and, of course, to Ceroni and his countrymen. The sickness killed many people, including Kaitoke, whose *hahunga*, that is, the ceremonial disposal of his bones, Te Pahi was now attending.

Since there was no help forthcoming at Te Puna, the Ngatimanu chiefs of Kororareka and Kawakawa, Tara and Tupe were approached. They volunteered the supply of timber and the provision of a hauling-out site and took the ship under their protection, assuring for themselves a share of the white man's business, which had hitherto been the monopoly of Te Pahi. Thus Kororareka, later a stronghold of Ngapuhi, commenced its reign of commercial pre-eminence. There, the ship's bottom was completely resheathed with 'plank made of New Zealand pine'; and the refit completed, the *City* left the Bay at the end of May 1809 for Fiji. Not, however, before Ceroni had again done his watch trick, dropping it into the sea to the horror and consternation of the beholders, who were undoubtedly convinced of the shocking result of the Whangaroa incident. Obviously given to the perpetration of provocative infantile tricks, Ceroni disappears from the scene unlamented. He did, however, leave an interesting account of an incipient attack on the ship as she lay on the beach. He stated that Berry had frustrated an attack by 100 armed men 'lurking about a quarter of a mile from the tents,' by leading an armed party against them, upon which they fled, and were later scattered by musketry. The account implicated Te Pahi, but no evidence in support of this is given. In fact, it is unlikely that his people would be assembling in force in the Kororareka district, which, for political purposes was foreign territory, and in which he could hardly do such a thing without the complicity of the inhabitants. The Kororareka Maoris are more likely to have been involved in this incident. Naturally enough they would attempt to implicate their rival Te Pahi in the event of the failure of their own *coup*.

This is the first recorded use of Kororareka for the purpose of refitting, but it is interesting that the *Southern Cross*, reporting on the death, in 1852, of Captain Stewart, of Stewart's Island, stated that he was the first white man '. . . who ever set foot on the beach of Kororareka.' This would no doubt be in 1805, when he was at the Bay in command of the *Venus*.[10]

In October *The City of Edinburgh* returned to the Bay of Islands to load spars, and it was found that during its absence Te Pahi's son Matara had died. Again Tara and Tupe lent their assistance, and the work of felling, trimming and loading the spars proceeded, but was delayed when an intertribal disturbance took place. But this lapsed into insignificance when, in the last weeks of 1809, Berry learned from Tara of the calamity that had occurred at Whangaroa. These events could have ended Maori-European relations at the Bay. As it was, they did destroy Te Pahi's stable little empire there.

---

1. Smith, S.P. *Maori Wars of the Nineteenth Century,* p.51.
2. McNab, *Historical Records,* v.1, p. 302.
3. Ibid, p.316.
4. Ibid, p. 322.
5. McNab, *From Tasman to Marsden*, pp.113, 139.
6. McNab, *Historical Records*, v.1, p. 423.
7. McNab, *From Tasman to Marsden*, p.116.
8. Ibid, p.117.
9. Ibid, p. 114.
10. *Southern Cross,* 13 January 1852.

7

The *Boyd* and its Aftermath

On 12 November 1809 the *Boyd* sailed from Port Jackson bound for the Cape of Good Hope with a cargo of sealskins, coal and timber. The captain, Thompson, intended first to call at the newly-discovered harbour of Whangaroa to complete his load with spars, which were said to be readily available there. In addition to the cargo, the *Boyd* carried a dozen or so passengers, among them Te Puhi's brother Te Aara,[1] or George, who was returning home after serving on the sealer *Star* with Captain Wilkinson, who, in the same ship, had discovered the harbour two years earlier.

At the Bay, Alexander Berry was initally sceptical of Tara's account of the events at Whangaroa following the arrival of the *Boyd*, but by the time he had finished loading spars, further information had come in which persuaded him and Captain Pattison, the master of *The City of Edinburgh*, to equip an armed party for an expedition to the harbour to rescue possible survivors. The Bay Maoris refused to have anything to do with this venture, asserting that active support by them would certainly cause war between the two groups. The party started for Whangaroa with three of the *City's* boats and about 20 men, and surprisingly, the ship was left under the armed protection of Tara and Tupe. Bad weather delayed the expedition, and when a second, and successful departure was made, it was with the addition of a Bay chief, Matengaha (or Matingaro), who volunteered, and acted as intermediary in the subsequent negotiations with the Whangaroa people.

Upon entering the harbour, the rescue party found the *Boyd* burned to the water's edge, lying near the island Motu Wai, now called Red Island.[2] Matengaha initiated discussions with the people concerned in the massacre, persuading them by an offer of axes to produce the survivors, and was assured that they would be delivered next day. The Whangaroans did not appear upset when accused of the murders and taking the ship. Clearly, they considered their action justified by the provocation of Captain Thompson — a valid view in Maori terms. These discussions were conducted at the Ngatiuru settlement at Kaeo, and here, the rescue party were invited to dine and stay for the night. But they had seen 'the mangled fragments and fresh bones of our countrymen, with the marks even of the teeth remaining on them,' and the prospect of dining, sleeping and fraternising with these unrepentant cannibals had no appeal. A camp was therefore made on Red Island, and there the expedition spent the night. Next morning the survivors were given up. There were four: Anne Morley and her child, another child, Betsy Broughton, and a 15-year-old apprentice, Thomas Davis. Betsy's mother had died with the others.

Having accomplished its objective, the party returned to the Bay of Islands. The members had displayed much courage and resolution and were rewarded by a successful outcome. Berry had also had the hardihood to seize and take some Whangaroa people back to the Bay, but they were later released. Although it seems likely that without the guidance of Matengaha the affair might not have reached its satisfactory conclusion, we have only Berry's account to rely on, and in it he shows up to best advantage. Unfortunately, his subsequent behaviour took on a truculence and vindictiveness that does him no credit, and may cast some doubt on the impartiality of his accounts of the affair. In fact, we may well speculate as to how much the role of Captain Pattison contributed to the success of the venture.

The four survivors were not returned to Sydney, as *The City of Edinburgh* sailed early in January 1810 for South America and the Cape of Good Hope. Anne Morley died in South America, from where Davis was returned to England. Two years elapsed before the children were taken back to Sydney from Lima. *The City of Edinburgh* foundered in the Atlantic in 1812.

Early in 1810, Captain Chace of the sealer *King George*, encountered the whalers *Ann* and *Albion* off Cape Brett. These vessels had been at the Bay of Islands, where they had been told of the *Boyd* by Tara and Tupe. Although Chace had intended to call at the Bay, he abandoned the idea on hearing of the tragedy, and sailed for Sydney, and when he arrived on 9 March 1810, he bore the first news there of the fate of the ship.

Evidence suggests that during the voyage of the *Boyd* from Sydney to Whangaroa, Te Aara had been harshly treated, and perhaps flogged by Captain Thompson. On reaching his home, he had immediately informed his brother and his people. As a further aggravation, it appears that Thompson had a Maori flogged for petty theft while the ship was lying in the harbour. Retribution was swift and savage. On the third day after his arrival, Thompson, his first mate and some seamen left the ship in three boats, and pulled up the Kaeo River in search of spars. They were accompanied by a party of Maoris, who made a pretence of leading the captain to the timber country. When his men landed at a spot which tradition has determined as the river flat near Kaeo township, they were quickly dispatched to the last man. Later, the ship was attacked and the slaughter completed. During the subsequent celebration on board, the *Boyd* caught fire due to a gunpowder explosion and drifted to its present resting-place.

Although a number of accounts generally agree on the details of the massacre, the only significant point of contention is whether or not Te Pahi was an active participant in the attack on the ship. Only Berry's account finds him culpable. Even Te Aara, the probable instigator of the attack, did not implicate Te Pahi in his version given to Samuel Marsden at Matauri Bay in 1814, and his innocence was confirmed by Marsden's friends, Hongi Hika and Ruatara. All the evidence is, of course, from Maori sources, but only Berry claims that Te Pahi directed and inspired the slaughter of the crew and passengers remaining on the ship. The other accounts while conceding that Te Pahi was on the ship, maintain that he tried to save the lives of some of the victims, and had to be forcibly restrained when the killing was done. It seems certain that Te Pahi was there, having arrived from the Bay on the morning of the attack, which was not unusual in view of his relationship with the Whangaroa people. It is also clear, that whether an active agent in the murders or not, he accepted loot from the *Boyd*, which was later found at his island home at Te Puna.

Berry's version was given to whalers at the Bay by Captain Pattison and the Bay of Islands Maoris. This they readily accepted without further investigation, and here again we find Te Pahi's reputation at the mercy of a rival faction. Consequently, although the attack took place at Whangaroa, it was on Te Pahi's people that retribution descended.

Those who took it upon themselves to deal out the punishment were Captains Kingston, Walker, Morris, Parker and Hasselberg, of the whalers *Speke, Inspector, Atlanta, Diana* and *Perseverance*, which were lying at the Bay in March 1810. On 26 March they raised an attacking party, ostensibly to look for further survivors from the *Boyd* on Te Pahi's Island. But, regardless of innocence or guilt, they destroyed the village, slaughtering 60 people who were unable to escape. When a search of the island was made, the *Boyd's* longboat and some clothes of the ship's people were found. Te Pahi himself was severely wounded in this encounter, but escaped by swimming to the mainland supported by women. He abandoned the island, which has never since been inhabited. Some five years later, Samuel Marsden, touched by the spectacle of ruin of what had once been the citadel of a powerful chief, wrote:

> I never passed Tippahee's Island without a sigh. It is now desolate, without an inhabitant, and has been so since his death. The ruins of the little cottage, built by the kindness of the late Governor King, still remains. . . I think it probable the mistake, if there was one, which I am inclined to believe, originated in the affinity between the name of Tippahee and the chief of Wangaroa who was principally concerned in the destruction of the *Boyd* and whose name is Tippoohee. This chief I saw and conversed with on the subject.[3]

Although Te Pahi was not mortally wounded in the encounter, he died as a result of it in the course of the battles with the Whangaroa people which arose out of the *Boyd* disaster. And all this originated from Captain Thompson's arrogance, and perhaps, Ceroni's mindless antics with his watch.

Judging from his presence and behaviour, Te Pahi must indeed have been a chief of character, and one with great influence, since in his time he clearly maintained his authority firmly in his district, in spite of the infiltrating Ngapuhi. The extent of his influence is uncertain, but perhaps can be gauged by the attitude of the more northerly people during his progress down the coast in 1806 on the *Lady Nelson*, as recorded in the ship's edited logs.[4] Significantly, during the early Ngapuhi attacks on the eastern side of the Bay, his district was not threatened, and it was not until after his death that anything was heard of Hongi Hika, even then a notable fighting chief of Ngapuhi, and perhaps some 40 years old. It is likely that at about that time he began to make use of Kororipo *pa* at Kerikeri, in order to have contact with the shipping at the Bay.

With the old chief went the power of the people at Te Puna. When, in 1834, HMS *Alligator* visited the Bay, it was remarked that the *pa* adjacent to Te Pahi's Island, was then, 'in comparative disuse and consequently out of repair.'[5]

Echos of the *Boyd* tragedy resounded throughout the North for many years, and loot from the ship filtered into many parts of the northern peninsula. In 1815 Marsden was shown a fragment of a letter to Captain Thompson,[6] and at this time, dollars from the ship were freely circulating among the Bay Maoris and had found their way as far south as the Waitemata. In the Hauraki Gulf area, Marsden's friend, J.L. Nicholas, saw some suspended by cords around the people's necks.[7]

The first attempt to form a trading settlement based in New Zealand was frustrated by the events of 1809 — 1810. An expedition with this as its objective arrived at the Te Puna anchorage on 5 April 1810 in the brig *Experiment,* under the direction of William Leith. He was instructed by his Sydney employers, with the sanction and blessing of the Governor of New South Wales, to establish trade with the New Zealanders for flax.[8] To this end, small settlements were to be established in suitable localities. The timing was grossly inopportune, since at the same anchorage lay four ships whose crew had, a week or so earlier, savagely attacked Te Pahi's Island.

In a letter to his employers, Leith advised while at Te Puna:

All the natives of this bay being at war with each other, added to the extreme poverty of the place, gave me poor hopes of meeting with success at this bay; even potatoes are not to be procured . . . The quantity of flax is very small indeed — the whole I have seen would not produce one cwt. when manufactured.[9]

Later in his report he stated that 900 men had gone to war eastward from the district, no doubt to the Te Rawhiti locality, and that it was no longer safe for two ships to lie at the Bay by themselves.

The notorious Bruce had originally been selected as one of the party to have settled in New Zealand under this scheme, but when his undesirability became apparent he was dropped. Leith wrote of him: '. . . Bruce has certainly grocely(sic) deceived you by his false representations.' No attempt was made to establish a settlement of Europeans here, and Leith did not even land his settlers.

But he did make an interesting journey inland toward Whangaroa in the hope of finding four white men '. . . who are supposed to be concerned in the seizure of some ship or other.' This was obviously not the *Boyd*, since he was well aware of the events concerning her, but his expedition is important, being the first to penetrate so far inland at the Bay. The party went to the 'head of the river' — clearly the Mangonui Inlet — and travelled, by Leith's account, 10 miles inland, or not half-way to 'the place of abode of the white men.'

It is likely that only after the death of Te Pahi did the final conquest of Te Rawhiti occur, and with this Ngapuhi domination of Paroa and Kororareka. There was now incessant warfare at Hokianga, Whangaroa and the Bay of Islands, and there is consequently a hiatus in the narrative. But although the shipping fell away and avoided the Bay for a time, stability had been regained by 1814. The whalers returned, and with them, the missionaries. So, in that year, where business enterprise had failed to find a foothold ashore, success attended the efforts of the Rev. Samuel Marsden, Principal Chaplain of New South Wales and a Magistrate of the Colony. Financed only by scanty

57

Church Missionary Society funds, his settlements achieved little during their first 15 years or so, but the settlers did establish themselves firmly and gained the respect of the Maori people, although they failed to convert them. Forces more persuasive than they could muster were at work, and civilisation, such as it was, came to the Maori people through the trade and commerce generated by the whaling industry. The whalers had initiated this process, and their influence was at all times the strongest.

---

1. Kelly, L.G. 'Some New Information concerning the Ship *Boyd*,' *JPS*, v.49. For full accounts of the *Boyd* massacre, refer: McNab, *Historical Records*, v.1, p.293-389; McNab, *From Tasman to Marsden*, p.126 — 147; Sherrin, R.A. & Wallace, J.H. *Early History of N.Z.*, p. 146 et seq. Additional information is found in: Dillon, P. *A Voyage in the South Seas to Ascertain the Actual Fate of La Perouse's Expedition*, v.1, p.215 — 225.
2. Her remains still lie in a few feet of water about a mile west of the present township of Whangaroa.
3. Elder, J.R. *Letters and Journals of Samuel Marsden,* p.87-8.
4. Lee, *Log-Books,* p. 283-294.
5. Marshall, W.B. *A Personal Narrative of Two Visits to New Zealand in HMS Alligator, 1834*, p.8.
6. Nicholas, J.L. *Narrative of a Voyage to New Zealand,* v.1, p.359.
7. Ibid, p.404.
8. McNab, *From Tasman to Marsden,* p. 138 et seq.
9. McNab, *Historical Records,* v.1, p.302.

8

Mission Settlement at Oihi

In 1794 THE Rev. Samuel Marsden took up his appointment as
Assistant Chaplain at the convict settlement at Port Jackson,
and became Senior Chaplain after his superior's resignation. It
was his initiative that led to the founding of a Christian mission
at the Bay of Islands in 1814, and he alone nurtured it jealously
in its early years. Some histories have tended to over-emphasise
the importance of Marsden's mission in the growth of the Bay
of Islands. In the rigid class-concious England of the day
Marsden would have been regarded as a man who 'rose above
his station', and this may to some extent explain his difficulties
with the upper-class dominated administration in Australia.
But as the son of a tradesman-farmer, he was well equipped for
his subsequent activities in New Zealand.

Much debate has focussed upon the character and activities
of Marsden. He was, according to some, a mercenary settler, a
harsh taskmaster and a flogging magistrate, regarded with fear
or aversion by a large section of the New South Wales public.
Governor Macquarie himself was certainly not among the
Chaplain's admirers. This view is most often found expressed
in Australian histories, while those originating in this country,
perhaps influenced by persistent Church views on the subject,
portray him as a saintly and charitable Man of God. But
vilification and fatuous eulogies tend to obscure his qualities as
a pioneer, explorer and agriculturist. His saintliness and charity
may be questionable, but his courage and enterprise have never
been in doubt. It is these qualities, and his prestige as a
European *tohunga* and *rangatira,* which explain his popularity
with the Maori people, although for some 15 years or more they
rejected his religious beliefs.

In 1807 Marsden travelled to England to persuade the

Anglican Church Missionary Society for Africa and the East to establish a mission in New Zealand. In August 1809, having obtained the necessary authority from the Society, he returned to Australia in the convict transport *Ann*, accompanied by two volunteer catechists, William Hall, a carpenter, and John King, a ropemaker. Both were prepared to go to the Bay of Islands and combine the duties of teaching the Maoris civilised arts and crafts and the propagation of the Anglican faith. In a letter of 1808 to the C.M.S. Committee in London, Marsden explained his choice of tradesmen as missionaries. 'Commerce and the arts have a natural tendency to inculcate industrious and moral habits, open a way for the introduction of the Gospel, and lay the foundation for its continuance when received.'[1]

The *Ann* arrived at Sydney at the same time as Captain Samuel Rodman Chace's gloomy tidings of the *Boyd* disaster. This event was entirely unforeseen, and such was the feeling of revulsion at the settlement towards the Maoris that Marsden had to postpone his project. Strangely enough, the chief Ruatara[2] who was later to assume Te Pahi's authority at Rangihoua, had been discovered aboard the *Ann* by Marsden, in a weak and debilitated condition. This young man, whom the Chaplain later regarded as the mainstay of his New Zealand mission, had little for which to thank many of the Europeans with whom he had come into contact. After some 12 months of service in the *Argo* whaler in 1805, he was discharged at Sydney without pay, but managed to return to the Bay in the *Albion* whaler after six months service on her. In 1808 he again went to sea on the *Santa Anna* sealer, and he, with 13 others, were left almost without provisions on Bounty Island to catch seals. After nine months of acute suffering for want of water and good food, during which three men died, the remainder were relieved by the return of the ship. Ruatara then joined the same vessel as a sailor, since he wished to visit England and to see King George III. But in London in 1809, he found himself stranded and friendless in this strange land, and ill, penniless and disillusioned, he was sent aboard the *Ann*, where Marsden found him.

In October 1810, having remained for six months at Marsden's home at Parramatta, Ruatara and three other Maoris secured a passage aboard the *Frederick*, bound for the

New Zealand whaling grounds. Although this ship touched on the northern coast, and later lay off the Bay of Islands, the captain, perhaps reluctant to lose four useful men, evaded their requests to be put ashore. He later called at Norfolk Island where Ruatara and two of his companions were left destitute and without their share of the catch, which should have amounted to about £100. The other lad, a son of Te Pahi, was forcibly taken on to the ship and was not heard of again, since the *Frederick* was later taken at sea by an American privateer.

From Norfolk, the men were by chance rescued and taken to Port Jackson by the *Ann* whaler. There, Marsden attended to their needs until a passage was found for them on another of the numerous *Ann*s which then plied the Pacific. On this occasion, after five months on the whaling grounds they landed home safely with seed-wheat and garden tools donated by Marsden. This was in 1812, Ruatara having been absent for some four years, during which much had occurred. Te Pahi was dead, and his island home destroyed, but the adjacent settlement of Rangihoua was unharmed, and here Ruatara stayed, apparently taking over control in the absence of a better claimant. He may well have been supported by the influence of Hongi Hika, who apparently exerted an authority in this district derived from his mother and his wives.[3]

The wheat was shared out among his relations, and planted, but all except Ruatara and Hongi, having no knowledge of the nature of the plant, destroyed the crops before they matured. Since the problem of how to grind the grain arose, Ruatara borrowed a small coffee-mill from Captain Barnes of the whaler *Jefferson*, then at the Bay. This was not a success, and another year elapsed before a mill was obtained.

Early in 1813, Marsden, firmly believing that without grave provocation, none of the attacks on shipping in New Zealand would have occurred, decided that he could proceed with his mission scheme given Ruatara's support. Since 1810, when Hall and King had been recruited for New Zealand, Kendall, a schoolteacher by profession, had volunteered his services, and had been sent out to join the venture. Although Marsden now had reservations about King and Hall, he decided to send Hall and Kendall to the Bay of Islands to explore the possibility of establishing his mission.

The experiences of Ruatara, and of others similarly ill-used, demonstrated that reliable communications with a settlement in New Zealand could not be maintained without the use of a vessel in the direct employ of the Society, despite the increase in the shipping at the Bay. Accordingly, Marsden on his own initiative, and at his immediate expense, purchased the brig *Active* for the use of the C.M.S. and for trading on his own account. As things turned out, the brig's trading activities left the New Zealand settlement still very much dependant on the whalers for supplies and communication.

Undoubtedly, the experiment about to begin might involve considerable personal risk. In the view of J.L. Nicholas, Marsden's friend, the Maoris were 'dreaded by the good and assailed by the worthless, their real dispositions not ascertained; the former dared not venture to civilize them, and the latter only added to their ferocity.'[4]

In March 1814, Thomas Kendall and William Hall sailed from Port Jackson in the *Active*, going via Tasmania to reconnoitre the Bay of Islands and discover the attitude of the Maoris to the proposal to form an English settlement among them. Captain of the *Active* was then Peter Dillon, an Irishman who was in his time one of the most notable characters in the Pacific. The mate was Rodman Chace who appears to have been the same man who brought the news of the *Boyd* to Sydney in 1810. There were two related men of this name in these waters at this time.

The investigation was promising. Assurances of support were given by Ruatara, Hongi Hika, then resident at Kerikeri, the old chief Tara at Kororareka, and Pomare Nui,[5] who lived at Matauwhi Bay. At Ruatara's 'farm' at Motu Tara, some miles from Te Puna, wheat was growing, and in his 'storeroom', the catechists saw rum, tea, sugar, flour, cheese and chests of European clothing. Here, surely, was an 'enlightened savage'.

The *Active* loaded spars from the Kawakawa River and departed for Sydney on 25 July, taking with her Ruatara, Hongi Hika and one of his sons, Korokoro [6] of Paroa Bay, and other less distinguished Maoris.

During the absence of the *Active*, Marsden had been granted leave by Governor Macquarie to proceed to New Zealand to see his mission established. Thus, on 19 November 1814, when the brig, in charge of Captain Hansen, again left for the Bay, it carried the whole mission complement. The settlers were Thomas Kendall, his wife and three sons, Mr and Mrs Hall and their son, and Mr and Mrs King, also with a son. These were the catechists. Also on board, were Hongi, Korokoro, Ruatara, and, as a passenger, the New South Wales farmer, J.L. Nicholas. A few stock were also carried, namely a stallion, two mares, a bull, two cows, a few sheep and poultry, the cattle being a present from Governor Macquarie.

Before his departure from New South Wales, Kendall had been appointed a Justice of the Peace in New Zealand, and at his discretion, he was given authority to permit or forbid vessels to take Maori people away from the country, or to discharge sailors or others there. Any such action taken without the requisite permission was a punishable offence. The appointment and powers had been created by a New South Wales Government Order of 9 November, and Hongi, Ruatara and Korokoro were, at Kendall's discretion, empowered to act under this authority. Offences were to be tried in the Colony or in England, but in the absence of any effectual policing, the Order was little more than a gesture.[7]

On the way to the Bay the *Active* called at the Cavalli Islands, from where some 20 years previously, Tuki and Huru had been kidnapped by the *Daedelus*.

Since Marsden was resolved, if he could, to terminate the warfare between the Whangaroa and Bay people which had arisen from the *Boyd* massacre, he went ashore at Matauri in company with Ruatara, Hongi, Korokoro, Nicholas, Kendall, King and Captain Hansen. He met Te Aara (George), Te Puhi and others involved in the affair, and was given their own account of it. So as to gain their confidence, he, with Hongi and Nicholas, remained on shore overnight, undeterred by Te Aara's villainous countenance, and the recent violent history of his people. Happily, however, Te Aara told Marsden that night that he wanted peace, and when the position of the settlers was explained to him, with emphasis on the fact that they were under the protection of the Bay chiefs, he also assured Marsden

63

that his people would do them no harm.[8]

On Thursday, 22 December 1814, the *Active* arrived at the Bay of Islands and anchored in the cove of Oihi, under the massive *pa* of Rangihoua, Ruatara's home. A brooding silence now lies over this eerie and lonely place, but the now desolate shore was then full of life, for here dwelt a strong chief and a prosperous people. Rising from the little stream that runs out of the steep hills at the south end of the cove, is the great terraced hill of the *pa,* where, on Christmas Day Ruatara planted the Union Jack as a gesture of goodwill. On the little flat below, Marsden preached his inaugural sermon. A rough outdoor chapel had been erected, with canoes for forms, and the chiefs and their people from Kerikeri and the Kororareka side attended in force, listening politely in deference to their guests. Not to be outdone, 300 warriors danced a furious *haka* around Marsden at the close of the service.

Work was quickly commenced to construct houses for the settlers, and terraces for them were excavated in the steep hillside. These terraces are still visible, the only evidence, other than recent formal memorials, of the occupation of these courageous people. Had Marsden and his catechists searched the whole coastline, a more dismal location for their settlement could scarcely have been found. The choice of the site at Oihi, when better ones existed within a mile or so, was either a hasty decision or one imposed upon the settlers by a cautious Ruatara, unwilling to part with any good land at Te Puna, and even then doubting the wisdom of his decision to play host to the mission. So here they were, on a poverty-stricken strip of beach, entirely at the mercy of the people of the land, which may indeed have been the way Ruatara wanted it.

Having constructed a temporary communal building for the immediate use of his settlers, Marsden sought timber to build permanent houses at Oihi. He and Nicholas visited the chief Tara, whose authority was required to bring timber from the closest source, the Kawakawa River. There the *Active* was able to load sufficient timber in about 10 days.

On 10 January, Hongi Hika, who was probably then assessing the value of missionaries in terms of warlike supplies, conducted Marsden and Nicholas up the river to Kororipo *pa* at Kerikeri, where they met Hongi's senior half-brother Kaingaroa.[9] From there they travelled inland to the Waimate district where they visited the Okuratope *pa*, inland stronghold of the brothers, and found wheat growing there, and they later walked to Lake 'Morberree' (Omapere) where Te Hotete had died. Waimate, it should be remembered, had been the springboard for the Ngapuhi invasions of the coast, and several chiefs had *kainga* both there and at the Bay.

Shortly after the party's return from the inland exploration, a small incident occurred at Rangihoua. The wife of one 'Wurree', said to be the brother of 'Gunnah', a chief (Kana?), was suspected of adultery with Hansen, son of the captain of the *Active*, for the very reasonable return of one nail and the promise of another. Wurree, finding his wife in possession of this fabulously valuable article, at once suspected the worst, and complained. Marsden, regarding this as an excellent opportunity to demonstrate that such abuses would not be tolerated by the missionaries, at once convened an enquiry to deliberate on this matter. After due examination, the suspected parties were exonerated. 'But,' the sceptical Nicholas mused, 'however pertinacious the lady was in insisting upon her innocence, I am much inclined to believe that the husband had just grounds for his suspicions; and that the nail had effected an easy compliance'.[10]

A cruise down the east coast was now undertaken, and such was Marsden's confidence in his Maori friends, that the ship's complement on this voyage was 28 New Zealanders and only seven pakeha. Contrary winds prevented a visit to Whangaroa, and the *Active* proceeded down the coast to the Thames, visiting the people there with a good deal of amiability displayed on both sides. In the Hauraki Gulf, the party were told of the depredations of the *Venus*, which had made away from there with the daughter of the chief Houpa. At Bream Bay, on the return trip to the Bay, the *Active* was visited by John Savage's protege, Moehanga.

Good progress had been made at Oihi on the vessel's return, and preparations were therefore made for the return voyage. The *Active* now loaded timber in the Kawakawa River and, on the invitation of a Waikare chief, Marsden went on an exploratory jaunt up that river to Waikare itself. Considering the time at his disposal, he completed a very impressive examination of the Bay of Islands, some inland areas, and the eastern coast from North Cape to the Thames.

On his return from Kawakawa to Rangihoua, he went with Kendall by canoe to the anchorage of the whaler *Jefferson*, lately arrived, and lying, it seems, at Kororareka. Here Kendall was called upon to exercise his judicial function to examine a dispute between Maoris and the crew, the particulars of which Marsden duly reported to Governor Macquarie. Barnes was notorious for his treatment of Maoris.

To the consternation of all, on the party's return to Oihi, Ruatara was found dangerously ill and likely to die. This was a very serious matter for the new settlers, since no other chief was committed to their cause to the same extent as he. Ruatara had been most anxious that civilisation should come to his people, until it had been suggested to him at Sydney, 'with the most dark and diabolical design', as Marsden put it, that 'our only object was to deprive the New Zealanders of their country and that as soon as we had gained any footing over there we should pour into New Zealand an armed force and take the country to ourselves.'[11] Clearly Ruatara had no wish to be the author of such a calamity, but as history has demonstrated, the 'diabolical' prophesy was a true one. Ruatara's scheme for a town of European design to be built on the rising land at the back of Te Puna beach was never realised, although he and Marsden had examined the site and had even decided the location of the buildings.

On 21 February 1815, a few days before the departure of the *Active*, Mrs King gave birth to a son at Oihi, the first fully white child born in this country. That she was making history probably had little significance for the poor lady at the time, as the birth was not easy. On 24 February he was christened Thomas Holloway by Marsden[12] but sadly, he lived only four years.

On the day of the baptism, a deed[13] was executed by which the title of the Oihi land was granted to the Mission Society. The deed describes the boundaries of the land, which on later survey was found to be 60 acres. The price was 12 axes. The island

Moturoa, at the mouth of the Kerikeri River, had also been offered by the chief Te Morenga[14] but was declined. It was apparently quite fertile at the time, and the modest asking price was two muskets.

The signatories to the Oihi document were 'Ahoodee O Gunna' (Turi O Kana), reputedly the son of the chief Moka of Hokianga, a Maori witness, Nicholas and Kendall. Turi appeared as the vendor, but it is not clear how he came by the title. It is conceivable, as Marsden asserted, that he was related to Te Pahi, perhaps through his mother, and apparently by marriage through his wife. No Maori at that time had any appreciation of the European concept of title or its transfer, and it was probably understood that the mission people would occupy the land, not necessarily exclusively, while they required it. Although Turi seems to have been a chief of some sort of standing, this would not have given him the right *per se* to dispose of land unless he had a demonstrable personal interest in it.

After having received the assurances of local chiefs, and particularly that of Hongi Hika, that should Ruatara die they would protect the mission settlement, Marsden and his entourage sailed for Port Jackson on 25 February. Te Morenga, the old chief Tara and his kinsman Tupe were among the Maori passengers to Australia on this occasion.

The settlers were now left to work out their own salvation, and a grim prospect confronted them. The picnic atmosphere soon dispersed, and their struggle for a tolerable existence in this poorly located and equipped station commenced. Only 21 Europeans remained at Oihi. They were Mr and Mrs Kendall and their three children; a servant, Richard Stockwell; Mr and Mrs Hall and one boy; and Mr and Mrs King with two boys. These were the Society's people — Mrs Hansen, wife of the *Active's* captain, and her boy, stayed on their own account. There were also two sawyers and a blacksmith employed by the Society. Three runaway convicts who had been at the Bay during the catechist's first visit were left to assist the settlers until they could be returned to New South Wales. The smith and one of the sawyers had their wives and two children sent over by the *Active* on her next trip, making the total then 25 settlers.

At the time, Marsden was confident of the good faith of both his missionaries and the Maoris, so that at the conclusion of his first New Zealand journal he observed: 'At the Bay of Islands I consider a vessel to ride equally as safe as in the harbour of Port Jackson should ever any difference take place between the natives and the crew, but for any other part of the island I won't answer.'[15]

In his book, Nicholas made some interesting observations. The 'Indians', as he called the Maoris, were even at that time using the word 'pakeha' for Europeans. They were avid traders and he speculated on their Asiatic origin, perhaps being the first to expound that theory. He also judged them to be inveterate liars, particularly in adducing sinister motives to such of their fellow-countrymen as suited their notions at the time. It is a view consistent with the behaviour of the Kororareka people as to Te Pahi's involvement in the *Boyd* affair. Both Nicholas and Marsden were shown an interesting document by the chief Te Koki.[16] A tattered paper evidently given him by the rescue party which discovered the *Boyd*'s survivors, it authorised his possession of that ship's jolly-boat in payment for services rendered at the time of the rescue.

Nicholas observed hosts of dogs, very much like Old English sheep-dogs, which the Maoris kept and used as a source of clothing and food. They also painted their faces with a blue pigment, and when he enquired as to its source, he was told that 'they dug it up in the lands bordering the Cowa Cowa, which were full of it . . . But they were obliged to dig to a great depth before they could get at it.' Some of the pigment Nicholas took away, and subsequent analysis showed it to be manganese, a mineral that in recent times has been worked in the area between the Waikare River and one of its tributaries, the Manawaora.

Nicholas mentions a Hindu deserter from Berry's ship, *The City of Edinburgh*, apparently still happy and contented after four years' living with the Maoris. His book also contains a vocabulary, list of numerals, and sentences in Maori – certainly the most comprehensive published to that date – comprising some 25 pages.

In many respects, the mission at Oihi was a failure. Nevertheless the limited success of its successors at Paihia and Waimate owed much to these early laymen. While their evangelical success was nil, they maintained their sporadic school and their trade-teaching to some effect, and consolidated their position with the Maori people. But to Kendall must go the credit for communicating with them on their own level, by assimilating, with considerable ethnological background, a knowledge of the language which led to its early written form. Although his downfall arose from this, his work was invaluable to his successors.

---

1. Elder, *Marsden's Lieutenants,* p.16. For further accounts of the mission at Oihi, refer: Elder, *Letters and Journals*; McNab, *From Tasman to Marsden* and *Historical Records*, v.1.
2. See Appendix 1.3.
3. See Appendix 1.2.
4. Nicholas, *Narrative of a Voyage,* v.1, p.2.
5. See Appendix 1.11.
6. See Appendix 1.10.
7. McNab, *Historical Records,* v.1, p.328-9.
8. The old stone cross, which fell from the monument erected to Marsden in recent times at Oihi, now lies on Matauri Beach marking the place where this meeting occurred.
9. See Appendix 1.2.
10. Nicholas, op.cit., p.368.
11. Elder, *Letters and Journals*, p.141.
12. Waimate Birth Registers, Diocesan Office, Auckland.
13. Elder, op.cit., p.123.
14. See Appendix 1.7, and Nicholas, op.cit., v.2, p.81.
15. Elder, op.cit., p.130.
16. See Appendix 1.2.

9

Southseamen and Missionaries

It should not be assumed that the treatment dealt out to the Maoris by visiting seamen was uniformly ruthless and dishonest. Despite the recurring incidence of such behaviour, a friendly, if wary, intercourse had developed prior to the advent of Marsden's missionaries. The Maori and the southseaman understood each other, met on clearly understood terms, and each was able to gratify the other's needs. The missionary, who could offer nothing that the whaler could not, other than a baffling doctrine and behaviour, was at a sad disadvantage. Until the 1820s the whalers and sealers exerted the only significant pressures which encouraged the adoption of European techniques and ways of life among the Maoris. Their relationship had begun towards the end of the eighteenth century, and despite setbacks had continued until the founding of the mission. Such pakeha habits of industry acquired by the Bay Maoris and whatever knowledge of European languages and customs, resulted from this intercourse with the shipping. Opportunities to travel were eagerly grasped by the many Maoris who were recruited as seamen, and who on their return made their small contribution to their people's knowledge of the affairs and ways of the outside world. In the 1820s some seaman-settlers ashore added their small influence, and these, together with the shore-based traders and merchants, dominated the scene at the Bay until 1840.

The excessive emphasis on missionary activity at the Bay of Islands by uncritical commentators over a period of more than a century, has obscured this significant development, and while the efforts of the missionaries were by no means unrewarded, the fashion has been to consider the history of this place in terms of mission stations, leaving the story less than half told. The mission situation in the early 1820s is well described in evidence before Commissioner Bigge, in 1821.[1]

Cannibalism, the most unacceptable Maori custom in European terms, did not survive the decline of the tribal wars at the end of the 1830s. This was obviously due to the falling-off of the supply of victims, the weight of whaler and settler opinion against it, and the Maori acceptance of the British sovereignty in 1840. Oddly, they appear to have been coy on this subject since early European contacts, except when inflamed by war.

Much has been said also about infanticide, but with little evidence to support the contention of its practice to any very significant extent. It could well have been used, as appears logical in a community which had no sanctions against it, as an extension of abortion for specific reasons, but there appears to be little likelihood that it reached serious proportions. Among others, Ensign McCrae in 1820,[2] Augustus Earle in 1827[3] and J.S. Polack in 1831-37[4] noted the custom, and believed that it applied particularly to girls, but to suggest an extensive incidence of this is inconsistent with the practice of polygamy, which was universally practised. However, Earle notes happily that the European demand for Maori wives brought an end to the undesirable practice.

Although prostitution, which was endemic at the Bay of Islands from the time of the first visitors, has been frequently described as the most destructive social evil attributed to the seamen, there is little evidence that this had any significant or long-term effect. Dr A.S. Thomson, Surgeon-Major of the 58th Regiment, found that 'the [venereal] disease is generally mild, and yields to cleanliness and medicine . . .' although he noted that it was more prevelant among Maoris.[5] Dr Fairfowl, in evidence before Commissioner Bigge in 1821, believed that the Maoris themselves kept the disease reasonably under control by *tapu* of the persons afflicted.[6] There were no social pressures in Maori society giving rise to prostitution, and the satisfaction of the demands of large numbers of visiting seamen was clearly not considered undesirable, but instead an opportunity to acquire European commodities at no significant cost and within a pleasant social context.

There is no doubt that, apart from the incidence of tribal

warfare, the Maoris lived in a well-ordered society which forbade only such things as threatened it, but this order inevitably collapsed under the pressures imposed on it by the alien European culture.

As we have seen, the association between seamen and Maoris had reached a fairly advanced stage at the time of the founding of the first mission. This had developed into an easy relationship, if one occasionally marred by unpleasant incidents. Some ships were notorious for their ill-use of native people, notably the *King George*, Captain Lasco Jones, the *Jefferson*, Captain Barnes and the *Vansittart*, Captain Hunt. Such cases invariably attracted the attention of the New South Wales authorities. Generally, however, the relationship had developed to the advantage of both parties. The Maori was quick to realise this, and his appetite for muskets, lead and powder, of all trade goods the most in demand, grew apace.

By this time, escaped convicts from New South Wales and Tasmania had begun to infiltrate into the Bay, settling in the more remote parts of the Bay. They came with whalers or sealers as stowaways or crew, sometimes having been illegally employed by shipmasters because of the difficulty of recruiting seamen in this part of the world. The most notable recorded case of illegal recruiting of convicts occurred in 1820, when Captain Riggs of the *General Gates*, an American sealer, took away a dozen or so from Sydney, only to be arrested at the Bay by HM Storeship *Dromedary*.[7] Such people often sought asylum among the Maoris, who would harbour them or give them up as they felt inclined. The convict problem was in its early stages at the advent of the missionaries.

Into this scene, Marsden's catechists fitted uneasily. The Maori, knowing little of the pakeha's religion and caring less, regarded the unimpressive little band as a source of iron, tools and other goods they desired, and inevitably came to expect muskets, ultimately precipitating a major crisis at the settlement. A flimsy sort of power might have been wielded by withholding supplies, were it not that the Maori had few scruples about helping himself. It could perhaps have been foreseen that parsimonious salaries and poor communications with Sydney would make constant trade with their hosts a necessity, to the point at which it became an overriding factor in the missionaries' lives.

In this difficult situation, Kendall, Hall and King took up their work. About a week after the departure of the *Active*, the *Phoenix*, Captain Parker, visited Rangihoua Bay to obtain supplies of wood and water. Parker, in command of the *Diana*, had been among those responsible for the massacre of Te Pahi's people, and must indeed have been insensitive or over-confident to beg provisions from the relations of his victims. On that same day, 3 March 1815, Ruatara died. The erstwhile enthusiast and mainstay of the mission was gone, but in accordance with his promise to Marsden, Hongi Hika assumed a vicarious responsibility for the safety of the mission people. Although he displayed no interest in the spiritual objectives of the mission, and died unconverted 13 years later, Hongi was a man of his word, although an element of self-interest proved later to be present. Kendall wrote: 'Our friend Shunghee [Hongi] is strongly attached to our interests. Whenever he hears of strong parties paying us a visit, he is sure to bring his men for our protection.'[8] Ironically, then, Marsden's venture was for many years obliged to lean heavily for protection on a man whose later activities accounted for the death, devouring and slavery of countless numbers of his countrymen. His friendship with Kendall was clearly not without thought for Kendall's assistance in his interests. Hongi had not at this stage achieved the authority he later had, on the death of his powerful half-brother Kaingaroa,[9] but his *mana* was high in the Kerikeri, Waimate and Kaikohe districts.

The arrival of the *Active* in the Bay in May 1815 coincided with the purchase by Kendall on behalf of the Society of 50 acres of land at Waitangi[10] from the Ngatipou (or Ngatirehia) chief Waraki, reputedly the late Ruatara's father-in-law.[11] Waraki was then in a difficult political situation with the encroaching Ngapuhi, and his early death had serious results. Although well-disposed toward the settlers, he was also concerned, as Ruatara had been, that eventually the Europeans would have all of his people's land. However, despite his pessimism, he was apparently unable to resist the princely offer of five axes for the land that he parted with.

About a week later, Mrs Hall gave birth to the first girl of European parentage to be born in New Zealand, and late in July, Hall went over to Waitangi with the sawyers Conroy and Campbell to build a house. It was not as difficult to procure timber here, Waitangi being much closer to the source at Kawakawa. No sooner had building begun, than Waraki died, and some disturbances occurred, but the work was continued, and on 5 September Mr and Mrs Hall went to live there.

Although this move had been made contrary to Marsden's advice, the four months which followed appeared to vindicate local judgement. In this short time, Hall claims that he had '. . . almost every useful kitchen vegetable in the highest state of perfection.' He also reaped small crops of both wheat and barley, and cleared two acres for wheat. 'Wythangee (Waitangi),' he declared enthusiastically, 'is the garden of New Zealand.'[12] Hall was undoubtedly a diligent worker, but unaware of the political situation, he reckoned without his Ngapuhi. It seems that even his own people, whom he employed in his agricultural work, constantly pilfered everything portable containing iron, although he paid them in axes, chisels, etc. The collapse of the venture came on 25 January 1816, when a party of Maoris came from the Kororareka side and plundered the house. With Hall unable to effectively protect his home, it was stripped of everything removable, while he was violently attacked in attempting a defence. Mrs Hall, upon coming to his rescue received a serious injury to her head which impaired the sight of one of her eyes. But for the arrival of the local people, who drove the raiders off, the affair might have ended tragically. Captain Graham of the *Catherine*, then lying at Paroa, assisted the battered family, and returned them to Oihi. The reason for the raid is obscure, but was certainly related to other recent Ngapuhi conquests. Later, the Waitangi house was also removed and taken over, thus ending the first brief period of European residence there. Hall continued to crop the land with wheat and barley, working from Oihi, until his departure from New Zealand in 1824.

Visitors to the Bay of Islands in 1815 included the brig *Trial* and the schooner *Brothers* on their way to the south, where attempts were to be made to form trading settlements for the newly-formed New South Wales New Zealand Company. As with the previous attempt in 1810, this venture, floated in Sydney by the same people, was a total failure. The ships returned to the Bay in August, after a disastrous encounter with the Maoris of the Thames district, which, in Kendall's view, was the fault of the Europeans, since they had dealt fraudulently with the Bay Maoris before they left for the south.

Kendall, the most intelligent of the missionaries, and the dominant personality, was now engrossed in an investigation into the Maori language and social usages, which in 1820 resulted in a systematic attempt to reduce the language to writing. Although this work undoubtedly contributed to his downfall, it was of inestimable value to his successors. In 1815 he had already had his *A Korao New Zealand* published at Sydney, but the adoption of a system of orthography troubled him, as well it might, for although the form now used is simple and reasonably accurate, it is still not perfect.[13]

The situation at Oihi at the close of 1815 was not promising. The Maoris were interested only in the white man's amenities to the exclusion of his religion, and the missionaries lived in constant fear of harassment from itinerant Maori parties. Differences had arisen between Kendall and Hall in regard to private trade, which Kendall considered weakened the communistic principles on which the settlement was founded. Hall voluntarily detached himself from the others, and the strained relationship between King and Kendall surfaced in a letter written by Kendall to his colleague in January 1816. This remarkable document consists of one noble sentence of 94 words, in which King is accused of holding Kendall's magisterial authority in contempt. It informed him that only the most formal relations would in future be maintained between them. King was apparently impressed by this feat of penmanship, for, as Kendall later notes with satisfaction, 'Since I wrote the above, Mr and Mrs King have not been so personal.'

The constitution of the small colony could have been responsible for this dissension. They had no appointed head, and consequently no decision-maker who could deal with situations summarily as they arose. Marsden, apparently unwilling to delegate his authority, did not appoint anyone to be in formal charge of his project. This failure of the settlers to co-operate seems odd in people of a pitifully small community, in a wild and strange land where they undoubtedly and quite frequently feared for their safety.

In November 1815, Captain Parker and the *Phoenix* were again in port, further contributing to Kendall's magisterial problems. The *Phoenix* and the *Cretan* had arrived and anchored at Rangihoua on the 22nd and a week later were ready to leave. In the meantime Parker had sent a man named Fop ashore to remain there until he could secure a passage to Port Jackson. In accordance with the relevant proclamation, a verbal request was made by Captain Parker on Fop's behalf to Kendall. Kendall refused on the grounds that Fop's presence on the ship was irregular, since his name was not mentioned on the clearance papers. Furthermore, Parker was not prepared to underwrite Fop's food and lodging during his stay ashore, and lastly, the Te Puna Maoris wanted nothing to do with any of Parker's crew. This categorical refusal was conveyed to the Captain in an official letter which he contemptuously returned by his first mate on 30 November. Having roundly abused Kendall, the mate ordered his boat's crew to pull down his house, and they were doing so when about 100 Maoris arrived, at the sight of whom Kendall reported with satisfaction, 'they [the crew] were glad to repair to their boats and go quietly away.' The *Phoenix* and the *Cretan* departed at once, still encumbered with the disputed Fop.

But the importance of the Te Puna anchorages had been declining for some time, and by the end of 1815, the days of the 'north harbour' as a whaler's rendezvous were drawing to a close. Apart from the shipping having business with the missionaries, the harbour was little used. This situation was made clear when in an entry in his journal in 1823, the Rev. J. Butler wrote: 'As soon as I heard of the arrival of ye ship in the north harbour, I immediately set off to see what she was, fully believing, from her coming into the north harbour, she must have missionaries or stores on board, or both.'[14]

76

For a short time, Korokoro's stronghold at Paroa, on the outer side of the Kororareka peninsula, succeeded the Te Puna-Mangonui locality as the favoured anchorage and supply base in the Bay, but it too had succumbed to Kororareka by the early 1820s.

---

1. McNab, *Historical Records*, v.1, p.545-58. McCrae and Fairfowl, who resided in New Zealand for 10 months during the visit of H.M. Storeship *Dromedary* in 1820, gave evidence before Commissioner Bigge concerning missionaries at the Bay. Bigge's charge was to examine conditions in New Zealand.
2. Ibid, p.539.
3. Earle, A. *Nine Months Residence in New Zealand in 1827*, p.195.
4. Polack, J.S. *New Zealand Being a Narrative of Travels and Adventures*, v.1, p.380.
5. Thomson, A.S. *Story of New Zealand*, v.1, p.214-5.
6. McNab, op.cit., p.555.
7. A description of this incident is given in Chapter 11.
8. Elder, *Marsden's Lieutenants*, p.112.
9. See Appendix 1.2.
10. The land appears to have been located between the present Residency and the Waitangi bridge.
11. Elder, op.cit., p.83.
12. Ibid, p.125.
13. A perusal of any written narrative of the early nineteenth century will show that the representation of consonants presented a formidable problem. An example is the almost unrepresentable Ngapuhi diphthong, now simply shown as H, whose sound could roughly be described as an H, heavily aspirated with the tongue close to the palate, and terminating with a tight palatal Y.
14. Barton, op.cit., p.308.

10

The Tribal Wars and the Missionaries

On Monday, 12 August 1816 New Zealand's first school was opened at Oihi. Since the Maoris did not object to their children attending, 33 pupils, among them a son of Te Pahi, were present. The children were fed by the mission, this probably accounting for the presence of many of them, since evidence suggests that food was not plentiful at this side of the Bay at that time. It seems that there were some wily old fellows who also wished to attend school, but Kendall believed that their apparent thirst for knowledge was, in fact, a hunger for mission food. The school was presumably one of the cluster of buildings on the high ground on the north side of the creek behind the Marsden Cross. Early in 1816 the staff was increased by the appointment of a Mr Carlisle as assistant to Kendall. However, in 1818 the school was closed temporarily, since the mission was no longer able to feed the pupils, who would therefore not attend.

The education of adults was a thankless task. Hall complained that while he was working with them, his tools vanished progressively until he had none at all, and the interest of his pupils in any one job could not be long sustained. At Waitangi, his wheelbarrow was chopped up for the nails, together with a small shed, and even boats acquired by Maoris from the whalers suffered the same fate for the sake of the iron they contained. Iron could quickly and easily be fashioned into efficient tools or weapons and was thus highly valued by a people who only 20 years earlier had emerged from the Stone Age.

The subjects taught were mostly handiwork, an emphasis which continued in Maori schools until their abolition in recent times. In conformity with the rather odd C.M.S. mission practice in New Zealand, the language used was exclusively Maori. The pupils appear to have had things rather much their own way, since Maori parents imposed no discipline on their children, and were indulgent in the extreme. This, it was considered, ensured the independent and aggressive spirit inseparable from a warrior people. However such children would scarcely have been promising material for a teacher to work with. In the school register for October 1816, Kendall noted: 'We have also been under the necessity of following several of our people into the bush, where we have taught them their lessons.'[1] A tenacious man, he was undismayed by obstacles, as his later activities testify. His school, 70 strong when the Rev. J. Butler took over the mission in 1819, was then the only tangible result of five years work among the New Zealanders. In his nine years at the Bay, Kendall established and maintained a school, wrote a book on the Maori language, collaborated with Professor Lee of Cambridge University in the production of the first authoritative work on the subject, investigated Maori psychology more thoroughly than was good for him, and finally took Holy Orders. Between times, he contrived to act as a business colleague of Hongi Hika, did considerable exploring, and traded in pork and muskets, besides performing his not very onerous duties as a Justice of the Peace. More importantly, and fatally for him, he gained the friendship and confidence of many Maoris, particularly Hongi Hika. A strong, aggressive personality, he constantly chafed under the restraints which his position imposed upon him. But Kendall was indeed a scholar, if not a gentleman, as Marsden later confirms.

Toward the end of 1818, Oihi had assumed a more permanent and tolerably comfortable aspect. The fear of sudden assault was not so constantly in the minds of the settlers, no doubt due largely to Kendall's relationship with Hongi, whose influence at Oihi was great, since his mother and his wives were members of this coastal tribe. However, little effort was directed to converting the heathen, and, indeed, it was Marsden's policy first to influence the Maori by percept rather than preaching, in the hope that conversion would follow. This policy failed, but when, in 1823, Henry Williams adopted a reversal of the procedure, he was equally unsuccessful, and only the inexorable erosion of the Maori culture under European pressure finally achieved what the mission had struggled for so long and so hard.

At the end of 1818, Captain Thompson, who had replaced Hansen as captain on the *Active*, gave the number of mission settlers at Oihi as 10 adults and 15 children, that is, five families: the Kendalls, Kings, Halls, Gordons and Carlisles.[2] Gordon was described as 'Superintendant of Agriculture' — a sinecure, surely — but the tradesmen who had followed the first contingent in 1815 had by this time been withdrawn.

The inability of the settlers to agree among themselves was now causing Marsden much alarm and led him to conclude that private trade, beyond that necessary to sustain life, was the cause of the trouble. This may have been so, but his expectations of the conduct of the missionaries exceeded that which might have been reasonably anticipated, considering the conditions imposed upon them. They were marooned among a people, the possibility of whose conversion must have appeared to them to be remote. Not being ordained clergy answerable to the Church, the settlers were at the mercy of the Missionary Society, and directly responsible to Marsden, a man not noted for his Christian charity or understanding. To live, they had to trade, but were expected to do so only to the extent that would sustain the community. It is to their credit that there was apparently some response to an appeal from Marsden to limit their commercial activities; Hall, however, appears to have been particularly rebellious.

In this respect Marsden was scarcely a model of the behaviour he required from his missionaries. He was himself a businessman of no mean ability, having interests outside his religious appointment from which he derived financial gain, and these activities have been the subject of much divided opinion. But here we are not concerned with this aspect of his character, for his influence and activities in New Zealand, aside from his relations with his missionaries, are difficult to fault. He did good service in exploration in the North, and in recording his observations of people and places he earned well-merited distinction. Always the champion and friend of the Maoris, he enjoyed great prestige among the chiefs. In fact, had he shown as much sympathy with the problems of his settlers, he might perhaps have had less trouble on his hands.

Since the founding of the mission, when Marsden had vainly hoped he had made peace, warfare between the Ngapuhi and the southern tribes had been almost continuous. In this the Whangaroa people and Ngatimanu were sometimes allied to Ngapuhi, so that the local peace had only promoted remoter wars. The mission had therefore settled down in an atmosphere of alarms and excursions generated by minor tribal skirmishes and threats of war, but in January 1818, the large-scale war expeditions got under way.[3] As seen in Chapter 5, parties were led to the east coast region by Te Morenga and Hongi Hika, soon to become the most successful, if not the most astute of the Maori generals. His advantage lay in the use of firearms and their adaptation to tribal warfare. Between 1818 and 1824, the people of Hauraki, Bay of Plenty, Kawhia, Taranaki and Wellington suffered onslaughts which seriously depleted their numbers. Whole settlements were entirely depopulated, and thousands were killed or enslaved. C.O. Davis quotes a visitor to Mokoia, one of these battlefields near Auckland, as having seen the bones of 2000 slain whitening the ground. Here, at West Tamaki in November 1821, Hongi and his Ngapuhi had defeated the Ngati-Paoa chief Te Hinaki.[4]

The 1818 expedition was not, however, as conspicuous a success as later ones, and in it the musket did not play a decisive part, but for all that, it was a victory for the northern people. Hongi told Marsden that when his forces joined those of Houpa, a Thames chief and an ally on this occasion, the total number in the war-party was 800. The expedition, it may be recalled, arose from the activities of the *Venus*, which in the hands of mutineers had visited the Bay in 1806, and had abducted women, relations of Hongi and Te Morenga, who were later taken by the East Cape Maoris from the ship and never returned to their homes. It was against these people that the expedition was directed. Hongi claimed that 500 villages were destroyed and 2000 prisoners taken.[5] Since this adds up to two and a half prisoners to every member of the attacking party, it suggests either a gross exaggeration or docile prisoners, but many may have been consumed as they came to hand. The Oihi missionaries do confirm, however, that a canoe loaded with about 70 heads landed on their beach on its return from this raid. Hongi's party got back to the Bay in January 1819.

It seems that his over-riding ambition, to the point of obsession, was conquest for revenge, rather than the acquisition of territory. He is reputed to have declared that, as there was one king of England, so there would be only one in New Zealand, and insofar as military pre-eminence may be considered kingship, he attained his ambition in his lifetime in the areas in which he could conveniently wage war.

Of all the war chiefs, Hongi was probably the least formidable in appearance. Of him, Nicholas said in 1816: 'Shunghi...had not the same robust figure as Duaterra, but his countenance was much more placid, and seemed, I thought, handsomer, allowing for the operation of the tattoo, which it had undergone, while it wanted that marked and animated severity which gave so decided a character to the face of his companion.'[6] Earle, who saw him in 1827 a few months before his death, had much the same to say: 'His look was emaciated, but so mild was the expression on of his features, that he would have been the last man I should have imagined accustomed to scenes of bloodshed and cruelty.'[7] Such was the manner and appearance of Hongi, under whose protection the Rangihoua mission sheltered, while he spread terror and death throughout the land.

It is difficult to determine accurately when firearms, so essential to Hongi's aspirations, first came to be acquired at the Bay of Islands in sufficient quantity to equip a sizeable war-party. The process must of necessity have been a slow one, if only due to the high barter prices demanded for them. Nevertheless the events of 1818-19 initiated a period in which the musket assumed great importance for Maoris throughout New Zealand. Sadly for those in other districts, the Bay at this time enjoyed a virtual trade monopoly with the outside world, and to the Maori, trade meant muskets. Ensign McCrae, of H.M. Storeship *Dromedary*, estimated that in 1820 there were 500 stand of arms at the Bay, with bullet-moulds, a great many of which had been acquired from whale-ships.[8] Many would have been brought in by Maori seamen and others visiting Sydney, and there is no doubt that from sheer necessity the missionaries contributed. Major Cruise, also of the *Dromedary*, observed that at the same time the Thames people had none, with the result that in the recent battle there, Hongi lost only four men to the enemy's 200. At Whangaroa the people were said to be terrified at the prospect of an invasion of a party with twelve muskets. Cruise added: '. . . the name of Krokro [Korokoro of Paroa, at the Bay], who is known to have fifty stand of arms, is heard with terror 200 miles from the Bay of Islands.'[9] The introduction of firearms was a calamity indeed. No innovation had such dire results, and an immense amount of Maori labour was expended to procure arms. It was not so much the efficiency of the musket itself which gave the user an advantage, as his ability to kill or wound at a distance, however short, when fighting an enemy armed only with hand-to-hand weapons.

By 1820, the missionaries, finding that their hoes, axes and other tools had become very small change in the trading world, felt obliged to deal in muskets, and the situation got out of control. While the settlers were largely dependent on the Maoris for food, it was difficult, without powder, lead and guns to acquire it, since little else was acceptable as exchange. Had they not been later able to grow more food, and to trade away from the Bay, their situation could have become untenable.

Augustus Earle believed that the Maori passion for muskets was the best insurance for the safety of those who traded in them. 'I know, from experience,' he wrote, 'that the New Zealanders will rather put up with injuries than run the risk of offending those who manufacture and barter with them such inestimable commodities.'[10] He quotes the ruling price for one musket in 1827 as 120 baskets of potatoes or 10 large hogs.

In 1819, Ngapuhi, sometimes with Hongi's Whangaroa relatives as allies, were entering into a phase of successive invasions against the conventionally armed tribes to the south, which lasted nearly 20 years. The acquisition of firearms was therefore a matter of paramount importance, and the energies of the Bay people were to an increasing extent directed towards re-arming. By the 1830s, the place was a veritable arsenal of small arms. Polack states that at that time 'almost every free native possesses at least one of these weapons.'[11]

F.E. Maning, 'The Pakeha Maori', in his whimsical narrative of early New Zealand times, described the consequences of the musket-boom as he saw them.[12] The fortified *pa* on hills and ridges, many hundreds of which occur in the North, fell into disuse on the introduction of firearms, since they were not designed for the new style of warfare, and whole populations abandoned the high, healthy dry places to live on the flats. While this removed the necessity of transporting provisions, fuel and water on to the hills, and in many cases brought them closer to the flax swamps and gardens from which they derived their means of trade, it was also, so Maning claimed, the cause of a serious decline in the people's health. The usual squat *raupo* houses, while tolerably healthy on raised ground, became pest-houses on the damp flats. Within his personal experience, he knew of a whole community of 40 persons which was destroyed by disease in eight years. In this settlement, water lay in depressions *inside* the houses, where people lay on rushes that rotted beneath them, and nothing could convince them that it was this that was killing them. This was at Hokianga, but Maning asserts that such conditions were universal. While there is more than a suggestion of ill-concealed contempt for the Maori race in both Maning's and Polack's writing, there is no reason to believe that such conditions as they describe did not exist.

Thus the musket, apart from directly causing countless deaths, may well have killed an indeterminate number by disease and starvation. The contending tribes had to have firearms or be exterminated. One of the ruling prices for a musket was a ton of flax stripped by hand. Anything that would purchase guns was sold. Agriculture as an industry among Maoris, which had been developing progressively since about 1800, was now to a large extent reduced to a means of procuring firearms to prosecute the warfare of Ngapuhi and its allies.

Almost incessant strife racked the northern part of the North Island. With the Bay of Islands as headquarters, Ngapuhi war parties reached as far south as Wellington. And when, after the deaths of Pomare Nui and Hongi Hika, Titore Takiri emerged as a successful war chief, fighting resumed, and continued until the end of the 1830s.

The export from New Zealand of baked or cured human heads prospered during these events. In fact, so brisk did this trade become, and so openly carried on, that Marsden records the visit of a chief to the ship *Prince of Denmark* at Port Jackson, where he saw on the cabin table 14 heads of his former friends, which had been brought over by Europeans for sale.[13] Thomas Dunbabbin[14] gives the date of the arrival of the first head at Sydney as 1811, brought by one William Tucker probably from Foveaux Strait, but the heyday of this commerce was between 1820 and 1830, when copious supplies were available, and prices went as low as £2-2s.

The preserving of human heads was a practice that had had significance of its own, but when the Maori came to appreciate their cash value, it quickly became an industry. Obviously the most desirable head from the European viewpoint was an elaborately tattooed one, but normally this would only be the head of an important chief, and the supply necessarily had limitations. Crafty devices were resorted to overcome this obstacle. Maning relates an incident in which 'a scoundrel slave had the concience to run away with his own head after the trouble and expense had been gone to to make it more valuable. . .' In another case, ignorant of the important transaction, a man had his head bought and paid for while he was still using it.[15] Heads were also reputed to have been tattooed after death, but this shoddy device was apparently easily detected by an expert.

The process of preserving heads is described by the Rev. William Yate, a missionary at Paiha and Waimate until the early 1830s:

When the head has been cut from the shoulders, the brains are immediately taken out, through a perforation behind, and the skull carefully cleansed inside from all mucilaginous and fleshy matter. The eyes are then scooped out; and the head thrown into boiling water, into which red hot stones are continually cast, to keep up the heat. It remains till the skin

85

will slip off, and it is then suddenly plunged into cold water; whence it is immediately taken, and placed in a native oven, so as to allow the steam to penetrate into all the cavities of the interior of the skull. When sufficiently steamed it is placed on a stick to dry; and again put into an oven, made for the purpose, about the dimensions of the head. The flesh, which easily slips off the bones, is then taken away; and small sticks are employed, to thrust flax, or the bark of trees, within the skin, so as to restore it to its former shape, and to preserve the features. The nostrils are then carefully stuffed with a piece of fern root; and the lips are generally sewn together; though sometimes they are not closed, but the teeth are allowed to appear. It is finished by hanging it, for a few days, in the sun.[16]

When in 1831, as a result of the *Prince of Denmark* incident, Marsden brought this unpleasant commerce to the notice of Governor Darling at Sydney, a General Order was issued forbidding the traffic, which, officially at least, then ceased.

---

1. Elder, *Marsdens Lieutenants,* p.128.
2. McNab, *From Tasman to Marsden,*p.210.
3. Smith, *Maori Wars of the Nineteenth Century,* pp.89 and 93.
4. Ibid, p.185.
5. Elder, *Letters and Journals,*p.173.
6. Nicholas, *Narrative of a Voyage,* v.1, p.25.
7. Earle, *Nine Months Residence,* p.58.
8. A description of the *Dromedary's* visit to New Zealand is given in the next chapter.
9. Cruise, R.A. *Journal of Ten Months Residence in New Zealand,* pp.36 and 282.
10. Earle, op.cit., pp.55 and 72.
11. Polack, *Narrative of Travels and Adventures,* pp.35-6.
12. Pakeha Maori (Maning), *Old New Zealand,* p.160 et seq.
13. McNab, *Historical Records,* v.1, p.716.
14. Dunbabbin, T.*Sailing the World's Edge,* pp.221, 224.
15. Pakeha Maori (Maning), *Old New Zealand,* p.150.
16. Yate, W. *An Account of New Zealand,* p.132 et seq.

11

Inland Exploration

MARSDEN MADE HIS second visit to New Zealand and the Bay of Islands in 1819, when, on 29 July he sailed from Port Jackson in the American brig *General Gates*, accompanied by the Rev. John Gare Butler, who had been appointed in London to be Superintendent of the New Zealand mission. The appointment was intended to resolve the vexed question of authority and control, but due to Butler's temperament and the remoteness of his chosen base from the main body of the missionaries, this objective was never achieved.

The most notable event during Marsden's three months' stay, was the Society's acquisition of 13,000 acres of land at Kerikeri from Hongi Hika. Here a second mission station was established and occupied by Butler. Called the Town of Gloucester, after the bishop, for a short time it became the headquarters of the Society in New Zealand.

It is difficult to conceive of any benefit which might accrue to the Maori people, for whose benefit the mission existed, from the acquisition of so vast a tract of land, so little of which was ever used for the betterment of the race. However, the choice of the locality was influenced by its agricultural possibilities. Forty-eight felling-axes was the purchase price, and for good reasons of his own, Hongi was satisfied with his bargain.

Hongi possessed this land by right of recent conquests by senior members of his family, as we have seen. The other signatory as vendor was 'Rawha', who was probably the Ngapuhi kinsman Rewa (Maanu). The land immediately to the south and east of this was owned by the Hokianga people, or by those having a Hokianga background, who later sold it to the Mission Society for the benefit of the mission children. Its Maori title derived from the raid on the Bay by the Hokianga people, mentioned in Chapter 1. As to Marsden's purchase, neither possession nor occupation of the land was established other than in the vicinity of the station, and on the assumption of British sovereignty in New Zealand, no claim was entered with the Land Claim Commissioners for the 13,000 acres.

A useful outcome of the 1819 visit was the inland exploration undertaken with the Bay of Islands as a starting-point. The Hokianga expedition was particularly valuable, since apart from a brief visit in June by Kendall and King, it was at that time *terra incognita* to Europeans, but when knowledge of it was gained it soon attracted commercial and pioneer settlers. In fact, the exploration of much of the northern half of the North Island was carried out from the Bay, and Marsden himself and the missionaries were responsible for a large proportion of it.

An interesting map appeared in the Church Missionary Register for 1822, which shows all that was then known of the Northern peninsula.[1] The Kaipara, Waitemata, Manukau and Whangarei harbours do not appear at all, and it is notable that of these, only the Waitemata was explored from the sea. The others, like Hokianga, were first approached by Europeans from inland.

Before embarking on his journey, Marsden busied himself getting the new station under way, and was a little apprehensive on discovering that his decision to make the Society's head-quarters station on land under the influence of Hongi Hika, had earned for him the disapproval of Korokoro, the Ngare-Raumati chief at Paroa, and one of the early supporters of the mission project. Since he anticipated the advantages that Hongi would gain from such a decision, Korokoro was greatly offended, complaining eloquently of Hongi's infamy and general unsuitability, in an attempt to persuade Marsden to reconsider his decision in favour of Paroa. Hongi and Korokoro were very distantly related, and Hongi's father, Te Hotete, had taken part in the earliest battles between Ngapuhi and the coast people, perhaps 20 years previously. But Te Hotete's family had not shared in the spoils. This was possibly because the actual occupation of the coast by Ngapuhi took place after his death. Dates of Maori events are difficult to determine, but to an ambitious man such as Hongi, his family's exclusion must have rankled. It may be recalled that during Alexander Berry's visit in *The City of Edinburgh*, the people on the eastern side of the Bay had been openly hostile toward Te Pahi, Hongi's relative through his mother and wives.

In an attempt to resolve the problem, Marsden visited Paroa, and his journal reveals that the site for a settlement was actually selected at Manawaora, near Paroa, and close to the scene of du Fresne's death. 'On our landing,' the journal reads, 'I selected a small spot of ground to sow a little English flax seed upon, which was immediately cleared and broken up, and afterwards I sowed the seed. I then examined the ground for building upon, and staked out a house about forty feet by thirteen for the workpeople, and in the evening returned to Rangeehoo.'[2] But the station never materialised, although the Rev. Butler recorded in his diary in June 1820 that an employee of the mission, James Boyle, a saltmaker, lived there alone in a rush hut for a while, making salt for the purpose of curing fish which the mission brig *Active* caught for the Sydney market. His occupation was brief, however, as he was forced to leave in the following February owing to the rough treatment meted out to him by the local Maoris, who were openly sceptical of Butler's vague undertakings concerning the proposed station. Only Marsden's deviousness and some diplomatic handling of Korokoro averted what could have developed into an unpleasant confrontation. A patch of flax (if it grew) and the corner marks of a house, either sustained hope or nurtured a smouldering resentment for four years, but until his death in 1823, Korokoro does not appear to have re-opened the matter. In the course of Marsden's discussions at Manawaora, he encountered Huru (or Woodu), one of the Maoris kidnapped by Captain Hanson from the Cavalli Islands 25 years earlier.

In 1819 Marsden, unaware of tribal undercurrents, and no doubt feeling that he had successfully disposed of Korokoro, began building at Kerikeri. On 28 September he set off for Hokianga, about which he had heard so much, accompanied by Kendall and Puckey. His route seems to have been up the Puketotara River and Kerikeri to the southern end of the Puketi Forest, and thence down the Waihoanga Stream to the Waihou Valley. Kendall had previously briefly examined the Hokianga for its suitability for a mission settlement, but neither he nor Marsden seem to have been impressed by its possibilities, and it later became a Catholic and Wesleyan stronghold. Marsden's rendition of the name — Shokee Hangha — he apparently found offensive, for he renamed it the River Gambier, as it appears on the map of Northern New Zealand in the Church Missionary Register. Mercifully, the name was never in general use. During the visit, much of the southern side of the river was examined, and the party met chiefs who figured largely in later events, notably Muriwai and Taonui, and also Patuone,[3] who was reputed to have seen Captain Cook.

Before returning to Sydney, Marsden undertook another inland journey, this time in the direction of Kaikohe. His party, which included Kendall, left the Kerikeri River, journeying up the Okura, and then went overland to the Waitangi River. They crossed near the Puketona *pa*, on the way to Paihia. They followed the Waitangi and its tributary, the Waioruhe, to Taiamai, Ngawha Springs and Pukenui (Te Ahuahu). At Taiamai he heard the tale of Captain Stivers, who is said by Maoris to have been the first European to visit New Zealand, and who introduced the potato here — hence 'Taewa,' one of its Maori names. On his return to the Bay he found the *Active* there, and on 9 November he embarked on her and departed.

In his account of this expedition, much is said of the place Taiamai, a name now seldom used. It applies specifically to a curious volcanic stone in the open ground about a quarter of a mile south of the present village of Ohaeawai. It is 'Te Tino o Taiamai,' that is, the precise place of Taiamai, a mythical bird associated with the rock, and after which the locality was named. In 1827, Earle spoke of it as a '. . . town of great size and importance, called Ty-a-my. It is situated on the sides of a beautiful hill, the top surmounted by a *pa*, in the midst of a lonely and extensive plain . . .'[4] The 'beautiful hill' could have been Maungaturoto, about one mile south of the stone, since this agrees with the description, but the possibility that it was Pouerua that Earle referred to cannot be dismissed, although it is some three miles to the south of the route that he appears to have taken. This almost certainly followed the old Maori track from Taheke to Kaikohe, thence to the north of Ngawha

Springs, and thus to Taiamai, or the present village of Ohaeawai.[5]

At the time of Marsden's 1819 visit, the few settlers at the Bay were confined to the coast. After some 20 years intercourse with whalers and other shipping, only one European settler not in the employ of the Missionary Society is definitely known to have been resident there. This was Hansen, who had commanded both the *Lady Nelson,* and the *Active.* He, with his family, lived with the missionaries, and acted as agent for trade between whalers and Maoris. Mention is frequently made, however, of runaway sailors or convicts living with Maoris before this time, so no doubt some of these were about, but would not, of course, make themselves conspicuous. However by the early 1820s, the missionaries' isolation at this Bay was coming to an end. From this time, the presence of other settlers is recorded, and Kororareka was the place at which they gathered.

Meanwhile, at Kerikeri, Butler had commenced his duties. The rules under which he functioned made it clear that the Society intended to remove the anomaly which had been the cause of so much dissent among the catechists, that is, the equal status of all, with none having over-riding authority. Those who drafted the Rules and Regulations of the New Zealand Mission no doubt had this in mind when they required that Butler should '... superintend, direct, order and manage all and every matter and thing whatsoever, and of any kind, nature and degree belonging to, affecting or concerning the Mission in New Zealand...'[6] Having erred in its former policy, the Society now made it abundantly clear who was to be in charge. However, as Butler later discovered to his sorrow, both Kendall and Marsden failed to comply with the directive. Butler was a hard-working and conscientious clergyman, but unable to satisfactorily assume such authority. Administratively he was not a success, and he received no help from the volatile Kendall who openly defied him. Worse, Marsden in spite of the terms of Butler's appointment, rode rough-shod over him. In theory, Marsden was the Society's Agent in New South Wales, but the New Zealand mission was his brain-child and it seemed that he had no notion of leaving it to the mercy of the man subsequently appointed to administer it.

In addition to the powers conferred on him by his employers, Butler held Governor Macquarie's warrant, issued on 24 July 1819, as a Justice of the Peace in New Zealand. In this capacity he earned some distinction in having heard before him depositions on the first murder charge formally brought against anyone in this country. He committed the accused, four soldiers of the 84th Regiment, to trial in New South Wales. The soldiers belonged to the *Dromedary,* and the victim was murdered on board on 21 November 1820 while the ship was in the Whangaroa harbour, apparently in a quarrel over a girl.[7]

In October 1819, temporary mission quarters having been built at Kerikeri, Butler and his wife began fencing and planting a garden with vegetables, indian corn and an orchard of 100 trees. Several attempts were made to burn bricks, but it was two months before suitable clay was found. George, a Maori who had learned the trade at Sydney, then succeeded in making 8000 bricks.

Not the least of the difficulties now confronting the missionaries was their inability to obtain sufficient meat. This was one of the 'little inconveniences' referred to in a letter written by Marsden to the Rev. J. Pratt, the Secretary of the Society in London. 'They have suffered a little inconvenience, a few privations while residing among the heathens, but some of them must in the common course of things have suffered more had they lived in England and had their families to maintain there.'[8] A startling statement, made surely with tongue in cheek. Otherwise it was a serious indictment of the conditions and values in contemporary England, which presumably the mission proposed to implant in New Zealand and impose upon the unsuspecting heathen. Another 'inconvenience' is mentioned by Butler in his diary on 18 March 1820:

> During this last week we have been severely tried by the natives. They are very insolent, and enter our houses with impunity. They abuse us, and if any of the chiefs ask for an axe or anything else that we have as trade, we dare not deny them. This morning . . . we had a complete skirmish in my yard, by the natives, one against the other. Mrs Butler fainted

with fear, and we are obliged to give several axes, hatchets, and other things to the chiefs in order to pacify and get them out of the yard. They plainly tell us if we will not issue powder and muskets, we must go away, which appears the only alternative.[9]

The meat shortage was, of course, caused by the preference of the Maoris to trade with the whalers, who had no scruples about trading in muskets and powder. In 1820 the *Dromedary*, under charter to the Navy, was unable to obtain meat for the same reason. The whalers got whatever they required of whatever was available and the missionaries such left-overs as there were. In the six months up to February 1820, five whaleships had been at the Bay, two of them twice, and Captain Spence of the *Echo* informed Butler, to his dismay, that 11 more were on the way. The summer months during the Pacific hurricane season, was the peak period for visiting whalers, and in the next year there were 17 ships on the coast. Each would stay perhaps two months at the Bay, and many made two or more visits in the year.

Mr Kendall's awakening business acumen did little to improve the meat situation, for by this time he had a prosperous sideline in pork-dealing with shipmasters. The net result, as Butler put it, was that '. . . the Bay of Islands is becoming very thin of pork.'[10] But at this period there was not the open hostility between whalers and missionaries that later developed under the administration of the Rev. Henry Williams.

Butler appears to have been a pleasant and sociable person, although subject to violent fits of temper, perhaps justified. He entertained ship's officers who visited him, one of whom was Captain Kent, whose name was given to the passage between Moturoa and the mainland, at the mouth of the Kerikeri River.

After about 1820, due to C.M.S. insistence that its members refrain from private trade, the missionaries ceased to have much economic significance for the Maoris. But as trade with the whalers increased, the missionaries, as compatriots of the now economically important whalers, enjoyed the same treatment and respect. Later, the same could be said for the Wesleyans at Hokianga, where the timber trade had become profitable to both Maori and pakeha, but at Whangaroa, where there was no regular trade between Maoris and shipping, the missionaries were unsafe and were finally obliged to abandon their station there. Such tenuous influence as the missionaries enjoyed was due to the recognition by the more discerning of the Maori chiefs of their sincerity and integrity, however ill-directed. In 1840 this, of course, led many Maoris to accept missionary advice to sign the Treaty of Waitangi, an action which a large proportion of them lived to regret.

The whalers, now the spoiled favourites of the Maoris, soon became the lifeblood of the many mercantile ventures established on the harbour shores and at Kororareka itself. Before 1840 and beyond, the many European settlers and merchants in business at the Bay depended almost entirely for their livelihood on the whale trade and its ramifications. Similarly, the early missionaries were largely dependent on the whalers for various domestic requirements, and for communications with the outside world. This no doubt accounts for the good relationship between them. Later, when under Williams, they had for various reasons achieved greater independence, and operated almost in isolation from all but the few of their compatriots whom they considered to be 'respectable'.

Early in 1820 Marsden arrived back at the Bay on the *Dromedary*, ostensibly to promote the interests of the vessel in dealing with the Maoris and obtaining a load of spars for the Navy. On board the *Dromedary* were nine Bay Maoris who had been visiting Sydney, and a contingent of regular British troops, the first to be seen here. The *Dromedary* was the first naval vessel to visit these shores since Cook.[11] She anchored at Kororareka on 27 February 1820, the pre-eminence of which, as a port, had not at that time been established. Three whaleships were observed lying at Paroa, but the days of this place as a haven for shipping were now numbered, and on the death of its chief Korokoro in 1823, it ceased to be a place of importance to the whale trade. But in 1820 it was certainly still in business, for on 6 September Butler noted an impressive list of ships which he observed all lying there together. They were the *Dromedary,* the English whalers *Catherine* and *Anne*, and the Americans *Indian* and *Independence*. After this, however, we hear little of Paroa and increasingly more of Kororareka, or 'The Beach', as it came to be called. Sheltered from northerly and easterly winds, it also offered good holding-ground. These features and the amiability of the resident Ngatimanu chiefs, Whareumu (or King George), the younger and elder Pomares[12] and Kiwikiwi, also contributed to this growth of Kororareka into a sizeable European township. So complete was the decline of Paroa following the destruction of the *pa* Kahuwera by Hongi Hika after Korokoro's death, that in 1827 Dumont D'Urville found the place abandoned, and the whole of the district deserted.[13]

It was from Kororareka then that the preliminary examination of the Bay's timber resources was made by the *Dromedary*. Negotiations to procure spars from the Kawakawa were initiated, but owing to their bad quality and the ungracious response of the people there to the princely offer of one axe per spar delivered to the ship, it was decided to try Whangaroa. The schooner *Prince Regent*, a tender to the *Dromedary*, tried for spars at Manawaora, but the swamps mentioned in 1772 by members of the du Fresne expedition, also made this source unsatisfactory.

Before the *Dromedary* left the Bay, an incident occurred which impressively demonstrates the capacity of the nineteenth century Royal Navy to enforce law and order almost anywhere it pleased. Captain Riggs, in command of the American brig *General Gates*, had again entered the Bay in 1820, and information that he had escaped prisoners aboard was conveyed by Butler to Captain Skinner on the *Dromedary*, which was then lying near Opua. Acting upon this, the second master and a sergeant's guard of the 84th, arrested Rigg's ship on 12 April, and five days later the *General Gates* was sailed under guard to Sydney. Riggs, although a man of bad reputation, was nevertheless the unlucky one among many masters equally culpable, and had reason to be dismayed at this untoward outbreak of law-enforcement.

Apart from these incidents, the *Dromedary*'s four months at the Bay of Islands produced little of note, and on 5 March Skinner, unimpressed by the local timber resources, sent the second master and the carpenter overland to Hokianga to make a survey of the possibilities there. They were accompanied on

95

this journey by Marsden, whose capacity for such jaunts was insatiable. On their return a fortnight later with a favourable report, Skinner decided to take the ship around before investigating Whangaroa. However Hokianga proved unsuitable, a four-day examination of the harbour and bar having convinced the Captain that so large a ship could not safely be taken in, and he took her back to the Bay. Later events did not, of course, support his judgement.

The few remaining weeks spent at the Bay of Islands was devoid of incident other than the death of a child of a sergeant of the 84th Regiment, who was buried on 27 May in Mr King's garden at Oihi.

On 19 June the *Dromedary* proceeded to Whangaroa, where an examination was made of the wreck of the *Boyd*. The stump of her mizzen-mast was found to be standing, and her rudder, which was sound, was unshipped and got aboard, and her wood and copper were also found to be sound.

Before leaving the Bay, a grisly reminder of the *Boyd* tragedy was seen at Te Puna, where a naval officer was presented with a carved human rib bone, said to be that of one of the *Boyd* victims. But if the approach to Whangaroa was cautious, the reception by the people there was considerably more so. However, Te Puhi, although in a very chastened state of mind, realised that a profit could be made from the ship's activities, and thereafter there was little difficulty in inducing these people, who 10 years previously had been responsible for the massacre, to supply the required spars.

A party from the *Dromedary* was conducted to the *pa* of Te Puhi and his brother, Te Aara, situated on the conical hill, Te Pohui rising abruptly from the flat immediately behind the Police Station in the present township of Kaeo. Captain Cruise, who was in command of the detachment of the 84th Regiment, observed that kauri was growing in abundance in this locality, and the valley floor around the *pa* was occupied by the village and cultivations. Near the summit of the *pa* were three of the *Boyd's* cannon, and a further three and an anchor lay on the banks of the river. It was from this locality, in a deep ravine about '. . . a mile and a quarter to the right,' that the spars were brought out, with the assistance of five pairs of bullocks which had been brought to New Zealand for that purpose.

Apart from the threat of a tribal skirmish, and a rumour of an attack to be made on the ship which was current among the Bay Maoris, the felling, trimming and loading of the spars proceeded uneventfully, while at the Bay, Marsden was planning further outings. Ostensibly, the reason for his visit had been to facilitate the procuring of spars for the *Dromedary*, but once here, he indulged in an astonishing orgy of walking tours. Before doing so, he delivered to Kerikeri some of his cattle, which had been brought on the ship from Sydney to graze on the Mission land. He also took there the famous first plough. In his diary on 3 May 1820 Butler noted: 'The agricultural plough was for the first time put into the land of New Zealand at Kideekidee, and I felt much pleasure in holding it after a team of six bullocks brought down by the "Dromedary".'[14]

Having witnessed this ceremony, Marsden set off on a trip into the interior, to Waimate and the Taiamai districts, returning to Rangihoua on 1 June to find that the *Coromandel*, Captain Downie, was in the harbour, engaged for the Navy on the same mission as the *Dromedary*. Downie intended to try the Firth of Thames for spars, and accordingly the *Coromandel* sailed on 7 June with Marsden aboard. On reaching the Hauraki Gulf it anchored in the harbour, which with the whole peninsula, now bears the ship's name.[15]

Tauranga now exercised Marsden's mind. It was thought that the *Brothers* may have been there in 1815, but there was no record of the visit, and so characteristically, Marsden decided to have a look for himself. From the Thames he travelled up the Waihou by canoe and thence overland to the Tauranga harbour. Returning within a week to the timber camp at the Thames, he went off on 25 July with the *Coromandel*'s launch, with the intention of going up the Waitemata and crossing to the Kaipara. On the morning of 27 July, his party, which apart from Maori guides included Messrs Anderson and Ewels of the *Coromandel*, reached the western limits of the harbour. Leaving Anderson behind with the launch, the others were conducted by the Kaipara people overland to a village on the Helensville River, where they arrived that night. During the few days they spent there, Marsden encountered a half-caste slave whose master said he came from the Bay of Islands, and that his father was a European. Since he was about 20 years of age, it is possible that he may have been the child Savage saw in 1805 (see Chapter 5). Marsden and his party returned to the *Coromandel* on 1 August, he himself having lived and slept in his clothes, wet and dry, for 24 days. But his appetite for exploring was as yet undiminished, and about a fortnight later he decided to return to the Kaipara, and to walk from there to the Bay of Islands.

Leaving Mokoia (Panmure) on 16 August, he set off accompanied by some of the Kaipara Maoris and the Bay of Islands chief Te Morenga, who was also among the *Coromandel* party. They followed a route from the head of the Waitemata to about Helensville, thence down the tidal river in canoes, across the open water where the many arms of the Kaipara unite, and up the Wairoa to Tangiteroria. There Marsden was advised to abandon his intention to travel up the Mangakahia and Awarua rivers, since both, he was informed, would have to be forded many times. Therefore, he, Te Morenga and their guides crossed to Whangarei, leaving the Kaipara people to return to their homes. At Whangarei, a local chief was induced to take them to Whangaruru by canoe, and from there the journey was completed on foot.

At the Kaipara, during this progress through the island, the party visited one of the greatest of the Maori generals of the traditional warfare era. This was Murupaenga of Ngatiwhatua, who was soon, however, to fall victim to the new musket warfare. At about the beginning of the century, he had led a war party to Moremonui, on the west coast south of Hokianga, and there slew Hongi Hika's brother Moka, and his sister Waitapu. It is likely that this event launched Hongi on his military conquests, for tradition has it that when he returned from England he had carved on the stock of a special musket, the words *teke tanumia,* to be a constant reminder of the indignity his sister suffered at Moremonui. It is said that all Hongi's campaigns were directed towards the final confrontation, when he and Whareumu destroyed Murupaenga's fighting strength at Te-Ika-a-Ranga-Nui, near Kaiwaka, in 1825.

Back at the Bay, after nearly a month of continuous walking,

Marsden transacted some business for the mission and then tramped over to Whangaroa to join the *Prince Regent* to return to Port Jackson.

But he was not alone in his urge to travel. On 31 August, four days before Marsden ended his journey from the Waitemata at Paroa, Mr Clark, the sealing-master of the *General Gates*, set off from the *Prince Regent*, which was then at the Waitemata and about to leave for Whangaroa. After the arrest of his ship, Mr Clark, apparently at a loose end, had gone down to the Thames in the schooner. On his overland tramp he covered new ground, for instead of going across the island from Kaipara to the east coast, he crossed the river and continued up the west coast to Hokianga, and from there along the river and over to Whangaroa, where he joined the *Dromedary* on 25 September.

In the meantime, the *Prince Regent*, with Marsden aboard, had left Whangaroa for Sydney so heavily laden with spars that when a gale was encountered near North Cape, Captain Kent decided that it was unsafe to continue. The vessel, now leaking seriously, returned to the Bay of Islands. From here Marsden again walked to Whangaroa to join the *Dromedary*, where he heard from Mr Clark of his journey from the Waitemata *via* Hokianga. Faced with the necessity of waiting six weeks for a ship to return to Sydney, he went off to explore Clark's route for himself. Mr James Shepherd, a newly arrived missionary, and Mr Butler, were persuaded to accompany him. On 30 October they left Oihi in a whaleboat bought for £30 from Captain Ker, of the ship *Saracen*. The journey down the coast took three days, and they re-joined the *Coromandel* at the Thames, where she was still loading spars.

Some days were spent on a visit to the Manukau, which hitherto had not been seen by Europeans, and on crossing the Waitemata isthmus the party climbed 'Wydakka' (Owairaka, or Mount Albert). From the head of the Waitemata they travelled overland to the Kaipara, and down the river to the heads to ascertain the navigability of the entrance. Satisfied on this point, Marsden decided to return to the Bay of Islands. The Rev. Butler and his attendants walked back to the Waitemata and returned to the Bay in the whaleboat, arriving home on 22 November, while Marsden and Shepherd travelled north taking Mr Clark's route. Arriving at Hokianga, they followed the southern side to the Upper Waihou River and took the track to Kerikeri which Marsden had previously used. Near Waipapa they parted, Shepherd going to Kerikeri and Marsden to Whangaroa to join the *Dromedary* once again. Having now obtained a full load of spars, the ship returned to the Bay of Islands, and on 5 December left for Sydney with Marsden aboard.

Valuable information was obtained during the 10 months' visit by the *Dromedary*. Much of this is recorded in evidence given in 1821 by Ensign McCrae of the 84th Regiment and Dr Fairfowl, Surgeon of the *Dromedary*, before Comissioner Bigge, who had been instructed by Earl Bathurst, the Colonial Secretary, to report on the general condition and treatment by visiting ships of the inhabitants of New Zealand. Much useful information on these matters is to be found in Bigge's report and Appendix, not the least of which is Kendall's statement of 8 November 1819 that there were at that date 52 European settlers in New Zealand (at the mission settlements), and his detailed list of ships visiting the Bay of Islands in the three years since 1816.[16]

---

1. Elder, *Letters and Journals,* p.252.
2. Ibid, p.156.
3. See Appendix 1.4 and 1.6.
4. Earle, *Narrative of Nine Months Residence,* p.75.
5. Ohaeawai's present site is not its original one, which was at the place now called Ngawha on the road to Kaikohe, some 2½ miles from its present location.
6. Barton, *Earliest New Zealand,* p.336.
7. Ibid, p.106; Cruise, *Journal of Ten Months Residence,* p.254-5.
8. McNab, *Historical Records,* v.1, p.492.
9. Barton, op.cit., p.78.
10. Ibid, p.87.
11. Although the *Daedelus* was on the New Zealand coast in 1792, there was no communication with the shore.
12. See Appendix 1.8 and 1.11.

13. Wright, O. *New Zealand 1826-1827,* p.179.
14. Barton, op.cit., p.80.
15. Elder, op.cit., p.253.
16. McNab, op.cit., pp.441-5 and 534-558.

12

Troubles and Changes in the Mission

Among the missionaries, Kendall's was the personality that compels most attention. Basically a scholar, more intelligent than most, though less astute and acquisitive than Marsden, instability flawed his character. In the English class-system, through single-minded and ruthless ambition, Marsden had got himself firmly established in the middle-class, whereas Kendall, wanting in education, was prevented from doing so. Too late he discovered that his talents were not those that could be most effectively used in the situation in which he found himself. Not an unusual situation, to be sure, but whereas resignation often succeeds such a realisation, Kendall reacted violently in many ways. Finally, probably more as an escape from frustration than because of his religious convictions, he decided to take Holy Orders. Kendall's career, if not high on proselyting fervour, was at least prolific in turbulent incident.

Few but the employers he had would have frowned upon most of his escapades, since their enormity was relative to his positon as a missionary, and had fate established him in the ranks of the intelligentsia, he could well have ended his career as a notable scholar, and died in an odour of sanctity.

Kendall's interest in Maori cosmological beliefs indicate an ability for subjective research despite the want of a formal education. He was a pioneer in this field in New Zealand, and had the unique opportunity of dealing with a more or less untainted primitive culture. It is unfortunate that in the upshot, he had insufficient time to extend and rationalise his researches, and indeed, he was discouraged from doing so. For his work in this area, and particularly on the study of the Maori language and its reduction to writing, which was so invaluable to his successors, he received little or no acknowledgement from his colleagues, mainly due to his moral lapses.

As a result of his urge to become an ordained Anglican priest, he took a passage on the whaler *New Zealander*, and was ready to leave for England when Marsden arrived on board the *Dromedary*, in February 1820. Bound for London with Kendall were his friend and evil genius Hongi, and the young Mawhatu chief, Waikato, from Kaihiki in the Mangonui Inlet. The journey occupied 17 weeks, a smart passage for those days, and during that time, Kendall was employed writing his *Guide to the Study of the New Zealand Language*.

When Kendall and the Maori chiefs arrived in London, the Society saw an opportunity to achieve a systematic spelling and orthography for the Maori language. They were sent to Cambridge to confer with Professor Lee, the oriental languages linguist there. Kendall no doubt had such an eventuality in mind on leaving New Zealand, since he had his research data with him, and the collaboration at Cambridge resulted in Kendall and Lee's *Grammar and Vocabulary of the Language of New Zealand* (1820).[1] This work, although later revised and modified, forms the basis of written Maori as we now know it. Kendall later produced another small work, *Easy Lessons in the New Zealand Language*, and continued writing on the subject until his death in 1832.[2]

Because Kendall's absence from New Zealand had not been authorised, he was censured by the Society, although disapproval was apparently tempered by the obvious advantages accruing from his presence in England with the Maori chiefs, and the knowledge he was able to make available to Professor Lee. He was received into Holy Orders during his brief stay, and remained an employee of the Society. In England, J.L. Nicholas, who accompanied the original settlers to New Zealand in 1814, renewed his acquaintance with his old friends, and at Cambridge, Kendall met the Baron de Thierry, from whom he was said to have received a large sum of money, with which he was later alleged to have purchased 40,000 acres of land for the Baron at Hokianga, from the chiefs Muriwai and Patuone. However, de Thierry was unable to substantiate his claim on his arrival to New Zealand in 1837,[3] a matter which we shall come to later.

Politically, the most significant aspect of this visit was the presence of Hongi Hika, who undoubtedly undertook the journey with the sole object of promoting his warlike ambitions by securing further arms. He and Waikato were shown every consideration and were presented to King George, who gave them valuable presents. These were later traded in Sydney for arms, which when added to those received in England, are said to have totalled 300, enabling Hongi on his return to the Bay of Islands to muster a fighting force armed with over 1000 muskets.[4] With King George's presents, Hongi had received a suit of armour from the Tower of London. This he retained and later wore into battle, where it is reputed to have saved his life many times.

Although Hongi was desperately ill, Kendall and his party left England for Australia in the convict ship *Speke*. In Sydney town, Hongi, having recovered, encountered Te Hinaki, the Ngati Paoa chief of Mokoia (Panmure), and Te Horeta of Ngati Maru (Thames). They were plainly informed that in revenge for the Ngapuhi defeats at Waiwhariki (Bay of Islands) and other battles, the destruction of their people was imminent – an accurate assessment as things turned out. On 11 July 1821 Kendall and his Maori friends arrived at the Bay in the *Westmoreland*. Repercussions from this jaunt to England were immediate and dramatic.

Kendall, in spite of undertakings to mend his ways, now resumed his musket trade. In a letter to the Secretary of the Church Missionary Society in January 1822, William Hall asserted that 'the conversation of the bretheren' was that Kendall had brought back 'cases of muskets and barrels of powder,' and was trading them to the Maoris for meat, which he then in turn sold to various ships in the harbour.[5] Hall, then a sick man, appeared to derive a sort of melancholy glee from frequent recitals of Kendall's misdemeanours. However, Butler had already noted the same thing in a journal entry of 5 September 1821, where he listed 17 chiefs who had received 21 muskets and two pistols from Kendall, with whom he was then at loggerheads.[6]

When Marsden charged him with arms dealing in a letter

from Sydney in June 1821, Kendall defended himself in his characteristically resourceful way:

> On the part of the New Zealanders I believed that they had an undoubted right to seek such payment as they might think most conducive to their own interests or convenience, or else how could they be a free people? And they consider themselves free, whatever we may think to the contrary... Nor can we dictate to them which of these they must receive in payment for their property and services. They dictate to us. ... The man who wants a musket will not be put off with axes or fish-hooks. .. Reflect for a moment that we are not only connected with, but we are the subjects of, a heathen government.[7]

Apparently shaken by this masterpiece of polemics, Marsden replied somewhat lamely: 'May I not ask you, are not we equally free? If we have no authority to compel them to leave off this traffic, they have none to compel us to carry on.' A valid comment in other circumstances, but it evaded the distasteful reality that in New Zealand the missionaries were painfully dependent on the Maoris for labour and most of their food, and of course, even for their continued existence in the country.

Kendall now estimated that there were 2000 stand of arms in the Bay of Islands – a startling increase on McCrae's estimate of 500 only 12 months before. The Bay had become an arsenal of small arms, but this in itself relieved the pressure on the mission people, since the insistent demand on them for muskets receded as the supply from whalers and others increased and the demand was satisfied. So that when the Rev. H. Williams took over the mission two years later, the musket syndrome no longer affected it significantly.

Upon his return from England, Hongi had quickly assembled his war-party. The Rev. Butler was unfortunately involved in these preparations, since Hongi's headquarters was the *pa* Kororipo, at Kerikeri, which later was regarded by the warring Bay people, due to its *mana*, as the only point of departure for raids – *Te waha o te riri*, or The inlet of war. Calamities would surely occur if any other route were taken. On this occasion, the aroused warriors became arrogant, making free of Butler's house and workshops, so that it was with relief that he wrote in his diary on 5 September 1821: 'This day, about noon, Shunghee, Rewah, and all their chiefs set off on a war expedition to the River Thames — indeed, the whole country for a hundred miles or more, are already on their way, and Shunghee and Rewah, and Wykato, and their men, are the last, in order to bring up the rear.'[8] The point of assembly was at Whangarei, and according to Butler, such a confederacy for war had never before been seen in New Zealand.

This situation had developed a scant two months after Hongi's return from England. It seems that during his sojourn abroad he had come to appreciate that missionaries had little influence among the mighty, and did not rate highly in the English social hierarchy. This undoubtedly coloured his attitude to the New Zealand mission, particularly since he himself had been treated with much affability by the great and powerful in England.

Due largely to a disproportionately small number of firearms among the Ngati Paoa defenders of the Mokoia and Mauinaina *pa* at Panmure, the assault by Ngapuhi and their allies was successful, and by one account over 1000 of the defenders were killed.[9] Hongi himself narrowly escaped death, but the army returned in triumph to the Bay, bringing with them Te Hinaki's head. In a letter Butler wrote that the raiders '. . .depopulated several very large districts. . . The moment they landed at Kiddee Kiddee they killed in a most brutal manner many slaves. . . The slaves thus slaughtered were afterwards eaten as common food.'[10] This victory encouraged further military operations to avenge old grievances, and early in March 1822, some weeks after Butler's return from a visit to Sydney, another party of about 1000 men left Kerikeri on its way back to the devastated district to extend the earlier operations to the Ngati Maru people at the Thames. A scintillating array of the most influential chiefs at the Bay and the north coast took part, and the strong *pa* at Te Totara was taken by a stratagem. Again some 1000 of the defenders were killed, and the defeat at Waiwhariki was avenged.[11] Unfortunately a nephew of Te Rauparaha, the Ngati Toa chief of Kawhia and a former ally of

Ngapuhi, was killed in this action. This led to a later murderous killing of a Ngapuhi party on a friendly visit to Rotorua, which in turn resulted in the Ngapuhi destruction of the island *pa* Mokoia in the lake, in 1823.[12]

With tremendous slaughter the wars continued unremittingly down the east coast as far as Wellington, and in the Waikato until the mid-1820s, when the defeat of Pomare at Te Rore, near Pirongia, put an end to Hongi's southern expeditions, although other minor actions continued for many years. Tradition has it that Pomare's death was due to his disregard for Kerikeri's *mana* as a point of departure, since his party left independently from Taumarere, in the Kawakawa River, on his Waikato raid.

When the first Thames onslaught was in progress in November 1821, Butler was visiting Sydney. His diary and letters at this time disclose a deterioration in his relations with Marsden, to the point of mutual acrimony. Marsden accused Butler of profiting in trade as a result of his position as Superintendent, and Butler insisted that Marsden was defrauding him financially. Marsden then got Butler's resignation as Superintendent, since Butler considered that he was not allowed to function as such. When the erstwhile New Zealand Superintendent returned home, simply as a resident ordained missionary, he found his now famous wooden house at Kerikeri almost completed and ready for his occupation. The building was commenced in June 1821 by Messrs Bean and Fairburn, and was more or less complete by about March 1822. Today, it seems to be good for many more years, and in its unpretentious appearance there is little to support the charges made against Butler at the time, of squandering the Society's funds on a palatial residence for himself. As the headquarters of the New Zealand mission it does not appear to be unduly luxurious. The timber for it came from the upper reaches of the Kawakawa and Waikare rivers, and although it is now known as 'Kemp' house, this is due only to Kemp's early occupation of it as an employee and tenant of the Church Missionary Society, and his purchase of it from the Society later in the century. But the house was originally built for and to the order of Butler, who occupied it until November 1823.

Kerikeri was now presumably the chief settlement of the Society in New Zealand, but the Oihi station was still maintained with its original personnel, although little missionary activity appears to have taken place there for some time. The school was practically defunct, owing to the want of food with which to lure the scholars into the classroom — a situation which Hall claimed was due to Kendall trading pork to the shipping.

Dire warnings of Kendall's general behaviour at this time were included in letters written to the Secretary of the C.M.S. by William Hall, whose dreary epistles reflect his disillusionment and deteriorating health. In April 1822 he wrote, apparently with some relish:

> If I were but an hour in your company I would tell you absolute facts respecting the conduct of Mr Kendall that would make your hair lift your hat ... And since he came home from England he took a native girl into his house and sleeps with her in preference to his own wife, publicly known to both settlements. Now if this is not sufficient to induce you to take off his gown, I can give you more of the same at some future times should you require it.[13]

It is difficult to warm towards Hall, in spite of his afflictions. Kendall did not deny this charge, and admitted his adultery with the young girl Tungaroa, the daughter of Rakau, a local chief, in a note to the Society Secretary of 27 March 1822.[14] Even in this extremity his mental agility did not entirely forsake him, as his explanation for this lapse demonstrates. His mind, so he explained, was corrupted by the obscenity he encountered in his study of the esoteric and religious conceptions of the Maori. Kendall showed considerable skill in justifying his various misdemeanours and apparently succeeded in convincing himself, at least, of his own basic rectitude. Against this background he was earnestly soliciting Marsden's permission to build a church at Oihi. But in the upshot, his ingenuity was unequal to the burdens he imposed on it, and Tungaroa completed his downfall. In June 1822 when he was at Hokianga with Captain Herd of the *Providence,* examining the district for a suitable site for a mission station, a letter arrived from Marsden suspending him from his duties until the decision of the parent Committee should be known. His dismissal was confirmed in a letter from the Committee of 22 September 1822, which reached him by Marsden in August 1823.

Kendall had for some time found his position at Oihi untenable due to his unconventional behaviour and disputes with his colleagues. He left there in March 1822 and taking Tungaroa with him went to live at the Hikutu village at Te Kaihiki in the Mangonui inlet. This he called Bethel. But driven by anguish and confusion, he moved from place to place, finally shifting to the Kororareka side in February 1823, where he lived under the protection of Pomare Nui, one of the great fighting chiefs of the Bay. He thus became the first known permanent European resident there. His home was at Matauwhi, a bay a few hundred yards east of 'The Beach,' and he called the place 'Pater Noster Valley.' There, in an ambivalent situation, being an ordained priest of the Church of England marooned in New Zealand with no employment as such, he continued his ethnic studies, but without the collaboration of Tungaroa. His association with her had lapsed some months earlier. Until the end of his life, the only further charge brought against him was a taste for 'ardent spirits' — an inconspicuous failing in those times under the prevailing conditions.

In August 1823 Marsden again visited the Bay, in order to establish another mission station with entirely new personnel. With him on the *Brampton* were Wesleyan missionaries, Messrs Turner and Hobbs, bound for Kaeo, Whangaroa, where a mission had been established by the Rev. S. Leigh. Also on board were the Rev. Henry Williams and his family. A newly ordained minister, aged 41, Williams had served for nine years in the Royal Navy, a factor which influenced his administration of the mission in New Zealand. Williams was to be responsible for holding together the tottering structure of the mission here and transforming it into a disciplined organisation.

Marsden's first action upon his arrival was to establish Williams at Paihia, although he had considered Whangaroa. Having visited Oihi, they crossed to Waitangi, recently taken over by Ngapuhi. Although Marsden and Williams favoured the place, they were unable to come to an arrangement with the occupiers, since their chief, Kaiteke,[15] was away in the south with Hongi. On the next day, therefore, a site was selected at Paihia. By the end of the month buildings had been erected to accommodate Williams and his family. Although the principal chief, Te Koki, a brother of Hongi's mother, was also away at the wars, Marsden knew him and was confident of his agreement. From Oihi, Mr Hall supplied 1500 feet of timber for the buildings — Kawakawa and Waikare timber, towed to Oihi in rafts and there pitsawn. The new station was called 'Marsden Vale', a name that struggled vainly for general acceptance but in due course peacefully and mercifully expired. Again Marsden considered acquiring Moturoa Island, as he had nine years earlier, but again the proposal lapsed. At Paihia, 733 acres were purchased between 1823 and 1831.

There were now three Church Missionary Society settlements, at Oihi, Kerikeri and Paihia, and the last became the headquarters after Butler's departure from New Zealand. Ten years of missionary occupation at the Bay of Islands had produced no satisfactory return, and another barren half-dozen years or more lay ahead. However, in the meantime the mission people contrived to make themselves tolerably comfortable, their position assured by the growing rapport between the whaling fleet and the Maoris.

A major problem facing Marsden now was the continued presence of Kendall at the Bay. He was alarmed at the prospect of leaving him in his old stamping ground answerable to none, with a grievance against most of his colleagues, and a powerful influence over Hongi Hika. Hongi was at the time ignorant of his friend's dismissal, being engaged in his wars in the South Auckland district. Therefore, removing Kendall before he could make trouble became Marsden's first objective, and he succeeded to the point of persuading Kendall to leave with him on the *Brampton*.

Meanwhile, 'in the Missionary House at Mata Hui' (Matauwhi), in the words of the Register, Kendall had performed the first Christian marriage service in New Zealand, on 23 June. The bride was a Maori girl, Maria Ringa, and the

110

bridegroom Philip Tapsell, first mate of the *Asp*. The ceremony was witnessed by Captains Brind of the *Asp* and Willson of the *Royal Sovereign*. In the Register, Kendall described the bride as a (baptised) native female, and himself as a 'missionary', in spite of his suspension.[16] That the bride vanished immediately after the ceremony and was never seen again by her husband, robs the occasion of much of its charm, if not of its significance, but we may be consoled a little by a Maori tradition which asserts that she did bear a child from this brief romance.

As Dillon noted in 1827, the missionaries held strange views on such mixed-marriages. His friend Captain Duke was then living with the daughter of the chief Whareumu at Kororareka.[17] Dillon asserted that had Duke applied to the missionaries for a Christian marriage to be performed, he would have been refused on the grounds that the girl was 'unchristian'. Two of the mission's sawyers had been refused marriage to their Maori women, '. . . notwithstanding their [the missionaries] abhorrence of concubinage.'[18] They severely rebuked Kendall for marrying Tapsell to a Maori woman. This abhorrence of such marriages in a land where the only available women were heathen and Maori, appears to have been an obsession with the Williams administration, but was one to which Marsden did not subscribe. When in 1830, Marsden again married Tapsell, he wrote: 'Some persons may condemn the act of marrying them as she is a native heathen, but . . . I felt no objection in my own mind against their marriage.'[19] Thus Marsden, who clearly demonstrated a good deal more common sense in such matters than did some of his New Zealand missionaries, and perhaps because of this, enjoyed a greater reputation among shipmasters than his narrower-minded brethren at the Bay. This marriage, again to a Ngapuhi girl, Karuhi, the sister of the Rangihoua chief, Wharepoaka, ended with her death at Tauranga. Tapsell brought her back, and her brother buried her on the summit of Rangihoua *pa*.

In the meantime, Hongi, once the hope and the declared protector of the mission, had by now become an embarrassment to Marsden. In turn, Hongi's attitude to him was characterised by a marked coldness, due to his refusal to allow his settlers to trade in arms, and his condemnation of his friend Kendall. The tension was not relieved by the appointment of George Clarke as a catechist to the New Zealand mission. Clarke had been a gunsmith, and Hongi was delighted on hearing of the proposal to send him here, thinking that Marsden was providing him with an armourer, and his dismay on discovering that the new man was just another missionary can well be imagined. According to Duperrey, commander of the *Coquille* on its visit to the Bay in 1824, Hongi's disgust was conveyed in the brief observation: 'A good workman was what I wanted, not yet another priest; I have too many of those already.'[20] Clarke did join the mission, but not as an armourer. Greatly worried by Hongi's influence and warlike activities, Marsden was willing to subscribe to the idea of Hongi assuming kingship in New Zealand over the contending tribes. But in this he displayed a poor understanding of the intensity of tribal rivalries and the clan feuds that gave rise to them. It was revenge, conquest and power that Hongi craved, not territorial gains.

On 7 September, still concerned about Hongi, but hopeful that the mission was now on a better footing, Marsden embarked on the *Brampton* with Kendall and his family to return to Sydney. The anchor was weighed, and Captain Moore prepared to beat out against an easterly blowing across the Bay, but the ship, high out of the water, and lazy on the helm, made much leeway on the first tack and lay in irons when an attempt was made to put her about. Twice she thus missed stays, and the captain, finding that he now had only three fathoms of water under him, dropped the anchors. The ship was then lying at the fringe of the reef which now bears its name, approximately between Waitangi and Moturoa Island, and when the tide ebbed, she began to strike heavily. Although the vessel remained habitable for a week, when she first struck some of the passengers abandoned her and landed on Moturoa. Kendall and his family and the remainder of the ship's complement remained on board, there being no immediate danger.

By the next day the *Brampton* was grinding violently on the rocks, the bottom was out of her, and the foremast was gone, but she still remained on an even keel. She seems to have been in this condition for a week, during which the rest of the passengers and crew, luggage, and everything of value was removed to Moturoa Island. On 17 September she was abandoned and went to pieces. At no time was life imperilled, but during the unloading, some 500-600 Maoris surrounded the ship in canoes, and it appeared that looting might occur. This was averted by the intervention of the Ngatimanu chief Whareumu, father-in-law of Captain Duke. In a persuasive oration he pointed out to the inland Maoris who were intent on plunder, that the Bay was his home and that at Kororareka, Europeans and their shipping were under his protection. Either his oratory or his military capability convinced the invaders, and order was restored. The incident illustrates the status then enjoyed at the Bay by Europeans associated with the whale trade. Whareumu also reminded his audience of the unpleasant consequences suffered by the Bay people following the taking of the *Boyd*.[21]

Also on board the *Brampton* when she went ashore were some of the survivors of the wreck of the American schooner *Cossack*, which had been lost at Hokianga some months previously. Her captain, Dix, had made a short visit there to purchase provisions, and attempted to leave the harbour on the outgoing tide, with a light wind. But the tide turned before the vessel was clear, and carried her ashore with all sails set, where she broke up within two hours. Maori chiefs informed Marsden that had not sailors, when on shore, struck with hammers sacred rocks at the south head, the catastrophe would not have happened, but as it was, the presiding god of the rocks engineered the wreck by rendering the vessel's anchors unserviceable. The survivors turned up at Butler's place at Kerikeri five days later, on 2 May, all exhausted, and many half clothed, after walking from Hokianga Heads. Butler supplied them with their immediate needs, and they proceeded to Kororareka, intending to get passages on the whalers *Sarah* and *Mary Anne*, then lying there. Some remained at the Bay and embarked on the *Brampton* in September to be shipwrecked twice in a little over four months.

From Marsden's viewpoint, the most serious development following the wreck of the *Brampton* was Kendall's decision to remain in New Zealand. He would now, reasoned Marsden, be left in a position to incite Hongi against the mission, and particularly against Butler, to whom both he and Hongi were implacably hostile. Well aware of the position, Butler, by the end of October, had agreed to return with Marsden to New South Wales. However there was no indication that he intended his departure to be permanent. Permanency was clearly Marsden's intention, however, and from this point onwards his conduct towards Butler appears questionable, to say the least. Marsden was not a forgiving man, and there can be little doubt that the ill-feeling engendered between them at Sydney remained with him.

On information from Captain Moore of the *Brampton*, he later accused Butler of drunkenness on the brig *Dragon*. Moore was later described on oath as '. . . extremely lewd and profane . . .' and a man '. . . who would take pleasure in exposing and exaggerating the infirmity, and in misrepresenting the manners and conversation of any man making a profession of religion.'[21] Marsden undoubtedly knew Moore's character, but engaged him to testify against Butler before a special committee of missionaries at Kerikeri, which obligingly found him guilty. However, affidavits sworn after this faceless committee had done its work, seem to make nonsense of its decision. Nevertheless, the affair concluded to Marsden's satisfaction, and the permanent departure and discrediting of Butler achieved, he wrote complacently in his journal: 'I consider him a ruined man.'

After the *Brampton* wreck, Kendall's bout of penitence was succeeded by one of defiance, so that when passages for him and Butler were arranged by Marsden on the *Dragon*, he refused to go. The *Dragon* sailed on 14 November carrying, besides a shocked Butler, a worried Marsden. He wrote: 'If Mr Kendall puts his threat in execution and goes to live with Shunghee, his mind must be bent on evil, and it is impossible to see what may be the consequences.' Rewha (Rewa?) the Kerikeri chief, told him that Hongi and Kendall had come to this arrangement on their return from England, and were only prevented from ousting Butler then and there by Rewha's intervention. Kendall, however, continued to live at Matauwhi, while Hongi, who returned from the south before the *Dragon* sailed, made no secret of his displeasure at the treatment of his friend, and displayed a coldness toward Marsden which did nothing for his peace of mind as he left New Zealand. But Hongi, preoccupied with his conquests, let the matter rest.

At Matauwhi, Duperrey and the men of the *Coquille* found Kendall and were impressed by his grasp and treatment of the Maori language. Duperrey was at that time engaged on a world voyage of exploration and discovery, and his two week stay at the Bay of Islands in April 1824 was the first official French visit since Marion du Fresne over 50 years before.

How Kendall supported his family from 1823 until his departure in 1825 is not clear, but on 3 February 1825, apparently convinced of the futility of remaining in New Zealand, he left the Bay with his family for Valparaiso on the *St. Patrick*. Here he acted in his professional capacity for two years, until his departure for Australia. He maintained his interest in Maori matters to the end of his life, and proof that his labours had gained recognition in some quarters is afforded by the decision of Governor Darling to make him a grant of 1280 acres in the Ulladulla district. At this stage he bought a small vessel, and took part in the timber trade on the Australian coast, where in 1832 he was drowned.

---

1. Binney, J. *Legacy of Guilt*, pp.55-69, 181.
2. Ibid, p.177.
3. Archives, Wellington, de Thierry's Old Land Claim, No.455.
4. Binney, p.68.
5. Elder, *Marsden's Lieutenants*, p.245.
6. Barton, *Earliest New Zealand*, p.173.
7. Elder, p.172 et seq.
8. Barton, p.172.
9. Smith, *Maori Wars of the Nineteenth Century*, p.187-90.
10. Barton, p.216.
11. Smith, pp.190 et seq.
12. Ibid, p.200, and Appendix 1.20.
13 Elder, p.246.

14. Binney, p.92.
15. See Appendix 1.9.
16. Waimate Registers, Diocesan Office, Auckland.
17. See Appendix 1.8.
18. Dillon, P. *Narrative of a Voyage in the South Seas*, v.2, p.323.
19. Elder, *Letters and Journals,* p.486-7.
20. Sharp, A. *Duperrey's Visit to New Zealand in 1824,* p.36.
21. In 1826 Dillon obtained a number of oak dead-eyes, said to be a portion of the wreck. Four of these were used to replace those damaged on his ship, the *Research.*
22. Barton, pp.343-4.

13

Kororareka

WITH THE APPOINTMENT of Henry Williams, Marsden left the conduct of the New Zealand mission largely in his hands. With his influence here now minimised, Marsden's achievements and failures can be assessed. He emerges from his New Zealand venture as a man lacking in compassion for those under his control. Devious and ruthless when he thought himself threatened, or if his motives or actions appeared to be questioned, he was not overly scrupulous in his business and trading activities. Williams was an industrious, conscientious, and competent administrator with influence in a restricted field, whereas Marsden, despite his failings, was a giant among men. Benefactor of Polynesians, explorer, businessman and pastoralist, he was big enough to face powerful enemies in the highest places, and still survive. He was a man of charisma, broad in his outlook, with friends and enemies at all levels of society. Sadly, he failed in the areas where a clergyman should have succeeded best.[1]

The 10 years or so of his relations with his missionaries were characterised by sporadic but unremitting strife but with Williams in charge, Marsden had to deal with a dour authoritative personality unlikely to repeat the errors of his predecessors. His own influence on the activities of the mission therefore diminished. The musket trade with the Maoris, one of the persistent causes of trouble, had ceased to loom large as a problem due, among other things, to an adequate supply from other sources. In this, and in other ways, Williams' task was a considerably lighter one than that of the early workers, since it was they who had to grapple with the unknown, and had demonstrated that the missionary was acceptable and in no serious jeopardy in New Zealand. But as Marsden's activity diminished, so too did the practical significance of the mission itself, as shipping and commercial interests came to dominate the scene. These had an impact on the Maoris which was never achieved by the missionaries, who, under Williams, progressively withdrew from contact with any but a few of the newcomers. These, in the course of time, settled at various localities at the Bay, but the commercial centre was Kororareka. There were good people and bad among these, and since for practical purposes they were subject to little or no enforceable law, it is remarkable that major disorder did not threaten the town's survival and its ability to fulfil its essential functions.

Mission eulogists, of which there have been many, are inclined to ascribe to Williams and his missionaries any improvement (in European terms) in the way of life of the Maori people, but there can be no doubt that changes that did occur were due to their association with Europeans of all descriptions, and the Maori belief that such changes that they tolerated were to their advantage. This belief, no doubt, was also a significant factor in many Maori conversions to Christianity, which would have appeared to many to be a religion which endowed its adherents with material advantages much superior to those they enjoyed themselves.

A group that needs to answer to its employers for its actions, as the missionaries did, may tend to magnify its problems so that their solutions appear more impressive, or so that failure is more acceptable. Any claim to missionary influence on the decline of Maori warfare needs to be closely examined since the wars continued on a reduced scale until most of the old fighting chiefs were dead, and the tribes within striking distance had acquired firearms. Disillusionment, revulsion and the satiety following an orgy of killing over a period of many years, must surely also have affected the Maori attitude to musket warfare. Trade and the adoption of the European values that it encourages, inevitably contributed. But there is no doubt that the *rangatira* Maori respected the mission people for their integrity and personal qualities as they did other sections of the permanent or temporary Bay community who merited respect for one reason or another. Williams ultimately gained a secure place for himself as did some of his colleagues, due to tenacity and force of character. To him was accorded the respect that intelligent chiefs, being members of an aristocratic society themselves, considered due to him as a pakeha *tohunga* and *rangatira*. Thus on occasions they were able to use him as an arbiter in local disputes, avoiding personal responsibility for decisions, which had they made them themselves, might have damaged their own *mana* or prestige, and perhaps further aggravated situations.

In this period, the attitude of the missionaries to Kororareka itself, the shipping, other settlers and visitors, and even to the Maoris, hardened into the characteristic form noted by Earle (1827), Dillon (1826), Marshall (1835), Lang (1839), Commander Wilkes, U.S.N. (1840), and finally de Thierry (1845).[2] The consensus appears to have been that as a body they were cold and inhospitable to strangers, and although tolerably comfortable and well provided for, were somewhat deficient in Christian charity towards those not connected with the mission. They held themselves aloof from the Maoris and were considerably less successful in their conversion than other Polynesian missions. The general stance of the mission was apparently a deliberate one, intended to disassociate its employees from the trading activities and 'fornications' of the early mission people, and from the association of Maori girls with shipping personnel. Perhaps the best considered comment came from Wilkes:

It is true that the situation of these missionaries of the Church of England is different from that of any we had heretofore seen, and equally so that they do not appear to have succeeded as well in making proselytes as those in other Polynesian islands; but I am persuaded that they have done, and are still endeavouring to do much good. They are, however, separated, as it were, from their flocks, and consequently, cannot have that control over their behaviour that would be desirable. Many scenes, therefore, take place at the pas or strongholds, that might be prevented if the missionaries mingled more with their converts . . . The missionaries of the Episcopal Church [C of E] appear to keep aloof from the natives, and an air of stiffness and pride, unbecoming a

119

missionary in most minds, seems to prevail.

Their dilemma must indeed have been a very frustrating one. Their potential converts, male and female, were being lured away from the regimented environment of the mission stations — no difficult achievement for the whalers — where they otherwise would have been engaged in household and other tasks, and in the maintenance and development of the station.

Edward Markham, a visitor to the Bay in 1834, and a man with no anti-missionary bias, summarised the position in his journal:

> The Missionaries hate the Ships to come into the Bay; the Reason is this. Thirty to five and Thirty sail of Whalers come in for three weeks to the Bay and 400 to 500 Sailors require as many Women, and they have been out one year. I saw some that had been out Thirty two Months and of course the Ladies were in great request, and even the Relations of those who are living as Servants with the Missionaries go to Pihere and bring them away, in spite of all their prayer lessons. These young ladies go off to the Ships, and three weeks on board are spent much to their satisfaction as they get from the Sailors a Fowling piece for the Father or Brother, Blankets, Gowns & as much as they would from the Missionary in a year. Therefore they prefer going on board the Ships 'Kipookys' when they come in, to the annoyance of the Missionaries. I believe the Missionaries are right, that They go too young, and are very often Barren, and that is one Reason of the decrease of population independent of any disease they may get. They have very few Children in the Villages. . . I do believe the Sailors have done as much towards Civilising the Natives as the Missionaries have, or more, but in a more worldly view as now a Man may go from one Village to another, and the Children do not hoot them as they did formerly, and such a number have been in Whalers, as each Ship takes eight or ten New Zealanders and the Seamen pick up the Language from them.[3]

Markham observed, as others did, that the attachments

between sailors and Maori girls were by no means always transient and promiscuous. Men had their wives here, women who remained in their way faithful to them.

I have known a Woman Tabooed to an European for Years, he coming every year to New Zealand for the last fifteen or so, then settling there altogether and Catching and salting fish, Salting Hams, Pork for sale and going to pass the remainder of his days there. . . The Tigris Whaler had arrived, and three Women of that Village had Tarnes [tane] or Husbands on Board; they drove three large Pigs down to the Bay of Islands and put them on board Canoes, and went to live with the Men they had been with for Voyages and made these Men presents of the only thing they had in the shape of property; I call that affection.[4]

The Maori was not easily led except in the direction of his inclinations, and his natural independence, gregariousness and ebullience led him toward a more colourful life than that to be found at the mission stations. Neither knowing nor caring about the ethics of the matter, some expressed astonishment at the hostile attitude of the missionaries to their fellow countrymen.

Apart from the people at the mission establishments, there were broadly speaking two groups comprising the white population at the Bay of Islands in the 1820s. Numerically, the largest was the shifting population from the whalers that Markham describes. These in turn gave rise to the presence of a more or less permanent group composed of former seamen or tradesmen associated with whaling or sealing. There was also a sprinkling of runaway convicts, all of whom lived with the Maoris at various parts of the Bay.

The reputation of the whalers as a whole had earlier suffered due to the barbarous manner in which some of them had dealt with the Maoris. However, as the advantages of a stable relationship became apparent this situation improved. Although whale crews were still much maligned by the missionaries, they were clearly held in high esteem by the Maoris, no doubt for the trade-goods and social amusement they provided, and for the opportunities they offered the young men to work and travel on the ships. The association undoubtedly also had its residue of harm, but it was inevitable that Maori life would be disrupted from the moment New Zealand was discovered by Europeans. The old ways were irrevocably doomed, and social chaos was certain. Against this, missionaries everywhere struggled in vain.

But small credit has been given to the fleet of small ships and their crews, who between 1800 and 1830 were the pathfinders of the Pacific Ocean. The Pacific whale-trade was originated from the convict settlement at Port Jackson, when the first whale-ships were the cleared convict transports *Mary Ann, Matilda, Britannia, Salamander* and *William and Ann*. In October 1791 they hunted for whales off the Australian coast, but with small success. The first four of these returned to port, but the *William and Ann,* under Captain Bunker, got as far as the New Zealand coast, and at the request of Lieut. Governor King attempted unsuccessfully to induce New Zealanders to accompany him to Norfolk Island. Bunker's vessel, then may have been the first to try for whales on the New Zealand coast.

Later, the East India Company's charter rights in the Pacific were relaxed, and the little ships ventured further into this relatively unknown ocean. They discovered hitherto unknown islands and encountered hostile and unheard-of people in the course of their work. Such men as Magellan, Cook, du Fresne, Byron, Vancouver, Bellingshausen and Malaspina travelled and mapped the highways. But the detail was filled in by the merchant marines of England, France, the United States and other nations. They initiated relations with hitherto unvisited peoples, albeit often roughly, and charted rocks, atolls and islands. As explorers in the plying of their trade, they did invaluable work, and one of these, the colourful Irishman, Peter Dillon, solved the riddle of the fate of the French explorer La Perouse and his expedition, where a well-equipped official attempt had failed.

Out of this whale trade grew Kororareka. Although the *City of Edinburgh* had used it for a major refit in 1809, Kororareka was not generally favoured by shipping until the early 1820s. It will be recalled that, when HM Storeship *Dromedary* visited the Bay in 1820 in search of spars, it did anchor there, but on that occasion Major Cruise remarked upon four whaleships lying at anchor at Paroa. Later the ship was moved and taken there also, 'the anchorage at Kororareka appearing too much exposed.'[5] Butler's journal for the years 1819 to 1823 contains many references to his journeys to Paroa to visit shipping there, and Polack[6] also testifies to Paroa's popularity. But we have already noted that the death of its chief Korokoro in 1823, and his brother Tuhi (also known as Katikati and Tupaea) only a year later, left Paroa deserted and without a patron. The *pa*, Kahuwera, had been plundered and destroyed by Hongi Hika due, it seems likely, to a long-standing resentment by Hongi and his relatives to the Ngare Raumati Korokoro's occupation of this favoured locality. The destruction ended, as it was no doubt meant to, the exercise of any authority other than Ngapuhi in the Te Rawhiti, or eastern districts.

The pre-eminence of Kororareka was therefore now un-challenged. Its chiefs were the Ngatimanu Pomare Nui [7] (formerly known as Whiria or Whetoi), domiciled at Matau-whi, Kendall's Pater Noster Valley, and Whareumu (also known as King George, or Shulitea), who lived at Kororareka itself. Both these chiefs also had interests further up the Kawakawa River. On the death of Pomare at Te Rore, he was succeeded by his nephew, also Whetoi, who too assumed the name Pomare.[8] Thus after 1826, although the name of the resident chief is unchanged, he is a different person, but unlike his uncle, he was not a great warrior. 'The Beach', as Korora-reka was to become known to shipping, never lost its place as the commercial capital of the Bay.

Before 1830, development was slow. Its settlers were then mostly working tradesmen, but the merchant traders who followed exploited the opportunities offered to supply and service the whalers not only with food and timber, but also with such commodities and services hitherto obtainable only at Port Jackson. With this development, Kororareka became a place of importance in the Pacific, and while it was the only settlement in the Bay that could ever have been described as a town, there developed along with it several sizeable trading establishments which were communities of their own.

But long before the advent of whaler or missionary, equally significant events had taken place at Kororareka. Originally Ngare Raumati territory, a change occurred in pre-European times when a party of Ngatimaru from the Hauraki Gulf, friends of Ngare Raumati, visited the Bay. At Paihia, coming upon Waipahihi, a chief of Ngatimanu, they killed him, and taking his body over to Kororareka, cooked and ate it. Ngare Raumati later patched up this breach of etiquette by ceding Kororareka to Ngatimanu as *utu*, or compensation, demonstrating the very Maori sense of what is just and seemly.[9]

The date of the advent of the first white settler at Kororareka cannot be determined with accuracy, but it will be recalled that Kendall lived nearby in 1823, and in the next year Duperrey saw 'several work men engaged in the construction of a new house.'[10]

In January 1826 Captain Stewart called at the Bay of Islands and induced a number of men living there to accompany him to Port Pegasus on Stewart's Island, where he intended to establish a timber and ship-building enterprise. These were the shipwright William Cook, John Leigh, Hugh McCurdy, Robert Day, Ben Turner, and three others. John Boultbee's journal[11] relates his encounter at Stewart's Island, probably in 1827, with a shipwright named Cook, eight men and nine women from the Bay of Islands, greatly distressed for want of food since Stewart had left them to return to Sydney, where he was reputed to have been jailed for debt. The party was at last able to escape from the island by building a small vessel. It is not clear whether all these men came from Kororareka, but it is likely. Turner, at least, lived there on his return, and was later one of the prominent personalities and land claimants in the town. He also lived to be a member of the Auckland Provincial Council. Cook had been picked up from Matauwhi, and his name is well known in the Bay to this day. His grandson, Bert, was born at Matauwhi, and in 1890 established the whaling station at Whangamumu which was in existence until quite recently.

Of the early references to European settlement at Kororareka, those recorded by Captain Peter Dillon are the most lucid and informative. Dillon visited the young town in July 1827, and has left an interesting account of conditions there:

About 10 a.m. I went ashore. . . We landed at the watering place, [at the western end of the beach] where we found the stream very scanty, owing to the long drought. The natives received us kindly, and conducted us along a path which they said led to an Englishman's house.

We shortly reached a very neat hut, surrounded with a palisading of about nine feet high. On entering it, we found the inhabitants consisted of an English cooper and his wife, a native of New Zealand. The man informed us that he had been cooper's mate to a whaler, and had been left on the island in consequence of ill health. . . He is sometimes employed by the shipping that touch here in repairing their water-casks, making buckets. . . for which he receives gun-powder, flints, musket balls, cutlery, ironmongery, &c., and barters those articles with the natives for hogs, fish, poultry, wild ducks, pigeons and potatoes, whereby he ekes out a very comfortable subsistence for himself and his wife.

[A little further along the beach was the home of a blacksmith and his Maori wife, and still further]. . . a third dwelling, occupied by four Europeans, employed in sawing plank. Johnston, the proprietor of it, was discharged from a whaler about three years ago, and forming the resolution to settle here, united himself with a native woman of the country, who had two fine children by him. He disposes of his planks to the ships which touch here, receiving in return tea, sugar, biscuit, flour, and such articles as the cooper accepts for his work.

At Matauwhi, Dillon found, in '. . . the village and fort of the late Boo Marray' [Pomare] a house which, for Kororareka, must indeed have been the latest thing in suburban homes. It was actually built entirely of plank, and even had glass windows. It had two rooms and was furnished luxuriously with chairs, a table, a bedstead and bedding, a looking-glass and dressing-case with various other necessaries. This was the shore home of Captain Brind, of the whaler *Emily*, '. . . son-in-law to the late Boo Marray, and at the time of my visit the gentleman and his

125

wife were absent at the fishery on the equator.'[12]

Johnson, the sawyer, was probably the first European to conduct a stable business at the town, since Dillon's account
implies that the other three men were employed by him.
Johnson's land claim is shown on Old Land Claim Plan No. 300
as situated on the present site of the Duke of Marlborough hotel
or thereabouts, and there, perhaps, was his saw-pit. But as a
matter of interest, the first recorded sale of land at Kororareka
was in 1814 to Thomas Hansen, the one time commander of the
Active who settled at Te Puna with the missionaries.[13]

On his return to Kororareka some months later, Dillon found
another settler in the little colony. Captain Duke, of the *Sisters*,
had taken up residence there to convalesce after an illness, and
Dillon spoke highly of his kind treatment of the great number
of sick in the *Research*'s crew, including Dillon himself.

Peter Dillon, a gregarious Irishman of engaging manners and
personality, had been a regular visitor to the Bay since his first
trip in the *Mercury* in 1808, and had commanded the *Active* on
her pioneering mission voyage in 1813. Many of his crew on his
1827 voyage were Maoris, and his popularity with Polynesians
was always apparent. He had a quaint conceit — he discarded
the Maori names of his friends in favour of such richly traditional Irish ones as Brian Boru, Morgan McMarragh, Phelim
O'Rourke, and Murtoch O'Brien, which unfortunately for the
historian renders many of them anonymous.

Dillon was at the Bay on his return from the Solomon Islands,
where he had succeeded in establishing the place and cause of
the destruction of La Pérouse's expedition in the 1780s. In the
next decade, a search by D'Entrecasteau had failed to do this,
but Dillon produced conclusive evidence that La Pérouse's two
ships had been wrecked, and their entire crews lost, at Vanikoro. In 1829, Dillon was awarded compensation by the French
Government, an annuity of 4000 francs, and the title of
Chevalier of the Legion of Honour.[14] Titore Takiri, the prestigious chief of Kororareka — Dillon's 'Marquis of Waimate' —
accompanied him on the voyage.[15]

The Kororareka population had also been increased when
four members of Captain Herd's expedition settled there. They

had been living with the cooper, but at the time of Dillon's visit were engaged by the Paihia mission in repairing their vessel. Herd's enterprise had been initiated by yet another New Zealand Company, which was formed in England in 1825 in order to establish a colony or trading settlement here, and early in 1826 the *Rosanna* left Leith with about 50 assorted tradesmen as the nucleus of the settlement. This was the forerunner of the Company which did, eventually, colonise Wellington and Nelson in 1839.[16] The Hauraki Gulf was first examined and land was acquired there, but the demeanour of the Maoris discouraged the colonisers. They then decided to try Hokianga, and on the way called at the Bay of Islands, where they were coldly received by the missionaries, who preferred them at Hokianga, hoping no doubt that they might there draw off some of the shipping from the Bay. At Hokianga, Herd purchased the point on which Rawene is now situated, but the same timidity exhibited by the settlers at the Thames re-surfaced here, and the entire project was abandoned. Until quite recently, Rawene was still referred to by old settlers as Herd's Point. Dillon asserted that the expedition failed due to Herd's inefficiency, while Marsden attributed it to the captain's former wicked ways with the Maoris.

Quite soon, however, a thriving timber industry developed at Hokianga, and Dillon commented on this: 'Messrs. Cooper and Levery, and Messrs. Raine and Ramsay, two respectable firms at Port Jackson, have each, I understand, an establishment at Hokianga for procuring pork, spars, flax, planks, & c., and are very well treated by the natives, who have permitted them within the last twelve months to build two or three small schooners.' Earle actually visited this dockyard at Horeke, in 1827, when the shipbuilding was in progress. The proprietors had named the place 'Deptford'.[17]

The *Rosanna* returned to Sydney in February 1827, where the tradesmen who so wished were discharged. A number of them returned to New Zealand, where, as Dillon noted, four took up residence with the cooper at Kororareka.[18]

At Kororareka in 1827, then, there were some dozen or so 'respectable' settlers, of whom two were semi-permanent captains, and the rest tradesmen. Eight more, probably former residents, were soon due back from Stewart's Island. All of these presumably had Maori wives. Earle mentions two other groups of European residents, one known locally as 'Beach Rangers', who had either deserted from whalers or had been discharged from them for crimes. They lived 'a mean and miserable life amongst the natives.'[19] How many of these there were Earle does not say. Similarly he made no estimate of his other group, the runaway convicts from the Australian mainland and Tasmania, with whom the Maoris refused all intercourse. The total European population, then, is difficult to assess, but was probably not considerable. Cook and Johnson probably qualify as the earliest settlers here.

No attempt was made by these early settlers to farm the land, although Captain Duke imported some sheep to Kororareka from Tasmania. What these animals lived on is hard to say, but their suffering was mercifully short. The local dogs soon killed most of the flock. Goats, however, abounded, and even a few sheep lived to provide broth for the sick men of the *Research's* crew. Earle also observed 100 fat cattle at Kerikeri, no doubt Marsden's private herd.

Money now appears to have been circulating fairly freely in the Bay of Islands, and the 'dollar', almost certainly the old Mexican eight *real* peces, or the newer *peso*, was apparently the most plentiful currency. These coins were in effect the international currency of the day. As early as 1823, Marsden had been worried by Maoris demanding money as payment, and had instructed his missionaries not to use money as a means of exchange, since he feared the practice would become general, and threaten the barter basis of Maori-missionary relations.

One of the more enterprising early settlers was Gilbert Mair, who settled at the Paihia mission station in 1825. In 1831 he purchased from the Ngatimanu Maoris 394 acres on the western side of Te Wahapu Bay,[20] mid-way between Russell and Opua. He farmed the land, and was among the more prosperous and 'respectable' businessmen in the Bay. He was a director of the New Zealand Banking Company, which started business in Kororareka in 1840, and is reputed to have exported from Te Wahapu the first shipment of kauri gum to leave New Zealand.

Mair assisted in the building of, and later commanded, the

first European seagoing vessel built at the Bay of Islands, and it seems that this may well have been his reason for first settling at Paihia. The mission stations had long been largely dependent on the whalers for communication with the outside world, due to the erratic service provided by the *Active*, Marsden's own property, which he complained was becoming a burden to him. He had used the vessel for trading and whaling as well as servicing the interests of the mission, but the venture had not prospered, and in 1820 he offered her to the Society. But the Committee was not interested, and he finally sold the *Active* in 1825. At the same time he authorised the New Zealand mission to build a vessel of its own.

Prior to 1826 the mission here had no vessel of its own, and had at times to rely on the generosity of whaling captains, even for small boats. On 2 January 1823 William Hall had noted: 'Received the loan of a boat from Captain Brind for the use of the settlement until he returns from the fishing grounds, in which time I mean to build one.' Build one he did — a boat 20 feet by 6 feet, which was completed by 27 January at Oihi.[21]

But a large vessel for deep-water communications was essential. On the last day of 1824 Hall commenced work on one, having been engaged on the plans for some months, but his health broke down early in the work. In spite of his failings, the Society had in him its most useful and versatile worker, and suffered a loss when his health caused him to leave New Zealand in 1825. Until his departure, he was the mainstay of the practical side of mission life, as housebuilder, boatbuilder, bushman and gardener, and although eternally disgruntled, he was a conscientious worker.

The *Herald*, as the new vessel was called, was about 55 tons burden, and took a year to build. Williams, Mair, five carpenters and several labourers accomplished the work, partly with materials from the wrecked *Brampton*, and the schooner was launched on 24 January 1826, from the eastern end of Paihia. With Mair in command it made a number of voyages, to Hokianga, Tauranga and Sydney, but the little *Herald* had a short life, being wrecked at Hokianga in May 1828, little more than two years after her completion. When wrecked she was a total loss, and was boarded and plundered by the Hokianga

Maoris.

Another incident, which resulted in the loss of a ship, took place at Whangaroa in March 1825, and demonstrates the widely differing attitude of the Maoris there from those of the Bay of Islands. On 5 March the brig *Mercury* entered Whangaroa for supplies and upon anchoring was immediately boarded and overrun by a great number of Maoris. [22] It was an unruly mob, insolent and aggressive, and remained in possession of the vessel all that night, to the great alarm of the captain and crew. The next day, Sunday, the Methodist missionary at Whangaroa, Mr White, boarded the ship and endeavoured to persuade the Maoris to leave. A few did so, and White left also. Thereupon, although a great number were still on board, the captain attempted to put to sea, and as there was no wind, two boats were put ahead to tow. This move apparently convinced the Maoris that they were about to be abducted, and some attacked the captain, who lost no time in escaping into the boats, with most of the crew. Then, in fear of their lives, they fled to the Bay of Islands for protection. At Oihi, Mr Hall gave them shelter until they found means to travel to New South Wales. In the meantime, White returned on board the *Mercury* and succeeded in taking possession of her. The mate, cook and steward, who had been abandoned by their shipmates, then managed with White's assistance to work the brig out through the narrow entrance of the harbour into the open water. But she was now in a bedraggled state. She had been aground at one stage of the fracas, and stripped of everything portable, including cargo and navigating instruments, she limped up the coast. The four men saw no hope of working her into the land, and abandoning her in White's boat, they eventually reached Whangaroa mission station. The *Mercury* later went ashore near North Cape.

Unlike the Bay Maoris, the Whangaroa people had not yet learned that it was to their advantage to remain on good terms with European shipping. Furthermore, they came very close to suffering a reprisal at the hands of Hongi Hika, ostensibly for their attack on the *Mercury*, although he may well have been using the incident as a pretext for a long-contemplated attack.

Meanwhile, shipping at the Bay was on the best of terms with the Maoris there. From various sources, a list can be compiled of some 17 ships which are known to have called there in 1823, and since their mention is only incidental, there could have been many more. At this time the influx of shipping was confined to a few months in the early part of the year, and in those unhurried times, visits in most cases ran into many weeks. In 1822 eight ships visited the port in seven weeks. But it was not until some years later that the port was used throughout the year, so that, except for occasional visitors, the mission stations were left in peace during the winter and spring months. In fact, such was his confidence that there was no competition in the offering that Captain Walker of the *Dragon* had the temerity in October 1823 to demand £1000 to return Marsden and his entourage to Sydney after the wreck of the *Brampton*. Walker finally settled magnanimously for $2800, perhaps a little over half his original demand, and Captain Moore of the *Brampton* and Marsden shared this expense between them. On the other hand, two years earlier in January, the Rev. John Butler had expressed dismay on being informed by Captain Thompson of the *Active*, that twelve ships were on the way to the Bay to snatch the port from the missionaries' mouths.

By the mid and late 1820s, European shipping was considered to be as safe from attack at the Bay of Islands as at Sydney, but a new problem was developing. Sailors, captivated by the prospect of an easy life ashore and the affection and loyalty of the Maori women, were deserting and finding refuge with the local people until their ships departed. This became a great nuisance to shipmasters, since labour was at a premium at Sydney, and the pool or surplus manpower was 12,000 miles away in the British ports. Maori seamen were therefore being employed by the whale-fleet, but they did not always undertake the voyage back to the home ports. That the native New Zealander made an excellent seaman is not surprising. As Elsdon Best somewhat fancifully observed when writing of Polynesian navigators: they were '. . . throwing the rolling sea leagues behind them even as our forebears paddled their dugouts across the Thames.' However, hiring Maori crew did not solve the problem of deserters, which had attained such proportions by 1838, that three of the resolutions, or 'laws' of the newly-formed Kororareka Association were devoted entirely to it.[23] Since five of the remaining 12 resolutions were constitutional ones, over 30 per cent of the 'criminal legislation' of New Zealand was directed towards deserting seamen. In British law, ship-desertion was, of course, a criminal offence.

Further official attention was given in 1824 to the enforcement of law in the Pacific area, because of the greatly increasing traffic between the native peoples and the whale-fleet, now traversing the length and breadth of the ocean. A statute was enacted in 1823 which conferred jurisdiction on the New South Wales courts over offenders in the Pacific. Pursuant to this, Governor Brisbane issued a Proclamation dated 17 May 1824 enforcing the execution of the provisions of the Act, and directed that it be read to all crews departing from Port Jackson for the Pacific, but there is little evidence that this measure was any more effective than previous ones having the same objectives. Under the prevailing conditions, the problems involved in obtaining evidence, or even knowledge of crimes, were difficult enough, let alone apprehending the offenders.

---

1. Yarwood, A.T., *Samuel Marsden, the Great Survivor,* passim.
2. Earle, *Nine Months Residence in New Zealand,* pp. 38, 55, 85, 181-7. Dillon, *A Voyage in the South Seas,* etc., v.2, pp. 321, 324-30. Marshall, W.B. *Personal Narrative of Two Visits to New Zealand, 1834-5,* pp. 113-116. Lang, J.D. *New Zealand in 1839,* p.32-3. Wilkes, C. *The United States Exploring Expedition,* pp. 383, 401. De Thierry, C.P.H. 'Historical Narrative of an Attempt to form a Settlement in N.Z.' (MSS) p.289-90.
3. Markham, E, *N.Z., or Recollection of it,* p.65.
4. Ibid, p.66.
5. Cruise, *Journal of Ten Months Residence,* p.34.
6. Polack, *Narrative of Travels and Adventures* v.1, p.250.
7. This name he took from the Tahitian King.
8. See Appendix 1.11.
9. Maori Land Court minutes, Tai Tokerau, Northern, No. 25, p.94.
10 Sharp, *Duperrey's Visit to NZ in 1824,* p.117.

11. Boultbee, J. (Journal of) p.168-9.
12. Dillon, v.1, p.184-248.
13. Bell, F.D. Schedule of Old Land Claims, No 1005.
14. Davidson, J.W. 'Peter Dillon of Vanikoro', p.154 et seq.
15. See Appendix 1.7.
16. Sherrin and Wallace, *Early New Zealand,* pp. 288-91.
17. Dillon, p.195, and Earle, op.cit., p.26.
18. Earle, who travelled on foot from Hokianga to Kororareka, mentioned these 'scotch mechanics' whom he had met during his sojourn on the 'Beach' in 1827, although elsewhere he mentions having met a further 'party of men' from the *Rosanna*, suggesting that more than the four mentioned above had returned to, or had remained in New Zealand. (Earle, p.47.)
19. Ibid, p.48-9.
20. Bell, F.D. No. 306.
21. Elder, *Marsden's Lieutenants,* p.228.
22. Ibid, p.238-9, and Owens, J.M.R., *Prophets in the Wilderness,* pp. 60, 69, 70.
23. Sherrin and Wallace, p.470-1.

14

The Last Years of Hongi Hika and Their Aftermath

IT WAS THE fate of the early missionaries in New Zealand to be plagued by the warlike activities of their closest Maori associates. Hongi Hika, the 'patron' of the Anglican missionaries at the Bay of Islands, had kept the mission dovecotes aflutter with his southern wars. But a much more serious situation arose, when, after his victory over the Ngatiwhatua at Kaipara in 1825, he directed his attention to local grievances. Those who suffered most were the Wesleyans at Whangaroa, where at Kaeo, with the active and willing assistance of the Church Missionary Society at the Bay, the Rev. Samuel Leigh and William White had established a mission station in June 1823. This they called Wesleydale, and they were joined later by Hobbs, Turner, Stack and Wade. Although Leigh had arrived at Rangihoua in January 1822, he appears to have done little until he founded the Kaeo station, but enjoy the hospitality of the settlement and share its activities. Although he did make excursions to Oruru and Whangarei to examine sites for a mission, he does not seem to have achieved much in 18 months. This inspired Kendall to pointedly remark that it would have been as safe for Leigh to settle elsewhere at that time as it had been for him (Kendall), to settle at the Bay some seven years previously. Indeed, Leigh's behaviour and activities, or want of them, were the subject of uncharitable comment by some of his Methodist associates, who also took a cynical view of his complaints about his health and general condition. Leigh seems to have been neither enterprising nor at all energetic in promoting his New Zealand mission, and clearly was not the pioneering sort. His various tribulations and perhaps his own realisation of his unsuitability forced him to depart with Marsden in the *Dragon* in November 1823, leaving his five colleagues to carry on at Whangaroa, where, with the departure of Mrs Leigh, the unfortunate Mrs Turner was now the only woman among them.[1]

The Whangaroa mission was under the patronage of Te Puhi and Te Aara (George), and although Te Puhi appears to have been moderately helpful, George's behaviour was erratic and a source of alarm to the missionaries until his death early in 1825. But these chiefs were in no way to be of much help. Their tribe, Ngatiuru, was weak and in constant fear of attack from its neighbours, the Ngatipou, or from Hongi Hika at the Bay. The mission enjoyed no success at all, and its people went in constant fear of molestation both from their nominal protectors and their enemies.

Hongi at this time was contemplating his attack on the Ngatiwhatua at Kaipara, to avenge various affronts to Ngapuhi, particularly the battle at Moremonui on the west coast near the Waipoua Forest early in the century, when his half-brother Moka and his sister Waitapu were killed.[2] Accordingly he assembled a force of some 500 at Kaikohe at about the end of 1824, and proceeded down the Mangakahia River towards the Kaipara. But a chief Hihi-o-tote who was related to both Ngapuhi and Ngatiwhatua, went ahead of the party and brought back to Hongi a very prestigious greenstone *mere* as a *tohu*, or peace-offering from the threatened people, and apparently marshalled such persuasive arguments that the invading *taua* returned and dispersed to their homes at Kaikohe and Waimate.

But Whareumu (King George), who was intent on avenging the death of one of his relatives was much put out at the abortive result of the expedition, and assembling 170 men of his own later in the year, proceeded by sea to Mangawhai with the intention of attacking Ngatiwhatua overland from there. He was followed in February 1825 by Hongi with 300-400 men. These forces assembled at Mangawhai, and the stage was set for the decisive battle of Te-ika-a-Ranganui.[3] The list of chiefs involved reads like a roll-call of the mighty of the day. Among them were Hongi, Te Whareumu, Kaiteke, Te Wera Hauraki,

Taiwhanga, Moka, Te Morenga and others from the Bay, Patuone, Nene and Moetara from Hokianga, and Tirarau from Mangakahia.[4] Hongi wore his coat of mail, and the war-party was almost wholly armed with muskets, while it is said that the 800-1000 men mustered by Ngatiwhatua under Murupaenga, had about 100 muskets, although the total is sometimes quoted as low as two.

The canoes were dragged overland toward the Otamatea River, a tributary of the Kaipara, and battle was joined a little to the east of the present township of Kaiwaka. Here Ngatiwhatua suffered a grievous defeat, which destroyed the power of the tribe and dispersed its people. Moremonui was indeed avenged, but Hongi had lost his son Hare,[5] and this led to further strife. At the end of 1825 Hongi departed from the Bay in canoes with 240 men to pursue the scattered Ngatiwhatua into the Waikato where many of them had fled. After many of the enemy had been searched out and killed, a peace was made with the Waikato people. Hongi then returned home, but on the way met a war expedition under the Ngatimanu Pomare Nui bound for Hauraki and the Waikato. Hongi told him of the peace he had made with the people there, but Pomare was adamant, and proceeded on his way to his death at Te Rore near Pirongia, as we have already noted.

Back at the Bay, Hongi went to live at the *pa* Tapuaeharuru, sometimes called Mawhe, on the eastern shore of Lake Omapere. Here, innumerable calamities overtook him. One of his daughters died, his favourite wife Turikatuku was now close to death, and another wife, Tangiwhare, commited adultery with Matuku, a member of his household, and upon detection hanged herself. Perhaps as a result of these disasters, Hongi now embarked on a policy of harrying the Ngatipou of Whangaroa, which by no means had the full approval of his associates, who considered this to be a 'mimi-whare' — a fouling of his own house — due to his close relationship with the Whangaroa people. However, tradition suggests that an underlying reason for his action may have been the Ngatipou murder, many years before, of his Ngatiuru grandfather, Tahapango.

In October 1826, therefore, Ngatiuru, the Wesleyan's tribe at

Kaeo, received a message from their relative Hongi to leave their food and fly into the woods, so that when he came he might not see their faces and kill them. On 25 October a *taua* from the Bay and the coast, comprising about 300 men, came up the river with the tide, destroyed the mission gardens and took away anything they fancied, including a servant-girl of Mrs Turner's. They broke down fences, scuffled with the missionaries and finally left with the tide next day. At the C.M.S. stations at the Bay the mission people also noted a strange mood and restlessness among the Maoris, but they were not seriously molested, although at Whangaroa the unease continued and increased. Te Aara (George) had died in April 1825, and his elder brother Te Puhi appeared to have little control over the local situation, which did not improve when Hobbs whipped George's son for stealing and was chided by Te Puhi for assaulting a chief's son. In all their tribulations the Wesleyans were loyally supported by their Anglican colleagues at the Bay of Islands, who had become apprehensive of the effect on their own affairs of the turbulent events surrounding Hongi Hika.

During the first days of January 1827, Hongi entered the Whangaroa Harbour with 400 men, and from that time Wesleydale was doomed.[6] He first took a Ngatipou *pa*, Pinia, near the heads. Te Puhi and his Ngatiuru hierarchy fled to Hokianga, although Hongi had not threatened them — on the contrary, he had warned them to keep out of his way lest they be hurt. The *taua* which plundered and destroyed the mission station at daybreak on 10 January was almost certainly a *muru* or stripping-party, bent on pillaging Te Puhi's former domain, following his abandonment of it, and the Wesleyans now had no recourse other than flight to the Bay. On the previous night Stack had gone ahead with some valuables, but in the early morning the Turners and their three children, Mr and Mrs Wade, Hobbs, Miss Davis of the C.M.S., together with some of the mission Maoris, started their 15-mile retreat to Kerikeri.

But their problems had not come to an end, since they immediately met a small number of Ngatiuru returning from Hokianga, who warned them that a larger party was on the way to defend Whangaroa and that they were likely to deal roughly with the mission people. Proceeding with some misgivings, they soon came upon Te Puhi's brother Ngahuruhuru, and Wharerahi (or Wharenui), whose wife Tari was the sister of Nene and Patuone;[7] and these turned back and escorted the fugitives until they met Patuone himself, with Te Puhi and 200-300 men. After assurances from Patuone, who allowed them to proceed, the missionaries were conducted by Wharerahi and Ngahuruhuru on the rest of their journey to Kerikeri, and they were shortly met and assisted on their way by H. Williams and others from Paihia and Kerikeri.

Hongi, who had been joined by the Roroa people from the south Hokianga head district, was now investing the *pa* at Taratara, at the head of the Whangaroa Harbour. Taking it, he pursued the fleeing Ngatipou through Otangaroa into the head of the Mangamuka Valley. However, Patuone had travelled to Whangaroa by the usual route from Hokianga, that is, up the Waihou Valley and the Waihoanga Stream on to the plateau at Puketi, thence north over the Pungaere ridge and down into Kaeo valley along the Upokorau and Kaeo streams. Of his subsequent movements and actions no record has been found. This party clearly did not engage Hongi's forces, since at no time did he threaten or attack Ngatiuru, and their defence appears to have been Patuone's only concern. On the other hand, the Ngatipou had suffered great loss, and Hongi returned, wounded grievously but victorious, to settle in Ngatipou territory at Pupuke, at the head of the Whangaroa Harbour.

Hongi fought no more wars, but the repercussions of this one seriously affected the mission community, and such was the prevailing mood that none knew what might result either from his death or his continued life. He remained at Pupuke until his death, but in his last battle, unprotected by his famous coat of mail, he had received a fatal wound, and although he lived for another year, he was during that time a dying man. Such events could only be contemplated with great alarm by the mission settlers at the Bay, particularly since rumours were abroad that Hongi, upon whose protection they had relied for so many years, was at the brink of death. But he did not die immediately and he and his allies at the Bay were now in a very strong position, having completely subdued their near neighbours at

138

the Kaipara and Whangaroa.

But the missionaries at the Bay were understandably apprehensive. Convinced that their district was about to become an arena for the activities of *muru* parties and general plundering, they put some 20 tons of their goods on Captain Duke's ship, the *Sisters*, for transport to Sydney with the Wesleyan missionaries who had decided to leave the country for the time being. Captain Herd of the *Rosanna* also volunteered his services, which, as things turned out, were not needed. Herd, as we know, was then at Hokianga engaged in acquiring land.

Now the Church Missionary Society's stations stood stripped, since, apart from the property sent away, all else not immediately required was concealed, put aboard a ship in the Bay, or buried. It seemed that these precautions were well-advised, when in January a considerable party of Maoris assembled near Paihia, and although it was believed that an attack was imminent, it dispersed without further action. It was a relief, then, when it was learned at the Bay that Hongi was not dead but only wounded. Later, the head of the chief Matapo, said to have been the principal in the plundering of the *Mercury*, was sent to the Bay and exhibited on a pole. Then Mr Clarke, one of the Kerikeri missionaries, brought a message from Hongi advising the Bay people to stay where they were, but adding that if he died, they should take leave of the country at once.[8] After anxious weeks it became apparent that Hongi would live, and by March it was considered that the immediate danger was over.

Smith[9] states that Hongi was shot, appropriately enough, by Maratea, who was connected with Ngatiwhatua, although his father was Ngatipou. This occurred at Oporehu, in the Mangamuka valley, in the fight known as Hunahuna. The wound was a curious one, which Dillon described on 13 November 1827, some four months before Hongi's death: 'About 10 a.m. I was visited by Shonghi . . . His wound is singular, a bullet having passed through his lungs, whence a hole appears in his breast and back, through which latter the wind issues with a noise resembling in some degree that from the safety-valve of a steam engine, which, however, he himself makes a subject of merriment.'[10] Dillon had a special interest in the chief, being, as

139

he claimed, '. . . the first person who took Shonghi from his native island, on the brig *Active* of Calcutta, to New South Wales in July 1814.'

Of this wound Hongi eventually died, on 6 March 1828, and it says much for his constitution that he survived as long as he did. He expired, according to tradition, exhorting his people to be brave and to withstand all attacks which might be made on them. He was clearly concerned about their survival and safety when bereft of his leadership, thus reinforcing traditional views that in spite of his single-mindedness and exceptional military talent in avenging affronts to his people, he was an affectionate family man of kindly disposition. Indeed, it may well have been this facet of his nature which led him to his career of conquest following the deaths of his closest relations at Moremonui. Be that as it may, during the last years of his life his enemies trembled at the mention of his name, and now his own people trembled, in fear of a future without him. In fact, so much were they in fear of an attack from the Hokianga people, that an attempt was made to suppress the fact of his death, by disposing of his body with indecent haste — an unprecedented proposal in Maori terms, which was vetoed by his lifelong comrade at arms Patuone, the Ngatihao Ngapuhi of Hokianga. 'I have only just become acquainted,' he said in reproof, 'with those who wish to bury their father alive.'[11] Since the only people now capable of attacking Hongi's tribe were those of Hokianga, it was due to Patuone's peaceful intervention that no serious hostilities followed Hongi's death, and his people were left in peace.

Hongi died at Pupuke, Whangaroa, at an age which a consensus of views puts at about 55 years. After the *huhunga*, or cleaning of his bones in April 1829 at Kaeo, his remains were laid successively at places near Te Ngaire, Matauri Bay, Waimate and Pakinga (Kaikohe), before being finally deposited at Wharepaepae, a traditional Ngapuhi burial-place between Kaikohe and Tautoro. However, his final resting-place is a matter of contention between Ngapuhi and the Whangaroa people. Neither fiercer nor more cruel than his contemporaries, he was without doubt an astute and enterprising general, and although he had the initial advantage in the use of firearms, he attacked warlike not peaceful people, who, had he not done so, would if given some assurance of success as willingly have attacked him. Twice, in fact, he is known to have made peace when he was in a manifestly winning position — once when on his way to attack Ngatiwhatua, and again in the Waikato. He was kind and considerate to Europeans, and without his early support the mission at the Bay of Islands could scarcely have survived.

The passing of Hongi had its sequel at Kororareka. His death had been anticipated and with it all kinds of disorders. However, as we have seen, due mainly to the influence of Patuone, such disasters did not eventuate. Nevertheless, at Kororareka, Earle[12] was told by one of the many chiefs who were present at his deathbed, that among Hongi's last utterances was a prophecy that Whareumu would not survive him by more than a week. At the time the patron of the Europeans at 'The Beach' was in perfect health and all was peace, but within the prescribed week trouble arose. Tiki, the only remaining son of the deceased Pomare Nui, had attempted to steal some pigs at Waima, Hokianga, where he had gone in order to complete a quota which he had undertaken to sell to the captain of a whaler. The rightful owners objected strenuously to this barefaced action, the upshot of which was that Tiki was shot dead by an outraged proprietor, concealed snugly behind a tree. A brawl then ensued between Tiki's bereaved friends, who were with him in some force, and the pig-owners, and seven more men were killed. Because of his relationship with Tiki and the great *mana* of Tiki's illustrious father, Whareumu reluctantly led a *taua* against the Mahurehure people at Waima, to exact such recompense as seemed appropriate to assuage Ngatimanu pride. The resolution of such disputes was frequently complicated by blood relationships and in spite of these, further bloodshed often resulted. And so it was this time. Three days later, news was brought to Kororareka that at first the meeting had been relatively peaceful, attended only by legitimate plunder of the offenders at Waima. However bickering broke out, culminating in the accidental death of Whareumu's wife and a nephew when he was returning home. A general fight then ensued, apparently mainly on the pretext that the deceased wife was related to the Mahurehure, during which Whareumu was first shot through both legs and then received a ball in the throat which killed him. The great Hokianga chief Muriwai[13] at this stage was shot in the thigh, sustaining a wound from which he died some time later. A very explosive situation now existed.

This skirmish, added to the general unease following Hongi's death, raised the possibility of a general war between the Hokianga and Bay tribes. This, of course, again threatened the C.M.S. missionaries. H. Williams therefore resolved to travel to Hokianga at the behest of the Bay chiefs, Rewa, Te Koki and others[14], in order to arbitrate if possible. But on their arrival at Waima they found that Patuone, and his brother-in-law Wharerahi, Rewa's brother,[15] had come down from the Upper Waihou, and in conference with Pi, the chief of Waima, had peace talks in hand. Messrs Clarke and Kemp from Kerikeri were also present, and it seems that the whole affair ended more or less happily, due to the reluctance of all parties to precipitate full-scale hostilities which were likely to do nobody any good. Patuone now seems to have established himself in the role of peacemaker, for which history remembers him.

Kororareka was now bereft of both the strong chiefs, Pomare Nui and Whareumu, and some sort of authority was assumed there by Pomare II (Whetoi) and Kiwikiwi, both Ngati-Manu. But Rewa (Maanu), and the very prestigious chief Titore Takiri clearly had much influence there, and spent a good deal of their time at Kororareka, although in the late 1820s they had *pa* in the Rawhiti district and the adjacent islands.

The customary turmoil usually attendant on the death of a chief was now, of course, likely to occur at Kororareka, and a menacing visit by a fairly large party did take place, but without incident other than a general and noisy debate on the sucession to Whareumu. Rewa succeeded in preventing this from deteriorating into armed conflict. In fact, the turbulence of the late 1820s did not affect European affairs at Kororareka to any great extent, and even Whareumu's death resulted only in minimal disturbance, this almost certainly being due to the anxiety of the local Maoris to preserve the place as an acceptable resort for whaleships.

In January 1827, when the Bay and Whangaroa missionaries were undergoing the trauma resulting from Hongi's Whangaroa adventure, the brig *Wellington* came to anchor off Kororareka.[16] The vessel was clearly not whaler, sealer or merchant – an unusual fact noted by H. Williams and by both Duke and Clarke, captains of the whalers *Sisters* and *Harriet*. When enquiries were made, the captain of the strange ship explained that it was a convict transport bound for Norfolk Island. Such ships were not customary visitors, in fact it is not likely that one had ever been here before. This fact, and the observed lack of proper discipline on board, aroused the suspicions of Duke and Clarke, who invited Williams to a conference on the matter. Suspicion crystallised into certainty shortly afterwards. When aboard the *Wellington*, Captain Clarke and the mission employee Fairburn received information by stealth from its lawful captain, Harwood, that the vessel was indeed a transport, but had been seized by the convicts while bound for Norfolk Island from Port Jackson. The bogus 'captain' then went aboard the *Sisters*, defiant and confident, and invited the captains to do their worst, promising retaliation. Williams, with his mission station open to attack, and all sorts of other troubles on his hands, had nothing much to lose, and was all for opening fire on the ship with the whalers' guns. However Duke and Clarke, who had the safety of their ships to consider, and having no obligation to engage in warfare with convicts, were naturally dubious about this. However, two days later, Williams was awakened at 5 a.m. by gunfire. The whalers had got their guns up out of the hold and had quickly subdued the *Wellington* pirates, but such was their fear of the Maoris that Duke sent to Paihia for Williams to see if he could keep them from molesting the prisoners. In spite of this, when they were landed on the beach from their ship, Maoris at once seized and stripped them of their clothes before they were sent as prisoners on to the whalers. Six of them eluded capture, and were at Kororareka a year later, where Earle surprised one, who had his face completely tattooed, lurking in his hut, which ten minutes later went up in flames.

So ended the convicts' dreams of a free life in some Pacific paradise. Three weeks later the *Wellington*, now under its lawful captain, left with the *Sisters*. At Sydney the 66 prisoners were tried in three lots and sentenced to death, although only five were in fact executed. The rest were sent to Norfolk Island, where, in the barbarous way of the times, they were faced with working in irons for life. So, in a sad way, they did finish up in a Pacific paradise.

A dispute now arose between Duke and his first mate, Tapsell, to whom our friend Kendall had married Maria Ringa at Matauwhi in 1823. Tapsell argued he was entitled to the claim of £5000 which Duke laid with the New South Wales Government for capturing and bringing back the prisoners. Although he was active in the incident, none of the accounts quoted seem to justify Tapsell's exclusive entitlement to the claim and it appears that he got none. Instead, Duke discharged him. Apparently, the easy capture of the mutineers was largely due to Duke's promise to turn 1000 Maoris loose to massacre them, which brought a prompt, if reluctant undertaking to surrender, provided that the canoes were called off.

In April, shortly after this incident, the British warship HMS *Rainbow* anchored off Kororareka, bringing Marsden on a very brief visit. Ships of war were not popular with the Maoris, since the discipline on board denied them the unrestricted inter-course with the crew to which they had become accustomed. The privilege of living on the ships during their stay did not extend to naval vessels. When whaleships arrived, large numbers of Maoris, mostly women, would crowd the ships, providing the social climate so necessary for the crews, who would otherwise have had no company other than their crew-mates for very long and difficult periods – sometimes years. Captain Gardiner of the *Marianne*, who claimed to be the oldest skipper in the trade at the time, told Earle that no trouble had occurred at the Bay for many years. Twenty years before, he said, ships that did venture to anchor here kept their boarding-nets rigged out, but in his view, this precaution was due to their ignorance of the true disposition of the Maoris. The presence of women on the ships was, of course, an infallible guarantee that no trouble was afoot.

There was indeed no hostility apparent now on either side. Whareumu and Pomare Nui had always been friendly, and

144

Sydney, now Kingston, on the south side of Norfolk Island, in 1793.
(Auckland Institute and Museum)

Whaling off the North Cape, New Zealand.
(Auckland Institute and Museum)

Whangaroa Harbour, showing position of the *Boyd* when seized by natives. *(Auckland Institute and Museum)*

Old pa and whalers at the Bay of Islands in 1820. *(Auckland Institute and Museum)*

By the 1830s, Kororareka was well established as a focal point in the Pacific for trade and industry, and missionary activities.

Hone Heke
(Auckland Institute and Museum)

Titore Takiri
(Auckland Institute and Museum)

Kororareka in 1843. *(National Museum)*

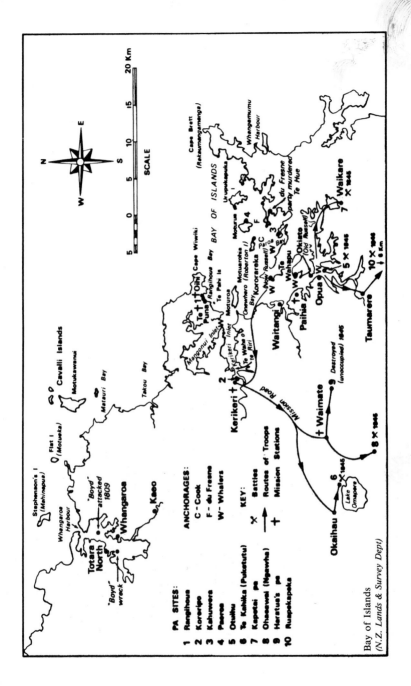

Bay of Islands
(N.Z. Lands & Survey Dept)

James Busby

Rev. Henry Williams

(All photos: Auckland Institute and Museum)

Bishop Pompallier

Hongi Hika

Baron de Thierry

James R. Clendon

(All photos: Auckland Institute and Museum)

William Hobson

Te Pahi

Okiato: Government House, Old Russell, 1840.
(Alexander Turnbull Library)

Pa at Lake Omapere: the Battle of Okaihau, 1845. *(Hocken Library)*

Ohaeawai pa, 1845. *(National Library of Australia)*

The bombardment of Ruapekapeka pa, 1846.
(Alexander Turnbull Library)

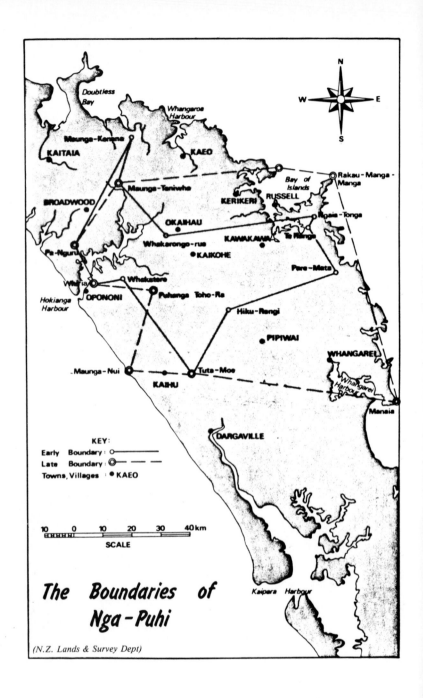

N

W   E

S

Doubtless
Bay

Whangaroa
Harbour

Maunga-Kanana

KAITAIA

KAEO

Maunga-Teniwha

BROADWOOD

Bay of
Islands

RUSSELL

Rakau - Manga -
Manga

KERIKERI

OKAIHAU

Rosia - Tonga

Whakarongo-rua

KAWAKAWA

Te Ranga

Pa-Nguru

KAIKOHE

Wairia

Whakatere

Pare - Mata

Hokianga
Harbour

OPONONI

Puhanga Toho-Ra

Hiku - Rangi

PIPIWAI

WHANGAREI

Maunga - Nui

Tuta - Moe

Whangarei
Harbour

KAIHU

Manaia

KEY:

Early   Boundary : ○━━━━━
Late   Boundary : ◎━ ━ ━
Towns, Villages   ● KAEO

DARGAVILLE

10   0   10   20   30   40 km
SCALE

Kaipara   Harbour

The Boundaries of Nga - Puhi

(N.Z. Lands & Survey Dept)

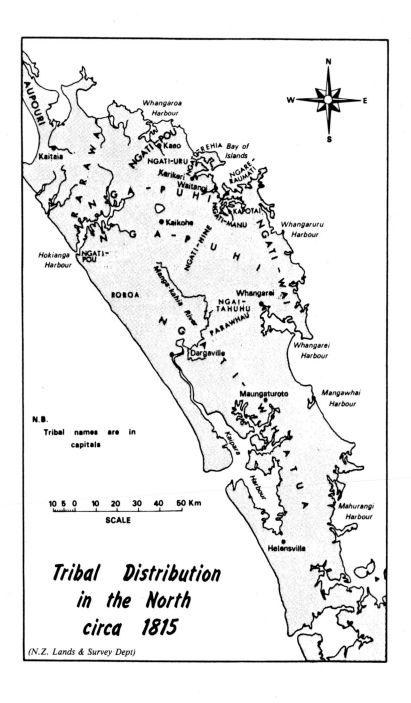

Tribal Distribution in the North circa 1815

(N.Z. Lands & Survey Dept)

Map labels:
AUPOURI

Whangaroa Harbour

Kaitaia

RARAWA

NGATI-POU

Kaeo

NGATI-URU

TE REHIA

Bay of Islands

Karikeri

Waitangi

NGARE-RAUMATI

NGA - PUHI

Kaikohe

NGATI-MANU

KAPOTAI

NGATI-HINE

NGATI-WAI

Hokianga Harbour

NGATI-POU

Whangaruru Harbour

ROROA

Manga-kahia River

NGA - PUHI

NGATI

Whangarei

NGAI-TAHUHU

PARAWHAU

Dargaville

Whangarei Harbour

N.B.
Tribal names are in capitals

Maungaturoto

Mangawhai Harbour

Kaipara Harbour

10 5 0   10   20   30   40   50 Km
SCALE

Mahurangi Harbour

Helensville

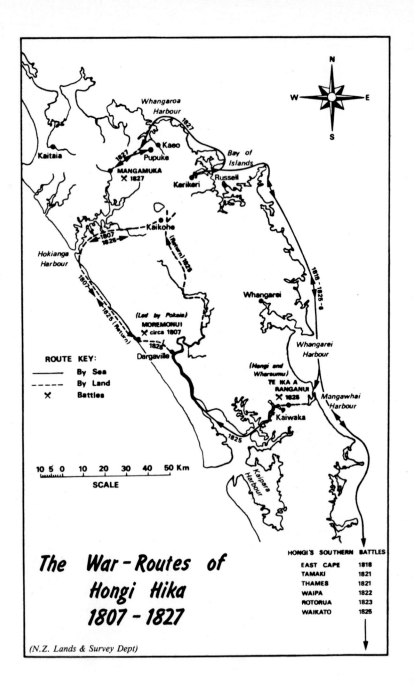

N
W   E
S

Whangaroa Harbour

1825

Kaitaia

1827

1827

● Kaeo
● Pupuke

MANGAMUKA
✕ 1827

Bay of Islands

Kerikeri   Russell

● Kaikohe

1807
1825

(Return) 1825

Hokianga Harbour

1807

Whangarei

1818 - 1825 - 6

1825 (Return)

(Led by Pokaia)
MOREMONUI
✕ circa 1807

1826

Dargaville

Whangarei Harbour

(Hongi and Whareumu)
TE IKA A RANGANUI
✕ 1825

Mangawhai Harbour

Kaiwaka

1825

Kaipara Harbour

ROUTE KEY:

— By Sea
- - - By Land
✕ Battles

10 5 0   10   20   30   40   50 Km

SCALE

The War-Routes of
Hongi Hika
1807 - 1827

HONGI'S SOUTHERN BATTLES	
EAST CAPE	1818
TAMAKI	1821
THAMES	1821
WAIPA	1822
ROTORUA	1823
WAIKATO	1825

(N.Z. Lands & Survey Dept)

Rewa and Titore were no less so. It was from the younger Pomare, Whetoi, who was 'of a friendly disposition and a gentle, kindly temperament' that in March 1827 Dumont D'Urville purchased the head of Hou, the father of Te Hinaki, the Panmure chief who died at Hongi's hands (see Chapter 12).

After the depature of HMS *Rainbow*, a sealer's long-boat arrived, manned by six men who had just completed one of the most notable open-boat journeys in European Pacific history.[17] Captain Swindells, who was in charge of the boat, had been in command of the sealer *Glory,* when on 15 January she went aground at her anchor at Pitt's Island in the Chathams. Since she was striking heavily, Swindells decided to put her ashore on the beach, and having done so, saved much of her gear and cargo. But as the Chatham Islands were little frequented at the time, and there was little chance of rescue, it was resolved to run for New Zealand, and the long-boat was fitted out for the voyage. Five men accompanied the captain, and the dangerous 800-mile run to the Bay of Islands was made without mishap. Here, all hands were taken on board the whaler *Samuel* which was coming out of the Bay when the long-boat entered. The party was landed at Sydney on 28 May.

The men who figured in such incidents probably accepted them as normal hazards, since the likelihood of these and similar hardships was always present when working the small seal and whaleships on the day. Whales had to be approached close enough to be struck and secured with a hand-thrown harpoon. Often the flimsy wooden boats were towed miles before killing the whale at closer quarters still with a lance wielded from the bow of the boat. It was common for these boats to be smashed by whales, leaving the men in the water for long periods. But the work was on a share basis, and with luck, comparatively large rewards might be forthcoming. The men toiled mightily at sea and lived for the day when ashore. The whole Pacific was their workshop. An example of the rigours of the trade is the *Ann*, which in 1827 came into the Bay for the third time in three years. During this period she had not once been in a civilized port. She had cruised from Japan and Timor to Hawaii and Tahiti, traversing the Pacific several times, and now, a full ship, she was at the Bay of Islands to refit for the voyage to England. It is probable that she would have been nearly four years out before returning to her home port, actively engaged in whaling for perhaps two and a half years to obtain a full cargo of oil.

So much for the growth of the already more than 25-year-old intercourse of whaler and Maori. The missionaries too, in their 15 years or so, had achieved some stability. In 1826, King, the last of the pioneers, still lived at Oihi, and with him was James Shepherd, a catechist and gardener, who later settled at Whangaroa where he founded families, whose descendants must now be the most numerous group in that district. Kemp, a smith employed as a storekeeper, occupied the house which the Rev. J. Butler had built and lived in at Kerikeri, and with him was George Clarke, another smith who later abandoned missionary work to become the Government 'Protector of Aborigines'. Messrs Puckey and Fairburn, whose names are now identified with the Kaitaia district, were carpenters, and with James Hamlin were employed according to their trades. Richard Davis, later to be ordained, was a farmer brought out to instruct the Kawakawa Maoris in European methods of agriculture. Gilbert Mair appears to have been attached to the Paihia station, employed as a carpenter, and one William Spikeman was described as a herdsman. The total mission population in 1826 was 59 including women and children. Of these 36 were children. While the total white population at the Bay might then have been around 100 people, Messrs. Davis and Shepherd had estimated the Maori numbers in the previous year at 3000.[18]

As the 1820s came to an end, the energies of the fairly extensive mission organisation, under the direction of the Rev. Henry Williams and his brother the Rev. William, were devoted to a large extent to supporting itself, which cost the Church Missionary Society about £1560 per annum. The little schooner *Herald* probably occupied much time in initially building and then working it on its voyages in search of supplies for the mission. In 1831, after she had been wrecked, another smaller vessel, the *Karere,* was built at Paihia. She was about 30 feet long. School teaching was undertaken, although Kendall's original school had lapsed. Maori parents allowed their children to attend school when it suited them, and there was therefore a variable supply of scholars, especially during the summer, when the whaleships were in. Maori children appear to have worked at various tasks around the mission at Paihia.

But there was no doubt that the nucleus of a permanent white settlement in the north was now established. At Hokianga, not hitherto much frequented, the economy improved almost overnight, when, as we have noted, a venturesome ship-building enterprise was established there in the mid-1820s. A flourishing timber industry was developing there. Some fine vessels were built at Horeke in the Hokianga, and in 1827, Mr Hobbs re-established the Wesleyan presence at Te Toke, near Rangiahua. Later, in 1828, the Mangungu mission station near Horeke was founded. These developments led to much increased communication between the two ports, and it may be interesting here to describe the routes which then connected them.

The main route taken by travellers to and from the lower reaches of the Hokianga used the tidal water of the Waima River as far as its abrupt end at Taheke, and from there the Maori track passed through Kaikohe and continued north of the volcanic hill Maungaturoto to Taiamai, near the present Ohaeawai. It then followed close to the State Highway to its intersection with the Old Bay Road, and continued generally down the Waioruhe and Waitangi streams to the Haruru Falls, where usually a boat or canoe completed the journey to Paihia.

A route from Mangungu passed up the ridge behind the mission site to Gile's Road, then descended into the valley which runs out towards Taheke, and on reaching the easy country, turned up towards Kaikohe, where it joined the main track.

From the upper Hokianga a track followed the Waihou Valley, passed up the Waihoanga Stream to the volcanic flats of Puketotara, and then generally followed the Puketotara Stream to Kerikeri, through the Waipapa district. From Kerikeri there was a track along the base of the hills inland from Kerikeri Inlet, to Waitangi. The track along which the Wesleyans fled from Whangaroa, joined this route.

147

Interestingly, although a permanent white settlement now existed in the Bay of Islands, remarkably few English place-names ever attained common usage, due no doubt to the influence of the Maori population, which was predominant until quite recent times. And, of course, there was a large infusion of Maori blood in the nominally European population. The name Marsden Vale was never generally accepted for Paihia, except by the missionaries at the time of their occupation, and Gloucester Town for Kerikeri was still-born. Busby's Victoria — Waitangi — for practical purposes was used only on Busby's letterheads, and on various occasions when attempts were made to sell portions of it. Matauwhi Bay was once called Brind's Bay, after Captain Brind, who married Pomare's daughter, but that name has gone the way of Point Pocock (Wiwiki), du Fresne's Point of Currents (Tapeka) and the Bay of Treachery. Gone also is One Tree Point, an early name for Opua, and even the ungainly (to the European ear) Kororareka held its ground until the Government decreed it was to be called Russell, although 'The Beach' was a common name applied to it.

So the 1820s drew to a close. Although in the past there had been causes for alarm, no well-disposed European had been seriously molested since du Fresne, except perhaps Mrs Hall, when she and her husband were unwittingly involved in tribal politics at Waitangi. That this period was so relatively free of violence was due in part to the missionaries' obvious good intentions, and also to the fact that they were compatriots of the whalers, whose good offices were carefully courted by the Maori people at the Bay. Intermarriage also gave white settlers and sailors immunity from interference. Whalers of all ranks intermarried with Maori women, and no relationship between races is more effective than this in establishing common ground.

---

1. Owens, J.M.R., *Prophets in the Wilderness,* passim.
2. L.G. Kelly, L.G. 'Fragments of Ngapuhi History,' *JPS,* v.47.

3. Smith, *Maori Wars of the Nineteenth Century,* pp.330-48.
4. See Appendix 1.13, 1.14, 1.15.
5. See Appendix 1.17.
6. Owens, op.cit., pp.94-99.
7. See Appendix 1.5, 1.6.
8. Rogers, L.M. *The Early Journals of Henry Williams,* pp.36-42.
9. Smith, p.398.
10. Dillon, P. *A Voyage in the South Seas,* v.2, p.332.
11. Elder, *Letters and Journals,* pp.442-3.
12. Earle, *Nine months in N.Z.,* pp.167-74.
13. See Appendix 1.4.
14. See Appendix 1.5, 1.2.
15. See Appendix 1.5, 1.6.
16. Earle, pp. 106-8. Rogers, op.cit., pp.34-6 and 41. Sherrin and Wallace, *Early New Zealand* pp.328-34.
17. McNab, *Murihiku,* pp.260-2.
18. Sherrin and Wallace, p.315.

15

The Transition Period

In THE 1820s permanent settlement by non-mission Europeans at the Bay was minor, and confined to a few tradesmen. But in the 1830s there occurred an influx of merchants and traders, who could, by their skills and services, exploit the needs of the whaling fleet. And in that period too, mission activities expanded. The C.M.S. hierarchy there extended its operations, and in order to achieve a measure of independence, established the successful agricultural station inland at Waimate.

There was also a technical advance, initiated by the Rev. William Yate, who had arrived in January 1828, and had been appointed to Kerikeri. He later returned to Australia and acquired a small printing press, with which, at Paihia in 1830, he pioneered printing in New Zealand.

Marsden, who had spent no time in New Zealand since 1823, apart from an inconsequential five-day visit in HMS *Rainbow* in 1827, turned up at the Bay in the *Elizabeth* in March 1830, and left again in May in the *Prince of Wales*. During his visit, dissent emerged among the missionaries as to the merit of retaining the old Oihi station. After some 16 years the buildings were delapidated. The point at issue was whether to transfer the station to a more suitable location at Te Puna, about a mile to the west, where it should originally have been, or to withdraw the personnel from that locality altogether. In anticipation of the closure of Oihi, some 16 acres of land had been purchased at Te Puna in 1828. Here, in 1814, it will be recalled, Ruatara had intended to build a town on the European pattern, but the idea had died with him, and Marsden now wished to re-establish the Oihi station there. He was not supported by the committee of the mission at the Bay, but Wharepoaka, the chief at Te Puna, exercised a powerful influence on Marsden, and his wish to retain a station in his district was respected. He may well, for purely materialistic reasons have been apprehensive at the prospect of losing his European contacts, since little shipping now frequented this part of the Bay. But whatever his reasons, in September 1832 Oihi was replaced by Te Puna and the veteran King was placed in charge.

But the change at Te Puna was of small importance to the mission in comparison with the projected station at Waimate, where Marsden initiated the establishment of a farm station by arranging for the purchase of two areas of land, in September and October 1830. Due in part to Te Puna's rapid decline in population and importance, a suitable location was now desirable, which would also supply the missions with fresh food for which they were dependent on Maori sources. The Waimate area was estimated to be 1035 acres.[1] Among the vendors were Rewa, Moka, Wharerahi, Titore, Tareha and Te Nana[2] — chiefs whose interests, due to earlier conquests, were now mainly elsewhere. This district was occupied in the mid eighteenth century by the Wahineiti and Ngatimiru, apparently Ngatipou people, who were overrun by Ngapuhi from the Kaikohe area, in retaliation for the murder of Whakarongo, the sister of the chiefs Auha and his half-brother Whakaaria. Her husband was affronted when, in his view, she favoured her brothers by serving them with the best kumaras at a meal they had with him, and this led to the murder. Reprisal for this was swift, when a Ngapuhi party drawn from the Ngaitawake, Ngatihineira, Ngatikuta and Ngatikura *hapu* invaded the Waimate district. They overcame the Wahineiti and Ngatimiru and drove them out of the *pa* Pahangahanga, Ngaungau, Whakataha, and Taumatatungutu. The defeated people fled to the Mangonui Inlet and to the south Hokianga head, and their land was divided among the Ngapuhi. This is how Te Hotete, who was Auha's son and Hongi Hika's father, and later Hongi himself, came to occupy Okuratope *pa*, near Waimate. An interesting incident arising out of the occupation concerns a group related to Auha, who came to the disputed area after the invasion occurred. They were apparently not involved in the fighting and were told firmly to leave the place they occupied and go to

Whakataha, the Waitangi valley *pa* mentioned above — hence its name, which means 'move over.'

To connect the new Waimate mission estate with the Bay, a road was built from Kerikeri, described in 1835 by W.B. Marshall, surgeon of HMS *Alligator*, as '. . . an excellent one, and would not disgrace McAdam himself.'[3] Marshall was an avid supporter of missionaries and prone to exaggerate their accomplishments. His description is therefore misleading, since, of the total length of the route, some eight to nine miles, perhaps only a mile or two would have required any significant earthwork, and the remainder would have taken wheeled traffic without any construction at all. But since the undertaking involved three bridges, it was no mean feat. Traces of the road may still be discerned within a few miles of Waimate, where the bridge spanning the Waitangi River below Waimate was located, measuring some 60 feet long and 40 feet above the stream. According to Yate,[4] the whole project was completed in a little more than three months by Maori labour, with the assistance of Messrs Clarke and Hamlin, who, with Yate and Davis were appointed to man the new settlement.

Yate, commenting on progress at Waimate early in 1834, reported the presence of a flour-mill, smithy and a brick kiln, from which 50,000 bricks had been produced. Some 700,000 feet of timber had been felled and sawn into boards and scantling, and 200,000 shingles split. From these, three 40 x 20 feet dwelling-houses had been erected, with stables, stores, a carpenter's and a blacksmith's shop, eight or ten 20 x 15 feet cottages, and a chapel. There were 30 acres cleared, grassed and paling-fenced around the houses, where orchards and gardens were thriving. Outside this area 48 acres were devoted to cereal crops. Three wells had been dug, and a dam and mill-race for the mill.[5]

The missionaries apparently had little trouble recruiting labour for this work, since in return, the station offered Maoris in the district a high standard of living in their terms. Yate states that the improvements described were achieved by a very substantial work-force numbering in all 80 Maori people. Many of these were now attracted to Christianity, no doubt influenced to a considerable extent by the apparent material benefits associated with it. The missionaries had indeed created a very comfortable little English world for themselves in a very short time, far from the rioting at the Bay; and there is no doubt that the first significant advances in the conversion of the Maoris dates from the establishment of this station. Davis, who as we have noted, was appointed in the mid-1820s as an agricultural instructor to the Maoris, was in charge of farming operations at Waimate.

When Waimate had advanced to this stage, Kerikeri could boast only three houses, a chapel, a bridge, a quay and pier and a boat house.[6] Agriculture was apparently confined to a subsistence level, enough to feed the people there. But Kerikeri had by now acquired the most impressive building in New Zealand, which, with Butler's house, still stands, and should remain there indefinitely with a minimum of maintenance. This, the stone store, was commenced in 1833, and was described by Edward Markham in the following year: 'It is very Substantial. The Walls above a yard thick of solid Stone, and above 10,000 Bushells of lime used in it, Three Stories high. On one end they were putting up a clock as the safest place and the Bell. The Mason came from Sydney. Arched windows, Doors Iron shod, Shutters too. In fact Stronger than is required. It is the only Stone building in the country.'[7]

The reference to the clock is interesting. Fitz Roy also noted its presence in 1835, in his narrative of his visit in the *Beagle*.[8] But the clock is now gone, although evidence of its former presence may be seen in the interior of the building.

Paihia, the remaining station, was essentially a residential settlement and headquarters for the Society. It consisted of the missionaries' dwelling-houses, other necessary buildings or shanties for schools and so on, and the chapel. In 1830 Yate was also operating the printing press, turning out hymns and other religious works. There were seminaries for girls and boys of mission parentage. The mission in New Zealand, under H. Williams, was now well set up, and in comfortable circumstances.

The inhabitants of Kororareka and other parts of the Bay had not aspired to stone buildings and clocks at this time, being under the constant necessity of earning their livings in a hard way. Early in the 1830s there were a few wooden dwelling-houses there. But it was not yet the commercial settlement it was soon to become. The notorious grog-shops were soon to appear, but the carousing and prostitution so frequently referred to by the mission people were as yet taking place aboard the ships at anchor off the town. 'Hell-side' was the contemporary name for this side of the river. It seems that one of the Maori girls from the Paihia mission could not be dissuaded from crossing the river when the ships came in, and was told in disgust to go to Hell in her own way. This she did, and told the story to her sailor friends, who completed the comparison by naming Paihia 'Heaven'.

The year 1830 was ushered in on 'Hell-side' with a beach squabble between girls, followed by a bloody battle, the famous Girls' War. This resulted in a major shift of power at Kororareka, and we are fortunate in having an eye-witness account of this affair. Our authority is Peter Bays, sailing-master of the whaler *Minerva*, which was wrecked on 29 September 1829 on what is now known as the Minerva Reef.[9] Bays, after adventures which included a 500-mile open-boat voyage, managed to get a passage to the Bay of Islands with Captain Brind of the *Toward Castle*, arriving there on 3 February 1830. Brind, according to the missionary version, is the villain of the Girls' War, but Bays stoutly asserts that he was neither as culpable as they claimed, nor was he the generally objectionable character portrayed in their accounts. For Captains Brind and Duke, depraved villains in missionary eyes, Bays had nothing but praise, and wrote at great length of their kindness to him. On the other hand, he was as generous in praise for the missionaries, which may invest his views with greater credibility than theirs. Indeed, Williams and some of his missionaries displayed an almost psychopathic aversion to seamen generally, and the seamen responded with irritation and an amused contempt. So prejudiced, in fact, were their stated opinions of each other, that the views of neither are acceptable.

When the *Toward Castle* dropped anchor at Kororareka, seven other ships lay there, the British whalers *Sisters, Royal*

Sovereign, Anne, Woodford, Elizabeth, and *Conway,* and the American ship *India.* Brind remained only three weeks before taking his ship out again, but in the meantime a quarrel had occurred on his ship between girls from the eastern and western sides of the Bay, called by Bays Amoongha and Akow (Munga and Kau?), probably Ngati-Manu girls. Bays refers discreetly to 'Captain [Brind?] whose girl was in the fray.' The quarrel, he says, was continued ashore, and all the females on the Beach seem to have been involved, abetted by Kiwikiwi's wife, Uru Mihi and other chief women.

We have it on Marsden's authority[10] that a long-standing feud was at the root of this affair. We have already noted the ill-feeling between the peoples on the opposite sides of the Bay, both 20 years earlier when *The City of Edinburgh* lay at Kororareka, and later when the *pa* Kahuwera was destroyed (Chapters 6 and 13). Hostility had surfaced on a number of occasions during the past 30 years and there is no doubt that the girls' fight was merely a catalyst which induced an inevitable fracas. However, probably advised by his missionaries, Marsden blamed Brind, and noted that the two girls involved were favourites of his. He also records the opinions of Rewa, Kiwikiwi and Wharepoaka, who claimed Brind was responsible for the whole affair; but since Maori chiefs had earned a reputation for deviousness, this could well have been a dubious ploy to shift the blame for a matter arising from their own deep-seated hostilities.

According to Maori tradition, one of the girls involved was Hongi Hika's daughter, Pehi, and another was Moewaka, a Ngapuhi, Rewa's daughter. Others, as above, were also involved.

The missionaries believed that before leaving the Bay, Brind, realising that a full-scale fight was likely and fearing that the Kororareka people were ill-equipped, had offered them muskets. However Bays asserted that another ship's captain did in fact supply arms to the opposing faction.

Towards the end of February, a meeting was held, presided over by Wharepoaka of Rangihoua and Rewa of Kororareka, in an attempt to resolve the matter. Kiwikiwi proved amenable, but Ururoa (Rewharewha), Hongi's brother-in-law from the north-west coast turned up, spoiling for a fight, ostensibly to redress the insult to Pehi, but he also nursed a long-standing grievance against the Thames people to whom Kiwikiwi's wife Uru Mihi belonged. He retired with his party to Paroa that night, but next morning came back over to Kiwikiwi's *pa*, indulging there in some ritual posturing. Following discussion a reconciliation appeared to have been achieved, when one of Kiwikiwi's young men fired a shot killing a woman in Ururoa's party. Fighting then became general.

The resultant battles were fought on the beach between Kiwikiwi and Pomare II and their supporters on the one side and Ururoa[11] and his people on the other. Both Rewa and Titore were present, but were not belligerents, although both were chiefs of the Ngapuhi faction supporting Ururoa.

The tension of weeks broke when the fighting erupted, since war-dancing and indiscriminate musket-fire had been going on ever since the girls' original quarrel. The battle commenced at 10 a.m. and continued until past mid-day. At one stage the exchange of shots was so furious that one of the *Elizabeth*'s boats, in which Captain Dean was about to leave the beach, was struck twice by musket balls. Two of his Maori boatmen were wounded, and Dean himself was obliged to run for shelter to the hut of one of the European sawyers, where he lay flat on his face to avoid being struck by stray bullets from the wild fusillade. Bays, who witnessed the whole affair, estimated that nearly 100 people were killed during the engagement, including Kiwikiwi's daughter, whose body, along with some of the wounded, was taken aboard the *Royal Sovereign*. A coffin was made for her, and the body was returned to her people. Some of the casualties died on board and others were attended to by the surgeon, who was forced in some cases to resort to amputation. All the vessels present were put in fighting trim, since no-one knew what the upshot might be.

The next day was Sunday. Bays wrote:

Yesterday we had hoped it was all settled, but at day light this morning the action recommenced and in this skirmish the great chief Henghee [Hengi], of the Ngapuis, was killed, whereupon they again retreated. Kivee Kivee and Pomurra

156

finding they were likely to be annoyed by the enemy, who it is said were three to one against them, tabooed the beach in honour of the deceased chief . . . and immediately set fire to the town, deserted the beach with all their tribe, and resorted to Kovva Kovva.

In this encounter, about nine men were killed on Pomare's side, and 40 on Ururoa's, and 24 in all were wounded; in an attempt to kill Kiwikiwi's wife, Uru Mihi. Bay's 'Ngapuis' were, in fact, Ururoa's people — the deceased Hongi's relations. Their adversaries at Kororareka were the Ngatimanu, Kiwikiwi and Pomare (Whetoi). They had lived there under the Ngapuhi domination of Titore, Rewa and others, who had conquered, and now occupied all the adjacent territory. Rewa was married to Titore's cousin, Te Koki, and he and Titore moved freely in the Kororareka-Te Rawhiti area. But the 'resort to Kawakawa' by Ngatimanu was at the express command of Titore, who stung into action by the death of Hengi, who was *hei matua* (as a father) to him, threatened to attack Kiwikiwi's *pa* if it were not abandoned. Ngatimanu's presence at Kororareka had been tolerated by Ngapuhi. They were an ancient tribe who had appeared in such widely separated places as Hokianga, Tautoro, Kawakawa, Kororareka and other even more distant places. They retained their identity despite their disintegration, and were inevitably related to Ngapuhi to a greater or lesser degree.

During Saturday's fighting Davis and Williams came over from Paihia and went ashore as it was terminating. They had previously made an attempt to avert hostilities, but without success. Now they could only do their best for the afflicted. Williams was not present at Sunday's renewal of the battle, but attended wounded who were either brought over to Paihia, or who later came with Pomare's party on its way to Otuihu, on the Kawakawa.

Perhaps as a result of Pomare's *tapu*, the dead remained on the beach. Bays wrote:

The slain in battle lay where they fell for days above ground to be eaten by dogs, till they stank so intolerably that from necessity they were compelled to burn them: these I saw as often as I went on shore, with the flesh partly eaten, their entrails out, the bodies mangled and swollen the size of two common men, while the flies had blown them in a state not to be described, and the boys were harpooning them with poles or long sticks and sporting over them with stones.

Bays, familiar with events leading to this massacre, suggests that one of the captains, '. . . under a cloak of chastity and religious influence among missionaries', spread slanderous accounts concerning Brind. He does not name the man, but his inferences are clear enough. He continues: 'But as it is true that the quarrel originated among themselves; so, from what follows, it may be seen, the natives were rather instigated to hostilities by laws of their own, than provoked to it by any allurement which a foreigner might throw in their way.'

Although Pomare and Kiwikiwi retired on 7 March to the Otuihu *pa*, at the junction of the Kawakawa and Waikare rivers, this did not put an end to the matter. Large reinforcements began to arrive from inland for both sides, and this was the position when Marsden arrived the next day on the *Elizabeth*, another vessel having the same name as Dean's, which was already there. The visit was Marsden's sixth since Kendall's exploratory voyage to the Bay in 1814, and in spite of his 65 years, he went to work with his customary vigour, in an attempt to defuse these warlike preparations.

Visits to the opposing parties commenced on 9 March when, with members of the mission and the captains of several ships, he visited Otuihu and lectured the embattled Pomare and Kiwikiwi on the evils of internecine warfare. He and his party then returned and crossed the Russell peninsular to Paroa, where Ururoa was camped, to ascertain his attitude. Ururoa, as did the other contenders, craftily laid all the blame on Brind. However, when Marsden suggested that he might be able to prevent Brind's return, Ururoa hastily vetoed this, saying that he preferred that he did return, so that he could deal with him himself. It was more likely, of course, that he was reluctant to offend any whaling captain for fear of losing his patronage and that of others. Since Brind continued to visit the Bay unmolested and later purchased land at Kororareka, Ururoa's threat was clearly an idle one. The distinction of having so many women quarrel over him, if indeed, this is what occurred, is not enjoyed by many men, and the equanimity with which Brind later exposed himself when ashore, to the supposed fury of so many affronted relatives, either marks him as no ordinary man, or casts doubt on the accusations levelled at him.

Be that as it may, from Paroa the deputation then went, accompanied by Titore and Tareha, on a similar mission to Moturoa Island, at the mouth of the Kerikeri, where newly-arrived allies of Ururoa were waiting in readiness to renew the fight.

Next morning, Te Morenga,[12] who was a relative of one of the girls originally involved, arrived at Paihia with a war-party to assist Kiwikiwi. After discussion with Marsden, he agreed to take no action, and on 11 March a meeting was held at Kororareka, at which Hongi's daughter Pehi, Moewaka, and Pehi's brother, expressed a willingness to settle the dispute. A lull followed, and on 17 March Marsden's peacemakers had a discussion with Ururoa's allies from Moturoa, and with emissaries from Ururoa, proceeded to Otuihu to arrange a truce. This was effected, and as a result a meeting of both sides was held at Kororareka, where it was agreed that the Ururoa faction should be compensated for the indignities suffered by their girl Pehi, by permanently depriving Pomare and Kiwikiwi of any title to the lands at Kororareka and Matauwhi. This decision merely perpetuated the situation then existing, and in the manner of such settlements, appears to have favoured the strongest party. But it probably averted an immediate large-scale war at the Bay, an event which could have had very serious, even calamitous results for the mission. But, in effect, the settlement only shifted the venue of the fighting, and led later to southern war-expeditions by the Hongi Hika-oriented Maoris at the west and north of the Bay.

The whaling skippers entertained little hope of any lasting peace, and their doubts were justified, but at least the Bay was spared for the time being the consequences of this incident, and some seven years elapsed before further hostilities occurred there. However, at the conclusion of the peace negotiations, the

Anne, the *Royal Sovereign* and the *India* put to sea, while the *Elizabeth* went up to the Kawakawa for water. As it was thought to be still dangerous for a ship to remain alone at Kororareka, the remaining vessel, the *Woodford*, was taken for safety to Te Puna.

The Girl's War marked the eclipse of Ngati-Manu as a tribal force in the North, but it also had the effect of establishing another resort for Europeans at Otuihu, where Pomare now presided. There was an excellent anchorage there, adjacent to the present port of Opua, but Otuihu attracted the more undesirable elements frequenting the Bay of Islands, such as runaway convicts and sailors, who lived under Pomare's aegis and enjoyed the brothels and grog-shops which later became established there. This development probably did Kororareka no harm, since the disruptive element would now, to some extent, be diverted to Otuihu, giving the more 'respectable' traders and merchants, who were now being attracted to the Bay, a more satisfactory climate in which to operate. In the event, however, the standard of behaviour at Kororareka was low enough, but it was not long before the Opua locality attracted two merchant traders of some standing. In 1832 J.R. Clendon established his trading station at Okiato, which was destined to become Russell, New Zealand's first capital; and in the same year, G. Greenway set up a similar business at the mouth of the Waikare River. Both of these provided for whaleships, which now had an alternative anchorage to Kororareka, where the shift of power had left Titore Takiri and Rewa in authority.

It was at this stage that Maoris, who, apart from Hansen's 1814 purchase at Kororareka, had hitherto sold land almost exclusively to the mission, began to dispose of considerable areas to individual missionaries, ship's captains, adventurers and others such as Clendon and Greenway. Most Maoris apparently considered that the pakeha manufactured goods, money and firearms which they received for the land were a fair bargain, but there can be little doubt that most purchasers were aware of the discrepancy. Unfortunately the Maori was not to know that only the retention of the land could guarantee his pride and ensure the survival of his status as an equal of the pakeha. The tradesmen and seamen gave little thought to such things, and the record shows that when they purchased, they mostly did so modestly. But many Anglican missionaries, even if they were aware of the significance of their actions in extinguishing the Maori title to very large amounts of land, did so apparently without any qualms. As to the growing body of businessmen, the ethics of the matter would have been of no concern to them.

Until this time, the Maori had been host to a small band of Europeans of various descriptions, who had wished for nothing more from them, or from the land, but a living. But now the speculators and traders were hovering, and they in turn attracted a host of similar opportunists. Thus, when the sovereignty of the land passed to the British crown in 1840, the Maori had parted with some 10⅓ million acres, or about a sixth of New Zealand's area.[13] Although, on Commissioner Bell's recommendation, the Crown allowed claims for only 292,475 acres. This was purchased at an average price of 5/6d per acre in money and goods on land granted, but only 3/- on what was claimed. Even the 10 million or so acres that the Commissioner dealt with had been reduced to that figure only by the disallowing or withdrawal of claims amounting to millions of acres, some measured in terms of degrees of latitude and longitude, or described by expressions such as 'as far as a cannon shot will reach'.

The arrival of the resident traders altered the economy of the Bay of Islands almost overnight. Their advent was the beginning of a middle class, to whom law and order were essential if their newly acquired estates were to be protected and be allowed to prosper. Yet their very presence and business activities created a situation least conducive to law and order, since the increasing commerce attracted the unscrupulous, who were eager to share in the new prosperity.

Under these circumstances, a social and commercial eminence based on land ownership was clearly a possibility. In 1839 we find J.D. Lang, Senior Minister for the Church of Scotland in N.S.W., suggesting the inevitable rise of '. . . an illiterate, narrow-minded, purse-proud, heartless colonial aristocracy —

161

one of the most intolerable nuisances on the face of the earth,'[14] created by the speculative acquisition of large tracts of land for later sale at exorbitant profits. This did in fact occur, but due to a strong stand by the Imperial Government the position did not turn out to be as serious as it could well have been. Sadly, though, the New Zealand Government later became the heaviest speculator.

From the nucleus of the settlers of the 1820s and the later traders, grew a European and American population, albeit a floating one, which expanded at such a rate that in 1834 the Rev. William Yate estimated it to be 1000 persons.[15] Accepting that this figure is reasonably correct, it is clear that in a few years an astonishing increase had taken place, and that the unattached population now greatly outnumbered the resident missionaries. Yate notes that at this time, 27 whaling vessels had lain at anchor in the Bay at one time and that barter was now giving way to exchange by currency — British coins and dollars, almost certainly Mexican, being most plentiful. Charles Darwin, a transient visitor in 1835,[16] commented sourly that the greater part of the English there, were the very refuse of society. His contacts were confined to Busby and the missionaries, and his attitude was a predictable one for a middle-class English scholar. It was tempered, however, by the observation that in several parts of the Bay little villages of square, tidy houses were scattered close down to the water's edge. He also noted that the mission had planted gorse for hedges at Waimate — ancestor of the prolific crops now flourishing in the North — and, interestingly, that kauri gum was then being sold to Americans at one penny per pound.

The first of the major trading and servicing establishments was Gilbert Mair's Te Wahapu. Mair had originally settled at Paihia, where he was employed by Williams as a carpenter, and also commanded the mission ship *Herald*. From 1831 Mair carried on a business at Te Wahapu as a general trader and a shipping agent, and established the first yard for ship repair, maintenance and refitting.[17] For the first 10 years at least, he had a flourishing business there. In 1836, his original house having been burned down, Mair erected a pretentious double-storeyed wooden building, and as an essential adjunct to his business, constructed a jetty from the point inside the island of Toretore, or 'Nobby' as it is now called, where fairly large vessels could be moored.

In 1832, Mair took as a partner William Powditch, who had arrived in New Zealand with his family in March 1831. Powditch also took up residence at Te Wahapu, acting as ship-agent, and, until his departure to Whangaroa in 1835, was 'postmaster' for the Bay of Islands, by authority of the Post Office Department of New South Wales, a task which Mair took over after that date.[18]

Another early settler who had interests in the same locality was the Jew, Joel Samuel Polack. Besides being a trader, he was an educated man whose books on New Zealand are valuable records of the times. Polack was probably the first of the merchant class to establish himself at Kororareka. For a year or two before this he had been at Hokianga, and from there he came to the Bay of Islands in 1833, and purchased 43 acres of land on that side of Te Wahapu Point facing Kororareka. Here he lived for two months and partly built a store which was later destroyed by a Maori raiding party. In the same year he moved to Kororareka, where he acquired five acres at the north end of the beach, and there he settled. This, interestingly enough, he stated had been owned by the Rev. H. Williams.

Polack's life on the 'Beach' was a stormy one. He made many enemies, among whom was Benjamin Turner, one of the first settlers there. A bad man to fall out with, Turner's origin was obscure, but he lived to become a member of the Auckland Provincial Council, having graduated by way of the hard school of Kororareka grog shops.

Another merchant trader of the period was Captain John Wright who, with Clendon and Mair, occupied all the north shore of the Kawakawa River from Okiato to Te Wahapu. Okiato, Clendon's property, was in a sheltered position with deep water close to the shore, and was admirably suited for a trading enterprise. Clendon built a small jetty there for the convenience of boats, and equipped the place with stores and all the facilities necessary for such a venture, including a stockade for defence. In 1839, undoubtedly with an eye for business, since 62 American whaleships had called at the Bay that year, Clendon accepted the acting consulship for the United States Government.[19] Although he had been a shipowner prior to this, the appointment established him as the most influential European in the Bay. This influence, and the merits of his establishment, no doubt led to Lieut. Governor Hobson's decision to purchase Okiato and to make it the first seat of Government in New Zealand. The trading stations of Clendon and Mair remained the most important in the Bay until the advent of Hobson, and the ensuing events which ultimately led to disaster for all Bay of Islands businessmen.

Captain Wright also deserves some mention, since he appears to have made some attempt to farm his land, Omata. He had been captain of the mission schooner *Active*, the second of that name, and with his wife and two stepdaughters he went to live at Omata when he purchased the land in 1832. In 1840 he haad 10 acres in wheat, which yielded, however, only 14 bushels from theacre, but he was having better success with vegetables. Aside from Busby and the missionaries, he alone among the early white settlers made any serious attempt to farm. But, as may clearly be seen today, his choice of land for the purpose was not a good one.

George Greenway, the other substantial trader hereabouts, seems to have had a prosperous trading-station, although more remote from the centres of activity, being on the south side of the Waikare River, upstream from its junction with the Kawakawa. He started his business in 1832, and earned additional distinction by brewing beer.

Thus, by 1833, quite abruptly there had appeared the makings of a well-serviced commercial port, where two years previously there had only been a resort where vessels were largely at the mercy of Maori supplies and suppliers. The whole of the Kawakawa estuary from Kororareka to Okiato had become a roadstead, as all the trading concerns had deep water adjacent to them. Contemporary observers have noted that it was common to see ships at anchor along the whole stretch of river from Greenway's to Kororareka.

None of the traders mentioned should be identified with the professional land-sharks and speculators who followed them, since their presence was amply justified by the service they provided for shipping, and the convenient clearing-houses they made available for Maoris to dispose of their produce.

Any account of the Bay of Islands at this time is incomplete without reference to the solid tradesmen whose services were equally as valuable as those of the merchants, and, indeed, contributed to their effectiveness. The tradesman and the versatile boatman was always in demand. Modest land claims for purchases at Kororareka were made by such men, among whom were Gray, Cooper, Cafler, Cook, Day, Leigh, McCurdy and Turner.

On his return to the Bay after the Stewart's Island incident, William Cook went into partnership with Robert Day, with whom he purchased 40 acres of land called Orari (Craig's Point) on the Waikare River, and there established a boat-building business. Cook lived at Orari and plied his trade as a builder and repairer of boats, until his death in 1874. He and his wife, Tiraha, a Kapotai woman also related to distinguished Hokianga chiefs, have many hundreds of descendants at the Bay and throughout New Zealand.[20]

The early 1820s also saw the arrival of the first resident doctor. Marshall[21] mentions meeting him at Paihia in 1835, where he attended the mission families for a small retainer. According to Marshall, Dr Ross came to New Zealand earlier as a settler. In 1833 he apparently purchased land at Waitangi, but was harassed by Maoris and retired thereafter to the mission-station.

At this time, the principal export from New Zealand was flax-fibre, with seal-skins next in value, although none of these, of course, originated at the Bay. A small proportion of the trade was in food-stuffs for the Sydney market. Flax suffered a sad decline towards the end of the 1830s; but as Maori lands were snapped up by speculators and the timber thereon worked, so significance of this as an export rose. New Zealand was not a British possession, and there were therefore tariffs levied in Sydney on imports from New Zealand. Timber, before Busby and Mair set up a saw-mill at Ngunguru in later years, was exported mainly in the log to the Sydney market. It is improbable that any significant amount of pitsawn timber was exported by the little band of tradesmen at the Bay, since their output would have been absorbed locally for boat-building and general use. All whalers employed boat-builders, who repaired or replaced damaged or smashed whale-boats on board. However, even in 1827, D'Urville mentioned having purchased 300 feet of kauri boards at Kororareka, for which he offered the sawyer 75 francs or 36 pounds of gunpowder. This the tradesman would have retailed to the Maoris at a high price.

Flax had had a spectacular career, but from the dealer's viewpoint had lost some of its charm by 1832. Prices over a period of 18 years were very erratic. The *Active* took over a few tons from the Bay in 1814, when Marsden estimated its value to be £12 per ton. In 1830 Polack quoted the New Zealand price of dressed flax prior to shipping as £5 per ton, and 160 tons cost £2,770 to land at Sydney, after adding ship-charter, collector's fees, insurance, etc. It was then sold at Sydney at £17 per ton, netting the owner a loss of £50.[22] Later, in 1832, the price, after a substantial rise fell to £20. Flax, then, was clearly an unreliable investment at this stage.

The Sydney Customs report of 1830 on New Zealand trade[23] discloses that imports to the port from New Zealand were valued at £18,426, while exports to New Zealand for the same period were £9,591. Some 2120 muskets, 11,052 pounds of gunpowder, 142 cartouche boxes and 836 pounds of shot accounted for £3,874. Flour valued at £787 came a poor second; followed closely by 4036 gallons of rum, some of which would have probably gone to the shore whaling stations in the South Island. Since Kororareka was not then a commercial town, New Zealand's export trade was then almost all from sealing, timber from Hokianga, and flax and foodstuffs from collectors established around the coasts by Sydney merchants. But times were changing, and soon, at Kororareka, New Zealand was to have a clearing-house for such trade, with vessels based there trading up and down the coasts.

Such was the situation when, in October 1831, the French discovery-ship *La Favorite,* commanded by Captain Laplace, sailed into the Bay. The Captain, as Dillon had been, was severely critical of the mission people for their indifference to the plight of his crew, most of whom were then in a sorry state through illness. Apprehension concerning the presence of a heavily armed French ship of war perhaps accounted to some extent for this attitude, since rumours abounded concerning the reason for its visit.[24] In the week he was there, Laplace surveyed parts of the Bay, which probably did nothing to re-assure the missionaries. According to Polack, '. . . a malicious and unfounded report. . .' was published at Port Jackson that Laplace intended to take possession of New Zealand in the name of the King of France, and he quotes the Captain as accusing those at the Bay of telling Rewa and other Maoris that his ship had come to take revenge for the death of Marion du Fresne. Strangely, *La Favorite* had dropped anchor at the Bay on the day after 13 chiefs had been induced, no doubt under missionary guidance, to send a letter to William IV, specifically voicing a fear of French annexation of New Zealand. A 'popish' invasion, no less, and to see a French ship drop anchor the very next day must have gone a long way to confirm the chiefs' faith in missionary judgement. The full text of this letter follows:

TO KING WILLIAM THE GRACIOUS, CHIEF OF ENGLAND

KING WILLIAM,
    We the chiefs of New Zealand assembled at this place, called the Keri Keri, write to thee, for we hear that thou art the great chief of the other side of the water, since the many ships that come to our land belong to thee.
    We are a people without possessions. We have nothing but timber, flax, pork and potatoes. We sell these things, however, to your people, and then we see the property of the Europeans. It is only thy land which is liberal towards us. From thee also come the missionaries who teach us to believe on Jehova God, and on Jesus Christ His Son.
    We have heard that the tribe of Marion is at hand, coming to take away our land. Therefore we pray thee to become our friend and the guardian of these islands, lest the bearing [sic] of other tribes should come near to us, and lest strangers should come and take away our land.
    And if any of thy people should be troublesome or vicious towards us — for some persons who are living here have run

away from ships — we pray thee to be angry with them that they may be obedient, lest the anger of the people of this land shall fall on them.

This letter is from us, the chiefs of New Zealand.

(The foregoing is a *literal* translation of the accompanying document — WILLIAM YATE, Secretary to the Church Missionary Society, New Zealand.)[25]

Appended were the signatures of 13 chiefs, whose jurisdiction extended over a limited area of the Bay of Islands and Hokianga, none of whom represented the adjacent districts of Whangaroa, Mangonui and Kaipara. The names of very influential chiefs, in the area from which the signatories came, are also missing; and the inference that those who signed represented the whole of New Zealand, together with the general tenor of the letter, suggest a degree of panic on the part of the authors. These could scarcely have been other than the Bay missionaries, who had clearly prevailed upon the more amenable of the local chiefs to lend their names to this dubious document. These were Patuone, Nene, Moetara, Matangi and Taonui of Hokianga, Wharerahi, Rewa and Titore Takiri, who had authority at the Bay of Islands and Waimate, and Te Morenga, Te Ripi, Te Haara and Te Atuahaere from Oromahoe and Kaikohe.

However, Yate sent the letter, which found its way in due course to the Colonial Secretary, Lord Goderich, after Governor Darling of New South Wales had despatched HMS *Zebra* to the Bay to investigate the unfounded rumours that Laplace had taken possession of New Zealand on 4 October.[26] Goderich replied with appropriate gravity, and despite its deficiencies it is likely that the letter was the catalyst which led, two years later, to the appointment of James Busby, a minor public servant at New South Wales, as British Resident at the Bay of Islands. However, he brought no protection, nor any other beneficial element of British rule or law, since, due to the political implications of his appointment and the restrictive terms of it, his influence was almost negligible. He was able, though, to keep the New South Wales and British Governments abreast of developments here and supply information to them. As Wards observes, 'He was left without legal authority, even in trivial matters, and his papers comprise a record of thieving and murder; of requests from the penal colonies of Australia to apprehend escaped convicts; of demands from ships' captains, including those of HM ships, to return deserters; of appeals from white settlers to adjudicate trading and boundary disputes; of self-righteous appeals from owners of public houses and brothels for protection from "ruffians", and of almost complete inability to do anything about any of these things.'[27]

Thus, the British Government took token action on a matter it had been vaguely concerned about for some time; and an attractive feature of its solution from Whitehall's viewpoint was that the colony of New South Wales was required to foot the bill for Busby's salary and expenses, which did nothing for his popularity there.

---

1. Elder, *Letters and Journals*, p.474. Turton, H.H. Maori Deeds of Old Private Land Purchases in New Zealand. No 83.
2. See Appendix 1.5, 1.7, 1.9 and 1.18.
3. Marshall, W.B. *A Personal Narrative of Two Visits to New Zealand in HMS Alligator in 1834*, p.99.
4. Yate, W. *An Account of New Zealand*, p.191.
5. Ibid., p.196-8.
6. Marshall, p.104-5.
7. Markham, E. *New Zealand or Recollections of it*, p.78.
8. Darwin and Fitz Roy, *The Surveying Voyages of HMS Adventure and Beagle*, v.2, p.606.
9. Bays, P.A., *A Narrative of the Wreck of the Minerva*, passim.
10. Elder, p.458.
11. See Appendix 1.2.
12. See Appendix 1.7.
13. Bell, F.D. Report of the Land Claims Commissioner, Appendices to the Journals of the House of Representatives, D-No.10, 1862.
14. Lang, J.D. *New Zealand in 1839*, (1873), p.64.
15. Yate, p. 103.
16. Darwin, C. *Journal of Researches during the Voyage of HMS Beagle*, pp.411-424.

17. Anderson, J.C. and Peterson, G.C. *The Mair Family,* p.15-16.
18. Robinson, H. *A History of the Post Office in New Zealand.*
19. Clendon's appointment, by letter only, was never confirmed; although he did, in fact, act as U.S. Consul. (Wards, I, *The Shadow of the Land,* p.14.)
20. See Appendix 1.20.
21 Marshall, p.244.
22. Polack, *Narrative of Travels and Adventures,* p.288-9.
23. McNab, *Historical Records,* v.1, p.713-4.
24. Elder, p.503.
25. Sherrin and Wallace, *Early History of New Zealand,* p.381-2.
26. Wards, *The Shadow of the Land,* p.7.
27. Ibid., p.9.

16

The Pace Quickens

ALTHOUGH GOVERNOR BOURKE'S attitude toward Busby has been considered vindictive, it could well have been that of a superior keeping an officer in his proper place. Busby, due to his personal views on his functions, was inclined to exceed his instructions. At the time, he was an unemployed New South Wales public servant, and he had promoted his appointment as British Resident in New Zealand by travelling to England and using his acquaintance with influential people there.[1]

He was sufficiently infected with the prevailing arrogant attitude of the middle-class Englishman, even when living on sufferance in a host country, to insist that its inhabitants treat him with the deference he considered due to him, or be dealt with severely. Henry Williams, on the other hand, possessed a native shrewdness, pragmatism and force of character that enabled him to influence some of the Maori chiefs, but Busby, wanting in these talents, was considerably less successful. The missionaries did, in fact, ride rough-shod over him in some matters relating to Maori affairs which Busby considered to be within his ambit, so that in the 1830s there was a coolness between them. Had he lived in a later age, his extreme sensitivity to criticism, and his conviction that he was being constantly victimised and attacked, would no doubt have labelled him as paranoic, as he may well have been. But there is little doubt that he did a useful job as a precursor of British rule, and established a reputation for honesty and fair dealing.

However, the confidence in the influence of the Bay missionaries, which is implicit in Lord Goderich's instructions to Bourke concerning Busby's appointment, was to some extent misplaced, due, no doubt, to their own or Marsden's reports, or those of sympathetic visitors. At that period, their influence over all but a few chiefs was not considerable in those matters about which Busby was most concerned. And, of course, such was the independence of the Maoris generally that the chiefs themselves had little control over them in such matters. Thus it seems that Goderich may have over-estimated the abilities of both the chiefs and the missionaries to promote order, and this may well have led him to establish Busby in the almost untenable position in which he found himself. Indeed, Yate's letter to William IV gave the impression that both chiefs and missionaries exerted significant control. Unlike the Tahiti missionaries under Henry Nott, who, due to the concentration of power in Pomare, were able to influence both religious and political matters there,[2] the C.M.S. in New Zealand was handicapped by dissension between the Maori factions. But within these limits, they had sufficient support from a section of the people to be of considerable assistance to Hobson, when in 1840 he negotiated the establishment of British sovereignty, and by that time, Busby himself was held in some esteem by the responsible Maori element.

Partly in response to the communication mentioned in the last chapter, HMS *Imogene* brought Busby to the Bay on 5 May 1833, armed with a letter of reply, expressing the benevolent sentiments of William IV. But the ceremonial landing, the reading of the letter, and the announcement of his appointment as British Resident in New Zealand did not occur until 17 May. If Polack can be relied upon, Busby was received by the Maoris with the customary exuberance they displayed on such occasions, but also with some reservations. They were 'with their usual fickleness, or perhaps maturer reflection on their present absolute power'[3] not too sure that they wanted any interference in their affairs.

Before leaving Sydney, Busby had been aware of the disabilities of his position, and also of his lack of support in New South Wales. This was partly due to the unpopularity of his family there, and the fact that the Colonial Government was responsible for financing his expenses. However, the strongest pressure for the appointment came from New South Wales. Recommendations were made to Lord Goderich in London by

Governor Darling, in despatches of 1830 and 1831, which were inspired, or at least precipitated, by Samuel Marsden's representations to him.[4] The Girl's War and its repercussions still loomed large, while European involvement with Te Rauparaha in the massacre of South Island Maoris at Kaiapoi, was a recent scandal. With the help of the missionaries, Busby was to put an end to such things, and bring law and order to New Zealand, a task which, without means of apprehending wayward Englishmen, he had no hope of accomplishing. But it is clear that the concern was not so much for Maori welfare, as the need to protect commercial and missionary activities in New Zealand. In affirming the interest of Great Britain in the area, it was hoped that some stability might be achieved. Marsden, a businessman himself, supports this view in a letter to the Rev. E. Bickersteth, of the C.M.S. in London: 'I have no doubt but the Governor will point out the necessity of a Resident being appointed to New Zealand to whom the natives may appeal for redress for acts of cruelty, etc., done upon them by Europeans. Something must be done, or all commercial connection must cease between New Zealand and the colony.'[5]

Busby, then, did not come here unaware of the shortcomings of the position he was about to occupy, since these had been clearly described to him by Bourke. The appointment had been made in anticipation of the enactment of New South Wales legislation deriving its authority from an Imperial statute, which would have enabled the Resident to arrest and bring British subjects to trial for offences against British law. But the proposed Act was never passed, and the luckless dignitary went to New Zealand with little prospect of achieving anything worthwhile. His total armament against law-breakers was a 10-year-old measure dating back to Governor Brisbane, which gave the New South Wales Supreme Court power to deal with offences by British subjects in New Zealand. The problem, however, was the apprehension of offenders upon detection; since no action could be taken until the Resident had applied for, and obtained from the Supreme Court, a warrant for the arrest of the offender, who, in the meantime, had gone beyond recall.

The Resident was provided with a salary of £500 per annum,

plus £200 as largesse to distribute to chiefs from time to time as necessary or expedient. He had no land upon which to erect the prefabricated house the New South Wales Government provided for him, but the Paihia missionaries came to his assistance, and housed and boarded him until he could fend for himself. At this stage they displayed toward him a solicitude in keeping with his instructions, implicit in which were directions to them to assist him. Later, their tendency to do this without reference to him, was a source of annoyance to Busby. Nevertheless, this helpful attitude, according to Marshall, was in marked contrast to that of the resident traders, who treated him with 'coldness and jealousy, not to say rudeness.'[6]

It was not until June 1834 that Busby purchased land for his house, although he had possession before that. He then bought 270 acres at Waitangi, and in the following November a further 25 acres. This cost him £197-16s[7] in money and goods at Sydney prices. These purchases were the first of those which ultimately expanded his Waitangi estate to some 9000 acres.

Polack, whom Busby loathed, considered that the Resident's authority was never allowed its fullest scope, even within its very narrow limits, as Busby early withdrew from association with 'respectable' Europeans, and lived in a locality remote from both traders and Maoris.[8] There may have been some truth in this, since by no means does he appear to have been a popular figure, nor one who mixed generally with the Bay's polyglot population, which his position surely required him to do. However, he did become a personal friend of Mair, and was later his partner in business enterprises.

Busby had not been in the country a year when he had his first brush with Maoris. On 1 May 1834 a party robbed an outhouse and fired eight or 10 shots at the Residency as Busby came to the front door, one striking the jamb and sending a splinter into his cheek. In October a meeting of chiefs was held outside the house to deliberate on this incident. Titore Takiri was conspicuous as a jurist, and the meeting decided that the chief offender, Reti, was to be banished and forced to give up 200-300 acres of his land at Puketona to King William as a punishment for this affront to his representative. The decision was, of course, never enforced, since the chiefs had no authority to do so, short of making war on Reti, and Busby himself was quite powerless. In fact, Governor Bourke failed even to acknowledge Busby's communications on the matter. It is on record that Mrs Busby gave birth to her first child prematurely, due to the fracas.

Although the goods stolen from the Residency were later recovered, the whole affair did little to enhance Busby's standing with both Maori and pakeha. Reti was a relative of Hone Heke, and his title to the Puketona was shared with Heke and many others, so that its confiscation would have adversely affected many Maoris not involved in the assault.

The attack on the Resident and Busby's failure to take immediate action worried the traders, who wrote to him in a hectoring tone. A letter, dated 6 May 1834, was signed by Messrs Powditch (Mair's partner), Ritchie, O'Connor, Mair, Stephenson, Clendon, Rogers, Greenway, Polack and Wright, all of whom could no doubt be classified as 'respectable'. The letter demanded that action should be taken against the Maoris responsible (this, of course, was before they had been identified, and the inquiry described above convened), and Busby was required to 'bring the natives of this country to a proper sense of the treatment to be observed to the representative of the British Government in a foreign country'.[9] Bold words from adventurers living on sufferance in the country of the 'natives', and from Busby's viewpoint the demand was quite unreasonable. Obviously, in the terms of his instructions he had no authority to meet such a demand, since his principal charge, and only explicit one, was to 'conciliate the good-will of the native chiefs, and establish on a permanent basis that good understanding and confidence which it is important. . . to perpetuate.'[10] He had authority only insofar as he could enlist the support of the chiefs individually, since they were as far from being a corporate body as it was possible to be. Highhanded or unsympathetic action could only bring him trouble, both from the Maoris and from the Governor, who himself was not competent to authorise such measures as the traders demanded. Busby's only weapon was his own diplomacy, which he used in the ensuing years with varying success. His reply to the traders was terse, and probably did nothing to

175

improve his relations with them.

If Busby did not succeed in 'bringing the natives to a proper sense' of their duty, he did undertake important routine duties, notably keeping shipping records, particularly of British whalers. Whale oil entering British ports was subject to customs duties unless it had been taken by British crews. One such example was the American ship *Erie,* crewed by English seamen who had taken its whole cargo of oil. Busby certified that the oil was 'British caught', enabling the *Erie* to pass through Customs without attracting penal duties.[11]

The first shipping summary from the Bay of Islands is, of course, that for 1833, and comprises a list of 89 ships, whose diversity is interesting:

One British ship of war	1
One ditto Government store-ship	1
Two Colonial Government brigs	2
British whaling ships	23
British merchant ships	6
New South Wales whaling ships	16
Van Diemens Land whaling ships	4
New South Wales trading vessels	19
Total British and Colonial vessels	72
American whaling ships	11
American trading vessels	4
Tahitian trading vessels	2
	17

(dated 26 February 1834)[12]

Only 15 American ships are recorded, but an indication of the rapid expansion of United States whaling activities in the western Pacific is to be found in the reports of Clendon, as Acting United States Consul, which show 62 U.S. whalers at the Bay in 1839, and 61 in 1840. By this time, the Americans had outstripped the British in the whaling industry here, and a contemporary opinion estimates the British and French ships on the coast in the same year at about 30 each, including those at the southern ports. The Bay of Islands record of 1838 [13] shows 56 American, 23 British, 21 French, 1 German and 30 Colonial vessels of various descriptions. Watkins, in his evidence on New Zealand given before the House of Lords Select Committee in 1838,[14] testified that during his visit to the Bay in 1833-34, 30 to 40 ships were in the harbour at once. There were both English and American vessels, which lay at Kororareka, Te Puna and in the Kawakawa River near the present Port of Opua.

A notable visitor to the Bay in March 1834 was HMS *Alligator*, on a special mission. She had brought three flags which had been designed by Busby, one of which was to be chosen by the local chiefs and officially recognised as the flag of New Zealand. Busby had advised Governor Bourke that such an arrangement was necessary, since ships were at this time being built in the country, and owned and operated by residents here. Hokianga was producing such vessels, and these, having no port of register, were unable to sail under any national flag; and as such were unprotected against piracy and liable to seizure in foreign ports. The large barque *Sir George Murray*, the brigantine *New Zealander*, the schooner *Enterprize* and others were built at the Horeke shipyard, and had been in this predicament. Registers of such vessels were now to be signed by the chief of the district in which they were built, and having been countersigned by the British Resident, they had the right to fly the flag of New Zealand.

The meeting at which the ensign was chosen was held at the British Residency at Waitangi on 20 March 1834; 30 chiefs assembled there with Captain Lambert of the *Alligator* and his staff, Busby, and other Europeans of the Bay. An oblong tent was erected, 'screened in at one side by canvass, and canopied by different flags; this was divided into two lesser squares by a barricade across the centre.'[15] The chiefs were called out of one square into the other to vote. Marshall witnessed the ceremony, and by his own account, figured largely in the choice of the flag, which was selected by Bay of Islands and Hokianga chiefs, whose votes were recorded by one of their number. For the chosen flag, 12 votes were recorded, 10 for the second, and six for the third. Two chiefs are stated to have refrained from voting. At the close of the proceedings, the flag was hoisted with the Union Jack at the staff, and saluted with 21 guns from the *Alligator*. But its brief period of national significance terminated, of course, in 1840, with the assumption of sovereignty by the British Crown. In design it consisted of the cross of St. George on a white ground, in the upper canton of which, next to the mast, was a small cross of St. George, on a dark blue ground; and in each of the small squares thus formed there was a small white star.

The Shaw Savill and Albion shipping line has fortunately preserved this flag almost in its original form, since the directors adopted it as their house-flag when the company was formed in 1859, and it has been used as such since that time.

With the increased tempo of politics and commerce, the Kororareka that has become legendary emerged — the bawdy drunken little town whose only law was expediency. Thomas Chapman noted the sudden access of opulence at the Bay. On 24 February 1834 he wrote: '... three years and a half ago when I arrived in New Zealand there was no European resident at Kororareka, save for a few sawyers and sailors who had left their ships; now there are five large wooden houses erected for Europeans and (I think) six more erecting, solely for the purpose of selling spirits.'[16] Marshall referred to Kororareka in the same year as 'a village once very populous [referring to the Maori population] but now almost depopulated from the influx of European visitors, and the ruinous effects of prostitution and ardent spirits upon the health and lives of the Natives.'[17] Some depopulation of the district was no doubt due to the eviction of Maoris as Europeans moved in on their newly purchased land, but the main reason for this was the departure of Pomare and Kiwikiwi with their people for Otuihu after the Girl's War, where Marshall states that he found Pomare 'surrounded by a set of the lowest and most debased Englishmen.'[18]

While Chapman's 'few sawyers and sailors' lived at Kororareka in a quiet and industrious manner, the place was quite wholesome. The merrymaking, debauchery and prostitution occurred on the ships at anchor in the Bay, and it was not until the prospect of large and easy profits encouraged the shrewd and the 'respectable' to sink capital into commercialising these activities ashore, that Kororareka was launched on its disreputable career. In 1834 Markham wrote: 'Some Sunday's (sic) 300 Men, from Thirty Whalers, have been on shore with their ladies and many a Row takes place.'[19] And shortly, of course, those who had enticed the revellers ashore were lamenting that their property suffered damage and that they themselves were endangered. Furthermore, they claimed, it was the obligation of the Crown to protect them from the perils of the situation they had created themselves.

Another description of Kororareka at this time is that of Captain Robert Fitz Roy,[20] later Governor of New Zealand, who on 21 December 1835 anchored HMS *Beagle* in Kororareka Bay. The *Beagle* was in a surveying expedition, and carried as a passenger the distinguished Charles Darwin. Two flags were flying at the Bay on the ship's arrival. On a tall staff in front of Busby's house was the Union Jack, while at Kororareka flew the brand new flag of New Zealand. Near the beach were some small cottages that had once been whitewashed, and at the foot of the hills were two or three houses of European design. The now venerable church was also there, and Fitz Roy observed a brisk passage of canoes to and from the Kawakawa River, loaded with firewood, pigs and vegetables for trade. An excellent sketch drawn by Polack in 1836[21] shows the extent of the township at that time. What is probably his own house is shown in the left foreground, a cluster of some 15 European or semi-European type buildings occupy the northern end of the beach, and at the extreme southern end are two large buildings, the furthest being on or near the land later purchased by Bishop Pompallier for his New Zealand mission. Between these and the northern group is the Maori village, palisaded and quite extensive, and to the rear, on the rising ground, are the Anglican church and some half-dozen or so shacks. The whole place has an orderly appearance, and there is clearly considerable activity afoot, since over 20 canoes of various sorts lie either on or off the beach.

Oddly enough, the erection of the church at this time coincided with the beginning of the lurid period of the town's history and its gravestones are a catalogue of successive settlers, famous and obscure, and a witness to events of over a century and a half. The church's construction does not appear to have been C.M.S. policy, but was due to the efforts of Charles Baker, who had arrived in New Zealand in 1828.[22] The care of Kororareka was given to this minor catechist, but when of necessity he was obliged to be away for some time, no effort was made to fill his place. However, on his return, a beginning was made on the building of the church. A chief offered land for the site, and subscriptions were made in generous amounts by settlers and whalers. Marshall noted that land was also offered by 'a Hebrew' — no doubt Polack — and £5 was donated by a Catholic settler. A truly ecumenical effort, it seems to have cost the Mission little or nothing and was thus Kororareka's own achievement. The church had not been built in October 1834, but was probably completed at the end of that year or at the beginning of 1835, and when Fitz Roy arrived in December of that year, it stood there in all its glory. But the Captain was not impressed, and unkindly described it as 'a slightly built edifice of bricks and light frame work, with an abundance of bad glass windows.'

With missionaries and 'respectable' residents now firmly established at the Bay, a social structure evolved on the English pattern, attracting the attention of John Dunmore Lang, who, as we noted in Chapter 15, made the scathing reference to this '. . . narrow-minded, purse-proud, heartless colonial aristocracy' in his 1839 pamphlet, which received publicity in England. Early in 1836 this stratum of Pacific society dreamed up an abortive temperance campaign in Hokianga and the Bay. While the missionaries no doubt supported the movement as a matter of principle, material considerations probably motivated the 'respectable' merchants and traders involved. Having acquired land and expended capital to establish profitable businesses, they had become vulnerable to the depredations of drunken rioters. They also feared, not without reason, that ships might avoid the port, to the detriment of business if this situation deteriorated. Since they were not heavily dependent on the sale of liquor for a livelihood, they could, with benefit to themselves, promote the aims and objects of a temperance society, at the same time appearing more virtuous than their less genteel and unrepentant colleagues.

A claim was made by the Temperance Society's supporters that shipping was avoiding the Bay because of the disorder there. In fact the peak of the whale-trade had been reached by 1836, although its subsequent decline was probably not so much due to the drunken revelry as the increased charges being made there by the business community.[23] In that year whaling vessels visiting the Bay of Islands were: British 25, New South Wales 35, United States 49, Van Diemens Land 4, French 3; totalling 116.

Whatever its motives or merits, the Temperance Society was a failure, perhaps because the sale and consumption of liquor was an important business for one section of the community, and a great consolation for another. The movement seems to have originated at the Bay, where the success of prohibition movements in missionary-dominated Tahiti and Hawaii had been discussed. In September 1835, a deputation headed by Henry Williams and James Clendon waited on Busby with a proposal to prohibit the sale of liquor. However, Busby rightly felt that he could take no official action since the matter was outside his jurisdiction, and in the terms of his instructions he could not in any case countenance any interference in the affairs of Maoris, who were implicated in the trade. However, he did appear as the chairman in the first, and as far as we know, the last, report of the Temperance Society.[24]

The first meeting of the society was held in the new Kororareka church on 11 May 1836. About 50 people attended. Nine rules were promulgated, but the Society seems to have been bankrupt of any new or effective ideas relating to the problem with which it was trying to grapple, and never again appeared as a viable concern. In fact, it is remarkable that such a project could have seriously been expected to succeed, since a significant portion of the economy of the Bay as a whole was reliant on the free flow of grog. At Hokianga, however, the Additional British Resident, McDonnell, had initiated direct measures for the prevention of the importation and sale of liquor, but these too were abortive.

McDonnell's appointment at Hokianga had been a painful thorn in Busby's side, and an affront to his dignity and pride. By lobbying in London, as Busby himself had, McDonnell promoted for himself this 'Additional' appointment; partly, it seems, by making the dubious claim that Hokianga was too far away from Waitangi for Busby to do justice to it. Not only was McDonnell appointed without Busby's, or even Bourke's, knowledge or approval, but in the execution of his duties he availed himself of every opportunity to undermine Busby both in Australia and New Zealand. Appointed in 1834, he certainly imposed his will and whims effectively at Hokianga, if not with any significant benefit, but does not appear to have done much damage, except to Busby's ego, before resigning in 1837. Nevertheless, he was a little unstable, and not a little dishonest in his dealings with, and concerning Busby.

But weighty affairs of state now arose to drive from Busby's mind the reformation of his compatriots and his feud with the Additional British Resident. As he had promised, the Baron Charles Philip Hippolytus de Thierry was now on his way to New Zealand to claim his South Sea Kingdom. It will be recalled that Kendall had, when in England in 1820, agreed to purchase land for the Baron in New Zealand, and that in 1822 he was alleged to have acquired 40,000 acres for de Thierry at Hokianga. Now it had come to Busby's notice that the Baron, styling himself King of Nukuhiva (in the Marquesas) and sovereign Lord of New Zealand, had issued a Proclamation notifying his intention of settling on his Hokianga lands and establishing the perfect political state. Busby, the representative of the British Government, was horrified at the very notion of a Frenchman usurping what he considered to be a British sphere of influence, although de Thierry was in fact a British subject, a matter that was not clear at the time. Accordingly, on 10 October 1835, Busby issued a warning to his countrymen to have nothing to do with the fellow's 'insidious promises' of utopian government, but to rely on the '. . . paternal protection of the British Government.'[25] He called upon them to '. . . inspire both Chiefs and People with a Spirit of Most Determined Resistance'. To this end, Busby called a meeting of chiefs at Waitangi, and displaying a talent for political manoeuvre worthy of the European school, proposed the Declaration of Independence of New Zealand.

Polack, however, volunteered the interesting opinion, that the settlers would gladly have embraced any form of government rather than endure the chaos then pervading, and that had the Baron been successful in forming a government, Busby would not have got much support in his opposition to de Thierry. This could, in fact, have been the view of the non-missionary-aligned section of the community.

Busby's fear of French influence was not altogether ill-founded, since lately France had displayed a rather more active interest in the exploration of the coasts and the study of the Maori people than England had. At the time the numbers of French and British whalers on the coast were about equal. French interest was sustained until the last, when, having established a settlement at Akaroa, the Nanto-Bordelaise Company suffered the indignity of seeing it annexed to the British Crown along with the rest of New Zealand. And in the 1830s our Chevalier Captain Dillon had settled at Tauranga, and styled himself French Consul, by authority of his honorary appointment as vice-consul to the islands of 'l'archipel de l'Ocean Pacifique'.

There is no doubt now that Busby regarded the de Thierry incident with more seriousness than was warranted, but in the circumstances his reaction does not appear an unreasonable one, since it seemed that, such as they were, the British Government's interests in New Zealand were threatened. Although Governor Bourke was unimpressed, and severely criticised Busby for his grand diplomacy, his authority clearly did not extend to this sort of policy-making, but the Imperial Government noted it at least with equanimity, if not guarded approval. Bourke's annoyance is understandable, for although the idea may have been good, his prior approval had not been obtained, and it was two more years before de Thierry actually appeared in New Zealand.

The Declaration was signed at Waitangi on 28 October 1835 by 34 northern chiefs, and 18 others from as far south as Hawke's Bay, signed it during the next four years. There were four clauses to the document, the first being the actual declaration of their independence by the 'hereditary Chiefs and Heads of the northern parts of New Zealand', who by this instrument established an independent state to be known as 'The United Tribes of New Zealand'. The second clause stated that the sovereignty of the area described was vested in the hereditary chiefs, who would, they declared, tolerate no infringement of their rights without their express permission. The third clause made provision for an annual meeting of these chiefs to be held at Waitangi to dispense laws, justice, etc., while the fourth provided that a copy of the Declaration be sent to William IV with a prayer that he should extend his protection to prevent any attempts on the Tribes' independence that might be made. Among the chiefs outside the Bay who signed were Nene, Patuone, Taonui and Tawhai (Hokianga), Nopera Panakareao (Kaitaia), Tirarau (Mangakahia), Te Hapuku (Hawke's Bay), and Potatau Te Wherowhero (Waikato). Henry Williams, George Clarke, James Clendon and Gilbert Mair witnessed the Declaration. Busby himself, as a public servant, discreetly refrained from signing.

The Maori tribal system, with its continuing background of bitter warfare, precluded any possibility of the proposal for self-government working. Indeed, there was little or no attempt to make it work, and it may be that even Busby had few illusions himself on the matter. But due to this ploy, he and the British Government were now at least armed with a document aimed at all intruders other than the British, and despite criticism, the term 'The United Tribes of New Zealand', coined for the Declaration, was later approved by Hobson, and perpetuated in the Treaty of Waitangi.

While these affairs of state were going forward, life on a humbler plane went on at the Bay of Islands. At Otuihu an unsavoury settlement had become established, based at Pomare's *pa*. Pomare was still a young man but had recently taken to 'ardent spirits' with such vigour that according to Marshall, 'his health and vigour of body are very sensibly impaired'.

Land was first acquired at Otuihu by Europeans in the early 1830s and there appears to have been a grog-seller in business there in 1836. Already it was a place of dubious repute. There were no doubt a few *bona fide* residents and tradesmen at

Otuihu, but no claims to land purchased there were allowed by the old Land Claim Commissioners in their final awards.

In 1837 Pomare's *pa* came to the attention of Samuel Marsden, who, with startling precision, asserted that the European population there numbered 131. In a letter of 27 March 1837 to the Secretary of the Church Missionary Society, Marsden wrote: 'These are generally men of the most infamous characters, composed of runaway convicts and sailors, and publicans who have opened grog shops in the *pa*, where every scene of riot and drunkenness and prostitution are carried on daily.'[26]

Although Kororareka was secure in its unsavoury reputation, and was likened by the missionaries to such places as Sodom and Gomorrah, Otuihu's claims to infamy appear to have been overlooked. Kororareka was, of course, a business town run by pakehas, and while there were sufficient brothels and grog shops there to meet the demand, legitimate business was of great importance. Otuihu, on the other hand, was a Maori settlement presided over by Pomare, who ran it as a commercial enterprise, offering liquor, the services of amiable ladies, and general merrymaking as commodities. In the deep water off-shore from his *pa*, where the Waikare and Kawakawa rivers join, ships would load timber or undergo refits. To these came canoe-loads of girls bringing joy to the crews. Pomare provided these and the grog to go with them, and even if these delights were spurned, all ships at anchor in his river were required to pay him a levy. In 1840, Commander Wilkes of the United States Exploring Expedition[27] was much disgusted when Pomare refused to let his people put on a dance until the whole of the American party had disgorged a shilling each. Although Wilkes described Pomare as a fine-looking man, six feet in height, he also says that he was avaricious, cowardly and much addicted to liquor. He attributed Pomare's influence to his tremendous eloquence, a means of dominance which still remains effective.

Later, Pomare arranged a full-scale exhibition of the war-dance for Wilkes, on Clendon's property at Okiato. Much bargaining over the food necessary to sustain the dancers took place, and the dance was then performed before the Americans and an audience of some 300-400 Maoris. A less violent exhibition was then given by the women, and 'it was not necessary to understand their language to comprehend their meaning... their tastes did not appear very refined'.

In 1839, Dr Lang observed at Otuihu 'a whole group of English public-houses of the most infamous description,' close to Pomare's *pa* 'which, during the late war in the island, contained upwards of fifteen hundred fighting men.'[28] McCormick, who visited the Bay in 1841 with the Antarctic Expedition, described the place:

> We landed on a small shingly and sandy beach, flanked on the right by two gin-shops, chiefly frequented by the whalers, and called the 'Sailor's Return' and the 'Eagle Inn', having the shutters and verandah painted green. A narrow path, with three or four peach-trees in their pink bloom, led up the face of the hill to the pah.[29]

At Kororareka, a wide variety of adventurers were now established, each pursuing his own chosen means of getting rich quickly. William Alexander, who in 1827 at Matauwhi assisted Earle and Duke in the burial of the partly cooked remains of a Maori girl, had a grog shop there in 1834. The other known residents in 1827 — Alexander Grey, John Piner, J.M. Chisholm, M.G. Johnston, John Johnson, Donald McKay, John Matthew and John McLean — were joined by the mid-1830s by Battersby and Turner, both known to have been grog shopkeepers. Also then present were Butterworth, Polack, Fitzsimmons, McDiarmid, Montefiore, Spicer, Moore, Hookey, Cunningham, Hull, Cole, Shand, Rose, Edney, Trapp, Poyner, Harris and others unknown, who had either bought land or were engaged in business of some sort. Polack, Montefiore and Spicer were apparently general merchants. Ross, the Bay's doctor, lived at Waitangi, loosely attached to the mission.

Commerce on a fairly large scale had now forced the general abandonment of the old barter system, which had worked well enough when commodities and payments were few and elementary. As we have seen, Yate noted in 1834 that exchange was then largely based British and other coin, but inevitably there was insufficient of this for large transactions, so that merchants had to resort to bills and promissory notes. Obviously those issuing such guarantees had to be well known and permanently settled, and a significant portion of the Bay's population could now be thus classified.

Having established themselves in the country, the traders, merchants and businessmen now required only the openly acknowledged protection of Great Britain, and with it recognition of the legality of their land purchases. It will be recalled that in 1831 a petition had been addressed to William IV praying for such protection, and this had produced only Busby. But by 1837, a minor explosion in the European population had occurred and another petition on this theme was drawn up, signed by nearly 200 persons in New Zealand, all Europeans, from obscure tradesmen to prosperous mercantile tycoons.[30]

---

1. Ramsden, E. *Busby of Waitangi*, p.34.
2. Kent, G. *Company of Heaven*, p.45 et seq.
3. Polack, *Narrative of Travels and Adventures*, v.2, p.219.
4. Elder, *Letters and Journals*, pp.497-501.
5. McNab, *Historical Records*, v.1, p.717.
6. Marshall, *A Personal Narrative*, p.55.
7. Bell, D-No. 14, 1863, Claims Nos 14 and 15.
8. Polack, v.2, p.221.
9. Sherrin and Wallace, *Early History of New Zealand*, p.433.
10. Ibid, p.430.
11. McNab, *The Old Whaling Days*, p.269-270.
12. Busby, J. 'Dispatch No.36 to Alex McLeay, N.S.W.,' (Aust. Nat. Lib.)
13. Lang, J.D. *New Zealand in 1839*, (1839), p.91-94.
14. 'Select Committee of the House of Lords on the State of the Islands of New Zealand.' B.P.P. No. 680, p.12-32. (Auck. Pub. Lib.)
15. Marshall, p.108.
16. 'Letters and Journals of the Rev. Thomas Chapman.' v.1, (Auck. Pub. Lib.)
17. Marshall, p.19.
18. Ibid, p.251.

19. Markham, E. *New Zealand or Recollections of it.* p.63.
20. Fitz Roy R. *The Surveying Voyages of HMS Adventure and Beagle,* v.2, pp.566, 576, 578, 582.
21. Polack, op.cit. v.1, frontispiece.
22. Marshall, p.271.
23. Sherrin and Wallace, op.cit., p.176.
24. Report of the Formation and Establishment of the New Zealand Temperance Society, (Auck. Pub.Lib.)
25. Sherrin and Wallace, p.460.
26. Elder, p.524.
27. Wilkes, C. *Narrative of the United States Exploring Expedition,* pp.390, 392-3, 402-3.
28. Lang, op.cit. (1873), p.4.
29. McCormick, R. *Voyages of Discovery in the Artic and Antarctic Seas and Round the World,* v.1, p.215-6.
30. Sherrin and Wallace, p.463-4.

17

Disorder and Confusion

ALTHOUGH THE GREAT land-purchase boom had not begun, and the professional speculators were not yet arrayed in force in New Zealand, the Maoris had still lost the title to much land. By the end of 1836 an impressive acreage around the Bay was in European hands. These titles, dubious in terms of British law, since they did not derive from the Crown, relied entirely on the good faith of the Maori vendors. The purchasers therefore needed the intervention of the Crown both to protect their newly-acquired estates, and to confirm their titles.

At Kororareka the buying began early, when Hansen, captain of the brig *Active*, bought two parcels of land there in 1814. This would have been the first land purchased in New Zealand, although the Crown did not subsequently recognise the claim. Until 1836 some 30 purchases had allegedly been concluded at Kororareka, including one each by the missionary W. Williams and his colleague C. Baker, who by this time also claimed to have acquired 5000 acres in the Mangakahia Valley, between Parakao and Titoki. Some properties had been bought by non-mission settlers in the outer bay, on the islands, and in the main tidal estuaries. Of these purchases, only Busby's, at Waitangi, could have been considered large.[1] Nevertheless, Church Missionary Society acquisitions, and those of the individual Anglican missionaries, were considerable. The society had, to this date, bought some 16,000 acres at Te Puna, Kerikeri, Paihia and Waimate, while mission personnel had purchased among them something over 30,000 acres, a figure that was considerably increased during the next few years. Apart from the 13,000 acres the society purchased at Kerikeri which it did not later claim, the figures are for those lands *claimed* to have been acquired; not those later confirmed by the Crown as *bona-fide* purchases. The areas are approximate, since some were estimated at the time of acquisition, and others were surveyed, but they are a good indication of the position at the end of 1836. The inland portions of the Bay of Islands and Whangaroa were favoured by the Anglican missionaries, who purchased much land around Kerikeri, Pakaraka, Waimate, Ohaeawai and Puketona. King, the most ambitious purchaser of them all, bought extensively on the coast between the Bay and Whangaroa. The Methodist missionaries, now well established at Hokianga, acquired no land, since this was forbidden to them by the Wesleyan Methodist Missionary Society.

This, then, was the situation when, early in 1837, a petition was submitted to William IV, requesting the British Government assume responsibility for the protection and government of the English population in New Zealand. Some hundreds, probably well over a thousand, Europeans, largely Irish, Scots or English, were permanently living throughout New Zealand. They had no political or other rights whatever, apart from those which they had the physical or economic power to assume and defend. If they were subject to any discipline, it was to the native custom. Although the Maoris at that time were tolerant, it must have been apparent to the more perceptive element of the white population that it was only a matter of time before the Maoris would become aware that they were losing their grip on the situation. Another consideration was the fear in the minds of the more prosperous English settlers of foreign intervention. But for the smaller tradesmen and settlers, whose only ambition was to earn a living, raise a family with their Maori wives, and exist more or less in comfort, the situation held few terrors. For the sake of cheap land, and the opportunities of making quick fortunes, the prosperous section of this strangely assorted community had voluntarily settled here, knowing the risks involved. Now, having attained their immediate objectives, they strove for the removal of the risks through the intervention of the British Government. Scant regard was taken of the fact that no foreign government had any moral right whatever to interfere, particularly since the sovereignty and independence of the chiefs had been officially recognised on the recommendation of Britain's representative in New Zealand. But the

Englishman of the time, of course, believed that His Britannic Majesty exercised peculiar rights in respect of native peoples, who, in the view of his loyal subjects, were incapable of governing themselves. That the Maoris had been rendered thus incapable by the influx of Europeans, and their activities, the conscientious Busby was fully aware; as his advice to the Colonial Secretary, of 8 June 1837, makes quite clear.[2] The missionaries held similar views, and, as we have seen, were heavily involved in land acquisition. Their mission activities were also in jeopardy, due to increasing lawlessness, and the want of control by the chiefs. The missionaries, therefore, lent their support to this further petition to the King.

The document represented a major organisational achievement, since according to Polack, it was signed by 192 residents, from such districts as the Bay of Islands, Hokianga and Whangaroa, and other places. There was no mention of the Temperance Society's grim prophecies of a declining whale-trade, and, to the contrary, it was stated that since 1833 shipping had increased considerably. In the words of the petition: 'The crews of vessels have frequently been decoyed on shore, to the great detriment of trade, and numberless robberies have been committed on shipboard and on shore by a lawless band of Europeans, who have not even scrupled to use fire-arms to support them in their depredations...' The object of the petition is summarised in one of the concluding sentences: 'Your humble petitioners would, therefore, pray that your Majesty may graciously regard the peculiarity of their situation, and afford that relief which may appear expedient to your Majesty.'[3]

The British government was by no means unaware of the situation in New Zealand, and was clearly being forced into deciding its future role there. Nevertheless it was concerned about the moral issues involved, although well aware of French and United States interest. Shortly, Clendon's appointment to act as U.S. Consul would have the effect of placing that country's official presence in New Zealand on a more prestigious footing than England's. Also, by the time the petition was presented, the New Zealand Association had been formed in London, with the avowed intention of colonising the country,

191

and its promoters included such influential people as the Earl of Durham.[4] In 1838 it sponsored a bill for the promotion of its objects, but although this failed, from its ashes rose the New Zealand Company in 1839.

Busby's inefficacy in regard to disorder was again demonstrated in January 1836 when a land purchase at Whananaki by two European settlers, Day and Bond, resulted in another brawl at Busby's Waitangi house. A meeting of chiefs contending the ownership of the land had been convened for the purpose of deciding who should receive payment for it, and at once sensitive tribal jealousies had reared their heads. Rival contenders were Ngati Manu of Kawakawa, represented by Noa, and Hongi's friend Waikato of Kaihiki, near Te Puna, although the latter is said to have admitted that his claim was not substantial. However, there is no doubt that he did have interests at Whananaki, so feelings at the meeting ran high, and since, unlike his rivals, Waikato's people were armed, they started shooting, killing two of Noa's men, the remainder of whom retreated into the Residency. There, on the advice of the Rev. W. Williams, they remained, and in spite of a general invasion of the house, order was restored, and Waikato and his cohorts decamped.

Meanwhile, Busby continued to share his office in New Zealand, to his chagrin, with Lieutenant Thomas McDonnell. Busby clearly regarded McDonnell's presence as a personal affront. Hokianga was developing in a different way from the Bay, and if a suitable Resident had been appointed there, he could have been quite effective, in spite of Busby's strenuous disclaimers. But such was the bitterness between the two men, that they spent the year until McDonnell resigned in 1836, hurling charge and counter-charge at each other, mostly through a third person.

After McDonnell's departure, Hokianga reverted to Busby's control. The highlight of his activities there was a murder trial in 1838, at which he presided over a tribunal of Europeans as jury, with chiefs as judges. This deliberated on a charge against a Maori called Kite for the murder by drowning of a European called Henry Biddle. After the jury had convicted the accused, the chiefs light-heartedly condemned him to death. On the island of Ruapapaku, off Horeke, he was seated on the edge of his grave and shot.[5] This judicial exploit, which Busby seemed to be quite pleased about, appears to have earned him little but official disapproval, as well it might, since it contributed nothing to the solution of the major problems facing him in New Zealand.

The fundamental difference between Hokianga and the Bay of Islands at this period was that which distinguishes a tradesman from a shop-keeper or merchant. At Hokianga, timber was being worked and ships built, while general commerce and ship maintenance predominated at the Bay. Kauri gum has already been noted as an article of trade there, and McNab records that early in 1835, Clendon exported a shipment of wool in his schooner *Fortitude*.[6] This could have been the first wool exported from New Zealand; and some of it had possibly been grown at Te Puna, where missionary King's son, now about 20 years old, had a small farm and a flock of sheep.

The nature of Bay of Islands trade is indicated in a letter written from Sydney by Gilbert Mair to his grandfather in May 1839. In it he sets out New Zealand produce then in demand on the Sydney market:

> The goods and prices of goods that we should wish you to purchase and get ready for us are as follows, viz —
> Sperm oil at or within £60 per tun)   Send up a certificate
> Black oil at or within £14 to 15 do.)   with the oil.
> Pork   Small quantity and must be good.
> Lard   good only 4d. per lb.
> Maize   Shelled dry & sound, for which we will send bags 2/6 to 3/-.
> Flax £8 to £10
> British Cordage & rope of all sizes 40/- & 45/- per cwt.
> Stockholm Tar filled 50/- per barrel.
> Whalebone good & clean for the London Market £80 per ton.
> Tortoise shell 15/- to 16/- per lb.
> Slush this must be well examined that it is good grade 20/- to 25/- pr. Barrel.

```
Timber  ½    inch not much                )
        1    inch as much as you can  )
        1¼   inch as much as you can  ) 10/- to 12/- per 100 ft.
        1½   do. as much as you can  )
        2    do. as much as you can  )
```

Spars — a few good ones if cheap.[7]

It will be noticed that the whale oil needed to be certified that
it was 'British caught'. The low price of flax is also interesting,
and two unexpected items occur — British cordage and
Stockholm tar. Apparently the Bay merchants were buying
these from ships coming there direct from England, and were
dealing with them wholesale to the Sydney market.

The late Mrs Louisa Worsfold, who as a child lived with her
uncle, the merchant George Greenway, wrote a colourful
description of the activities of the New Zealand traders of those
times:

George Greenway built a good big house, and a pier out to
deep water...He had a general store and a malt house...also
a brew house I have heard of...As to trade there was flax and
firewood for the ships — and general provisions for the same
— pigs for pork — also the ships brought other things from
other places — even from China...enamelled copper...tea in
lead-lined cases of cedar of some sort, red and scented, with
chinese writing on a sort of parchment — sugar in matting
containers. . .preserved fruits in willow-pattern jars, with
cane lattice overwork and handles. From the same source
were carved ornaments in ivory and jade — many of the
houses of my youth owned all these sorts of things — lac-
quered tea-caddies, with lead linings, chased in lovely patterns, and willow patterns in gilt and red enamel, and gilt
claws for legs. These were all trade. There was also Raupo for
trade — used for putting between the staves for making new
casks for ship's water supply — when these were empty they
used them for whale oil — wherever they called for water they
made new casks.[8]

194

Missionary and merchant alike owed their comfort and their very existence to the shipping. Eulogies of these people are commonplace in New Zealand's bibliography; although little but acrimony has been reserved for the masters and crew of those small and rugged ships — the Southseamen — that created and maintained the economy of the Bay of Islands.

Twenty to thirty vessels — brigs, schooners, barques and ships — frequently lay anchored at one time between Kororareka and the present Opua, with canoes passing and re-passing among them, trading in firewood and vegetables. Gaily dressed Maori girls thronged the decks, and ashore around the Bay 500 to 1000 Europeans went about their various affairs. Boats constantly passed between ship and shore, while at the various trading establishments commerce and industry thrived. And the metropolis was Kororareka. At Paihia, Kerikeri, Te Puna and inland at Waimate, life at the mission stations went comfortably on. Having created this, the Southseamen now maintained it with a steady stream of shipping — British, French, colonial and American — which brought the life-blood of the Bay of Islands from other lands.

Here, on the world's edge, with communications confined to the slow sea-lanes, was a community without leaders or law. While general, and often gross, disorderliness caused chaos, there is little evidence that major crimes of violence were any more prevalent than in the more orthodox communities of that era. Seamen behaved as such men are wont to do, and while many were turbulent, few appear to have been criminals. Escaped convicts and undesirables from Tasmania and New South Wales were in the minority, and apparently were for the most part concentrated at Otuihu. The Maoris had their own effective disciplines. While there was disorder at the Bay among Europeans, there was apparently little terrorism or major crime. If this had been present, the 'respectable' community could scarcely have survived. In fact, it was Thomson's view that the missionaries 'magnified and widely circulated' accounts of disorder. This is his description of Kororareka *circa* 1838:

It was the most frequented resort for whalers in all the

South Sea Islands; and its European population, although fluctuating, was then estimated at a thousand souls. It had a church, five hotels, numberless grog-shops, a theatre, several billiard tables, skittle alleys, finishes, and hells. For six successive years a hundred whale ships anchored in the Bay, and land facing the beach sold at three pounds a foot.[9]

In March 1838 Polack was in trouble in an unruly incident. For four years he had conducted a substantial business at Parramatta, his home at Kororareka. Having mastered the language, he appears to have established a good relationship with the Maoris, apparently one of the few settlers who paid them adequate prices for their land. This could have accounted for his unpopularity with other land-buyers, but he was obliged finally to make an ignominious exit from New Zealand, as a result of the prevailing lawlessness.[10] He had run foul of Ben Turner, one of the town's earlier residents, and a dozen years in the Pacific paradise had not softened Turner's nature to the extent that he would allow Polack to best him.

The antagonism between the two men arose from several causes. Polack clearly considered himself socially superior to his rivals, but, worse perhaps, he was suspected of sharp business practice, and here his undoubted intellectual superiority could well have put his rivals at a disadvantage. Dr Lang stated that one reason for Polack's downfall was his announced intention to open a grog shop in opposition to those already established. Apparently the competition was fierce in this business, so his competitors threatened to hang Polack at once, and accordingly made preparations to erect a gibbet for the purpose. It is unlikely that this was any more than an elaborate threat, but Polack took the point and reconsidered his grog-shop proposal.

His New Zealand career was terminated for the time-being by a dispute with Turner over land at Kororareka. Turner enlisted some aid and set about the disposal of his rival in the best way he knew how — direct action. One night in March 1837 a fight erupted at Polack's premises at the north end of the beach. Turner, Evans and Steward opened the attack and were later reinforced by Polack's partner, George Russell. Turner was shot in the mouth for his pains, but eventually Polack was soundly beaten. Convinced that his continued residence at Kororareka could do him no good, and having without success sought Busby's assistance, he left New Zealand in June, after leasing his store to Thomas Spicer and appointing Clendon as his agent.

Polack evidently went direct to England, where he published his books on his experiences in New Zealand. In 1841 he was back in New Zealand again and, what is more, in the next year he fought another duel with Ben Turner, in which this time Turner was wounded in the cheek and Polack in the elbow. But in 1849, having lived in Auckland for some time, he left New Zealand permanently.

The following amusing anecdote is again from Dr Lang, whose outraged though interesting comments on conditions at the Bay in 1839 are an excellent record of the times. In this incident, he relates how forthright methods were used in dealing with a situation for which there was no other remedy.[11] The captain of a French whaling vessel was preparing for sea when he received a demand from one of the publicans on 'The Beach' to pay a grog bill, which three of his crew, Englishmen, had run up when ashore. But the captain refused to pay, whereupon the publican seized one of his ship's boats as security for the debt. The captain had little choice but to leave it when he sailed, but shortly afterwards a French warship arrived, and on learning of the incident her commander informed the publican that if the price of the boat was not forthcoming at a certain hour, 'he would drag him, house and all, into the sea'. Having no reason to doubt the sincerity of this promise, the grog-seller paid up at once.

Such disorderly conditions were soon to be aggravated by a local Maori squabble early in 1837, which ended in an open war, if indeed it could be called such, between the Maoris attached to Titore Takiri, who was now permanently resident at Kororareka, and Pomare's followers.[12] Ostensibly, the cause, or *take* for this war was a casual act of cannibalism — a practice that was dwindling due to European disapproval, but was by no means extinct. But Pomare's resentment at his eviction from Kororareka seven years earlier was unabated, and this was undoubtedly the true cause. But whatever his motive he charged that a girl who had been living with a sailor aboard a whale-ship had been put ashore at Paroa when the ship left, and that a local chief passing that way in a canoe had seen her, and, being hungry, he and his friends had killed and eaten her on the spot. The chief, who was related to both the opposing parties, denied the accusation, claiming that the girl had been taken to Cloudy Bay in the South Island. But honour had to be satisfied, and regardless of the whereabouts of the girl, the matter went forward in the time-honoured fashion.

Titore recruited the most men, but Polack, who claimed to have witnessed the whole affair, observed the wind and fury of the campaign with some cynicism. His account states that Titore took an attacking party in 30 canoes up to Pomare's *pa* at Otuihu (Marsden's account gives the number of canoes as 42, and the number of men as 800). Upon arrival, terrific *haka* were performed, blood curdling threats were bandied about, and while this was occurring, to the accompaniment of the discharge of thousands of rounds of ball ammunition, Pomare appears to have simply sat tight. The procession of canoes between Kororareka and Otuihu continued for some time, at the expense of much powder and lead, and furious war-dances substituted for actual conflict. On one occasion, two opposing canoes actually engaged, and three of Titore's men were killed, this regretable incident marring an otherwise pleasant occasion. A leg belonging to a Rawhiti chief, Nana, was left behind by the attackers; and Polack, apparently feeling that this incident required some justification, said that Nana '. . . had always been a turbulent noisy chief'. He estimated that in all, some hundreds of thousands of rounds of ammunition were discharged during the three months of desultory warfare; but the casualties appear to have been confined to those described, since there was little, if any hand-to-hand fighting. At times there were many hundreds of Europeans close at hand, and 30 ships were at anchor within view of the operations. Although no European residents suffered harm, the contestants passed freely through their properties, and a little plundering occurred, notably at Greenway's, on the Waikare, where Titore's people had taken up a position facing Otuihu.

The warriors' hearts could scarcely have been in their work — in fact Polack uncharitably believed them to be showing off before the assembled Europeans. Missionary persuasion was of no avail in terminating this affair, but in June, Hokianga Maoris came over, and since they were undecided as to which side they should join, a peace was patched up with their assistance. The war thus ended without disturbing the Maori status quo at the Bay, although it was Busby's view that it had been Pomare's intention to regain his place at Kororareka.

There are conflicting accounts of Titore's death, but he may have been dying from natural causes while these events were occurring. He was, in fact, dead by the middle of the year, so that his people may have been without his leadership. This is certainly not the sort of campaign which might have been expected from him, a great warrior-chief.

Early in 1837, the aged and enfeebled Marsden came tottering into this scene of riot and confusion. This was his last visit, as he died in the next year, but he had lost none of his interest in his New Zealand mission. At the Bay, the organisation was still reeling under the impact of another scandal as traumatic as the Kendall affair. This time it was the Rev. William Yate, who was accused of homosexual relations with Maori boys, a charge which, unlike Kendall's, never seems to have been satisfactorily proved, and was certainly not admitted.[13] Nevertheless, Yate had been dismissed from the employ of the society, when he was in New South Wales in 1836, although in 1843 we find him employed as chaplain to a London workhouse. It was partly his case which brought Marsden here on his final visit to New Zealand. Accompanied by his daughter Martha, he came to the Bay by way of Hokianga, where he arrived in February 1837 on the timber ship *Pyramus*. From Hokianga he was carried on a litter to Waimate, possibly by way of the Waima River and Kaikohe, arriving when the local war was in full spate. He had little to say about it except in general terms, and remarked that the missionaries had made unavailing attempts to prevent the fighting. He also confirmed Polack's casualty list, and noted the large number of Europeans at Otuihu during the hostilities.

Busby's fears for the safety of Europeans due to this war, which he had confided to Bourke early in the year, turned out to be groundless; but reluctantly, the Governor despatched William Hobson to the Bay, in command of HMS *Rattlesnake*.[14] This vessel belonged to the East India squadron, and had been in Australian waters since 1836, engaged in survey and patrol work. She arrived at the Bay on 26 May 1837, towards the end of the war, and because the contending parties were making menacing noises at each other and would not be interrupted, investigation was difficult. However, Hobson spent a week interviewing missionaries, traders and chiefs, before sailing for the south to examine other parts of New Zealand that were frequented or settled by British nationals. Marsden sailed with the *Rattlesnake* to the Thames and Cook's Strait, from where the vessel returned to the Bay on 30 June. A few days later the ship left for Sydney, where Hobson reported his findings.

Apparently the New Zealand question was still rated as a nuisance in London at the time of Hobson's report, and another year was to elapse before any significant action was taken. His investigation was important, in that it was the first official field-examination of conditions in this country. The report, dated 8 August 1837, did, however, result a year later in the British Government's decision to dismiss Busby, who had been expecting to be appointed to any higher office decided upon, and appoint a fully-fledged consul in his place. Apart from the unacceptable disorder in New Zealand, persistent colonising proposals and a growing awareness of the possibilities of action by the French, had by now made the matter an urgent one.[15]

In his report, Hobson suggested that some remedial action should be taken to avert the disastrous consequences that might follow the undisciplined behaviour of many Europeans in their dealings with the Maoris. One of his recommendations was that 'factories' be established, similar to those formed during the exploitation of India by the East India Company. These were self-contained English communities amenable to British law, but with no overt political dominance over any other portion of the country. But this disguised colonisation of India was confined to military people and adventurers in the employ of the Company, and all were thus under some sort of discipline. By contrast, New Zealand's European population was more diverse, and furthermore, had already decided where it was going to live and what it was going to do.

While the *Rattlesnake* was in New Zealand waters, an isolated incident occurred, involving an attack on an inoffensive settler, which created a major *furore* both here and in New South Wales.[16] One Edward Doyle, and his henchman, James Goulding, entered Captain John Wright's house at Omata, between Te Wahapu and Okiato. They overpowered the captain, after menacing him with a pistol, and a general scuffle took place, involving his wife and stepdaughters, who joined the battle and were also assaulted. The men searched and plundered the house, escaping with tobacco and other goods to the value of £100 — a considerable amount in those times. But they were soon apprehended, apparently with Maori assistance, and Mr Busby took them in charge. He, in turn, handed them over to the *Rattlesnake*, and within a fortnight they were on their way to Sydney to stand trial under the provisions of the seldom-invoked Act of 1823. While the Act gave the New South Wales courts the power to deal with offences committed by British subjects in the Pacific, the problem had always been to catch the offenders. But this occasion was an exception, and on the evidence of John Wright, his stepdaughters, and the Rev. H. Williams, who all travelled to Sydney to testify, Doyle was hanged. The case against Goulding, all at great expense to the New South Wales tax-payers, was dismissed. After the hanging, a Proclamation was issued by Governor Bourke, in which His Excellency expressed the devout hope, '. . .that this example will afford a salutory warning.' Copies were distributed in New Zealand and throughout the Pacific.

In the meantime, the 'respectable' settlers at the Bay were daily growing more apprehensive of the disruptive forces at work, and of the possibility of foreign intervention. Although largely isolated from these events, the Anglican mission un-doubtedly suffered from the disorder. The achievements of the mission on behalf of the Maoris had not been particularly impressive in the 23 years since 1815. By the C.M.S. account there were now 35 accredited mission workers in New Zealand, who conducted 51 schools with 1431 scholars. A total of 2176 people were said to be attending public worship, of whom, however, only 178 were communicants.[17] This was from a Maori population, directly under the influence of the mission, estimated at 10-12,000. And now, over the missionaries hung the question of their dubious land acquisitions.

---

1. Bell, F.D., A.J.H.R., D-14, 1863, No. 547 (Baker) and passim.
2. Ramsden, *Busby of Waitangi*, p.171.
3. Polack, *Narrative of Travels and Adventures*, v.2, p.431.
4. Sherrin and Wallace, *Early History of New Zealand*, p. 408.
5. Ramsden, p.185.
6. McNab, *The Old Whaling Days*, p.133.
7. Mair Papers, ex-Mr Gilbert Mair, Torbay, Auckland, 1944.
8. Letter to the author from Mrs Worsfold.
9. Thomson, *The Story of New Zealand*, v.1, p.285.
10. Ramsden, p.173.
11. Lang, *New Zealand in 1839*, (1873), p.4.
12. Polack, op.cit., v.2, p.40 et seq. Elder, *Letters and Journals*, p.524. Ramsden, p.167.
13. Yarwood, *Samuel Marsden, the Great Survivor*, p.272-4.
14. Scholefield, G.H. *Captain William Hobson*, passim.
15. Wards, *The Shadow of the Land*, p.24 et seq., and McLintock, A.M., *Crown Colony Government in New Zealand*, p.26 et seq.
16. Sherri and Wallace, p.465.
17. Elder, *Letters and Journals*, p.545.

18

Chaos

It is not commonly realised that the French, who were then among the great maritime races, shared in the rising prosperity at the Bay of Islands. French whalers were at this time operating on the coast in numbers comparable to those of the English, although both were outnumbered by the Americans. A dozen French names appear among the Bay's early population; but apart from these, and a sprinkling of Jews, Germans and Portugese, the inhabitants were predominantly from the British Isles. Nevertheless, the naval strength both the French and the Americans in the Pacific was greater than that of Great Britain.

At this juncture, de Thierry, a man of ambivalent ancestry — an Englishman of French descent with a hereditary French title — materialised at Hokianga. His plans to establish his own principality in New Zealand were such as to make a thoughtful observer dubious as to his sincerity or his judgement. His coming had been long awaited with trepidation. As early as 1835, Busby had been intriguing industriously to confound the nefarious designs of the King of Nukuhiva. However, it was not until November 1837 that the Baron Charles Philip Hippolytus de Thierry landed at Hokianga with, by his own account, an entourage of 68 persons, to claim his estates there, and in accordance with his decree of 1835, to proclaim himself Sovereign Lord of his New Zealand lands.[1] The territory that he claimed as the nucleus of his kingdom was situated on the south-eastern side of the Hokianga Harbour, where in the Rangiahua district he claimed that Kendall had purchased 40,000 acres for him in 1822. In support of this, the Baron later stated that he had incurred expenses of £12,000 while in Europe, on account of his New Zealand venture.

When the unfortunate de Thierry arrived at Hokianga with his family and retainers, the chiefs Patuone and Nene[2] from whom, with the deceased Muriwai, his kingdom was purported to have been purchased, rejected his claim to the 40,000 acres. Nevertheless, shortly after his arrival, they did establish him on land near Patuone's village of Tarawaua, close to Rahiri, on the Waihou River. This was 'a present. . . to the Baroness in consideration of the regard we had for her', Patuone stated in his evidence before the Old Land Claims Commissioner.[3] Here, beside the Waihou River, where the Horeke road now joins State Highway 1, de Thierry raised his standard, which fluttered not over the rolling miles he had envisaged, but over a mere 814 acres, charitably donated.

He had never been the menace Busby believed him to be. When he met Bourke in Sydney, the Governor was not impressed, and apparently unmoved by the Sovereign Lord's pretensions, did not oppose his entry onto his Hokianga estates. An altruistic lamb in a wilderness of land-hungry wolves, poor de Thierry dreamed of an industrious community presided over by his benevolent presence. But the dream faded swiftly, and with it his retainers, many of whom deserted to McDonnell within weeks of his arrival. Neither lust for power nor greed for gain seem to have inspired him, but rather an overweening faith in human nature — a serious handicap in any situation, and particularly so in early New Zealand society. After his initial disillusionment, he and his family lapsed into poverty and oblivion, re-appearing occasionally as courteous hosts to travellers. De Thierry became an indefatigable writer of petitions, memorials and appeals to New Zealand Governors and Land Claim Commissioners, seeking redress for the injustices he claimed to have suffered. At Mount Isabel, the home he named after his adored daughter, the family led a drab life until their residence there was rudely terminated in 1845, when Hone Heke's destruction of Kororareka resulted in their flight to Auckland with many other refugees from the North.[4]

Two months after de Thierry's arrival, Hokianga became host to another, and very different sort of settler, when the 60-ton Tahiti-built schooner *Raiatea* sailed into the harbour. Owned by the United States Consul at Tahiti, the vessel was under charter to the Catholic Vicar Apostolic of Western Oceania, the Right Reverend Jean Baptiste Pompallier, who had come to establish a mission in New Zealand. A French Catholic dignitary could scarcely have expected a warm reception in this stronghold of hostile Protestantism, but calmly, and with determination, Pompallier went about his appointed task. It was estimated that there were less than 100 Catholics in New Zealand on his arrival, but these loyally supported him, despite the violent opposition which he was said to have encountered.[5]

The place which the Vicar first chose for his establishment was at Totara Point, on the north-west side of the Hokianga, at the junction of the Mangamuka and Te Karae rivers. When news of this reached Sydney, Captain Cecile of the French corvette *Heroine* sailed at once for the Bay of Islands, where Pompallier met him. The French captain accorded the Vicar Apostolic a most deferential reception. Nevertheless, opposition among the Anglican and Methodist missionaries was very bitter, and there were frequent dark references made to 'The Scarlet Woman' and 'The Whore of Babylon'. But the Church does appear to have made good early progress, particularly on the north-west side of the harbour, where no Protestant station had been established, and with French naval forces and whalers in the Pacific, it had ample moral support.

With the arrival of three priests and three catechists in June 1839, the location of a headquarters at the Bay of Islands became possible. Pompallier wrote of the land purchase for this purpose:

With the funds that were brought me I bought a wooden house at the Bay of Islands with a small bit of land. This house was situated at Kororareka... I fixed then my residence at this place, and made it the head of the whole Apostolic Vicariate. This new establishment served at the same time as a store and as the principle mission station of all the missions confided to me.[6]

Other land at Kororareka was also acquired by Pompallier

on behalf of the church, but there was no further Catholic establishment in the town, apart from a small chapel on the site of which the shrine of St. Peter Chanel now stands. At Hokianga, Te Karae was abandoned almost at once in favour of another site further down the river, at Purakau, near the mouth of the Tapuae River, where the Church was later awarded a grant of 104 acres.

There is little of general interest in the Bishop's later activities at the Bay, where his impact was not considerable, due to his energetic promotion of his missions elsewhere, in which he rivalled Marsden in his energy and application. By 1846 the number of baptised Maoris is given as 5000, but the diverse interpretations of Christian doctrine and the obvious rancour against Catholicism must have puzzled the Maoris. If there is any truth in anecdotes to be found on the subject, some Maoris were not slow in taking advantage of the situation, artfully soliciting from those expounding the rival creeds, such small bribes as were offered for their conversion. And there is a ring of triumph in the minutes of an old Waimate baptismal register, which records the 'decontamination' by re-baptism of a group of former Catholic converts. But the Maoris were now turning to the Pakeha God, their confidence in the old gods shaken. Although it was not clear to them which of the sects He favoured most, He seemed at least to be giving the Europeans a better deal than the Maori gods were giving them.

On 16 February 1838 the French whaler *Jean Bart*, bound for the Chathams, and commanded by Captain Gateau, anchored at Kororareka, and she had no sooner done so than the first in a series of tragedies occurred. Having brought his ship to port, Gateau committed suicide. This left the *Jean Bart* under the command of the first mate, but piloted by an Englishman called Thomas Grimwood, who knew the Chathams, and so shortly afterwards the whaler left for the south. Nothing was heard of the vessel until 28 September, when the United States whaler *Rebecca Sims*, under Captain Ray, arrived at the Bay with the news that she had indeed reached her destination, and lay at Ocean Bay, in the Chatham Islands, destroyed by fire. Of her complement of 40 crew, there was no sign.[7]

At that time the corvette *Heroine* was at the Bay, commanded, as we know, by Pompallier's friend, Captain Cecile. Three vessels, the French whaler *Adele*, the *Rebecca Sims* and the *Heroine*, left for the scene of the disaster on 6 October. The American ship made the fastest passage and arrived 13 days later. A chief and his wife, six others, and an Englishman, the husband of one of the women, were enticed on board, and a scuffle broke out. One Maori was killed and the remainder taken prisoner. But from the prisoners, Ray learnt of the events that led to the destruction of the *Jean Bart*. When the whaler anchored, about 70 Maoris peaceably boarded her for trade and socialising, but the captain became alarmed at their number and got under way. This frightened the Maoris, and led to general fighting, in which 29 of them were killed and a further 20 wounded. The ship was then pillaged and burned. Although the Maoris admitted to killing only two crew members, no survivors were ever found, and since some of the boats were missing, it was assumed that having escaped, they were lost at sea.

Having this information, on 20 October, 20 armed men went ashore from the three ships and totally destroyed the Maori village, but its inhabitants had been forewarned and escaped to the forests. Cecile was convinced that the captain had brought this misfortune on himself and his crew, as had happened so often in the past.

Such incidents demonstrate that business in New Zealand, particularly in the Bay of Islands, was no British or American monopoly. Indeed, in 1838 some 30 American and at least 16 French whalers visited the South Island alone. Ashore, British capital predominated, but around the coast French and American interests prevailed. As a result, in 1838 the United States Secretary of State notified Clendon of their intention to appoint him as Consul to ensure the protection and interests of American citizens. It is therefore not difficult to appreciate the attitude of the non-British involved in New Zealand affairs after 1840, when their customary free entry and trade practices were suspended, and they became amenable to British law and liable to pay British imposts.

In 1838 Captain J. Langlois had purchased from Maori chiefs

a large area of Banks' Peninsula, on a deposit of 150 francs. He contracted to return later, which he did, and upon making final payment to the value of £234, took possession of the land on 14 August 1840. Following Langlois' original contract and deposit, the Nanto-Bordelaise Company was formed, financed by interests in Nantes, Bordeaux and Paris, and acquired Langlois' interest. Supported by a treaty with the French Government made in December 1839, an expedition was fitted out to go to New Zealand and colonize the South Island. The vessel, the *Comte de Paris,* did indeed arrive at Banks' Peninsula with French emigrants, but, as we shall see, the venture was forestalled by official British action here. Plainly, the French, at least, had territorial aspirations in New Zealand.[8]

But events were also going forward at the Bay, where the Kororareka Association had arisen out of the disorderly and unstable conditions there. This Association, which has been variously described as republican or vigilante, could by no means be defined as a government in the accepted sense, although the British authorities plainly distrusted its intentions. The Association's functions were clear enough — to protect the persons, goods and property of the residents of Kororareka who were its members.[9] Apparently Busby approved in principle of such an organisation when its formation was under discussion, but on discovering that it intended to form what he considered to be a local government having authority not only over its own members, but anyone it could enforce its will upon, he withdrew his approval.

There is no doubt that in practice the scheme achieved its objectives to a large degree, subduing the more anti-social elements of the town's permanent and floating population, although obviously its decisions favoured the interests of its members. The Association confined its jurisdiction to an area comprising roughly the whole of the peninsula upon which the present town of Russell is situated, northward of Matauwhi and the eastern end of Long Beach. The original membership was confined to residents of this area, but it soon included most of the substantial settlers in the Bay, including Gilbert Mair, who was president for a time.

The penal code of the Association was nothing if not vigorous.[10] Punishments for infringing its decrees varied from fines to locking the evil-doer in a sea-chest, or stripping, tarring and feathering him, then marching him up and down the streets and finally drumming him out of the town. But many undesirable social irregularities which did not interfere with business were apparently not deemed offences by the property-owners' security club. At times its powers were used to further its members' interests, as on an occasion when a man came from Sydney to collect a debt from one of the leaders of the Kororareka 'government'.[11] Upon his arrival, the Association decided that he had offended against its laws, and he was thereupon tried, convicted and duly tarred and feathered — all strictly in accordance with the local code of justice.

Despite the partisan attitude of the Association, it probably did contribute to peace and order in Kororareka. But a private army controlled by men who were not all scrupulous, could not be tolerated indefinitely, and disorders that were supported by sufficient force were beyond its power to prevent. The most notable incident of this sort was a violent affray which occurred in the township in August 1839, when the Association was at the height of its power.

The matter started prosaically enough with the discovery by Captain Lewis L. Bennett, of the American whaler *Hannibal,* that two of his men had deserted while the ship was at anchor, taking with them a boy named Benjamin Savage, who was in the special care of the captain.[12] About a week later, Bennett saw one of the deserters at the house of a grog-seller called Chalk. Bennett demanded that he return to the ship but the man refused, and was supported by some bystanders. This annoyed the Yankee skipper, and in defiance of the local 'government', went around the other ships in the harbour and recruited a small army with which to recapture his men. When the muster was complete it consisted of about 12 men from the *Hannibal,* reinforced by five boatloads from the *William Hamilton* and the *Richmond,* both of New Bedford. The party landed armed with cutlasses, pistols and muskets, and marching to the front of Chalk's house, unfurled the Stars and Stripes with due ceremony, and demanded the return of the men, together with stolen clothes and effects. The occupants of the house, undismayed, abused the array of might outside. With true American enterprise, Captain Bennett then gave orders that the house be removed from the men, since they would not remove themselves from it, and the troops went to work tearing off the weatherboards. By this means, a view of the interior was gained, and the clothes stolen from the *Hannibal* were revealed.

At this point, the Rev. Henry Williams, who was present, suggested that, having thus shown its strength, the army would gain its objectives without further violence. But this possibility was ruled out by the appearance of Chalk, very drunk and enraged by the rough treatment of his property. He '... attacked the party with most abusive language,' with some justification, it seems, whereupon the work of demolition, which had no doubt been suspended with reluctance, was resumed with renewed vigour.

Busby and Clendon, in their official capacities, reported on this incident, Clendon, probably in deference to his employer, noting the 'praiseworthy conduct' of Bennett in the matter. The deserters were recovered, since their retreat was dismantled to the stage where all that remained was the back wall and a few studs supporting the roof. Predictably, two casks of spirits were staved, and the total damage, according to the owner, was £50 — a modest estimate even for those days.

The position of the acting United States Consul at this time was no sinecure. There were about 100 American whalers on the coast, and they undoubtedly gave him plenty to do. Unlike the office of British Resident, this appointment provided, among other things, an allowance to aid distressed nationals and for other approved purposes. In July and August 1839 he effectively provided for the crew and officers of two wrecked whalers, the *Atlantic* and the *Brilliant*,[13] both of Warren, Rhode Island. His returns for that year to the Secretary of State of U.S. shipping at the Bay record the arrival and departure of 62 American vessels with cargoes of oil valued at $1,636,335, but a sharp decline in these figures occurred in the latter part of 1840, and early in 1841.[14] The complement of these 62 ships would probably be 1800 men. Add to this perhaps another 2500 on the British, French, colonial and Pacific Island vessels, and it is apparent that the business potential of the whalers and their crews was very considerable.

Clendon's acceptance of the United States appointment had been a clever move by a man who was probably at this time the most generally influential of all the Bay's residents, lay or missionary. How long the creation of the office had been under consideration prior to Clendon's appointment, is not clear, but he was advised of it in a despatch from the Secretary of State, dated 12 October 1838, and took up his duties on its receipt, in May 1839. Once appointed he gained a hold on the American trade that he could not have hoped for otherwise. All U.S. shipping reported to him on arrival at his Okiato establishment, where they got his services and he got their trade. Unhappily for Clendon this did not last, for about 18 months later he supported the new British Lieutenant-Governor Hobson, and probably anticipating another triumph for his business acumen, negotiated with Government representatives for the sale of Okiato as the seat of government, a transaction that was as disastrous for Clendon as it was embarrassing for the British Government. Furthermore, this neglect of his United States obligations discredited him there.

Clendon retained his appointment until 1842, when he was also a member of the New Zealand legislature – a farcical situation, since there was clearly a conflict of interests between the two parties he represented.

American citizens did not settle in New Zealand in any significant numbers. Settlement by British subjects had been largely from New South Wales, and the absence of American settlers was probably due to the remoteness of the bulk of the population, which was then concentrated on the Atlantic coast. And, of course the boundless opportunities for adventurous men on the American continent did not encourage their emigration.

It is difficult to accurately assess the value of the whale-trade to the Bay of Islands during this time. In 1839, immediately before the cession of sovereignty to the British Crown, the number of ships, including coastal traders, to visit the Bay, must have been well over 150. Using the American oil-value figures as a basis, cargoes of a total value of over £4,000,000 may have passed through the Bay, and without this business its economy would have collapsed. The timber and gum trades were not considerable, and there remained only the wood, water and garden produce of the old days. Although capital was available for investment, opportunities were limited. Commercial enterprises existed in sufficient number for immediate needs, and those with capital were therefore looking for land. Land-buying was thus taking place on an unprecedented scale all over New Zealand, and local settlers and imported land-sharks were in full cry. As a result, the Kororareka Land Company was formed in March 1839.[15] There was nothing unusual about this company, which was formed simply to buy land cheaply, subdivide it and sell it dearly. The first president was one W.V. Brewer, an imported capitalist, and the treasurer was Captain Clayton, a man long associated with Kororareka, and a consistent land purchaser. In 1840, another newcomer, Cornthwaite Hector, became president and solicitor, and from that time handled all the company's business. Hector's 1842 report of the company's land claims, showed that it had 35 shareholders owning 99 shares. The company sold 48 subdivided lots and three blocks of unsubdivided land, and there were also two auction sales, one in October 1839, the other in March 1840. In all, 11 parcels of land were purchased by the company, whose last transaction appears to have been a land purchase at Kororareka in October 1840. O.L.C. Plan 300 shows the location of its holdings.

Lang commented on the sale of lots at Kororareka at this time. 'The price of land even at present in the neighbourhood of the Bay of Islands . . . is from eight to ten shillings per acre: and for building allotments near the anchorage ground in that Bay, as much as a pound sterling per foot of frontage has already been paid for land having an extent of sixty feet back.'[16] This works out at £726 per acre, but reports on the per foot price of town lots seem to vary, probably according to their lineal depth.

Although there was little merit in the company's activities, they are important as those of the first known share company to be formed at the Bay. However, like many Bay of Islands businesses, it foundered after the seat of Government moved to

Auckland.

Another notable enterprise was the New Zealand Banking Company. This was floated in 1839, and commenced business on 4 September 1840, with its head office at Kororareka.[17] It was thus the first bank in New Zealand, and unlike the Land Company, it had possibilities as a useful public utility. Cash was not readily available in sufficient quantities for all transactions, and promissory notes were in common use. A reputable bank, then, had a potential for the service of shipmasters, the business community, and any one requiring loan accommodation.

The advertisement announcing the opening of the bank was published in the *New Zealand Advertiser and Bay of Islands Gazette*.[18] The nominal capital was £100,000 in 10,000 shares of £10 each, of which only about £8000 was ever paid up. Clendon was president, and Gilbert Mair and an American master-mariner, William Mayhew, were among the eight directors. Interest rates were 10% and 12½% for short-term and long-term loans respectively. However, interest paid to depositors was 4% on current accounts and 5% on fixed deposits, so that, all being well, the shareholders could expect handsome returns on their investments. The Government was obliged to pay the bank 12½–15% on a loan made to it when it was financially embarrassed in its early formative stage.

The life of the bank was short, and its fortunes deteriorated rapidly when, after 1840, the tide of business ebbed from the Bay of Islands and flowed correspondingly to the new town of Auckland. A large proportion of its investments were at the Bay, but in 1842 it moved its headquarters to Auckland, since at that time the population of the Bay was largely bankrupt. In March 1843 a resolution of the directors contemplated 'with alarm the frightful amount of overdue paper exhibited by the late returns from the Branch at Kororareka.'[19] This was equal to the whole paid-up capital of the bank, some £8278. The directors also observed 'with great pain that apparently little or no exertion is made to reduce that amount.' It appears that most of the Bank's Bay of Islands business after the transfer of the head office to Auckland, consisted of foreclosing on its clients' mortgages.

The bank was located at Bank Square, Turner's Terrace, this

being at the corner of the present Strand and Pitt Street.

The most undesirable feature of the emergent New Zealand economy was undoubtedly land speculation. The avaricious speculator, thwarted by government action in Australia, had directed his attention to New Zealand, where the Maoris, still with an insatiable appetite for European commodities, had not yet realised the true value of their land. The buying started in earnest about 1837 and continued into 1840, but was rudely terminated by a Proclamation issued on 19 January 1840 by Sir George Gipps, successor to Bourke, stating *inter alia* that all purchases of land thereafter made in New Zealand by British subjects would be considered null and void. This stopped an auction of 2000 acres at the Bay of Islands being conducted in the rooms of Hebblewhite and Vickers at Sydney.[20] However, much of the land at the Bay of Islands had already been purchased, generally by *bona fide* settlers, before the imported speculator commenced his large-scale operations.

Elsewhere in New Zealand, three of the more spectacular Australian speculators claimed to have purchased in 1839 over 33,000,000 acres, or about half of all the land in New Zealand, most of it in the South Island. Of these, Mr W.C. Wentworth, against whom Gipps waged a relentless war, was the most notable, and he seems to have thwarted the Governor's efforts to conclude a treaty of cession with Maori chiefs who were in Sydney at the time. This unsigned treaty is dated 14 February 1840, and was drawn up without the knowledge that Lieutenant William Hobson had already negotiated a similar treaty at Waitangi with local chiefs. Wentworth claimed to have purchased some 10,000,000 acres in the South Island.[21] Two Sydney businessmen, Edward and George Weller, also claimed to have acquired 1,750,000 and 1,450,000 acres respectively,[22] and the New Zealand Company 20,000,000 acres.[23] Another settler and speculator, William Webster, an American citizen, claimed 132,300 acres, mostly in the Hauraki Gulf.[24] All these transactions took place after 1837, although the 50,000 acres claimed by Busby was for land purchased between 1834 and 1840.

Although the scale of the missionary purchases at the Bay of

Islands and adjacent districts does not approach these in magnitude, many of them were very considerable by normal standards. Such acquisitions were also very contentious, since there was a large and responsible body of opinion that frowned on the acquisition of large areas of land at the expense of Maoris, by people who were expected to be dedicated to their well-being. Apologists for the missionaries claim that they needed the land to provide for their families, and that since they were the earliest in the field, they had the best right to acquire land. Had modest purchases been made by all, as indeed they were by some, both these arguments may have been valid. However, Yarwood suggests, in discussing Marsden's Australian estates, that 'the ruling passion for respectability [was] measured by landed property, and the concern of the newly rich to establish heirs in unchallenged affluence.'[25] There is little doubt that this influenced some of the New Zealand missionaries, and it would be fair to say that subscribers to the funds of the Church Missionary Society did not expect their money to be used to send men out to New Zealand to establish a landed gentry through the acquisition of Maori land. In some cases this did occur, but in many it did not, and these confounded the arguments of the others. Some of the larger missionary claims are given below. After some 20 years of contention, these were mostly settled by Commissioner Bell, who did not always award the total amount claimed. Most of the areas are from actual surveys, and are given in round figures.

Claimant	F.D. Bell Schedule No.	Area Claimed (acres)
John King	603-6	21,000
James Shepherd	802-6	19,000
James Kemp	594-8	12,000
J.D. Orsmond	809	11,700
Rev. Henry Williams	521-6	11,000
George Clarke	633-4	10,000
Rev. Charles Baker	545	6,260
Rev. Richard Davis	773	4,613
John Edmonds	172	3,962
The Mission Families	734-6	6,780

The Church Missionary Soc. 658-71: 676-78 <u>2,600</u>

108,915acres

John King's land includes some in Whangaroa.
James Shepherd's includes his Whangaroa land.
Charles Baker's includes his Mangakahia claim.
Orsmond was with the London Missionary Society, but the land was acquired with the assistance of Shepherd, his brother-in-law.

In addition to these purchases, the Rev. Richard Taylor acquired a very large area near North Cape, and W.T. Fairburn another to the south-east of Auckland. These totalled many tens of thousands of acres, and both were claimed to have been acquired to prevent trouble among rival Maori owners. The mission families' land was acquired by the Mission Society for the mission children.

In his letters to the Earl of Durham in 1839, Dr Lang wrote:

> Yes, my Lord, it is mortifying in the extreme, to any man of the least pretensions to Christian philanthropy, to reflect, that instead of endeavouring to protect the New Zealanders ... from the aggressions of unprincipled European adventurers, the Missionaries of the Church Missionary Society have themselves been the foremost and the most successful in despoiling them of their land.[26]

Lang had his prejudices, but was an honest, conscientious churchman, and there is no doubt that his views were widely shared. It would be idle to suggest that men of the calibre of Williams were ignorant of the degradation which would inevitably follow if the Maoris were deprived of their land and reduced to dependence on the pakeha. Yet by extensive land purchases, these missionaries became identified with the process by which this could well have occurred at that time, but for resolute action by the British Government. By these purchases they tarnished their own image.

Missionary purchases at the Bay of Islands comprised generally the whole of the present district of Kerikeri and those of Waimate, Ohaeawai, Pakaraka and Puketona — a large and fertile area which included some of the best land in North Auckland. This was joined to the Mission land at Paihia by a further large block of Williams' land on the southern side of the Waitangi River, separated from the Kerikeri land only by the river and by one of Busby's claims, which extended on the northern bank from Waitangi itself, almost to Waimate.

The attitude of the speculators is well exemplified in a letter which was sent to Gilbert Mair from an aspiring land-baron in Aberdeen,[27] dated 30 September 1839. This gentleman, John Smith, no less, had paid a passing visit to New Zealand, and confident that the British Government would soon bring the country under its control, was determined to be in the hunt while the opportunity remained. 'I am not desirous of obtaining a large piece of land,' he wrote, 'some 2000 or 3000 acres will answer my views for the present. Nor do I wish to get it for nothing, or next to nothing...' Mr Smith's concept of a fair price for the modest 2000 or 3000 acres is interesting. The total value of the axes, hoes, fish-hooks, knives and the like, with which the land was to be purchased, was £70-14-5d in Aberdeen. The Maori vendor also had to accept the cost of transporting the goods to New Zealand — dock dues, duties, insurances, bills of lading and shipping expenses — as part payment. In addition, this hard-headed Scot assessed a profit for himself on the goods amounting to £14, bringing the total value in New Zealand to £100-9-7d, i.e. 9½ pence per acre. If this was not next to nothing, it was certainly the next thing to it.

A common and thoughtless view on this matter is that the undeveloped land was not worth more than the paltry prices paid for it. Obviously the buyers knew its potential, or they would not have scrambled so eagerly for it. They merely took advantage of the Maoris' ignorance of the relative value of their land, compared to that of European manufactured goods. Interestingly, however, the inland Ngapuhi sold very little land that had not been acquired by conquest within the preceding century, and by 1840 they were still in possession of the 'ancestral' lands west of Waimate and Pakaraka.

Of the local proprietors outside Kororareka, only Polack, Busby and later Clendon, appear to have promoted towns on their land by subdivision into small lots. In 1839 Busby employed the surveyor Florance to subdivide his land at the Residency, hoping to sell the block to the Government when it became established, as the capital town. Henry Williams, whose relations with Busby were strained, was unimpressed by the proposal, which was ill-judged due to the exposed situation and want of a safe deep-water anchorage. Busby hopefully named his 'paper' town 'Victoria'. Polack's proposal for his land adjacent to Mair's at Te Wahapu seems to have come to nothing, and Clendon's, which could well have been undertaken with the same motive as Busby's, was superceded when the Government did, in fact, take his place over.

Into this scene of frantic land speculation came the newly formed New Zealand Company, risen from the ashes of former colonising ventures, and most recently, the 1837 New Zealand Association. Neither the Association nor the Company gained any support from the British Government, and its preparations for the formation of a New Zealand colony had no official approval. It also found itself opposed by the moribund Company of 1825. Nevertheless, on 2 May 1839 the Company was formally incorporated, and its survey-ship, the *Tory,* sailed three days later. Although the vessel was safely on its way, and committed to its mission, the Government was apparently unperturbed, and continued with its preparations to send Hobson to New Zealand as Consul. He had been appointed to the office in February 1839, but by mid-May, the decision had been made to acquire if possible the sovereignty of New Zealand from the Maori chiefs. Thus, towards the end of that year Hobson left England with a warrant naming him Lieutenant – Governor under Sir George Gipps, so that he could assume the government of any lands ceded to the Crown. Authority extending the boundaries of New South Wales to include New Zealand was then issued under the Great Seal of the United Kingdom. The matter had now assumed some urgency, since a 'republican' settlement, similar to that believed to have been created by the Kororareka Association, was developing at Port Nicholson (Wellington), but on a large and well-organised scale,[28] with much British capital invested.

Before he sailed from Sydney for the Bay of Islands, Hobson

took the oath as Lieutenant-Governor. Although he had no territory to govern, and no assurance or offer of land from the Maoris, a sizeable staff accompanied him. Included were a Treasurer, a Collector of Customs, a Police Magistrate, a secretary, a clerk, and an unimpressive army comprising a sergeant and four troopers of the New South Wales Mounted Police. Also included was Mr Felton Mathew, as Acting Surveyor, from whose garrulous diaries much information has been gained.

On 29 January 1840, this entourage arrived at the Bay. Its task was, in some way, to acquire the sovereignty of the country from its people, and as it turned out, this responsibility rested on the shoulders of a man in poor health. Antagonism from some quarters was expected, since, as we have seen, Sir George Gipps' Proclamation of 19 January had invalidated the land titles held by British subjects, pending their confirmation and the issue of grants by the Crown. Hobson was to deal only with the Maoris, in whom it was presumed the sovereignty of all land was vested. The only advice available to him was that of Busby and the missionaries, particularly Henry Williams as their executive head. The Maoris, however, had no disinterested advice available to them, and had it been, it could have proved most embarrassing to Hobson.

---

1. Sherrin and Wallace, *Early History of New Zealand,* p.166-8.
2. See Appendices 1.4 and 1.6.
3. Bell, F.D. Old Land Claim File No. 455.
4. De Thierry, C.P.H. 'Historical Narrative of an Attempt to Form a Settlement in New Zealand.' (Auck. Pub.Lib).
5. Pompallier, J.B. *History of the Catholic Church in Oceania.*
6. Ibid.
7. McNab, *The Old Whaling Days,* p.250-9.
8. Wards, *The Shadow of the Land,* p.17., and Sweetman, S. *The Unsigned New Zealand Treaty,* pp.44-7.
9. Sherrin and Wallace, p.470-2.
10. See Appendix 5.
11. Martin, S. McD. *New Zealand in a Series of Letters.*

12. McNab, *Historical Records* v.2, p.608-9.
13. Ibid, pp.605-7.
14. Ibid, pp.604-622.
15. Ross, R.M., Personal records in A.I. Library derived from O.L.C. File No. 340, National Archives.
16. Lang, *New Zealand in 1839*, (1873), p.67.
17. Moore and Barton, *Banking in New Zealand,* p.5-7.
18. Issue of 8 September 1840.
19. Moore and Barton, *Banking in New Zealand*, p.5-7.
20. Sweetman, E. *The Unsigned New Zealand Treaty*, p.55-8.
21. Bell, op.cit., Nos. 497-509. Sweetman, p.65.
22. Bell, op.cit., Nos. 482-95.
23. Wilson, E.W. *Land Problems of the New Zealand Settlers in the Forties*, p.23.
24. Bell, op.cit., Nos 714-727.
25. Yarwood, *Samuel Marsden, The Great Survivor* p.226-7.
26. Lang, p.28.
27. Mair Papers. (Auck.).
28. Wards, pp.18-27.

19

Climax

THUS, THE 40 and more years of steadily increasing shipping and mercantile activity had brought the political situation in New Zealand to this interesting point, when HMS *Herald*, with Hobson and his staff on board, dropped anchor in Kororareka Bay.

The first visitors to the ship were Busby and three of the missionaries, who formed the 'ways and means' committee to deal with immediate problems. On the next day Pompallier came aboard, and his visit probably did little to relieve Hobson of his anxieties concerning French intentions here. In his diary, Felton Mathew noted that when the *Herald* arrived, the French tricolour was flying on a flagstaff on 'Kororareka Point'. 'The sight of this made our Governor look rather blue, for he begins to think that the French may have anticipated us, and that perhaps *L'Artemise* is lying at anchor in the harbour.'[1] But the flag, according to the missionaries, simply indicated the presence of Pompallier's church, although Hobson's reaction indicates the prevalent apprehension of French intervention.

Hobson immediately wrote to the Rev. H. Williams at Waimate, explaining his official business, and summoning him to return without delay. Then, despite Busby's opinion that the chiefs of the 'Confederation' could not be summoned in less than 10 days, Hobson, on the day after his arrival, went ashore and publicly read his Commission as Lieutenant-Governor and also the Queen's Commission conferring on the New South Wales Government jurisdiction over New Zealand. Governor Gipp's Proclamation relative to land tenure was also read.[2] This took place in the Kororareka Anglican church on 30 January in the presence of about 300 Europeans and 100 Maoris, whereupon Hobson became the executive head of a hypothetical territory in New Zealand. This was precipitate action, but obviously considered necessary due to the possibility of impending foreign action, since both French and United States naval strength in or close to New Zealand waters outnumbered Hobson's unimpressive force.

Apart from a polite semi-official welcome, the reception accorded the embryo government was not encouraging. The clamour for protection had subsided somewhat during the preceding two years, due to the Kororareka Association's activities. There was also a growing apprehension that a properly constituted government might threaten some avenues of enterprise, as indeed proved to be so. Dr Johnson, the Colonial Surgeon, who arrived in the *Westminister* in March, noted in his journal:

> The arrival of an established government caused universal consternation. The storekeepers and grog-sellers were not certain that their trade would be improved, the 'Land Sharks' saw their 'occupation gone'. . . the runaway sailors imagined that there might be a possibility of their being delivered up to their ships and the Convicts slunk off to the bush without delay.
>
> The officers of the Government were received therefore with fear and dislike which was very visible on our landing.[3]

There were those, however, who after the initial shock capitalised on the situation, and a short period of wild prosperity followed at Kororareka itself. But a sullenness prevailed among both Europeans and Maoris, an attitude that was to persist at the Bay throughout the five dreary years to come.

A meeting on 5 February at the Residency at Waitangi, between the officers of the Crown and the Maori chiefs, was attended by about 1500 persons, Maori and European, and on the following day, the Treaty was submitted to a further meeting for signature by the chiefs.[4] The Treaty itself has been discussed and dissected by many historians, and it is therefore not intended to discuss here, except in general terms, its merits or its subsequent interpretation, nor the motives behind the arguments advanced in its favour at the time. The missionaries and Busby were, of course, the main props of Hobson's debating team, and a good deal of rancour was aired. A crisis occurred in the lives of the missionaries, when at the opening of the talks, Bishop Pompallier appeared to be about to forestall them, by establishing himself in a privileged position at the meeting, but mercifully, this calamity was averted. 'No,' the Rev. Richard Taylor had declaimed, 'I'll never follow Rome.'[5]

The meeting of 5 February was held in a marquee of sails and spars set up in front of Busby's house. A rough draft of a treaty was first submitted to Hobson by Busby, and after consulting his advisors Hobson passed an approved draft to H. Williams, whose son Edward translated it into Maori. It was necessary that both versions should have precisely the same meaning, and convey the Governor's intention without ambiguity — something difficult to achieve, if indeed, it was achieved. Hobson then addressed the assembly and read the Treaty in English, and Williams followed in Maori. Busby then said a few appropriate words, and the assembled chiefs, ever ready for ceremonial oratory, took up the discussion. Te Kemara (Campbell or Kaiteke or Tareha) at once accused Williams and Busby of depriving him of his land. 'Thou, thou, thou, thou bald-headed man, thou hast got my land,' he roared at Williams. Mr Busby received similar embarrassing attention, and both men hastened to justify their land dealings. Here, Williams made his much quoted statement that the missionaries had a prior claim to land, as they had 'laboured for so many years in this land when others were afraid to show their noses.' This extravagant claim could not be substantiated, since we know that for more than a dozen years the missionaries had been a minority group in the Bay's European population, and that the whalers, upon whom the early missionaries had relied so heavily for their very existence, had freely used the Bay and mixed with the Maori people for 40 years. Indeed, the only real pioneer missionary left was John King, still at Te Puna.

Then Wai, a Ngaitawake Ngapuhi, spoke up: 'To thee, O Governor! this. Will you remedy the selling, the exchanging, the cheating, the lying, the stealing of the whites?' Oratory in similar vein continued. In fact, so little of the actual terms of the Treaty seem to have been discussed, that the meeting appears to have degenerated into an occasion for airing grievances and general preferences, such was the tenor of the discussion. There were several interruptions from Europeans who considered that Williams was not translating the Maori speeches for the Governor fairly and accurately, but none, on Hobson's invitation, seemed willing to assume the task. It is difficult to determine why, in fact, many of the chiefs signed the Treaty, or if they understood its implications at that stage. Most of the speeches appear to have been hostile, but Hobson seemed pleased when he adjourned the meeting until 7 February to allow the Maoris time to discuss and consider the Treaty, which was in its intent, a document calculated to preserve for the Maori his existing lands, rights and privileges. It did, however, contain a provision important to the Crown, and theoretically to the Maoris — since it was intended to protect them from land-sharks. This provided, or was certainly intended to provide, that Maori land was to be sold only to the Crown.[6] As time went on, however, the Maori discovered the disadvantages involved in having access to only one purchaser. The other two articles of the Treaty provided for the cession of the sovereignty of New Zealand by the Maori people, and the vesting of it in the Crown, and the extension of the Crown's law and protection to the Maoris and to their '. . . lands and estates, forests, fisheries and other properties . . . ' (English version.)

The day which Hobson allowed for discussion was vetoed by the missionaries, because they feared that the Maoris would disperse before the appointed resumption at Waitangi, due to a general shortage of food, since no one had come supplied for a protracted stay. The missionaries may also have suspected that the chiefs' interest could not be sustained, and that prompt action was necessary if success was to be achieved.

On 6 February, then, all parties assembled again at the marquee, and the chiefs were invited to sign. Hobson gave the important assurance that all religious persuasions would be on an equal footing, but at this point, William Colenso, the mission printer and probably the most talented of the mission people, expressed grave doubts that the Maoris understood the significance of the Treaty at all. This was by no means a remote possibility. The Maoris were an undisciplined people, and it is

224

unlikely that they contemplated, or even understood, sub-mission to government of any sort, since the only law they recognised or understood was their own custom. Colenso did not consider that they should be permitted to sign merely on the advice of the missionaries, whom they trusted, without having them carefully explain the Treaty. He felt that if they signed, it should be at their own free will and not on the prompting of the missionaries. Busby, on the other hand, had no qualms of conscience, and stated that he was quite happy that they should sign on his and the missionaries' advice.

The strange scene, the conflicting arguments, and the tension and uncertainty of the situation in which he was involved so deeply, and for which he alone was responsible, had no doubt worn Hobson's patience very thin; and he was clearly in no mood for Colenso's moralising, in spite of the disturbing matter it raised. 'If the Native chiefs do not know the contents of this Treaty it is no fault of mine,' he said. This was indeed true, for he had given a day for discussion but had been over-ruled by mission officials. So Colenso, having satisfied the dictates of his conscience was silent, and the signing began. The mark of the Ngatihine chief Kawiti appears at the head of the signatories, and is followed by others who affixed their names or marks — often a facsimile of their face tattoo, or *moko*, or part of it.

With such names as Kaiteke, Nene, Patuone, Heke, Kawiti, Rewa and other influential chiefs on the Treaty, the chances for its success at the Bay of Islands and Hokianga seemed good, but prior to the meetings, Hobson's situation had been very un-certain, since it was doubtful if the chiefs would have signed but for the persuasion of Busby, Clendon, and the missionaries. Pompallier, asserting that politics had no place in missionary activities, appeared entirely disinterested; although Rewa later told Colenso that the Bishop had advised him not to sign.

An active and patriotic United States Consul, with Clendon's influence, may have seriously embarrassed England's plans in New Zealand, but on his own admission, Clendon persuaded many chiefs to sign Hobson's Treaty. This drew comment from Commander Wilkes, who was at the Bay shortly afterwards:

The circumstances that have occurred at New Zealand fully

prove the necessity of having American citizens as our consuls abroad. Mr J.R. Clendon, our consul at New Zealand, an independent state, and the only representative of a foreign power, whose interest was at stake, was consulted by some of the most powerful and influential chiefs, who had refused to sign the treaty of cession to Great Britain. They came to Mr Clendon for advice, how they should act, and he admitted that he had advised them to sign, telling them that it would be for their good. He himself signed the Treaty as a witness, and did all he could to carry it into effect; but in doing this, he said, he had acted as a private citizen, by request of the Governor, thus separating his public duties from his private acts. At the same time he buys large tracts of land, for a few trifles, and expects to have his titles confirmed as Consul of the United States.[7]

Some days later, the Governor and his party proceeded inland to Waimate and Hokianga, where more chiefs appended their signatures to the Treaty. The entourage then went down the coast to the Waitemata, leaving the Bay of Islands on 20 February, and here the last signatures on the original document were obtained. Subsequent signings were on copies or loose sheets. At Waitemata, Hobson initiated an investigation of the harbour with a view to establishing his capital there, during which he suffered a paralytic stroke which left the administration, such as it then was, in the hands of officials for a month, under the direction of Willoughby Shortland. The contentious purchase of Clendon's Okiato for the temporary seat of government was negotiated while Hobson was at Waimate, tended by the C.M.S. surgeon, and in a serious condition.

A situation had developed between Hobson and Captain Joseph Nias of the *Herald*, arising from their incompatibility and the jealousy of each for the other's individual authority. Both held the same naval rank, but Nias was in command of the ship which was Hobson's only means of transport, and maintained his authority allegedly with scant regard for some of the Lieutenant-Governor's wishes. This led Hobson to take an unfavourable view of Nias' conduct, and finally to accuse him of obstruction. However, while Nias probably never in any way exceeded his authority, he does not appear to have been particularly helpful in the period preceeding Hobson's illness. On the other hand, Hobson was, according to one observer, '...very jealous of his authority and obstinate.'[8] An earlier incident that did nothing to improve the relations between the two men occurred prior to Hobson's initial landing at Kororareka, when he demanded a 13-gun salute, to which a Lieutenant-Governor was entitled. Nias refused this request, but accorded him 11 guns, although a Consul rated only seven, and a Consul was what Nias considered him to be, at that stage.

The sporadic clashes that followed resulted in a civil action in which the New South Wales Government, on Nias' behalf, sued the editor of the *Sydney Gazette* for libel. The journal had published an account of Nias' activities in New Zealand which was considered damaging to his status as a naval officer. This account was contributed by a correspondent at the Bay of Islands, whose intemperate reports, while no doubt improving the circulation of the *Gazette*, were the cause of its luckless editor being fined £200 and cast into jail for 12 months.[9]

The onset of Hobson's illness followed these disagreements, and thereupon Nias returned to Sydney to acquaint Governor Gipps of the situation in New Zealand, and to refit his ship. Gipps was, of course, very concerned lest Hobson's death should leave the infant colony without an executive head at this precarious stage of its life. He therefore instructed Major Bunbury, an ex-Governor of Norfolk Island, to go to New Zealand, taking with him a detachment of the 80th Regiment consisting of two subalterns, four sergeants, two drummers and 80 rank and file. He was to assume control should Hobson not be capable. This force, accompanied by Mrs Hobson, arrived at the Bay in HMS *Buffalo* on 16 April, at a stage when the Lieutenant-Governor had recovered sufficiently to resume some of his duties. The *Herald*, with Nias in command, also returned to the Bay in April, and under Hobson's instructions, proceeded with Bunbury on a voyage to the South Island, where further signatures to the Treaty were obtained.

On 17 March, the *Westminister* arrived at the Bay, bringing the tradesmen and labourers necessary to build a proper establishment for the Government. Also on this vessel, was the Colonial Surgeon Dr. John Johnson, who proceeded immediately to Waimate to attend Hobson, whom he found much improved.

At this time a murder occurred at Puketona, some seven miles inland from Paihia. The victim was a shepherd employed by the Williams family, and the deed was traced to a Maori named Kihi, whose case duly came up for hearing at Kororareka. At one stage of these proceedings, Maoris demanded Kihi so that they themselves might kill him, but it was only when Bunbury's redcoats intervened that the court was able to proceed, and Kihi was committed for trial. Kihi was clearly a man of no account among Maoris.[10]

A significant commentary on the mood of the local Maoris several months after the signing of the Treaty, is to be found in Dr Johnson's journal:

> It appears that the Tyami [Taiamai or Ohaeawai] tribe, wished to build a pah on a headland in a lake [Owhareiti] which was in the possession of Mr [the Rev. Henry] Williams and had commenced the stockade. The sons of this gentleman who had a fine farm near it at Pakaraka threatened to burn it down, it appears that had they done this, the Tyami people intended to have shot them, that a party had gone armed for that purpose, had they done so these savages (for they are a turbulent tribe) meant to have hurried on to Pakaraka to have murdered all there, to have pushed on to Waimati where all were to have shared the same fate and to have established themselves there until they could be joined by other tribes — also that it was mooted, to form a confederation to make a general attack on the English in December, when their potatoes would be ripe and they could have provisions.[11]

In April, Johnson went to Kaitaia with Shortland to obtain further signatures for the Treaty, and there, the story was corroborated by the chief Nopera Panakareao who informed them:

> ... that a conspiracy to compel the Governor to abandon the

Island had been attempted to be formed by some of the Ngapuhi chiefs who had not signed the Treaty of Waitangi, especially one named Kawiti who resides on the Kawa Kawa, some of the Hokianga chiefs had also been engaged and overtures had been made to him (Nopero), through his Wife who had lately been on a visit to Hokianga. He said they had been urged to it by the Pakeha Maoris who were bad men and had spread many falsehoods.[12]

Clearly, there were many disaffected Maori chiefs, nor was the assumption of government by Great Britain proving as universally popular as had been initially assumed when the Treaty was signed at Waitangi. An interesting situation now existed. But contrary to Johnson's information, Kawiti did, in fact, sign the Treaty. He and many like him probably signed, as Colenso had suggested, without knowledge of the significance of their actions, and henceforth he was to be the most bitter of the Government's enemies. Nor was this unrest a transient thing, as it smouldered, to the manifest alarm of the European settlers in the North during the ensuing five years, and culminated in Heke's War.

Such was the situation while Hobson was convalescing at one of the mission houses at Paihia. He had previously declined Busby's open-handed offer of his own house at Waitangi, containing at the time but two main rooms, at a rental of £200 per year — a princely sum in those times. This offer had been made, and accepted provisionally, soon after Hobson's arrival in January, no doubt with a view to also persuading the Governor to take over the Residency and turn it into the seat of Government.[13]

That Hobson never seriously considered the Bay of Islands as a permanent location for his capital is certain, and this was apparent when Mathew visited the Waitemata in April and explored the harbour with the object of selecting a suitable site for the future capital. On 23 March, in his capacity of Acting-Surveyor, he reported on his investigations to date in this matter, condemning the Bay of Islands as a possible site for the capital, mainly because of its position at the extreme end of the country.[14] Nevertheless, he did recommend that because of the concentration of European population, a Government establishment should be located there, which would serve until the permanent capital should be built. The report rejected Busby's Victoria out of hand, but negotiations for a site for a Government establishment at Kororareka were initiated. On this matter, Bunbury wrote:

> Unfortunately some differences had arisen between him [Hobson] and the inhabitants [of Kororareka], regarding particular sites he wished to be given up for the erection of public buildings; although with a little more conciliation, the difficulty might I think have been adjusted. As it was, it ended in his selecting a site for the principal town five miles up the harbour, which he called Russell, in honour of the minister, and had he succeeded in prevailing on the people to build, this would materially have injured the trade and prosperity of Kororareka.[15]

The purchase of the site of Russell at Okiato was evidently arranged between Clendon and Mathew, during Hobson's illness, and the transaction was approved by him on 23 April, while he was at Paihia. The buildings, a large store, a dwelling-house, two cottages, a blacksmith's and a carpenter's shop, were valued at £13,000, and the land at £2000. There was also a jetty in front of the store, which faced down the river towards Waitangi. Certainly, the price demanded for the buildings seems excessive for 1840, and for the land extremely so, since it had been bought by Clendon eight years earlier for £180.[16] As it was, the deal proved calamitous for both parties. Clendon received only the first instalment of £1000, before Governor Gipps intervened and refused to approve the transaction, primarily because Clendon's title to the land had not been established in accordance with Gipps' Proclamation. Mathew had already completed a survey, laying out the site of the town, and all was in readiness for the first sale of lots on 12 October, when the announcement of its postponement appeared in the *New Zealand Advertiser and Bay of Islands Gazette,* on 24 September. Despite this, the government remained in possession, and Clendon's claim was finally settled in July 1841 for a further £1250 in cash, and a grant of 10,000 acres of land between Papatoetoe and Manurewa. Nevertheless, the deal evoked piteous complaints from him for many years.[17]

Gilbert Mair also offered his well-developed property for £13,990, but Mathew did not entertain the idea. The survey of Okiato was carried out in July 1840, and the new town was named in honour of the Secretary of State, Lord John Russell. Some 80-90 subdivided building lots were set out in the township site, and larger allotments were allocated to the 'suburbs' in the higher ground. Jail, police station, church, customs, abattoir, hospital, cemetery and barracks were provided for. The street names were Bedford Street, Hobson Street, Melbourne Street, William Street and Emma Place,[18] none of which were constructed. Although clear ground evidence of Clendon's original establishment remained before it was obliterated some time after 1946, not one building, or for that matter, road, was built by the Government during the whole of its occupancy, from the beginning of April 1840, when the workforce was landed from the *Westminister* at Pipiroa Bay, until the whole place was abandoned in May 1842.[19]

On 20 April 1840 Bunbury's troops were put ashore, and made a camp '. . .near the proposed site of the Governor's residence and that of the police offices.' The soldiers' camp was a miserable and temporary affair, until September 1840 when most of the troops shifted to permanent quarters in Auckland. Until recent development occurred, there was clear evidence of their occupation, and round sites of their tents could be located. Numerous tunic-buttons and hat badges have been found on the property.

Hobson and his entourage, who had been accommodated in Kororareka lodgings, about which they complained bitterly, took possession of the new 'capital' at about the end of April or early May. It seems, though, that Customs still remained at Kororareka, and the office appears to have been built twice, the first attempt being stopped by the chief Rewa, who maintained that the site was *tapu* ground. It was finally located on a portion of Polack's land at the extreme north end of the beach. The Government bonded-store was later re-established at Koro-

231

rareka, its location at Russell being too remote to adequately perform its function. However the Post Office transferred from Kororareka to Russell in September, where it remained until the shift to Auckland in February 1841. Until that date, the government of New Zealand was conducted from Russell, although some officials remained there after the shift to Auckland.

Two ships of the United States Exploring Expedition were at the Bay to witness the birth-pangs of the new Government. Their presence, and that of other foreign naval forces visiting the harbour during the first few months of this period, demonstrate the embarrassing predicament Hobson now faced. While no overt hostile action was taken by any power, there was a growing apprehension, reflected in the precautions Bunbury took. The Major, alarmed by the superior French naval forces on the coast of New Zealand, wrote from the Bay to his Major-General in New South Wales, asking for instructions in the event of hostilities between England and France. He was ordered, in such an eventuality, to retire to the interior, but not to abandon the country. By this time his total force was only 109, including himself.

The United States naval vessels *Porpoise* and *Flying Fish* had been at the Bay since 24 February, two and a half weeks after the signing of the Treaty. On 30 March they were joined by Wilkes, the commander of the expedition, with the *Vincennes*.[20] The squadron left on 6 April, but had been gone little over a fortnight, when the *Astrolabe*, of the French Antarctic Expedition, dropped anchor at the Bay.[21] It was learned with relief by the almost defenceless Government that this expedition had not claimed any land for France in New Zealand. The ships did not stay long, departing on the 4 May without complicating Hobson's task in any way. He was now left in peace for some two months, and on 2 July, Nias brought the *Herald* and Major Bunbury back from the South Island, in company with HMS *Britomart*, under Captain Owen Stanley, which had come from Sydney. The *Herald* then left for Sydney, but Nias, aware of Hobson's situation, had spoken to the commander of HMS *Favourite* while in Cloudy Bay, instructing him to put himself at the Lieutenant-Governor's disposal.

In July, while the *Britomart* was at the Bay, the French frigate *L'Aube*, under Captain Lavaud, arrived. This did cause a stir, since *L'Aube* was acting in company with the French immigrant ship *Compte de Paris*, which was already on its way tò New Zealand to found a colony at Akaroa for the Nanto-Bordelaise Company. The situation was further aggravated by Lavaud's refusal to acknowledge Hobson's authority, having no instructions from his Government to do so. Discussions took place at Russell, and since neither knew the other's language, Pompallier acted as interpreter. Lavaud, of course, was concerned that the interests of the French settlement should be protected.[22]

Although Hobson had issued a proclamation at Russell in May, taking possession of the whole of New Zealand in the Queen's name, he was now alarmed at developments at Akaroa, and instructed Captain Stanley to proceed there at once and take formal possession. So, unknown to Lavaud, the *Britomart* unobtrusively left the Bay, and arrived at Akaroa five days ahead of him. On 17 August, two days after Lavaud, the *Comte de Paris*, with its hopeful immigrants, also made Akaroa. However, at that stage the issue of sovereignty was no longer in doubt. The incident was reported in the 1 October issue of the *Bay of Islands Gazette*. 'We understand,' the account reads, '. . .that the *Britomart* was considerably injured in her haste.' Although the French settlers were greatly upset by these developments, the Nanto-Bordelaise Company's claims were later settled, leaving them little worse off.

The problem of the New Zealand Company's 'republican' settlement at Port Nicholson (Wellington) had also been disposed of satisfactorily, when on 3 May, Hobson issued another proclamation requiring that the settlers acknowledge the Queen's authority. The trading vessel *Integrity* was chartered to take the Colonial Secretary to Wellington to publish the proclamation, and no difficulty was encountered here.[23]

The harrassed Governor now had a little time in which to direct operations at the Waitemata. By August a decision had been made as to the site of the capital and preparations for building were in hand.

Despite the hostile attitude of the settlers at Kororareka at the time of the Government's shaky inauguration, it seems that now the township had entered upon a period of considerable but transient prosperity, reflected in the columns of the *New Zealand Advertiser and Bay of Islands Gazette*. This folio-sized four-page paper was first issued in June 1840 by G.A. Eagar and Co. From its first issue, the paper had been used for the publication of Government Gazettes, and a notice to this effect signed by Hobson, and dated 12 June, appeared in the first issue. However, on 30 December 1840, a *Gazette Extraordinary* was issued by the Government, and printed on the mission press at Paihia, in which a notice appeared, announcing that '. . .in consequence of the editors of the *New Zealand Advertiser and Bay of Islands Gazette* having declined publishing any advertisements for Her Majesty's Government, all communications from this Government inserted in the *Gazette Extraordinary* are to be deemed official.' The next issue of this Gazette was published at Kororareka, presumably on a government press, and was called the *New Zealand Government Gazette*. The Gazette was published at Kororareka until late 1842, although the capital had by then moved to Auckland, eliciting bitter reproaches from the *Auckland Times* of 18 October 1842. The Government Printer, it claimed, was 'kicking his heels' up at the Bay, when he should have been grinding out his Gazettes in Auckland.

Until the end of 1840, business thrived at Kororareka. Properties changed hands, new businesses opened, and there appeared a flock of new names unheard of before 1840. In May 1840 Dr Jameson described the township:

I found the aspect of Kororareka considerably altered since I left it, two months previously. The British ensign was hoisted on the beach, numerous tents pitched beside the town, and, in addition to the 'old familiar faces', there were many newcomers, whose presence gave to the little settlement an air of bustle and animation. To complete the metamorphosis, the appearance of a policeman, sauntering along with an idle step, but with busy and searching eyes, indicated clearly that the occupation of the old tarring and feathering association was gone for ever. Moreover, the price of building allotments had more than doubled, and all the materials of building were in strong demand at exorbitant prices, circumstances strongly indicative of a prevailing impression that a numerous population would forthwith arrive in New Zealand. There was also an increased number of stores and shops. Bakehouses and butchers' stalls had been established, and regular ferry boats plied between Kororareka and the neighbouring settlements of Paihia and Russell, a locality four miles distant where, for the present, the Government offices were established, on the premises of the American consul.[24]

Nevertheless, there was still considerable resentment over Gipps' Proclamation, which denied legal title to land claimants until their claims had been approved by a Commission yet to be appointed. A correspondent for the *Advertiser* reported that he had '. . .lately heard it gravely stated by a Magistrate on the Bench, at Kororarika, that he "did not consider that there was such a thing as property at present in New Zealand to be protected by law, and that, therefore, the plaintiff [in the case being considered] could expect no redress".' Even the old Kororareka Association, with its raupo 'feathers' and tar, could do better than this.

Despite the uncertainty as to title, one William Wilson advertised that he would auction on 19 October, 'that well-known and highly desirable property, situated at the corner of Hobson and Victoria Streets, known as the Royal Hotel.' Another *Advertiser* notice announced the opening of the 'Hobson Hotel, Matavia Bay . . . on the high road to Russell Town . . .'

Mention is also made of a small settlement now called English Bay, close to Opua. It is called 'Tawkainga', and is described as situated 'Opposite Russell Town'. Here were in residence J.E. Bright, M.R.C.S., and Messrs Black and Green, who had unlimited qualities of timber for sale.

The character of the town had clearly changed in a few months. No longer was it a village of brothels and grog shops, but had instead become 'respectable' with the influx of ambitious businessmen. Its optimistic citizens now went about their affairs, with their newspapers, hotels, billiard saloons, Land Company and Bank, and most of the trappings of a small mercantile town — an economy preparing itself for the march of progress that never eventuated. By October 1840, reaction was apparent. For practical purposes the Land Company had already expired and those businessmen in a position to do so were now moving to Auckland. The whaleships, at least, kept coming, albeit in reduced numbers but they at least kept the town alive.

Probably the most ambitious business venture launched in the North till then occurred at this time. In 1839 Busby purchased some 40-50,000 acres at Ngunguru and Whangarei, and in partnership with Mair, imported saw-milling machinery at a cost of £730 to work the timber on the land.[25] An agreement was drawn up in March 1840, by which Busby was to conduct the business at Ngunguru on a salary of £150, and Mair, at the Bay of Islands, was to see to the disposal of the timber. The mill machinery cost about £750, and the total capital cost of the project, including the land, was nearly £2000. Mair's salary was to cover the use of his own 'timber yards, docks, wharves or premises.' A William James Lewington was appointed manager at £150 a year, given an equal share. He appears to have handled the shipping. Although assigned to Ngunguru, Busby spent the whole of his time from March to the end of 1840 in New South Wales. He reported in May that timber was on the rise there, but in June, when the first shipment of milled timber arrived at Sydney, he gloomily reported that there was little chance of realising the freight and demurrage charges incurred. But the mill had its part in the building of Auckland. A Government order of 12 December 1840 instructed Mair to deliver to the Superintendant of Works at Auckland, 16,000 feet of 'Koudi Plank' and 6000 feet of scantling. The venture deserved a better fate than it suffered. It apparently collapsed in the financial failure at the Bay of Islands in 1844, when the Bank applied pressure to its debtors there.

Nearly all enterprise in the North declined in the same way, once the fateful decision on the site of the capital had been made. On 13 September 1840, the barque *Anna Watson* sailed from the Bay with 32 tradesmen and labourers who had been camped in tents at Russell since March. These people were the founders of Auckland, some 80-90 persons including 28 children, of whom 19 were under 10 years old. On 18 September, formal possession was taken of the site of the town, and within two months of the arrival of the pioneers, Mathew had completed the survey of Auckland.[26] With its interesting, although much-maligned street layout, and its many hundreds of building lots, the plan was ready by November, and was approved by Hobson, who was now dividing his time between Auckland and Russell.

Although ambitious plans had been proposed for Russell, it was never more than a temporary expedient. The exodus of officials commenced in February 1841, when the Colonial Secretary and his department moved to Auckland. They were followed in March by the Governor and his family, who had been in residence at Russell for nearly a year. This left the erstwhile capital of New Zealand occupied by only small detachment of soldiers of the 80th Regiment left behind by Bunbury, and Mr Wellman, the Police Magistrate, and his retainers. Bunbury had transferred all but 20 of his men to Auckland, away from their camp in Russell. Since its inception, not one person had settled near the confines of Russell, which had become '. . .a city only in name.'[27] Bunbury's troops had lived in a primitive rustic barrack there, of which he complained, '. . . I dreaded in the delapidated condition our tents were, that the men should have to remain in that boistrous climate, another winter without cover.' Clearly Hobson did not intend to spend any money on his Bay of Islands town.

In the meantime, to the consternation of both *bona fide* land claimants and speculators throughout New Zealand, the intentions of Governor Gipps' Proclamation had been clarified by an Act of 22 August 1840, passed by the New South Wales Legislative Assembly. This provided for the appointment of a Commission to examine and report on land claims in New Zealand, and to recommend grants where it considered them valid. None, however, were to exceed 2560 acres (four square miles) unless in exceptional circumstances.[28] Messrs. Godfrey and Richmond were appointed as Commissioners. However, the Act did not arrive in England soon enough to receive the Queen's consent before New Zealand was erected to a separate colony. Hobson, now Governor, was obliged to enact legislation with similar objectives, which he did by introducing and passing his Land Claims Ordinance. This followed the New South Wales Act closely, and re-appointed Gipps' Commissioners. Under the ordinance, grants were allowed up to 2560 acres on the basis of a sliding scale of land values, so that land purchased between 1815 and 1824 was assessed at six pence per acre, and that in 1839 at four to eight shillings per acre, with land acquired in the intervening period valued *pro rata*.

Claimants were granted only such land as they had paid for at the scale quoted above. If, for instance, a claim was made for 5000 acres purchased in 1839, but payment of only £200 could be substantiated, a grant of 1000 acres was made (assuming four shillings per acre).

This system, and particularly the 2560-acre limit, was strenuously opposed by claimants until the Land Claims Settlement Act of 1856 promulgated new rules. In the meantime, Captain Grey, who had a savage dislike for land speculators, had been appointed Governor. The 1856 Act appointed Mr Francis Dillon Bell as Commissioner, who was responsible for finalising most of the grants. Where the amount granted was less than that which the applicant claimed he had purchased (in many cases it was very much so) then the difference — the 'surplus' — was vested in the Crown since its legal advice was that the Maori title to all the land claimed had been extinguished by the original deed. This became the cause of much discontent among the Maoris, particularly since the Government, after dealing so severely with its claimants, proceeded to excercise its pre-emptive right to Maori land by purchasing it at prices like six pence per acre.

---

1. Rutherford, J. (ed) *The Founding of New Zealand,* p.24.
2. Buick, L. *The Treaty of Waitangi,* p.87-8.

3. Johnson, J. Manuscript Journal (Auck.Pub.Lib).
4. Colenso, W. *The Signing of the Treaty,* passim.
5. Colenso, p. 13-14.
6. Buick, pp.63-4, 99-103.
7. Wilkes, *Narrative of the United States Exploring Expedition,* p.379-80.
8. Bunbury, T. *Reminiscences of a Veteran,* v.3, p.56.
9. Hall, T.D.H. *Captain Joseph Nias,* p.68-9.
10. Taylor, N.M. *Journal of Ensign Best,* pp.217-8, 406-8.
11. Johnson.
12. Ibid.
13. Rutherford, p.32.
14. Ibid.
15. Bunbury.
16. Rutherford, p.112-5.
17. Ross, R. *New Zealand's First Capital*, p.50.
18. Ibid, p.47-8 and plan opp.p.74.
19. Rutherford, p.184-6.
20. Wilkes, p.370.
21. Wright, O. *The Voyage of the Astrolabe, 1840*, p.65.
22. Scholefield G.H. *Captain William Hobson,* p.121-30.
23. Ibid, p.144-6.
24. Sherrin and Wallace, *Early History of New Zealand,* p.530.
25. Anderson and Peterson, *The Mair Family,* p.513.
26. Rutherford, pp.192, 196.
27. Bunbury, p.135.
28. Healy, T., *Old Land Claims,* N.Z. Draughtsmen's Journal, v.1, No. 6, March 1951.

20

Stagnation

THE DECISION OF the New South Wales Government to restrict land grants was probably first known at the Bay through a letter written from Sydney by Busby to Mair in August 1840. Busby was present in the Legislative Council chamber when this measure was announced, and hastily conveyed the dismal tidings to New Zealand.[1]

If hardship attended this arbitrary rule, it was scarcely financial, since little of the land had been acquired at any great cost. However, many disappointed purchasers were irate, having for some time lived in a fool's paradise, imagining that they had been successful in looting New Zealand's land resources. The blow could be absorbed without fatal results by the emigrés to the new town of Auckland, where other opportunities for making money were developing. For the settlers who remained at the Bay, however, the matter was more serious, since land speculation had been one of the causes for the recent boom there. Now this was no longer attractive, due to the legislation, and of course, no one now wanted land at the Bay. The community therefore had to revert to useful work for a living, and the economy slipped back many years. A fall in standards was inevitable, both for Maori and pakeha. 'Seeing that so many of the respectable portion of the Proprietors are removing to Auckland, I fear it will be impossible to get 8 directors sufficiently acquainted with business...to manage the business of the Bank with prudence. . .' Busby wrote to Mair from Waitangi in May 1841.

But whalers still used the Bay of Islands. U.S. vessels operating at the South Island invariably made the Bay their point of departure for home, and English and French whalers continued to use the port as before. So back into the arms of the

240

whalers went Bay of Islands business, after a brief time of philandering with flightier loves. Much of the traffic in general merchandise was now diverted to Auckland, although the buoyant appearance of the shipping returns for the Bay for 1841-2 suggests otherwise. The tonnage entered for that period was 22,206 — the highest in New Zealand — but the customs receipts of £3728-15-7d were below Auckland. The explanation of this is that shipping at the Bay consisted mostly of whalers, large vessels, averaging perhaps 300 tons, but handling little dutiable merchandise, and generating little business. On what they did generate, however, the settlers now relied for their livings.

The Bay people who had clamoured so long and loud for British rule now had it, but so far it had brought them little but grief, and their early triumphs turned to ashes in their mouths. British rule might now deprive them of land they considered to be their own, and worse, its effect on their port had been to strip it of its mercantile supremacy and divert its trade to Auckland. At the Bay all the luckless population had to show for the advent and passing of the Government was the ghost town of Russell and a few officials, who from their lairs at Kororareka extorted various imposts to nurture Auckland's administration. True, law and order was established, but as the *Bay of Islands Observer* plaintively observed in its issue of 2 June 1842, the Kororareka Association had done this, despite spiteful overseas opinion to the contrary.

At this stage, law and order was dispensed from Russell by Captain Beckham, the Police Magistrate, and Messrs Clendon and Mair had been appointed as Justices of the Peace. A police station had been established at Kororareka, but the jail was at Russell. Since mid-1840 residents had had the benefit of a mail service between the Bay, Waimate and Horeke on the Hokianga.[2] A hospital had been proposed at a meeting presided over by Hobson in May 1840, but no action eventuated. These services, with the handful of troops at Russell, the Government Printer and a few more officials, were all that were left when the tide of governmental activity receded from the Bay of Islands.[3]

Because of the peculiar circumstances in which Clendon now found himself, he could do little else but resign from his position as Acting United States Consul before he was removed from it by the Secretary of State. In his letter of resignation, Clendon stated that his inability to attend to his duties was due to his '. . .present residence being so distant from the seat of commerce in New Zealand. . .'[4] At this time he appears to have been living at his Manawaora property, now known as Clendon Cove, meditating, no doubt, on his recent follies. Bereft of his consular appointment and the American business that went with it, Clendon had also been deprived of the purchase-money for the Okiato property, and having no prospect of an early settlement, he was indeed in a bad way.

Concurrently with his resignation, he appointed William Mayhew, an American citizen, as vice-consul on 20 April 1841. From January 1842 Mayhew assumed consulate responsibilities,[5] although his appointment was never confirmed. Mayhew's first appearance in New Zealand waters appears to have been as captain of the U.S. whaling vessel *Warren*, which was engaged in bay-whaling at Cloudy Bay and Akaroa in July and August 1836. He was later in command of the U.S. whaler *Luminary*, which visited the Bay of Islands in 1839. In 1842 Mayhew appeared as captain of the brig *Atlas*, a tender to the *Luminary* and *Warren*. He appears to have remained in New Zealand after this, trading on the coast with the *Atlas* after the departure of the whaleships.[6] In December 1842 Mayhew was replaced by a properly accredited consul, the American J.B. Williams, an unscrupulous businessman by his own account. He was appointed on 10 March 1842, but remained in New Zealand only a year, leaving Mayhew again as vice-consul. By now, Mayhew had established himself as a prominent businessman at the Bay. In 1840 he had taken a lease of Gilbert Mair's property at Te Wahapu, as a going concern, and in September of the same year he appeared as a director of The New Zealand Banking Co. at Kororareka.

Thus the two leading merchants, Clendon and Mair, went out of business simultaneously. Mair abandoned Te Wahapu in order to make his home near Whangarei, a sudden decision, which suggests that the Ngunguru mill venture had even then failed to achieve its anticipated success. In occupying the Whangarei land, Mair believed that he could better establish his claim to it when his case came before the Commissioners.

The scope of the two merchants had been wide. Mair had owned the cutter *Glatton,* which traded up and down the coast. Clendon, with the schooner *Fortitude*, later lost at sea in 1835, had conducted a similar business in partnership with Stephenson. Mair and Clendon had also, as a joint venture, purchased the American vessel *Independence,* which had been stranded at the Bay. She was re-commissioned and named *Tokerau*, a Maori name applied to the northern lands, and sent away in trade. In 1839 she was whaling at Cook's Strait — one of the few New Zealand-owned ships to engage in the industry.[7]

Enterprise of this sort now lapsed, and the alteration in the tone of reports in the Bay newspapers in 1842 is very noticeable. In three or four years Kororareka had changed from a turbulent, prosperous community to a shabby colonial township, now dependent for its life-blood on the reduced whale-trade. The new Consul, Williams, depicted Kororareka and Te Wahapu between 1842 and 1844 as veritable dens of iniquity, and the behaviour of the population as sexually and generally morally depraved. An American, aggrieved at the losses incurred by the whale-fleet as a result of British rule, Williams was very prejudiced, and was also a very sanctimonious person.

A weekly paper, the *Bay of Islands Observer*, was now produced by the Bay of Islands Printing Co. at one shilling per copy. Its inaugural date has not been determined, but it was publishing in January 1842. A better printed and more sedate journal than the *Advertiser*, it disseminated little but sad news; and in place of the buoyancy and optimism exuded in 1840 by the older newspaper, gloom pervaded the editorials and letters to the editor in the *Observer*. This advertisement in the 'To Let' column speaks for itself:

> That well-known and commodious Hotel the Victoria, containing fourteen rooms, a good well of water, with an acre of land, and other useful outbuildings.[This hotel was at the North end of the beach.]
>
> ALSO:

243

> Other houses and gardens which will be given
> to any respectable tenants rent free, by taking
> care of the property.

The 2 June 1842 issue contained a complaint concerning the proposed official survey of Kororareka. There was apparently fear that proposed roading would sever properties, further complicating the land claims and title boundaries. The actual survey does not appear to have been done, however, until about two years later, and the layout then achieved did not differ substantially from that adopted by W.J. Wheeler in 1890, and which is retained to this day.[8] The approximate date of the first survey can be determined by a remark made by Mayhew in a latter to Mair on 16 August 1844. In this he stated that 'The Surveyor General arrived to cut up Kororareka township'.[9]

As for Russell, Mathew's town on Clendon's old estate, its extinction occurred in such a way as to relieve Hobson or his successors of the necessity of making a distasteful decision upon its ultimate fate. On the night of 1 May 1842 the former Government House caught fire and was burned to the ground in 30 minutes, despite the efforts of Captain Beckham and Mr Wellman, a handful of troops, and a boat's crew.[10] The house was occupied at the time by the two officials mentioned, who then evacuated the Town of Russell with their retainers, and took up residence at Kororareka. This was the end of Russell. Only a few weeks before the fire, another of its functions had been transferred to Kororareka, where a rented building was acquired for the Government bonded-store. Complaints from businessmen about the expense and delays arising from the distance of the Russell store from the centre of commerce had been effective, and Hobson had agreed to its transfer.

Another newspaper, *The Bay of Islands Advocate*, commenced publication on 4 November 1843, but expired in February 1844.

By late 1844, Russell was already an historical incident. When Andrew Sinclair, the new Colonial Secretary, visited the Bay in January 1845, he found Russell completely deserted, and all the remaining buildings, with the exception of Clendon's old store, in ruins, and not worthy of repair.[11] So

Russell remained for over 40 years, deserted and in ruins, until in 1891 most of it was purchased by G.E. Schmidt. Even though it is now inhabited, no traces of its illustrious past remain.

The status of Kororareka, which had hitherto been equivocal, was finally clarified, when in January 1844 a Government Gazette tersely announced that the boundaries of Russell were to be extended to include Kororareka, which henceforth would inherit its name,[12] and become the port of entry to the Bay of Islands. Until then, official correspondence from Kororareka to Auckland had been indiscriminately headed 'Kororareka' or 'Russell', but the official elimination of the old Maori name was to put an end at least to official confusion. Henceforth, if it were necessary to refer in correspondence to the former seat of government, it was to be called 'Old Russell', as opposed to the new Russell (formerly Kororareka).

By now, the position of the settlers and businessmen at the Bay was desperate. In 1844, as we have seen, the New Zealand Banking Company, in its death-throes, concerned itself largely with foreclosures, and selling its securities at the Bay of Islands.[13] £8000 of overdue paper was held by the branch there, and in December 1843 Busby confided in a letter to Mair: '...I confess, however I am not without fear of the Bank while that fellow Whitaker is at the head of it.'[14] Whitaker, later Prime Minister of New Zealand, was not a charitable man, and Busby's fear was justified by later events. In a letter written to Mair at Whangarei, Waetford, acting as attorney for Mayhew, described the state of affairs there:

Wahapu 15 June 1844

Dear Sir,
    When I promised to write you I did hope to have given you some cheering news, but things were much worse than I expected. On Thursday after you sailed the Sherrif seized all Busby's property even to Mrs Busby's and the children's clothes, the Gum[?] also that was shipped on board the 'Elizabeth' which now remains on board assigned to a merchant in Salem to be sold for account of the Bank to

245

whom the proceeds are to come. Mr H. Williams paid £10 to redeem his clothes [Mr. Busby's] so that he might sail on the 'Elizabeth' which he did. It is expected that everything will be sold by the Sherriff in 14 days for cash, so they will not realize much — this seems very cruel on the part of the Bank & shows that no mercy can be expected from them however kindly the Directors may talk to a person's face — indeed Clendon tells me that they will have from everyone the last penny & that they must force people in order to raise money; for all the Capital is sunk — Clendon has arranged I believe owing to some large remittance from England but Thompson had to give a covenant of Attorney & the Bank takes all — so the prospect for the country are very melancholy & nothing but ruin and beggary are before us.[15]

There followed a pitiful recital of the financial straits of the various properties, and the hardships incurred by the actions of the dying Banking Company. Mair was apparently in acute financial difficulties, and Busby was destitute. Clendon only remained in financial health by an injection of foreign capital. Two Kororareka merchants, Spicer and William Wilson, were ruined, and had left the town. One of the few solvent survivors, as one might expect, was the redoubtable Ben Turner. But bad as the financial situation was, it was not the only worry that the settlers had on their minds.

So far, no actual clashes of any significance had occurred between European settlers and Maoris. There had been the murder at Puketona, and the abortive plot described by Dr Johnson and mentioned in the last chapter. This conspiracy had harmed some white settlers, who had been suspected, even officially, of having a hand in encouraging the incipient insurrection. Oddly enough, the Government does not appear to have been greatly alarmed by the incident, although settlers at the Bay and elsewhere came in for some criticism, notably from Willoughby Shortland. Powditch, who had been in partnership with Mair, and who had moved to Whangaroa in the middle 1830s, later claimed that he was victimised by the Land Commission as a result of unfounded suspicions that he had a part in the affair.

A murder committed at Motu Arohia Island in November 1841 marked the commencement of the decline at the Bay. It created a considerably more dangerous situation than the Kihi affair, since the suspected murderer this time was Maketu, son of Ruhe, a Waimate chief of some standing.[16] Kihi's escapade had occurred when the infantile Government was in a thoroughly defenceless position and scarcely able to deal with normal business. Fortunately, the lowly Kihi had obligingly died from natural causes before he could be hanged.

The suspected Maketu worked on Motu Arohia for Mrs Roberton, widow of Captain Roberton, a whaling skipper whose treatment of the Maoris at the Chathams was said to have been a contributory cause of the *Jean Bart* massacre. In 1839 he had purchased Motu Arohia, but had drowned a year later while crossing in a boat to the island. The victims of the murder were Mrs Roberton, her pakeha manservant, Thomas Bull, and three children, including Captain Brind's daughter, Isabella, grand-daughter of the Kororareka chief Rewa. It seems that Maketu had been ill-treated and abused by Bull, and had taken the first opportunity to kill him, but when he confessed his crime to Mrs Roberton, she was apparently not at all understanding, and as a result suffered the same fate as Bull. Maketu, then thoroughly aroused, killed the three children.

A proud, undisciplined and murderous youth, Maketu was not given up by his Maori relations without considerable disorder. In Maori custom, Rewa was entitled to *utu,* or payment for the death of his grand-daughter, and probably this alone led to Maketu being surrendered more or less peaceably to the magistrate at Russell. The investigation of his case was conducted amid scenes of tension. The luckless Kihi and Kite had been Maoris of little consequence, but here was a Maori of considerable standing. In fact, the settlers in the district feared an attack, and since the French warship *L'Aube* was on hand at the time, it stood by in case of emergencies. HMS *Favourite*, of Sir James Clark Ross' scientific expedition, also supplied a guard to keep order at Kororareka. Nevertheless, despite considerable apprehension, no serious trouble occurred and in due course Maketu was tried at Auckland and hanged.

The Maketu affair was an isolated and violent incident, and had no direct bearing on the mounting unrest among a section of the Bay Maoris. There can be little doubt that, as Colenso suggested, the Treaty was signed by many chiefs who had only a dim comprehension of the significance of their actions, particularly relative to their acceptance of British law. It now seemed to them that although they were subject to its penal provisions, they reaped none of its benefits. The rancour left in the wake of Hobson's eventful passage had become an increasing source of alarm to the Europeans in the North.

The unstable state of affairs is reflected in a circular letter drafted by a committee set up at the Bay of Islands following a general meeting of property-owners. This committee had been formed to petition the Queen, informing her of the situation that now existed. In order to assemble relevant data for this purpose, the following questions were submitted to settters:

QUERIES

1st What number of years have you lived in New Zealand.

2nd Have you acquired a knowledge of the language of the natives, and of their general habits & disposition.

3rd Do you consider that the natives are satisfied with the proceedings of the Government, or that they have entertained, or do now entertain no distrust, or apprehension that it is the intention of the Government to deprive them of their Lands?

4th Do you consider that the safety of British settlers has been endangered by the proceedings of the Government with regard to the Land question and the proclamation prohibiting the cutting of timber on land purchased from the natives?

5th Do you consider that the active colonization of their Country by the British Government is consistent with the spirit of the Treaty, and that it is likely to be submitted to by the natives without opposition?

6th Do you consider that the natives are well affected towards the Government, or the contrary?

7th Do you consider that the natives hold themselves amenable to British Law, or that they will submit thereto without opposition?

8th Do you consider that in the event of any outbreak amongst the natives the well disposed amongst them could be relied upon to afford protection to the persons and property of British Subjects or that there is any adequate means of preserving the peace of the country?

(Signed on behalf of the Committee by James Busby.)[17]

The proposal to petition the Queen arose from a speech made on 31 January 1842 by Willoughby Shortland in the Legislative Council, concerning a similar petition that his Government had recently received from the North. The Colonial Secretary had ridiculed the settlers' fears, but as subsequent events proved, he was grievously misinformed on the matter. He boldly asserted that the Maori people were perfectly satisfied. In his speech he also implied that the settlers who now appeared to be so concerned were among those who had attempted to promote ill-feeling towards the Government on Hobson's arrival in New Zealand.

The questionnaire, inspired by recent incidents and the general demeanour of the Maoris, was circulated among the Northern settlers in November 1843, and in April of the same year, Powditch wrote from Whangaroa to Mair at Whangarei: 'We have frequent rumours of disturbances we hear that the people in the Bay are looking for some attack and with in these few days European men have been stopp'd and plundered somewhere abt. Tarko [Takou]. The inefficiency of the Government to overawe the natives and keep peace seems to me daily increasing and becoming more serious.'[18]

In 1846 ex-Governor Fitz Roy wrote of the causes of the unrest:

Eagerness to trade, and to have settlers near them, overcame all other considerations during 1840 and 1841; but in 1842 the tide began to turn. More settlers arrived in every ship. The natives were not only treated with less caution and less kindness then previously, but they were threatened, even on trifling occasions, with the punishments of English law [This is footnoted by Fitz Roy, 'To them unintelligible'], and they were told by ill-disposed or unreflecting whitemen that their country was taken from them, that they were now Queen Victoria's slaves, and that they could not even sell their own property — their land — as they pleased. These taunts were felt deeply. The natives had been so accustomed to pass freely across land or water, wherever they pleased in their own districts, that they were perplexed by seeing fences rising, and by finding that people were becoming averse to their company. They also found that land that they had hastily sold for a few articles, soon consumed or worn out, was resold for many times — perhaps more than thirty times the value which they had received. They discovered that the government understanding of the treaty of Waitangi not only bound them to give the Queen of England the first offer of land they wished to sell, but that they could not sell to any other person, even if the government, on behalf of Her Majesty, declined to purchase.[19]

Customs duties had also become effective, and soon affected the price of goods, while the private revenues from anchor and other dues, formerly levied by individual chiefs, ceased.

The acting U.S. Consul, William Mayhew, was accused, among other American traders, of fomenting unrest among the Bay Maoris. They were also accused of supplying arms to the Maoris after the outbreak of war. After Mayhew's departure, Waetford and his associate H.G. Smith did, in fact, deal in arms, and Waetford was actually jailed at Auckland for this, although he was not convicted. Williams, the U.S. Consul at the Bay since 1842, was also accused of supplying arms, but was later exonerated by an official inquiry. Nevertheless, American influence, albeit unofficial, was apparent by the Stars and Stripes that the chief Hone Heke flew on his canoe when he was visiting the Bay.[20] However, it is certain that none of this American support of Maori unrest was sanctioned by the United States Government. Nor is it likely that Mayhew, with a valuable business and £2300 invested at Te Wahapu, would deliberately incite a rebellion.

There was also a contemporary belief, never substantiated, that Pompallier was a focus of discontent; but such was the settlers' mood that they suspected anyone with a non-English background of plotting their destruction.

Following Hobson's death and Willoughby Shortland's

administration, the new Governor, Captain Robert Fitz Roy, who had commanded HMS *Beagle* on its visit to the Bay in 1835, arrived in New Zealand in the last week in 1843. He took no effective action on appeals from the North, although he was clearly disturbed by them. It was not, then, until the disaffected element found leaders in Heke Pokai (Hone Heke) and Te Ruki Kawiti, and took direct action, that Fitz Roy acted, sending 30 men of the 96th Regiment to Russell and appealing to New South Wales for additional military support. But his ineffectual attempts at conciliation failed, and war resulted.

---

1. Mair Papers, Auckland.
2. Robinson. H. *A History of the Post Office in New Zealand,* p.20.
3. Ross, *New Zealand's First Capital,* p.59.
4. McNab, *Historical Records,* v.2, p.618.
5. Ibid, pp.618, 620.
6. McNab, *The Old Whaling Days.* pp.189, 303-9, 314.
7. Ibid, pp.296-314.
8. Wheeler, W.J. Survey Office Plan No. 5602 (Auckland).
9. Mair Papers, op.cit.
10. Ross, p.58-9.
11. Ibid, p.61.
12. King, M.M. *Port in the North*, p.49.
13. Moore and Barton, *Banking in New Zealand*, p.7.
14. Mair Papers, op.cit.
15. Ibid.
16. Sherrin and Wallace, *Early History of New Zealand,* p.585-6.
17. Mair Papers, op.cit.
18. Ibid.
19. Fitz Roy, R. *Remarks on New Zealand,*p.11.
20. Wards, *The Shadow of the Land,* p.97.

21

War

HONE HEKE WAS NO amateur in war, despite his education by the missionaries at Paihia. His apprenticeship had been served in the Girl's War in 1830, and in 1837 he had been involved in the curious internecine battles against Pomare. He was a Ngapuhi of the Ngati-Rahiri *hapu*, and son-in-law of Hongi Hika, whose daughter Hariata Rongo he had married. The districts in which he had influence included Te Ahuahu, Waimate, Pakaraka, Oromahoe, Kaikohe and Te Tii Waitangi. Also Tautoro, in the district then known as Hikurangi, and the present Ohaeawai — at that time called Taiamai.

Although he had signed the Treaty, Heke had become the focal point of Maori discontent. He and his sympathisers roamed the country, often in armed bands, greatly alarming, if not actually menacing Europeans.

A significant factor in this discontent had been the realisation by many chiefs that their authority was gone — gone to the English Governor in a way they never anticipated — and with it their *mana* or prestige, both with their own people and Europeans. Their authority among their own people had already been eroded by the liberal aspects of Christian teaching, which, predictably, the underprivileged were by now embracing *en masse*. However, there were also chiefs such as Rewa, Nene (Tamati Waaka), Patuone, Taonui and Tawhai who were more pragmatic, and had realised the inevitable outcome of the pakeha influx. Heke, Kawiti of Waiomio, Kapotai of Waikare, Haratua of Oromahoe, Pene Taui and Heta te Haara of Ohaeawai and their allies appear more as idealists, since they seem to have believed that they would successfully right their wrongs by ejecting the Europeans. That many more did not join these was no doubt due to caution rather than conviction.

Nene, the so-called 'friendly' leader, who was anything but friendly to a large proportion of his own people, saw Heke's stance as a threat to his own standing as a dominant Ngapuhi leader, and when Heke finally committed himself with an act of violence at Kororareka, Nene's way was clear — this 'upstart' had to be put in his place. More importantly, Heke and his warriors were now a threat to Nene's Hokianga people. Heke, as we have seen, had married Hongi Hika's daughter, with whom he had a common ancestor,[1] and it was against Hongi Hika that Nene nursed his grudge. Thus, at this stage, Ngapuhi became divided into pro-Hongi and anti-Hongi factions. The anti-Hongi faction was later joined by Ngatipou of Whangaroa, who, although closely related to Hongi, had suffered grievously at his hands (Chapter 14). In correspondence with Sir George Grey, written after the war in the North, Kawiti stated that Nene was constantly 'naming his dead', and that he fought Heke and Kawiti, not because of the pakeha dead but to avenge the death of his own people — Kao, Te Tihi and Poaka.[2] Maning's old chief, recounting the battles of 1845-6 in which he took part on Nene's side, made no secret of his leader's motives, which to him were quite clearly to revenge Hongi's past depredations.[3] Nene was a chief having great influence in the upper reaches of the Hokianga, but little of any consequence at the Bay of Islands at this stage.

Heke himself, in contrast with some of his turbulent followers, was seen to be meticulous in his attitude to Europeans on most occasions, but the incident which precipitated his first major confrontation, occurred at Kororareka. Early in July 1844, he and a strong party came to the town in a truculent mood to recover a woman slave who was living with a shopkeeper, a man named Lord. On 5 July they took over Lord's house, and despite the efforts of Kemp, a Protector of Aborigines in the employ of the Government, and Nene himself, created a noisy demonstration. Empty threats of 'death to Europeans' were bandied about, and war was a dominant theme. Persuasion by the Rev. H. Williams and Captain Beckham, the Police Magistrate, was unsuccessful in dispersing this troublesome party, which continued to terrorise the town, throughout the next day, without doing anyone much harm. Heke harangued the Maoris on the beach with inflammatory speeches, recounting grievances that had come in the wake of the Europeans. Finally, on 8 July the flagstaff above the town, on Maiki Hill, was felled, chopped into pieces and burned. The British flag on the staff represented all that the disaffected Maoris resented, and to them, nothing could be more insulting to the authority that it stood for than to treat it thus. This was Heke's stance throughout the next few months.[4]

Beckham, with only a few policemen, had insufficient force to exercise any control over these events, and rejected offers of help from the more resolute of the town's citizens. However, having made his point, Heke retired with his party and his slave to Kaikohe. Fitz Roy reacted calmly. He sent an officer and 30 men of the 96th Regiment to garrison the town, and requested further military assistance from Governor Gipps at New South Wales, who, in due course, sent 150 men of the 99th. By August there was a force of 250 men camped at Matauwhi Bay under Lieut. Colonel Hulme. In August also, Fitz Roy himself arrived on HMS *Hazard*.[5]

The Governor proceeded cautiously, apparently appreciating the gravity of the situation, and adopted a conciliatory attitude at the meeting convened by him at Waimate. Here he met chiefs, who for various reasons supported him, notably Nene, who guaranteed the good behaviour of Heke — an arrogant and provocative gesture, since he had no authority whatever over him. Heke did not attend, but Fitz Roy accepted 20 muskets from the chiefs there as a gesture of allegiance. He seemed re-assured, particularly since Heke had written him a conciliatory letter. Later, as a token of good faith, Fitz Roy declared the Bay of Islands exempt from Customs dues. The Governor now made the fatal error of abolishing the Crown's pre-emptive right to acquire Maori land. This was one of the actions which led to his dismissal, but it did nothing to relieve the situation in the North. The meeting at Waimate, particularly Nene's guarantee of his good behaviour, served only to wound Heke's pride. 'Let Waaka keep to his own side of the Island, Hokianga,' was his comment on the pleasantly euphoric function at Waimate.

Apparently Fitz Roy now believed the flagstaff incident to be satisfactorily concluded, and he, with his troops, embarked for Auckland after instructions had been issued to Beckham to re-erect the staff. Fitz Roy was, however, under no illusion as to the hopelessness of dealing with such situations without adequate military support, but he wisely disapproved of the formation of a militia. This could only consist of settlers who at this stage were only too willing to provoke Maoris, and arming them would be seen as a hostile act.

A short lull now ensued before further minor disturbances occurred. At the Bay, eight horses were stolen from Captain Wright at Omata, as compensation for a slight injury to a Maori woman during a scuffle between the police and her pakeha husband. Inland, Hingston suffered similar losses, and Kawakawa Maoris were suspected of assaulting Europeans as far south as Matakana. It was at about this time that Te Ruki Kawiti of Waiomio, a non-Christian, and the most influential of the Ngati-hine chiefs,[6] allied himself with Heke. This alliance remained intact throughout the sorry military campaign which followed.

On his own initiative Heke again visited Kororareka in January 1845. He had lately written to Fitz Roy asking for a meeting to discuss matters at issue, but had received no reply. The symbolic flag was still there on its re-erected staff, and it was with the intention of again removing this affront to his principles that this expedition took place. On the early morning of 10 January 1845, the new flagstaff suffered the same fate as its predecessor. It fell to the axe and was burned on the ground, and Heke and his men departed quietly by canoe for their homes. Fitz Roy, now bereft of his borrowed troops, could do little but again send up 30 men of the 96th Regiment. By proclamation he offered £100 reward for the capture of Heke, to which the chief responded by offering a similar sum for Fitz Roy, and went on his way unmolested. Fitz Roy also forbade the flying of any but the British flag at the Bay — an oblique reference to the anti-British activities of the U.S. consular agents there — and again set about, albeit in a leisurely way, obtaining military aid from New South Wales.

Meanwhile, Sinclair, the new Colonial Secretary, came north in the brig *Victoria* with the men of the 96th, and contrary to the advice of the missionaries, ordered the re-erection of the staff. An absurd pre-occupation by both sides with the fate of this wretched pole seems to have obscured the significance of the events which gave rise to the assaults on it, but in accordance with orders, a small spar was set up and placed under guard. Ten days after the second staff fell, this, the third was cut down. Heke, with a party, again came to Kororareka, and leaving his men below, he walked up the hill alone, stalked composedly through the guard of Nene's men, brushing them aside, and the deed was done. Clearly, the 'friendliness' of Nene's people did not extend to shooting down one of their own for the sake of a pole. Untouched, Heke walked down the hill, boarded his canoe, and passing close to the *Victoria*, crossed the Bay.

This bold and courageous action did as much to increase his prestige with the vacillating 'friendly' chiefs as it did to lower that of the Government, and even the seasoned politician Nene wavered at this stage. But the missionaries now made a strong effort to avert open war. With their fingers to the pulse of local Maori affairs, they realised the necessity for decisive action. H. Williams attended a meeting called at Paroa Bay by Nene and other doubting chiefs, who were now asking whether, in fact, Heke was right in describing the Treaty of Waitangi as a 'trick'. But for missionary persuasion, their support could well have been withdrawn in the following year of war. This meeting polarised Maori opinion, and after it, Heke was in no doubt as to who were his friends. Great Britain, with its massive military resources, could scarcely have lost the war in the North, but without the assistance of Maori allies, active or passive, it might have taken a long time to win it.

Heke now went on his way unrestrained, flying the Stars and Stripes on his canoe when at the Bay. He had been friendly with Mayhew before the consular representative had returned to the United States, and remained so with H.G. Smith, whom Mayhew had left to look after the affairs of the consulate. Heke, therefore, had a useful base at Te Wahapu, close to Kororareka.

Early in the year, the Government forces at Russell consisted of 40 foot soldiers and the officers and men of HMS *Hazard*, commanded by Captain Robertson, whom Fitz Roy had ordered to the town in mid-February. A detachment of the 96th formed a guard for the new iron-encased flagstaff which had been erected on Maiki Hill with an adjacent blockhouse. Another blockhouse was constructed near Polack's house at the north end of the beach, and in the hands of this small force lay the responsibility of defending the town, or its flagstaff, against further indignities.

But soon Heke was on the move again. Both Williams and the Rev. R. Burrows had visited him at Kaikohe to persuade him of the error of his ways, but his single-minded aversion to the flagstaff, and his contempt for the 'trick' that he believed had been perpetrated by the Treaty, were uppermost in his mind. Both these men, and the Rev. R. Davis, who also attempted to move Heke from his stance, failed, and on 3 March 1845 he passed through Waimate with 150 followers, on his way to the Bay. Next day, at Waitangi, Williams again tried to dissuade Heke from his purpose, which was obviously another assault on the flagstaff, but his arguments were coldly received and he was accused of deceiving many chiefs as to the significance of the Treaty.

In the afternoon Heke and his men crossed the harbour and camped at Uriti, a small bay a mile south of Kororareka, on the same coast. Here he was joined by Kawiti with 100 men, and for the first time, a combined military exercise was planned. Heke's declared objective was the destruction of British authority. He publicly disapproved interference with either the settlers or their property, but the old man Kawiti had no such scruples, and his men antagonised some of the local settlers. But both had great *mana* at this stage, and further reinforcements were attracted to them. Minor brushes with the anxious defenders of Kororareka occurred during the next few days, and by 10 March the town was expecting a full-scale attack at any time. A gun was placed on the slope of Maiki Hill commanding the low saddle between Kororareka and Matauwhi. This was manned by civilians, of whom 110 were enrolled as special constables from the population of about 400.[7] Ninety marines and sailors had also been landed from the *Hazard* for the defence of the town. The Maori forces camped nearby were now estimated at

600-700.[8]

Kororareka was by no means unprepared for the attack, and indeed, very thorough preparations had been made in anticipation of it. The surprise lay in the tactics that the Maori forces employed. The *Hazard* commanded the town with its guns, and now three guns ashore were laid on the pass to Matauwhi Bay, adjacent to the church, from where it was anticipated the attack would come. Beckham, the Police Magistrate, was, at least nominally, in command of the defence, supported by the 96th's troops and Captain Robertson, with his sailors, marines and guns. The action commenced on 11 March, when some 200 of Kawiti's men attacked as expected from Matauwhi, but later, a similar force of Waikare Maoris came over the saddle from Oneroa (Long Beach) into the attack. Severe hand-to-hand fighting took place near the old Anglican church, resulting in losses on both sides, including the Kawakawa chief Pumuka. Captain Robertson was seriously wounded. In the meantime, Heke's own party had approached Maiki Hill in force from Long Beach, having waited there since the night before, and without losses to his own force, took possession of the flagstaff. Iron-sheathed though it was, it fell an hour and a half later. The military guard had been caught outside its blockhouse enjoying the spectacle of the Matauwhi battle and was completely routed, retiring to the lower blockhouse on Polack's land with the loss of four or five men. The signalman was also killed in the initial confusion, and, by accident, a young half-caste girl.

The fighting at the other end of the town continued until noon, but the wretched episode closed after a conference on the *Hazard*, when Lieutenant Philpotts, who now commanded the vessel following Robertson's injuries, ordered the evacuation of the town. It is not clear who, in fact, authorised this, but it was strongly opposed by the dashing Cornthwaite Hector, lawyer and man of affairs, whose spirit on this occasion did him credit. He appealed for 40 men, with which, he asserted, he could save the town. However, he was over-ruled, and Philpotts made a present of Kororareka to the raiders. This decision was an odd one, since the evidence suggests that the battle was by no means lost when the town was abandoned, and it is still doubtful whether taking it was an objective of the attack.

The refugees were taken on board the *Hazard*, the United States warship *St. Louis*, the British whaler *Matilda*, the schooner *Dolphin*, Bishop Selwyn's *Flying Fish*, and the Government brig *Victoria*. No sooner had the unfortunate inhabitants been evacuated, however, when the powder-magazine at Hector's house mysteriously exploded. The invading Maoris, being now at a loose end, and having nothing better to do, entered the town and took charge. They plundered at their leisure; while Philpotts, for no obvious reason, bombarded the town from the *Hazard*, damaging the Anglican church. The looting Maoris displayed no rancour, and allowed householders to land and regain some of their belongings. They even ferried some of the refugees to the anchored ships for evacuation. But the unpredictable Philpotts again bombarded the town while people were ashore salvaging their belongings. During this curious performance, Henry Williams ascended Maiki Hill, and with the help of Heke's men, carried down the European bodies to the *Hazard*. Some of the dead of the battle were buried at the church, near where they fell, and there, at the church, their monument may still be seen. Like Hector, Williams, an ex-naval man himself, did not conceal his distaste of Philpotts' strange behaviour.

The destruction of the town by fire was well under way when, on the following day the refugee ships left for Auckland. The Rev. Robert Burrows, who arrived at Kororareka on 14 March, when the plundering and burning was continuing,[9] described how Heke had indicated a point towards the south end of the town, beyond which no buildings were to be destroyed. Thus, the Anglican church, the Catholic chapel, Pompallier's headquarters and printery, and a few cottages and buildings survived. On Monday 17 March the invading forces abandoned the town, recrossed the harbour and dispersed, Heke to Pakaraka and Kawiti to Waiomio. By the end of the month Heke was engaged in refurbishing one of Hongi Hika's old *pa* at Mawhe Kairangi, called Tapuae-haruru, but now known as Mawhe, on the shores of Lake Omapere.

Thus ended the Kororareka incident. Almost the whole population moved to Auckland, leaving the Bay virtually deserted. But this was only the first of a dismal succession of indifferently equipped and ill-directed military actions, which were relieved only by the final decisive defeat of the Maori allies at Rua-pekapeka, where the British troops gained their first and only significant victory in the whole unhappy campaign. Kororareka, and the official view that Fitz Roy had mismanaged both the economy and the military defence of the colony, broke him and led to his dismissal. He had indeed adopted a rather philosophical view of his problems when perhaps they merited more urgency than he realised. He had a low opinion of Kororareka and upon reflection considered the destruction of this 'house of corruption' to be a blessing in disguise.[10] But he now issued a proclamation declaring martial law at the Bay of Islands and in an area within a radius of 60 miles from Kororareka. In another proclamation, he called on 'loyal' Maoris in the Bay of Islands and neighbouring districts to separate themselves from 'the ill-disposed natives' and gather around their chiefs under the British flag. No Maori was to approach a military establishment except with a missionary or 'protector', and under a white flag.

For some six weeks following the battle at Kororareka, no direct military action was taken in retaliation, since Fitz Roy rightly refused to act until he had adequate military support. During this period almost continuous sparring and skirmishing took place in the Okaihau-Omapere district, between the forces of Heke and Kawiti and those of Taonui and Nene. Nene had established himself in a *pa* at Okaihau, strategically situated for attacks on Heke and the defence of the Hokianga people at Waihou and Utakura. Pre-occupation with this situation may have been partly responsible for preventing an attack on Auckland by the disaffected northern tribes, which had been openly threatened. However, the postponement of this was also due to the reluctance of many Maoris to take part, since they were then engaged in digging kauri gum, for which a sudden demand had arisen.[11]

By the end of March the *North Star* had been sent from Auckland to evacuate any of the remaining families who might wish to go to the capital, and to give notice to all concerned that the port was about to be blockaded. Nothing could better describe the desolation of the once thriving Bay of Islands than the following extract from a letter written on 12 April by Henry Williams from Paihia to Mair at Whangarei.

> My Dear Sir,
> I did not see the person by whom your communications were given. He called at Mrs. Wright's and passed up the river for which I was sorry. The recent disasters here have totally brought our work to a stand. It is a serious distressing affair. . . Since the destruction of Kororareka I have scarcely been out of the settlement not having anything to say. They trampled on my advice and must now follow their own. It is my purpose to sit still and keep myself as close as possible to my Mission work strictly speaking. My boys of course partake in the general loss, their houses having been broken tho not destroyed. I understand that Cap. Wright's cattle have been shot to present[?] supplies to the Men of War. I am sorry Mrs. Lewington has gone from her place, yet do not see what else she could do — Waitford is still here with the Pikopos [Catholics]. Mrs Clendon is here. Mrs. Wright Hingstone *Heoi ano* [that's all]. The Bay is clear and on the appearance of any military the remainder of my family will remove somewhere I hope to stand my ground.[12]

At the end of April, Fitz Roy's punitive force, drawn from the 58th and 96th Regiments, most of which had lately arrived from Sydney, assembled at Kororareka to the accompaniment of much band-playing and royal-saluting. There were about 500 in all, transported here by the *North Star* and *Slains Castle*. In the meantime, Heke had been negotiating with Nene, but they could not come to terms, and the *status quo* was maintained. Nene, with his *mana* at stake, now had the tiger by the tail, and was committed to the decision he had made.

Lieutenant-Colonel Hulme, the commander of the military force assembled at Kororareka, apparently held the view that something should be done at once, and found an easy mark at Otuihu. Here, the unfortunate Pomare was Hulme's military objective. Innocent of any complicity in recent events, he was suspected on very flimsy grounds of having incited Potatau Te Wherowhero of Waikato to oppose the Government. Hulme took the *North Star* up the river and stood off the *pa*, but before attacking it, he took Pomare prisoner by inviting him aboard the ship. Then a shore party was landed, and since the occupants had fled, it had much sport looting the *pa* before it was destroyed by fire. Thus the Bay's second most notorious pestspot was purified by the flames. Pomare was taken to Auckland and was well treated, but was subsequently released upon Nene's request when no charge could be proved against him. After this bloodless victory, Hulme proposed a move on Kawiti at Waiomio, attacking by way of the Kawakawa River, but he was strongly advised by Williams not to attempt such a drive deep into enemy country. A meeting was therefore held at which Nene was present, and the decision was made to attack Heke at his *pa* at Lake Omapere.

Another ill-fated military exercise now began. The *Slains Castle* and HMS *North Star* stood across the Bay to the Brampton Reef, but instead of transporting the troops up the Kerikeri River in boats, from where there was a good road inland, the 420-strong assault force was landed at Onewhero (Red Beach), for the march to Lake Omapere. But due to bad weather, the force was diverted to Kerikeri, where it arrived on the second day. During this exercise the *Slains Castle* struck a rock at the mouth of the Kerikeri River which now bears its name.

On 6 May 1845 the march to Okaihau began. There was no wheeled transport or artillery on this journey, which was fortunate, since to reach its objective the force had to leave the Kerikeri-Waimate road at the Waipapa bridge, some three miles from Waimate, and follow the stream up onto the high land to the north-east of Okaihau. Here the going was easier, although the men had to endure considerable discomfort due to their heavy loads and the bad walking conditions before arriving at Nene's *pa* that evening.

The ensuing indecisive battle, fought without active participation of Nene's or Taonui's men, left Heke still in possession of his *pa*. He had chosen a good site some 2¾ miles south of Okaihau, and had built the pa with its unusual stone *pekerangi* (base), overlooking Lake Omapere. He had abandoned his work on Hongi's old *pa*, and had built this entirely new one, which he called Te Kahika, on what was undoubtedly the best defensive position in the locality. Although Hulme outflanked it on the lake side at considerable risk, his men were menaced by Kawiti's forces who were guarding the rear of the *pa*, and it was clear that the structure was too strong to be taken by assault, or breached by the ineffective Congreve rockets Hulme used. So he wisely decided to withdraw, with 13 of his men dead and 39 wounded, and on the next day the whole expedition returned to Kerikeri. The Maori losses were uncertain, but 20 or so were believed to have been killed in the fighting outside the *pa*. They were buried temporarily on the lakeside, about a mile south of the battle-site, and were later taken across the lake by canoe to a point near Putahi, now called Piraunui. Here the bone-scraping or *hahunga* took place before the bones were deposited in the Putahi cave. In this encounter Kawiti was wounded, and his son Taura killed. Heke, with the assistance of the Rev. Burrows, buried the English dead, since they had been abandoned on the field on the day of the battle. Heke and Kawiti then left the *pa* and retired: Heke to the Ohaeawai district and Kawiti to Waiomio.

By 13 May the bedraggled red-coats returned to Kororareka, and three days later, Major Bridge of the 58th led an attack on Kapotai's people at the head of the Waikare River. This was undertaken in small boats with some difficulty, due to the tidal nature of the river. The party burned the *pa* at Waikare, and when the occupants took to the bush they were engaged by Nene's people with casualties. The young Whirinaki chief Hauraki, of Hikutu, died from wounds sustained in this fight. His presence here was due to his relationship with the Kapotai people, who, in fact, were also closely related to Nene. Later, Nene's people and some soldiers raided and burned Maori settlements at Kaipatiki, about a mile from Paihia.

In the meantime, Nene's men were dismantling Heke's *pa* at Lake Omapere, and were using the materials to strengthen two stockades near the big hill, Te Ahuahu (Pukenui). Kawiti and Heke had now agreed where to make the next stand. On 21 May the Rev. Burrows observed Kawiti laying out a new *pa* at Ohaeawai (Ngawha), but he was, in fact, enlarging and strengthening the old *pa* of the Ngatirangi chief Pene Taui. The present church of Saint Michael now occupies its site.

At Kororareka, Major Bridge, on Nene's advice, was planning to attack Ohaeawai before the *pa* was built, but decided against this upon hearing from the Rev. Williams that Heke wished to negotiate. In due course a letter from Heke arrived, but although it appeared unsatisfactory, Sir Everard Home returned to Auckland with his troops, and delivered the letter to Fitz Roy.

Inland, matters were still going forward. Taonui had now moved up to Te Ahuahu and had taken a *pa* of Heke's there, with all its provisions, while Heke and his men were away. Nene joined him later, and the stage was set for a major battle. Heke approached before dawn with a large force, but an old woman who had been gathering firewood outside the *pa* raised the alarm, and the defenders reversed the roles by making a sortie and attacking. This, the battle of Whatitiri, went decisively to Nene's side, and in it Heke was himself badly wounded, losing many of his old war chiefs. Both sides, in fact, suffered such heavy losses that they were now content to remain where they were, Nene at Te Ahuahu, to the north of the hill, and Heke and Kawiti to the south of it, in the Maungakawakawa district.

At Auckland, towards the end of May, Fitz Roy had finally decided to subjugate the hostile northern people by force of arms, and now believed that he had sufficient fire-power to do so. A further 200 officers and men from the 99th Regiment had lately arrived from Sydney in HMS *British Sovereign,* with their commanding officer, Lieutenant-Colonel Henry Despard. As the senior officer in New Zealand, Despard was now in command of all the forces here, and by 10 June was at the Bay with his troops. But Despard displayed no more aptitude for warfare under New Zealand conditions than his predecessors had. The first mishap in the campaign occurred when the *Royal Sovereign* went ashore on the Brampton Reef when transporting soldiers and equipment to the Kerikeri River. A delay of two days resulted, but the vessel was refloated without damage, and the troops and their gear were taken up to Kerikeri in boats. Having endured similar difficulties to those suffered by the expedition to Lake Omapere, this force arrived at Waimate on 16 June. It consisted of detachments of the 58th, 96th, and 99th

264

Regiments and Auckland Volunteers, and had been preceded by marines and sailors of HMS *Hazard*. All forces were billetted in unoccupied buildings at the mission station. This time they had artillery with them — two six-pounders and two 12-pounders.

On 19 June Nene called to pay his respects to Despard and to offer his services, but to these overtures the Colonel replied with old-world courtesy that when he wanted help from savages, he would ask for it. Fortunately there were no volunteers with the temerity to translate this remark. Pomare also turned up with a following and offered his services, after requesting a glass of rum. However, he retired unobtrusively before action commenced. Four days later the force left for Ohaeawai with high hopes of breaching the fortress with its artillery. Here, Pene Taui and Kawiti were in command, since Heke was absent at Tautoro, incapacitated by the wound he sustained in the battle with Nene and Taonui. The route from Waimate to old Ohaeawai then followed approximately the present road to the State highway, and from there, the road into the Remuera district, which passes over the southern flank of the hill Te Ahuahu.

Ohaeawai turned out to be practically impregnable, using the artillery available. Its heavy stockade was constructed of large trees, and inside were bomb-proof shelters five or six feet underground. For a week, to the derisive comment of the defenders, Despard hurled his six and 12-pound cannon-balls at the defences without significant effect. By the end of the week, some of the defenders, apparently finding the affair tedious, sallied out in sorties and almost succeeded in putting out of action a 32-pound cannon, which Despard had ordered be brought up from the *Hazard*. Meanwhile, over 800 men were standing idle, including some 250 Maori allies. On 1 July at his wits end, due to the failure of his artillery to breach the palisades, Despard ordered the *pa* to be stormed.

British military prestige gained nothing from the war in the North. The Maori chiefs attached to Despard disassociated themselves from such a foolhardy proposal, and their men took no part in the slaughter which now ensued. The orders were to charge across the open ground before the *pa* under murderous musket-fire, carrying scaling-ladders which were to be placed against the stockade. By this means, the attackers, with muskets now firing at them at point-blank range, were to enter the *pa*, or at least surmount the first obstacle, since there was another palisade inside. In spite of this, no trouble was met in obtaining volunteers for the 'forlorn hope', and in due course, carrying their full packs, they charged. Five minutes later, 40 had been killed and 80 wounded out of the storming party of nearly 300, and the horrified Despard ordered the retreat. In this action, the eccentric Lieutenant Philpotts, whose peculiar behaviour at Kororareka a few months earlier had attracted so much adverse comment, lost his life, leaving behind his eyeglass hanging on top of the palisade as a witness to his personal courage. Philpotts seems to have disagreed with practically everything Despard proposed, particularly with the assault in which he died. Next morning, under a flag of truce, a defender asked Henry Williams to come and collect the dead. Except for the officers, who were taken to Waimate for burial, the dead were buried on the field. Predictably, Despard blamed the Auckland Volunteers and the sailors, who were in charge of the scaling-ladders and tools, for the failure of the exercise. They apparently did not turn up where they were required, but clearly, their presence would hardly have affected the issue.

The stalemate continued for another week, to the accompaniment of plunging artillery fire. By now, ammunition was running low, and Despard was ready to leave the besieged in possession and retire with his force to the Bay, when Clendon, now Resident Magistrate at Hokianga, persuaded him to hold on for a while. This advice shortly proved to be good, when, just after midnight on 11 July the *pa* was found to be abandoned, after having been held without difficulty for nearly three weeks. Having served the purpose of the defenders, it was of no further use to them, and undefeated and almost unscathed, they retired to Kaikohe, to where Despard's Maoris later pursued them. But only the burning of a house of Heke's rewarded them there.

The enemy was gone and the *pa* was in British hands. After destroying it, Despard returned with his troops to Waimate. Here he organised a party to attack the *pa* of Haratua, Heke's ally at Oromahoe (Te Aute). This, too, was found to be abandoned, and the men had no more heroic task to perform than to burn it. Despard remained with his troops until after this exercise, when it was proposed to attack Kawiti's unfortified *pa* at Waiomio. However, he was recalled to Auckland on military business, leaving detachments of the 58th and 99th camped at Waimate under Major Cyprian Bridge.

At about this time, Nopera Panakareao,[13] who had been so co-operative in signing the Treaty of Waitangi visited Nene to offer his services in the fight against Heke. Fitz Roy, however, suspected that Nopera was more interested in fighting against Heke than fighting for the Government, and discouraged him with suitable blandishments, believing that Nopera's participation could, in fact, have the effect of attracting more people to Heke's standard.[14] Nopera, the paramount Rarawa chief in the Mangonui district, had fallen foul of Ngapuhi over his sale of Mangonui land to the Government in 1840. This sale was disputed by a Ngapuhi chief, Pororua, who was then living on the land, on the grounds that it was Ngapuhi territory by right of conquest. This led to fighting between the two tribes in 1842.[15] Nene was left to deal with Nopera on this matter at a *hui* near Okaihau, apparently at Taumata Parororo, on the Waiare road.

Having attended to his business in Auckland, Despard collected artillery and ammunition and returned to the Bay in the *Slains Castle* at the end of August, escorted by HMS *Daphne*. He arrived at Waimate with reinforcements on 1 September 1845, and found the place a shambles. Fences had gone for firewood, and pilfering was rife. It was a very delapidated mission station that the soldiers left behind them when, in the middle of October, they returned to Kororareka in the *Slains Castle* by way of Kerikeri.

The withdrawal arose from recent political developments. Despatches from Lord Stanley dated 30 April, had notified Fitz Roy of his recall from his appointment as Governor of New Zealand, for 'defects in circumspection, firmness, and punctuality'. Another reason was Fitz Roy's temporary abolition of customs duties at the Bay and elsewhere — the sop he had offered after the fall of Kororareka. In his place Captain G. Grey, recently Governor of South Australia, was appointed, who arrived at Auckland on 14 November, and was installed as Governor four days later. Fitz Roy's failure demonstrated that New Zealand could not be governed without military and other assistance from Great Britain. Grey had this of right, whereas Fitz Roy did not.

Grey was, however, a different character to Fitz Roy in every respect, and although greatly better equipped personally, financially and militarily than his predecessor had ever been, from then onwards he missed few opportunities to ascribe New Zealand's difficulties to Fitz Roy's mismanagement. He came to the Bay on the *Elphinstone* within ten days of his landing in Auckland. A meeting of chiefs was convened, and with a firmness to which they had not been accustomed in a Governor, he made known to them his policy and intentions. He found the troops in good heart, camped near Okiato, Old Russell. At this time missionaries were attempting to effect a reconciliation, and until this peace offer had been accepted or rejected, Grey would not act against the disaffected chiefs. The Rev. Burrows carried a message from Grey to Heke, but neither he nor Kawiti responded, and instead decided to build a *pa* in Kawiti's territory at Rua-pekapeka in the Akerama Hills, on the ridge called Tapuae-haruru, where they would make their next stand. This was to the east of Kawiti's village of Waiomio. Advised of this, Grey sent to Auckland for all available troops and ships, and issued orders for an assault on Rua-pekapeka, after taking personal command. Lieutenant-Colonel Despard no doubt found such a decision by a captain distasteful. By early December Grey had an available force of 68 officers and 1100 men, consisting of elements of the 58th and 99th Regiments, sailors and marines, the East India Company's artillery from the *Elphinstone,* and Auckland Volunteers. He also had at his command 450 Maori allies under Nene, Patuone, Tawhai, Repa and Nopera Panakareao, supported by Taonui, whose task was to watch the movements of Heke, then recovering from his wound at Hikurangi (Tautoro).

Under Grey's leadership, the campaign for Rua-pekapeka went without a hitch. Again the *Slains Castle* and HMS *North Star* were pressed into service to take the troops up the Kawakawa River, where they were encamped temporarily at

Pomare's old *pa*, which he had abandoned for his inland *pa* at Karetu, called Puke-tohunoa. This time the expedition was to travel up the Kawakawa to the attack, and on the advice of a local chief who offered to act as a guide, the first stage of the march was made from a promontory on the west bank of the Kawakawa River, through which the railway tunnel now passes. To this point, the main body of the soldiers were ferried in boats from Otuihu, and from there the march took them to Taumarere by a Maori track, although some were ferried all the way up in boats. Heke and his allies did not harry the troops with guerilla tactics. Had they done so in this and previous actions, it could have proved difficult for the invading columns, particularly during the march to Okaihau, when they were particularly vulnerable. But the defenders were obviously concerned only with testing their opponent's strength when pitted against the Maori defences.

Having returned to Auckland, Grey again made the journey to the Bay, and remained with the forces throughout the ensuing campaign. On 27 December, 700 troops marched from Taumarere on a Maori track, which had been recently improved by the Auckland Volunteers so that it was now passable for wheeled traffic. So Grey's army came to the *pa*, by now a formidable defensive work which later drew admiring comment from military experts. Kawiti had been occupying Ruapekapeka with his own people and some of Heke's, but two days before the fall of the *pa* he was joined by Heke, himself from Tautoro, some seven miles south of Kaikohe. He had evaded Taonui and his watchdogs, and had brought 60 men, but the besieged force apparently never amounted to more than a few hundred, and had no chance at all. Arrayed before them towards the end of December were well-equipped military, naval and Maori forces numbering over 1500, armed with seven pieces of artillery and four mortars. The defenders had two small cannon which fired only two shots between them before they were silenced by a preliminary bombardment on 30 December.

After the bush had been felled between the soldiers' camp and the *pa*, a carefully planned and concentrated artillery barrage opened on 10 January 1846, and although the defenders had adequate shelter underground, the palisades were extensively damaged by this battering. There was no infantry attack that day, and the defenders stood firm. The next day was Sunday and they naively assumed that the Christian pakeha would not fight. In this, their missionary teaching had deluded them, for that day, Grey's troops carried the assault into the *pa* itself. Most of the garrison were at religious worship in the bush at the rear, but the old heathen Kawiti was in the *pa,* and he and some followers fought bitterly. But caught thus, separated and disorganised, the defenders were soon overcome, and by nightfall the stronghold was in the hands of the Government forces, which had lost 12 killed and 30 wounded — 26 of whom were seamen or marines.

Although Kawiti and Heke and their people remained at large, the war in the North was over. For 18 months Heke and Kawiti had defied the might of the Queen's Government with no prospect of ultimate success, hoping, no doubt, that an honourable solution might result. But now, with this decisive defeat, with forces greatly superior in equipment and technology poised to crush any further hostile action, the patriotic war in the North came to an end. These people honestly believed that they had been deceived, but they never again produced a leader willing to do anything about it. Among the chiefs mustered by Heke and Kawiti for the war were Whe, Te Haratua, Pene Taui, Hare Te Pure, Hautungia, Te Awa, Kuao, Te Haara, Tohua, Hori Kingi, Maru, Kokouri, Hikitene, Haumere and Tukerehu.

At the end of January Despard left Auckand to return to Sydney. Although the main body of his troops left the Bay, a detachment of 300 from the 58th under Major Bridge was left as a garrison at Busby's estate, where the house, now the Treaty House, had been damaged during the war. In May, sickness broke out among the soldiers, whereupon Bridge decided to find a more suitable camp. He selected Mair's old estate at Te Wahapu which the garrison occupied in July. Te Wahapu remained a military establishment for 11 years. During this time the garrison was engaged for some of its time in building roads in the district. The road from Paihia to Ohaeawai was almost certainly one of these. Part of this was the half-mile stone causeway across the mouth of the Kaipatiki Creek, about a mile from Paihia.

By the time it was occupied by the military, the affairs of Te Wahapu were in disorder. Mayhew had taken a lease in perpetuity from Mair, but later assigned it to Henry Green Smith, who in turn assigned it to one Burr. Waetford remained throughout attorney for the estate in New Zealand. In order to finance his original purchase of the lease, Mayhew had paid £300 in cash and had raised a mortgage for the remaining £4700 with a Captain Robert Milne. It was to Milne that the £400 annual rent for the military occupation was paid as a result of these transactions.

In a proclamation gazetted on 24 January 1846 Grey revoked Fitz Roy's proclamation of martial law, and by a further proclamation he issued a free pardon to all concerned. Kawiti responded to this, but it was not until 1848, only two years before his death, that Heke met the Governor and shook his hand. He died a bitter and disillusioned man.

Meanwhile, Kororareka lay in ruins. As an economic entity, the Bay of Islands, so prosperous and promising in 1840, had ceased to exist. The flagstaff on Maiki Hill, the focal point of the trouble, remained where it fell, now having neither use nor significance. But a new one was erected with full Maori ceremony and honours in January 1858. For his services, Nene received a pension of £100 per year, and the Government built a house for him at Kororareka, which he occupied in 1846. The Government continued to shower other gifts on him from time to time.[16] Nene never again lived at his proper home at Utakura, in the Hokianga, where, it has been suggested, his life may have been in danger. When he died, a memorial was erected to his honour in the Russell churchyard.

Grey, as are all such strong-headed men, was either loathed or fulsomely praised by those acquainted with him. He had an obvious affection for the Maori people, but his implacable hatred for land grabbers did not endear him to many settlers. It was unfortunate that on the land issue he fell foul of the Rev. Henry Williams, who had worked hard at the Bay of Islands for over 20 years for what he deemed to be right. Grey's attack on

Williams was directed mainly at his weakest point, his extensive land purchases,[17] and was clearly calculated to damage the political influence of the Church Missionary Society. Since he now had military strength, he no longer required the intermediary services of the missionaries. At the same time, he also accused them of subversive activities during the war, but these charges were not proved, nor, indeed, was any justification found for them. Nor did Pompallier escape unscathed; since, as a 'foreigner' he was widely suspected of not discouraging Heke, even if he did not actively encourage him in his campaign against British rule.[18]

Among Williams' failings was his predilection for politics. He had been prominent among those missionaries and settlers whose influence had contributed to the success of the Waitangi negotiations in 1840. To be accused of traitorous activities, having so willingly supported Hobson and his Government, must indeed have been a bitter blow to him. His brush with Grey eventually led to his dismissal from the Church Missionary Society in 1849.

Curiously, Williams' eulogists have tended to elevate him to the status of patron saint of the Bay of Islands, a notion that he himself would probably have rejected. This seems to have arisen from his ill-advised martyrdom by Grey, who stated in a despatch to the Colonial Secretary, 'that these individuals cannot be put in possession of these tracts of land without a large expenditure of British blood and money' — the notorious 'Blood and Treasure' despatch.[19] It cannot be denied that Grey's views on the ethics of excessive missionary land purchases were soundly based, despite the fact that they never looked as if they would lead to bloodshed. Nevertheless, he was intemperate in his attacks on these transactions. In attempting to depict Williams as a heartless exploiter of Maoris he was so far astray that he directed undue attention and much sympathy towards him, leading to a spate of pro-Williams eulogies, commencing with that of his son-in-law, Hugh Carleton, in 1874, and continuing to this day. These have tended to overshadow the contributions and often brilliant talents of many of his co-workers, such as his brother William, Octavius Hadfield, Richard Taylor and William Colenso. The Methodists at Hokianga, Hobbs, Stack, Woon and Whitely, to name a few, made equally significant contributions to Maori-pakeha relations, as indeed, the Catholics did also, but it is of the Church Missionary Society we hear most.

Williams arrived in New Zealand after eight years of hard work and privation had been endured by the men and women who preceded him. It was they, not him and his comfortable flock, who broke the ground, opened the way, and bore the heat and burden of the day. In retrospect, Williams appears as an authoritarian, competent and conscientious administrator for the Society, who industriously built the New Zealand Anglican mission on the hard-won foundation laid by his predecessors, and on Samuel Marsden's dynamic personality and enduring prestige with the Maori chiefs. His loyalty was unquestionable, and in his devotion to the maintenance of peace and order at the Bay in the troubled period between 1840 and 1846, he was tireless. It must therefore have been a matter for great satisfaction both to him and his family when the Church Missionary Society re-instated him in its service in 1854.

When the blockade was lifted in 1846, the whaleships drifted back in reduced numbers, and for some years the slowly re-built port, now called Russell, lived again on this trade in one way or another. Coal, discovered on Kawiti's land in 1864, was the next source of work and revenue, when the mines were opened up at Kawakawa by John McLeod in 1867. The timber trade then revived, and supported the population for a time, with fishing, farming and horticulture.

Today, the Port of Opua continues to have importance as a potential outlet for the products of the farms and forests of the North, while thousands of New Zealanders and overseas tourists enjoy the beauty and romance of the Bay, and they love it for itself, not for its commercial potential.

---

1. See Appendix 1.3.
2. Wards, *The Shadow of the Land*, p.194.

3. Pakeha Maori (Maning, F.E.), *Heke's War in the North of New Zealand,* p.200.
4. Wards, p.102-4.
5. Accounts of the war may be found in: Buick, *New Zealand's First War, passim;* Burrows, R. *Heke's War in the North, passim;* Cowan, J. *New Zealand Wars,* v.1, p.7-87; Meurant, E. 'Meurant Papers', (Auck.Pub.Lib.); Pakeha Maori, op.cit., p.183-274; Rutherford J. *Hone Heke's Rebellion,* 1844-6, *passim*; Thomson, *The Story of New Zealand,* v.2, p.95-130; Wards, op.cit., p.102-202; White, J. 'White Papers', (Auck.Pub.Lib.).
6. See Appendix 1.8.
7. Wards, p.120.
8. Ibid, p.119.
9. Burrows.
10. Buick, p.96.
11. Sherrin and Wallace, *Early History of New Zealand,* p.699.
12. Mair Papers, Auckland.
13. See Appendix 1.19.
14. Wards, p.188-9.
15. Wilson, *Land Problems of the Forties,* p.73-5.
16. Wards, p.205.
17. McLintock, A.H. *Crown Colony Government in New Zealand,* p.199-200.
18. Wards, p.98-9.
19. McLintock, p.201.

Appendix 1
Northern Maori Genealogies (Whakapapa)

These genealogies are not intended for the uses to which Maori people normally put such records, and the author does not presume to inform Maoris on these matters. What follows, then, is intended for the information of Pakeha readers, and to show the relationships of some of the great Maori families to each other. This in turn throws light on otherwise inexplicable alliances, and on some of the actions these people took, or refrained from taking. Maoris may notice things with which they disagree, and if so I apologise to them, and can only say that I have done my best to preserve information, the knowledge of which is important to the New Zealand historian. I do not think there are errors that would affect this objective.

The author's association with the Northern Maori people extends back nearly fifty years, and the genealogies have been collected by him as a result of that association and during that time, from many sources.

SOURCES

1) Many Maori people have, in the course of the above period, contributed valuable traditional matter bearing on these records.
2) Extensive genealogies in the author's possession by Mita Wepiha, and by Pere Wihongi (1847-1928) Ex A. Cole, Awarua.
3) John White, incorporated in his map showing the location of Ngapuhi *hapu*, and apparently used to illustrate his lectures on Maori customs, A.J.H.R., E No. 7, 1861 (A.P.L.)
4) The Aperahama Taonui Manuscript, 1849 (A.I.L.)
5) Extensive Bay of Islands and other genealogies incorporated in what are clearly the Block Committee Minute books relating to the Rawhiti and Islands cases in the Maori Land Court (A.I.L. Mss. 895).
6) Hare Hongi Stowell papers (T.L.). Use with caution. By local standards not very reliable in some respects.
7) Milligan papers. (T.L.) Scrappy.
8) Tai Tokerau Maori Land Court Minutes.
9) Leslie Kelly, from Bay of Islands sources (Te Rawhiti) and published by him in various J.P.S. and in *Marion du Fresne at the Bay of Islands*.
10) *The Peopling of the North* and *Maori Wars of the Nineteenth Century*, by S.P. Smith.

275

6) and 7) are of interest, but not recommended, and in regard to 5) and 8) it must be understood that the desire to succeed in applications for title to land sometimes led to deception to support false claims, but the Court, or a later appeal to the Appelate Court in most cases corrected errors that occurred in this way. The student must therefore be sure to refer to appeal cases. The author has carefully checked his sources against one another, and is satisfied with the result. A remarkable consistency exists among most sources, at least as far up as Rahiri, which, in practical terms is as far back as we need to go.

Many of these genealogies are composite, that is, they may be derived from more than one source, but in some cases this has been necessary to order to demonstrate the relationships mentioned above. Sources for individual genealogies are therefore not given.

The reader is warned against accepting relationships stated to exist by the early visitors, and sometimes even missionaries, between Maoris of their acquaintance. The Maori then, and to a lesser extent even now, belonged to an extended family group in which precise relationships were not always important. Uncle and cousin were very general terms, and in-law relationships could also have confused early writers. Therefore true relationships can be deduced only from the study of reliable genealogies (whakapapa).

1.1 The relationship between Te Puhi (of Whangaroa), Te Pahi, and Hongi Hika.

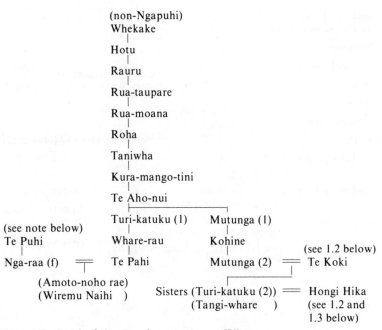

(non-Ngapuhi)
Whekake
|
Hotu
|
Rauru
|
Rua-taupare
|
Rua-moana
|
Roha
|
Taniwha
|
Kura-mango-tini
|
Te Aho-nui

Turi-katuku (1)   Mutunga (1)
(see note below) | |
Te Puhi   Whare-rau   Kohine
| | | (see 1.2 below)
Nga-raa (f) ══ Te Pahi   Mutunga (2) ══ Te Koki

    (Amoto-noho rae)   Sisters (Turi-katuku (2)) ══ Hongi Hika
    (Wiremu Naihi   )   (Tangi-whare   )   (see 1.2 and
                                                               1.3 below)

Note: Te Puhi of the *Boyd* massacre, at Whangaroa.

277

1.2 The relationship between Hongi Hika and the Coastal Ngati-rehia.

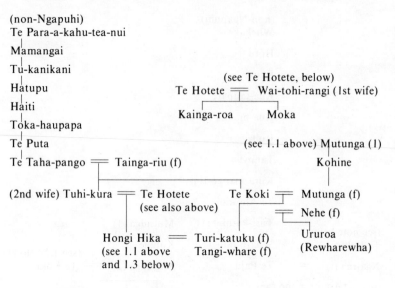

1.3 The relationship between Hongi Hika, Ruatara (no descendants) and Hone Heke.

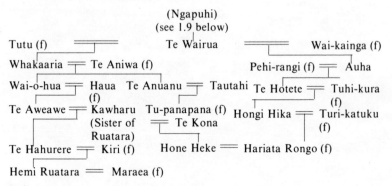

1.4 The marriage of Makoare Taonui (Hokianga) into coastal Ngati-rehia.

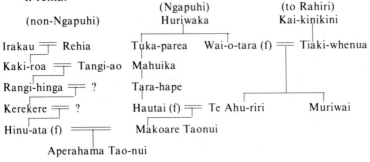

                                (Ngapuhi)   (to Rahiri)

  (non-Ngapuhi)   Huriwaka   Kai-kinikini

Irakau == Rehia   Tuka-parea   Wai-o-tara (f) == Tiaki-whenua

Kaki-roa == Tangi-ao Mahuika

Rangi-hinga == ?   Tara-hape

Kerekere == ?   Hautai (f) == Te Ahu-riri   Muriwai

Hinu-ata (f) ========== Makoare Taonui

      Aperahama Tao-nui

1.5 Rewa (Maanu), Whare-rahi (Whare-nui) and Moka (Kainga-
mataa)

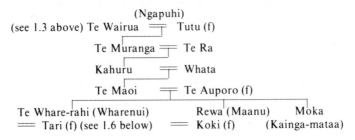

                      (Ngapuhi)

(see 1.3 above) Te Wairua == Tutu (f)

          Te Muranga == Te Ra

          Kahuru == Whata

          Te Maoi == Te Auporo (f)

Te Whare-rahi (Wharenui)   Rewa (Maanu)   Moka
  == Tari (f) (see 1.6 below)   == Koki (f) (Kainga-mataa)

279

1.6 Tapua, Nene (Tamati Waaka) and Patu-one (Eruera Maihi)

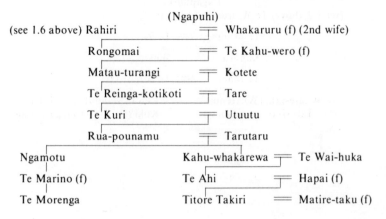

(see 1.7 below)   (Ngapuhi)
Rahiri ══ Ahua-iti (f) (1st wife)

Uenuku Kuare ══ Kare-ariki (f)

(see 1.11   Maikuku (f) ══ Hua-takaroa   Te Wairua   (see 1.3 above)
below) Te Ra ══ Whaka-kopapa (f) ══ Whare-toru (3rd w)

Kamama ══ Papatu   Te Ngawa ══ Kuta (f)

Papa-ora ══ ?   Te Patu

Ripia ══ Takare (f)   Tua

Tapua ══ Kawe-hau (f)

Patu-one (Eruera Maihi) Nene (Tamati Waaka)   Tari (f)
══ Whare-rahi
(see 1.5 above)

1.7 Titore Takiri and Te Morenga (see also 1.19 below)

(Ngapuhi)
(see 1.6 above) Rahiri ══ Whakaruru (f) (2nd wife)

Rongomai ══ Te Kahu-wero (f)

Matau-turangi ══ Kotete

Te Reinga-kotikoti ══ Tare

Te Kuri ══ Utuutu

Rua-pounamu ══ Tarutaru

Ngamotu   Kahu-whakarewa ══ Te Wai-huka

Te Marino (f)   Te Ahi   Hapai (f)

Te Morenga   Titore Takiri ══ Matire-taku (f)

280

1.8 Kawiti (Ngapuhi) and Whare-umu (Ngatimanu)

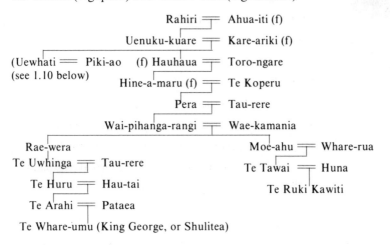

Rahiri ═╤═ Ahua-iti (f)

Uenuku-kuare ═╤═ Kare-ariki (f)

(Uewhati ══ Piki-ao   (f) Hauhaua ═╤═ Toro-ngare
(see 1.10 below)

Hine-a-maru (f) ═╤═ Te Koperu

Pera ═╤═ Tau-rere

Wai-pihanga-rangi ═╤═ Wae-kamania

Rae-wera   Moe-ahu ═╤═ Whare-rua

Te Uwhinga ═╤═ Tau-rere   Te Tawai ═╤═ Huna

Te Huru ═╤═ Hau-tai   Te Ruki Kawiti

Te Arahi ═╤═ Pataea

Te Whare-umu (King George, or Shulitea)

1.9 Kai-teke (or Tareha, or Kemara) (Ngapuhi)

		Rahiri ═╤═ Whakaruru (f)
(see 1.8 above)		
Hauhaua (f) ═╤═ Toro-ngare		Kaha-rau ═╤═ Hou-taringa (f)
Te Aonga-taua ═╤═ Rangi-heke-tini (f)		Taura-poho ═╤═ Ruaki-whiria (f)
Toko-wha ═╤═ ?		Mahia ═╤═ Hau (f)
Te Ao ═╤═ Taurekareka		Nga-hue ═╤═ Tau-tahi
Mangere ═╤═ Te Awa		Te Wairua ═╤═ Tutu (f)
Haro ═╤═ Te Kiri		Kawhi (1) ═╤═ Tango
Mano ═╤═ Whee		
Kai-teke ══ Puatea (f)		

281

1.10 Korokoro (or Te Kauae) (Ngare Raumati)

```
        Ue-whati ══ Piki-ao (see 1.8 above)
Ue-mata-ngerengere ══ ?
             Pare ══ ?
         Te Haua ══ ?
          Ohuha ══ Te Tawheta
       Tukawau ══ Muri-tere          (Ngapuhi connection)
    Mau-hikitia ══ Te Awhi          Hui-po ══ Raumati (f)
          Korokoro (Te Kauae)       (Ngare Raumati (Ngapuhi)
```

1.11 The two Pomares, commonly Pomare Nui and Whetoi (Ngatimanu)

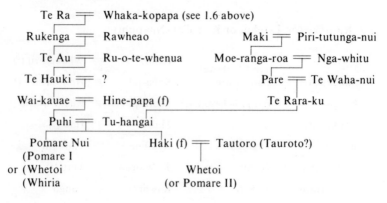

```
        Te Ra ══ Whaka-kopapa (see 1.6 above)
     Rukenga ══ Rawheao              Maki ══ Piri-tutunga-nui
        Te Au ══ Ru-o-te-whenua   Moe-ranga-roa ══ Nga-whitu
     Te Hauki ══ ?                         Pare ══ Te Waha-nui
   Wai-kauae ══ Hine-papa (f)            Te Rara-ku
         Puhi ══ Tu-hangai
     Pomare Nui         Haki (f) ══ Tautoro (Tauroto?)
     (Pomare I
  or (Whetoi                 Whetoi
     (Whiria              (or Pomare II)
```

282

1.12 Tupe of Kororareka

Te Wairua ══ Tutu (f) (see 1.3 above)

Whaka-aria ══ Te Aniwa (f)

Kawhi (2) ══ ?

Tupe ══ Moe-waka (f)

Koki (f) ══ Rewa (Maanu) (see 1.5 above)

1.13 Moetara, chief of Pakanae, Hokianga (Ngapuhi)

Rahiri ══ Whakaruru (f)

Kaharau ══ Hou-taringa (f)

Taurapoho ══ Ruaki-whiria (f)

Tupoto ══ Kauae (f)

Korokoro

Whitiki

Tangaroa

Te Haunui

Te Hunga

Aitu

Moetara

1.14 Tirarau, chief of Mangakahia (Ngapuhi)

```
Rahiri              ══  Ahua-iti (f)

Uenuku-kuare        ══  Kare-ariki (f)

Hauhaua (f)         ══  Toro-ngare

Tama-ngana          ══  Rangi-heke-tini (f)

Rua-ngaio           ══  Ika-o-te-awa

Taura-haiti         ══  Whare-angiangi

Te Pona-harakeke    ══  Whaari

Tataia              ══  Tara-mai-nuku

Haumu               ══  Tokai-tawhia

Kukupa              ══  Whitiao (f)

              Te Tirarau
```

1.15 Waimate — Kaikohe chief Tai-whanga (Ngatimiru)

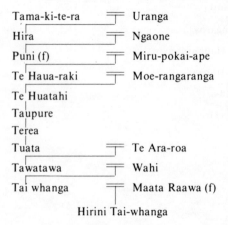

```
Tama-ki-te-ra       ══  Uranga

Hira                ══  Ngaone

Puni (f)            ══  Miru-pokai-ape

Te Haua-raki        ══  Moe-rangaranga

Te Huatahi

Taupure

Terea

Tuata               ══  Te Ara-roa

Tawatawa            ══  Wahi

Tai whanga          ══  Maata Raawa (f)

              Hirini Tai-whanga
```

284

1.16 Muru-paenga, chief of Kaipara (Ngatiwhatua).

Rahiri ╤ Moe-tonga (f) Note 3rd wife.

Tangaroa-i-te-whakamanama

Hine-te-wai

Hau-maua-rangi

Rango

Moe-rangaranga

Tira-waikato

Muru-paenga

1.17 The two Hare Hongis (Ngapuhi)
    (see 1.12 above)

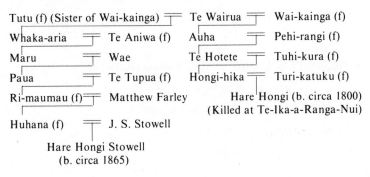

Tutu (f) (Sister of Wai-kainga) ╤ Te Wairua ╤ Wai-kainga (f)

Whaka-aria ╤ Te Aniwa (f) Auha ╤ Pehi-rangi (f)

Maru ╤ Wae Te Hotete ╤ Tuhi-kura (f)

Paua ╤ Te Tupua (f) Hongi-hika ╤ Turi-katuku (f)

Ri-maumau (f) ╤ Matthew Farley Hare Hongi (b. circa 1800)
                                (Killed at Te-Ika-a-Ranga-Nui)

Huhana (f) ╤ J. S. Stowell

    Hare Hongi Stowell
      (b. circa 1865)

1.18 Te Nana, chief of Rawhiti (Ngapuhi)

Rahiri = Whakaruru (f)
|
Kaharau = Hou-taringa (f)
|
Taura-poho = Ihenga (f)
|
Tupoto = Tawa-keiti (f)
|
Kairewa
|
Te Miringa
|
Uru-karito
|
Tere-whare
|
Wai-kawe-kee
|
Kopipi
|
Huri   Kemara (Kaiteke) see 1.9 above
|
Te Nana = Here (f) (Celia)   Takarua
|
Himi (Clendon ?) = Kiritapu (f)
|
Heta (Clendon or Te Nana)

1.19 Nopera Pana-kareao, chief of Kaitaia (Rarawa)

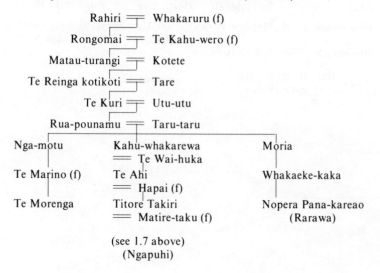

Rahiri = Whakaruru (f)
|
Rongomai = Te Kahu-wero (f)
|
Matau-turangi = Kotete
|
Te Reinga kotikoti = Tare
|
Te Kuri = Utu-utu
|
Rua-pounamu = Taru-taru

Nga-motu   Kahu-whakarewa   Moria
                   = Te Wai-huka
|
Te Marino (f)   Te Ahi   Whakaeke-kaka
| = Hapai (f)
|
Te Morenga   Titore Takiri   Nopera Pana-kareao
                  = Matire-taku (f)   (Rarawa)

(see 1.7 above)
(Ngapuhi)

1.20 Ko Te Whakapapa O Tiraha Papa-harakeke Tenei

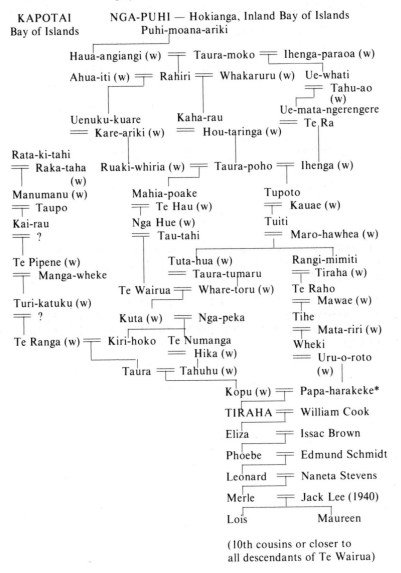

KAPOTAI   NGA-PUHI — Hokianga, Inland Bay of Islands
Bay of Islands   Puhi-moana-ariki

Haua-angiangi (w) ══ Taura-moko ══ Ihenga-paraoa (w)

Ahua-iti (w) ══ Rahiri ══ Whakaruru (w)   Ue-whati
                                                ══ Tahu-ao
                                                   (w)
        Uenuku-kuare   Kaha-rau   Ue-mata-ngerengere
        ══ Kare-ariki (w)   ══ Hou-taringa (w) ══ Te Ra

Rata-ki-tahi
══ Raka-taha   Ruaki-whiria (w) ══ Taura-poho ══ Ihenga (w)
   (w)
Manumanu (w)   Mahia-poake   Tupoto
══ Taupo   ══ Te Hau (w)   ══ Kauae (w)
Kai-rau   Nga Hue (w)   Tuiti
══ ?   ══ Tau-tahi   ══ Maro-hawhea (w)

Te Pipene (w)   Tuta-hua (w)   Rangi-mimiti
══ Manga-wheke   ══ Taura-tumaru   ══ Tiraha (w)
                Te Wairua ══ Whare-toru (w)   Te Raho
Turi-katuku (w)   ══ Mawae (w)
══ ?   Kuta (w) ══ Nga-peka   Tihe
                                            ══ Mata-riri (w)
Te Ranga (w) ══ Kiri-hoko   Te Numanga   Wheki
                            ══ Hika (w)   ══ Uru-o-roto
                Taura ══ Tahuhu (w)   (w)

                    Kopu (w) ══ Papa-harakeke*

                    TIRAHA ══ William Cook

                    Eliza ══ Issac Brown

                    Phoebe ══ Edmund Schmidt

                    Leonard ══ Naneta Stevens

                    Merle ══ Jack Lee (1940)

                    Lois   Maureen

                    (10th cousins or closer to
                    all descendants of Te Wairua)

OTHER RELATIONSHIPS
(Tiraha is 5th cousin or closer to the chiefs in capitals.)

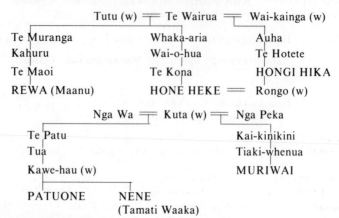

```
              Tutu (w) ══ Te Wairua ══ Wai-kainga (w)
Te Muranga            Whaka-aria         Auha
Kahuru                Wai-o-hua          Te Hotete
Te Maoi               Te Kona            HONGI HIKA
REWA (Maanu)          HONE HEKE ══ Rongo (w)

            Nga Wa ══ Kuta (w) ══ Nga Peka
  Te Patu                      Kai-kinikini
  Tua                          Tiaki-whenua
  Kawe-hau (w)                 MURIWAI

PATUONE        NENE
            (Tamati Waaka)
```

*Papa-harakeke and his party were murdered in 1822 at Rotorua at the instigation of Te Rau-paraha. Hongi Hika's war expedition to Rotorua in 1823 avenged this.

The *patu*, PAPA-HARAKEKE, was made to effect this vengeance, but was never used. It is now the property of the ARAWA TRUST BOARD, but in the custody of the AUCKLAND INSTITUTE MUSEUM — Ref. No. 19424.

Appendix 2
Te Iwi Nga-Puhi

There are two components of the Nga-Puhi tribe, that is, Hokianga
Nga-Puhi and inland and Bay of Islands Nga-Puhi. Of these, there is
an old saying:

Ka mimiti te puna i Hokianga —
Ka toto te puna i Tau-marere.
Ka mimiti te puna i Taù-marere —
Ka toto te puna I Hokianga.

(From Hemi Pou, Whangarei)

That is to say — When the spring at Hokianga dries up, the spring
at the Bay of Islands flows, and when the Bay of Islands spring is dry,
that at Hokianga flows.

This is a reference to the age-old obligation of the two components
to each other — the Taumarere and inland Bay of Islands descendants of Rahiri's wife, Ahua-iti, through her son, Uenuku-kuare, and
Rahiri's descendants through his son Kaharau, from his Hokianga
wife, Whakaruru. The saying implies that when support is required
by one of the groups in trouble with enemies, the strength of the other
can be relied upon. Hone Heke, when the Hokianga people did not
come to his aid during his actions against British troops in 1845-6,
referred to the failure of this principle, asking bitterly, "Where is
Kaharau?"

There are chants which describe the boundaries of the territory
occupied by Nga-Puhi. The first chant below probably dates back to
the mid-eighteenth century. Then, Nga-Puhi had not expanded in
strength to the east coast, or Te Rawhiti, as they knew it, from their
home territory inland and at Hokianga. The second chant clearly
reflects the dramatic change in Nga-Puhi fortunes in the time of Auha
and Te Hotete, Hongi Hika's grandfather and father. This occurred
at about the end of the eighteenth century and the early part of the
nineteenth, by which time the whole of the Bay coast between Takou
and Rakau-mangamanga (Cape Brett) was under the tribe's domination. However, the inclusion in the chant of the Ngati-Wai and
Ngai-Tahuhu lands to the south does appear a little ambitious.

Both these chants, and that above, demonstrate that Nga-Puhi
considered itself to be a corporate group, despite ill-formed Pakeha
opinion which depicts it as "a loose confederation of tribes". It is no
more this than any other tribal group in New Zealand. The common
ancestor of all of consequence in the tribe is Rahiri, the grandson of
Puhi-moana-ariki, who appears to be the eponymous ancestor.

Here are the chants:
> Titiro e Whiria ki Pa-nguru
> Maunga-kenana, ki Maunga-taniwha
> Ki Whakarongo-rua, ki Ngaia-tonga
> Ki Te Ranga, ki Pare-mata, kapo ai
> Titiro Hiku-rangi, ki Tuta-moe
> Whakatere, Puke-huia, Rama-roa.

> Ko nga maunga enei o Nga-Puhi, e
> E nga kawe korero, a nga tupuna, e
> Ka tau ratou o haki ete iwi
> Whakapono, tumanako, aroha.
>
> (From Graham Rankin, Kaikohe)

Translated:
> Look from Whiria to Pa-nguru
> Maunga-kenana to Maunga-taniwha
> To Whakarongo-rua, to Ngaia-tonga
> To Te Ranga, to Pare-mata, reach out
> Look to Hiku-rangi, to Tuta-moe,
> Whakatere, Puke-huia, Rama-roa.

> These are the Mountains of Nga-Puhi
> The story brought to us by our ancestors
> Our challenge of the pride of our people
> Truth, longing, love.

This is the older chant. Unlike that below, it apparently includes a Nga-Puhi occupation at the south of the Mango-nui Harbour — perhaps the land taken there by Te Hotete before his initial attack on Te Rawhiti. Land thereabouts was later involved in the Government's notorious Mango-nui purchase, when its ownership was in dispute between Nga-Puhi and Rarawa.

The second chant:
> Te Whare o Nga-Puhi.

> He mea hanga
> Ko papa-tuanuku te papa-rahi
> Ko nga maunga nga poupou
> Ko te rangi e titiro iho neu te tuanui.

> Puhanga-tohora titiro ki Te Rama-roa
> Te Rama-roa titiro ki Whiria
> Ki te paiaka o te riri, ki te kawa o Rahiri
> Whiria titiro ki Pa-ngu-ru, ki Papata
> Ki te rakau tu papata i tu ki te Tai-ha-uru

290

Pa-nguru Papata titiro ki Maunga-taniwha
Maunga-taniwha titiro ki Tokerau
Tokerau titiro ki Rakau-mangamanga
Rakau-mangamanga titiro ki Manaia
Manaia titiro ki Tuta-moe
Tuta-moe titiro ki Manga-nui
Manga-nui titiro ki Puhanga-tohora
Ko te whare ia tenei o Nga-Puhi.

(From Eru Pou, Kaikohe)

Translated:

The House of Nga-Puhi

This is how it is made:

The earth is the floor, the mountains the supports, the sky we see above is the roof:

From Puhanga-tohora look toward Te Rama-roa: Te Ramaroa toward Whiria — the seat of our war-like prowess, the ancestral line of Rahiri:

From Whiria look toward Pa-nguru — to Papata, to the thickly growing trees which extend to the western sea:

From Pa-nguru and Papata toward Maunga-taniwha: from Maunga-taniwha look toward the Bay of Islands: from the Bay to Cape Brett and from there to Whanga-rei Heads: (Manaia)

From Manaia to Tuta-moe: from Tuta-moe to Manga-nui Bluff: and from the Bluff look toward Puhanga-tohora.

This is the house of Nga-Puhi.

Appendix 3
Nga Hapu O Te Iwi Nga-Puhi

HAPU	LOCATION
	North Hokianga
Wai-Araki	Whakarapa (Pa-nguru)
Ngati-Manawa	Whakarapa (Pa-nguru)
Ngai-Tupoto	Motiti
Ngati-Here	Motu-karaka
Ngati-Hau	Motu-karaka
Uri-Kopura	Rangiora
Ngati-Hua	Motu-runa
Mahurehure	Tute-kehua
Te Uri Mahoe	Manga-muka
Uri-Kopura	Manga-muka

Ihu-Tai	Manga-muka
Te Uri o Te Ahu	Omahuta
Ngati-Wharara	Koko-huia (?)
Kohatu-Taka	?
Pehi-Kauri	Te Tio
Ihu-Tai	Rau-kapara (Orira)
Te Popoto	Rangi-ahua
Ngati-Hao	Wai-hou (Upper)
Patu-Po	Wai-hou (Upper)
Te Ngahengahe	Wai-hou (Upper)
Mata-Pungarehu	Puketi

South Hokianga

Te Popoto	Uta-kura
Whanau-Pani	Ho-reke — Uta-kura
Ngati-Hao	Ho-reke — Uta-kura
Ngati-Toro	Motu-kiore
Te Ngahengahe	Motu-kiore
Te Honihoni	?
Ngati-Rauawa	Lower Waima
Mahurehure	Waima
Uri-Kopura	Omanaia
Ngati-Hau	Omanaia
Ngai-Tupoto	Omanaia
Ngati-Here	Oue
Ngati-Hurihanga	Manawa Kaiaia
Te Hikutu	Whirinaki
Ngati-Korokoro	Pa-kanae
Ngati-Wharara	Pa-kanae
Pouka	Pa-kanae
Ngati-Pou	Omapere (Hokianga Heads)
Ngati-Korokoro	Waima-maku
Te Roroa) Border-line —	Waima-maku
Te Roroa) Ngati-Whatua ?	Wai-poua

South Inland Hokianga

Ngati-Te Rahape	Waima
Ngati-Kaihoro	Waima
Ngati-Te-Rouowe	Waima
Kohatu-Taka	Waima
Te Uri Kai-Whare	Waima
Po-Kare	Taheke
Ngati-Pakau	Taheke

Ngai-Tu	Taheke
Ngati-Kaihoro	Punaki-tere
Ngati-Moe	Punaki-tere
Ngati-Ue	Punaki-tere
Ngati-Tautahi	Punaki-tere
Ngai-Tu Te Auru	Otaua
Ngati Te Ra	Otaua
Ngati-Wai-Hengehenge	Otaua

Western and South-Western Bay of Islands

Ngati-ue-Taora	Kai-kohe
Te Uri o Hua	Kai-kohe
Te Tako Toke	Kai-kohe
Ngati-Whakaeke	Kai-kohe
Ngati-Tore-Hina	Kai-kohe
Ngati-Kura	Kai-kohe
Ngati-Tautahi	Kai-kohe
Ngati-Hika-Iro	Kai-kohe
Te Mata Rahurahu	Kai-kohe
Whanau Tara	Kai-kohe
Ngati-Wai-Haro	Mata-raua
Ngai-Tawake	Mata-raua
Te Whanau Koata	Mata-raua
Uri-Kapana	Tautoro
Ngati-Rangi	Tautoro
Ngati-Moerewa	Tautoro
Ngati-Ueoneone	Tautoro
Ngare-Hauata	Tautoro
Ngati-Whakaeke	Tautoro
Ngati-Mahia	Awa-rua
Te Whanau Koata	Awa-rua
xNgati-Manu) Pre-	Awa-rua
xWhanau Whero) European	Awa-rua
Ngati-Toki	Manga-kahia
Ngati-Horahia	Manga-kahia
Ngati-Whakamana	Manga-kahia
Ngati-Tau-Potiki	Manga-kahia
Ngati-Terino	Manga-kahia
Ngati-Aka-Mau	Manga-kahia
Te Ku-Mutu	Manga-kahia
Te Parawhau	Manga-kahia

Central Bay of Islands

Ngati-Koro-Hue	Puke-tapu (Ngawha, or old Ohaea-w
Ngare-Hau-Ata	Nga-whitu
Uri-Kapana	Nga-whitu
Ngati-Rangi	Ohaea-wai (now Ngawha)
Ngati-Kiri-Pakapaka	Te Ahuahu
Uri-Taniwha	Te Ahuahu
Ngati-Matariki	Okaihau
Ngati-Koro-Hue	Te Ma-tira
Ngai-Tawake	Te Kauri
Waikato (Maioha family)	Te Urupa
Ngati-Whakaeke	Te Urupa
Te Whiu	Ranga-unu
Ngati-Rehia	Ranga-unu
Whanau Tara	Manga-taraire
Ngati-Tautahi	Wai-mate
Ngati-Hine-Ira	Wai-mate
Te Motu Koraha	Wai-mate
xNgati-Miru) Pre-	Wai-mate
xWahine-Iti) European	Wai-mate
Nagti-Kawa	Oro-mahoe
Ngati-Rahiri	Oro-mahoe
Ngati-Kawa	Te Tiu-wai

Southern Bay of Islands

Ngati-Hine	Otiria, Wai-omio, Mota-tau
Te Uri Ongaonga	Kawakawa
xNgati-Manu	Kare-tu
xTe Uri Karaka	Kare-tu
xNgati-Kahununu	Kare-tu
xKapotai	Wai-kare
Uri o Hikihiki	Wai-kino
Ngati-Pare	Wai-kino

Eastern Bay of Islands

xKainga-Kuri	Mata-pouri
xTe Parawhau	Mata-pouri
xTe Whanau Whero	Whana-naki
xTe Aki Tai	Whana-naki
xTe Panu Puha	Whana-naki
xTe Panu Puha	Whanga-ruru
xNgau-Paiaka	Whanga-ruru
xTe Tawera	Owae

xNgati-Wai	Tutu-kaka
xNgati-Wai	Mokau, Whanga-ruru
xNgati-Kahu	Puna-ruku
Ngati-Kura	Motu-rua
Ngai-Tawake	Rawhiti
Ngati-Kuta	Rawhiti
xWhakatohea	Rawhiti
xNgare-Raumati	Rawhiti
xNgati-Wai	Rawhiti
xNgati-Kopae	Korora-reka, Motu-arohia
xTe Uri Haku	Korora-reka, Motu-arohia
xPatu Tahi	Paroa

North-western Bay of Islands

Ngati-Rahiri	Waitangi
Mata-Rahurahu	Waitangi
Te Whiu	Waitangi
Ngati-Rahiri	Hau-o-tapiri
Te Whanau Tara	Hau-o-tapiri
xMata-Kakaa	?
xNgati-Rehia	Te Tii Mangonui
xNgati-Rehia	Takou
xTe Ra-Waru	Wai-ana
Mata-Popore	?
Te Ihutai	Puke-whau
xNgati-Mau	Puke-whau
Te Hikutu	Pata-nui, Te Tii Mangonui
Ngati-Tore-Hina	Pata-nui, Te Tii Mangonui

Sources

1) Appendices to the Journals of the House of Representatives: 1862, E No. 7: 1870, A No. 11: 1878, G No. 2. Use cautiously, sometimes unreliable as to spelling and location of *hapu*.
2) John White papers — Auckland Public Library. (Map)
3) Maori Land Court Minutes — Tai Tokerau.
4) Personal communications to the author over some 40 years.

Note: *Hapu* shown thus x cannot be properly described as Nga-puhi, but were closely allied to that tribe by blood and marriage, and in the early nineteenth century all came under the influence and domination of Nga-Puhi. The tribes to which they belonged included Ngai-

Tahuhu, Ngati-Kahu, Ngati-Manu, Ngati-Wai, and Kapo-tai. Ngati-Rehia was closely related to Ngati-Uru — itself a sub-tribe of Ngati-Kahu.

Appendix 4
Old Land Claims at the Bay of Islands
Sources

Published Works
Turton, H. H. — Maori Deeds of Land Purchases, etc (1877)

Cadastral Plans
Deposited Plans (D.P.) and Deeds Records Plans (Lands and Survey Department, Auckland)
Maori Land Plans (M.L.) (Lands and Survey Department, Auckland.)
Old Land Claim Plans (O.L.C.) (Lands and Survey Department, Auckland)
Survey Office Plans (S.O.) (Lands and Survey Department, Auckland)

Land Records
Land Transfer Title Registers (Auckland Land Registry)
Crawford's Index to the Deeds Indexes (Auckland Land Registry)
Wither's Index to the Deeds Indexes (Auckland Land Registry)
Old Land Claim Plan Index (Lands and Survey Department, Auckland)
Crown Grants (Auckland Land Registry)
Deeds Indexes (Auckland Land Registry)
Deeds Registers (Auckland Land Registry)
Old Land Claim Awards (Dillon Bell) Appendices to the Journals of the House of Representatives, 1863, D No 14
Old Land Claim Files, Copies of. (Lands and Survey Department, Auckland)

O.L.C. Plan	Claim No	Area Claimed acres	Purchaser	Area Granted acres	Grantee
1	634	8957	*G. Clarke	6531	Clarke family and Hopkins

2	736	1997	*C.M.S. Families	945	C.M.S. Families
3	734-5	4783	* do	4450	do
4	773	4613	*Rev. R. Davis	4308	Davis family
5	270	1500	T. Joyce	508	H. Hopkins
12	116	1699	J. R. Clendon	1362	J. R. Clendon
13	116	1643	do	1323	W. B. White
15	809	11741	*J. D. Orsmond	5014	Orsmond family and J. Shepherd
16	59	1827	T. Bateman	1157	W. S. Graham
17	804-6	1187	*J. Shepherd	255	J. Shepherd
18	353	355	B. Nesbit	230	A. & W. Scott & J. Hart
19	603-6	20516	*J. King	11788	King family
20	863	157	E. Bolger	157	E. Bolger
21	1309	25	T. Hansen	24	T. Hansen
21	603-6	710	*J. King	710	J. King
24	594-8	82	*J. Kemp	14	J. Kemp
25	803	6300	*J. Shepherd	4195	J. Shepherd
27	227	1595	W. G. C. Hingston	1276	W. G. C. Hingston
28	803	3863	*J. Shepherd	1528	J. Shepherd
29	862	513	E. Bolger	437	C. H. Davis
30	278	151	J. Leitch	151	J. Leitch
33	56	29	T. Bateman	29	J. R. Clendon
34	597	13	*J. Kemp	13	J. Kemp
38	599-02	4464	do	2722	do
39	672-3	345	*Church Miss Soc	345	Church Miss Soc
40	697-9	219	do	141	J. King (incl. land in OLC 56)
41	650	71	H. Day	71	H. Day
42	65	136	*J. Bedggood	136	J. Bedggood
43	529-34	28	*Rev W. Williams	28	H. Williams Jnr
44	51-5	158	J. Barber	158	J. Barber
45	521-5	130	*Rev H. Williams	130	Williams family
46	521-5	187	* do	187	do
47	529-34	1460	*Rev W. Williams	1460	H. Williams Jnr
48	676	977	*Church Miss Soc	977	Church Miss Soc
52	594&6	356	*J. Kemp	356	W. Kemp
53	67	310	Black and Green	310	Black and Green
54	521-5	5528	*Rev H. Williams	5287	Williams family
55	633	1488	*G. Clarke	1463	Clarke family & C.M.S. (37 ac)
56	697	60	*Church Miss Soc	60	J. King (see OLC 40)
57	698	16	* do	16	Church Miss Soc
58	521-5	186	*Rev H. Williams	186	Williams family
59	521-5	1413	* do	1413	do
60	595&8	7125	*J. Kemp	6967	Kemp family

63	1327	588	J. White	588	F. White
65	399-01	53	G. F. Russell	53	Webster & Campbell
66	399-01	117	do	117	do
69	878-80	1896	W. Spickman	1896	W. Spickman
71	871	640	Johnson & Henderson	640	J. Johnson
72	202	117	G. Greenway	117	C. A. Waetford
73	537	262	J. Wright	262	J. Wright
78	939	483	Wesleyan Miss Soc	483	Wesleyan Miss Soc
79	940	77	do	77	do
80	941 943 944	36	do	36	do
81	938	103	Wesleyan Miss Soc	103	Wesleyan Miss Soc
85	513	462	W. White	462	W. Russell
87	512	8	do	9	F. White
91	556	12	W. D. Brind	12	W. D. Brind
96	247-8	937	H. Jellicoe	837	Webster & Campbell
102	1032 1033 1035 1038	916	T. McDonnell,	300	T. McDonnell
106	81	54	J. Byron	54	J. Bryon
117	814-6	217	J. McLeod	217	R. McLeod
122	311	99	F. E. Maning	100	F. E. Maning
123	312-6	523	J. Marmon	523	J. Marmon ·
125	700-3	461	S. H. Ford	461	R. Blaezard
126	607-9	6	*P. H. King	6	P. H. J. King
128	554	504	W. D. Brind	398	F. McMillan & ors
130	969	75	A. & W. Birch	75	A. & W. Birch
131	120	222	J. R. Clendon	222	J. R. Clendon
134	383-5	837	W. Powditch	742	J. Shepherd
135	545	1260	*Rev C. Baker	1260	Rev C. Baker
136	126-7	226	Cook and Day	226	Cook and Day
140	117	23	J. R. Clendon	23	J. R. Clendon
142	122	200	D. B. Cochrane	200	Jane Clendon
150	1045	109	Baron de Thierry	109	Baron de Thierry
158	65	49	*J. Bedggood	49	J. Pugh
172	200-1	89	G. Greenway	90	G. Greenway
175	51-5	20	J. Barber	20	J. Hill
176	1030	11	J. Hargreaves	11	J. Hargreaves
181	881	465	J. Hayes	465	J. Hayes
183	173	4¾	Hemmings & Edney	4¾	J. Johnson
186	277	58	J. Leef	58	J. Leef

194	818	390	S. Harvey	390	S. Harvey
197	951	104	R. C. Mission	104	R. C. Mission
209	637	43	J. S. Polack	43	J. S. Polack
213	172	3962	*J. Edmonds	72	J. Edmonds
217	954	85	R. C. Bishop of New Zealand	85	R.C. Bishop of New Zealand
226	805-6	1187	*J. Shepherd	22	J. Shepherd
228	610-11	3276	P. H. King	3276	Mrs E. Stephenson
229	444-5	25	S. Stephenson	26	S. Stephenson
231	1306	83	H. Sturley	83	H. Sturley
245	526	2000	*Rev H. Williams	2000	Rev H. Williams
251	660-9	733	*Church Miss Soc	733	Church Miss Soc
275	1043	814	Baron de Thierry	No Grant	Scrip in
300	Var		A composite of Kororareka Claims		compensation
353	58	67	T. Bateman	67	T. Bateman
358	789	114	Joubert and Murphy	114	D. N. Joubert
431	1304	596	J. Irving	596	J. Irving
436	89-90	416	C. H. Chambers	416	J. I. Montefiore

M.L. (Maori Land Plan)

3401	51-5	32	J. Barber	32	J. Barber

C. T. (Certificate of Title) V = Volume : F = Folio

V. 37)					
F.224)	409	363	J. Salmon	363	J. Salmon
V. 504)					
F.257)	1307	49	W. Butler	49	W. Butler
V. 501)					
F. 253)	677	52	*Church Miss Soc	52	Church Miss Soc (Patetere)
V.595)					
F. 29)	678	200	*Church Miss Soc	200	Church Miss Soc (Waikuku)

DEEDS PLAN

C.33	—	—	H. D. Snowden	507	H. D. Snowden

SURVEY OFFICE PLAN

423	172	3962	*J. Edmonds	550	Edmonds family (Same claim as O.L.C. Plan 213)
930A	14-22	10315	James Busby	9374	James Busby
949D	—	273	J. Johnson	273	J. Johnson
1281	524	1643	*Rev. H. Williams	1643	Williams 763 Hadfield 440 Hutton 440
2050	393	224	F. Reed	106	Harriet Johnson

DEPOSITED PLAN

982	306	394	G. B. Mair	395	G. B. Mair
1167	—	—	T. Bateman	128	T. Bateman

12400	13	47	J. I. Montefiore	47 J. I. Montefiore
23065	952	—	R. C. Mission	Grant ordered but not made
				First R. C. Mission — Totara
				Point
27702	470	89	B. Turner	89 B. Turner

General Comment

1. With the exception of most of those in the last group, for which there are no O.L.C. Plans, and a few others, the grants are those ordered by the Old Land Claims Commissioner, Mr F. Dillon Bell, and the claim numbers are his sequence, as they are tabulated in his Schedule of Grants in the D-14 of the 1863 Appendices to the Journals of the House of Representatives.

2. Since it is one of the intentions of the compiler to illustrate the activities of land purchasers and settlers at the Bay of Islands, all the grants in that district, as defined by the present County boundary, are shown. It appeared desirable, however, to show also the claims or grants through, or near which, the main routes from the Bay to Hokianga and Whangaroa passed, and this has been done. In addition, the various mission claims and grants in those districts are shown, and those on the sites of modern townships, together with a few of general historical interest.

3. If further information on a grant is sought, its counterpart may be found at the Deeds Registry in Auckland, by reference to Crawford's or Wither's Indexes, and thence to the Deeds Indexes and Registers. The O.L.C. plans do not always show the correct area of the final grant.

4. Where a claim arising from an old land purchase was not settled by Commissioner Bell, and a grant was later made, a claim number may sometimes not be readily applicable. The grant can, however, be easily found in the Registers through the above indexes.

5. In the column 'Area claimed' is shown the area of land disclosed by a proper survey of the claim, (in most cases the O.L.C. plan) which was made for the information of Commissioner Bell, or another authority, not the amount of land originally claimed, which in most cases was merely an estimate, and frequently a very inaccurate one.

6. In the column 'Area granted' is shown the area of land which was granted pursuant to the order of Commissioner Bell, or an earlier or later authority. Some earlier grants were indefeasible, and were not disturbed by Bell.

7. It will be observed that, due to conveyance, or assignment of

interests, between the time of the purchase and the issue of the grant, the claimant was not always the grantee.

8. Since the matter of the land purchases of the Church of England missionaries has been, and remains, a contentious one, the claims of the Church Missionary Society and its personnel are identified by an asterisk. Also a claim by Orsmond, a member of the London Missionary Society.

9. As a matter of interest, it may be noted that at the Bay, the total of the alienated land, that is, the land claimed, is not greatly in excess of that granted, except in the cases of the larger claims of the Church Missionary Society personnel, and James Busby. The difference between the claimed and granted areas is the surplus, which vested in the Crown, a process which caused considerable resentment among the Maori people. However, in round figures, the Bay of Islands County contains 537,000 acres, and the Maori title to less than a quarter of this was extinguished by the Old Land Claimants.

Appendix 5
Petition to his late Majesty from British settlers in New Zealand.

To the King's Most Excellent Majesty

Sire,

May it please your Majesty to allow your faithful, obedient, and loyal subjects, at present residing in New Zealand, to approach the Throne, and crave you condescending attention to their petition, which is called forth by their peculiar situation.

The present crisis of the threatened usurpation of power over New Zealand by Baron Charles de Thierrry, the particulars of which have been forwarded to your Majesty's Government by Charles Busby, Esquire, the British Resident, strongly urges us to make known our fears and apprehensions for ourselves and families, and the people amongst whom we dwell.

Your humble petitioners would advert to the serious evils and perplexing grievances which surround and await them, arising, for the most part, if not entirely, from some of your Majesty's subjects, who fearlessly commit all kinds of depredations upon other of your Majesty's subjects who are peaceably disposed. British property in vessels, as well as on shore, is exposed without any redress to every imaginable risk and plunder, which may be traced to the want of a power in the land to check and control evils, and preserve order amongst your Majesty's subjects.

301

Your petitioners are aware that it is not the desire of your Majesty to extend the colonies of Great Britain; but they would call your Majesty's attention to the circumstances of several of your Majesty's subjects having resided in New Zealand for more than twenty years past, since which their numbers have accumulated to more than five hundred, north of the river Thames alone, many of whom are heads of families. The frequent arrival of persons from England and the adjacent colonies is a fruitful source of further augmentation. Your petitioners would, therefore, humbly call your majesty's attention to the fact, that there is at present a considerably body of your Majesty's subjects established in this island, and that owing to the salubrity of the climate, there is every reason to anticipate a rapidly rising colony of British subjects. Should this colony continue to advance, no doubt means would be devised whereby many of its internal expenses would be met, as in other new countries. There are numbers of landholders, and the Kouri Forests have become, for the most part, the private property of your Majesty's subjects.

Your humble petitioners would also entreat your Majesty's attention to the important circumstance that the Bay of Islands has long been the resort of ships employed in the South Sea fishery and the merchant's service, and is in itself a most noble anchorage for all classes of vessels, and is further highly important in affording supplies and refreshment to shipping. There are also several other harbours and anchorages of material important to the shipping interest, in situations where British subjects have possessions and property to a large amount. The number of arrivals of vessels in the Bay of Islands, during the last three years, has been considerably on the increase. At one period thirty-six were at anchor, and in the course of the six months ending June, 1836, no less than one hundred and one vessels visited the Bay.

Your petitioners would further state, that since the increase of the European population, several evils have been growing upon them. The crews of vessels have frequently been decoyed on shore, to the great detriment of trade, and numberless robberies have been committed on shipboard and on shore by a lawless band of Europeans, who have not even scrupled to use firearms to support them in their depredations. Your humble petitioners seriously lament that when complaints have been made to the British Resident of these acts of outrage, he has expressed his deep regret that he has not yet been furnished with the authority and power to act, not even the authority of a civil magistrate to administer an affidavit.

Your humble petitioners express, with much concern, their conviction that unless your Majesty's fostering care be extended towards them, they can only anticipate that both your Majesty's subjects and also the aborigines of this land will be liable in an increased degree to murders, robberies, and every kind of evil.

Your petitioners would observe that it has been considered that the confederate tribes of New Zealand were competent to enact laws for the proper government of this land, whereby protection would be afforded in all cases of necessity; but experience evidently shows that, in the infant state of the country, this cannot be accomplished or expected. It is acknowledged by the chiefs themselves to be impracticable. Your petitioners, therefore, feel persuaded that considerable time must elapse before the chiefs of this land can be capable of exercising the duties of an independent government.

Your humble petitioners would, therefore, pray that your Majesty may graciously regard the peculiarity of their situation, and afford that relief which may appear most expedient to your Majesty.

Relying upon your Majesty's wisdom and clemency, we shall ever pray Almighty God to behold with favour and preserve our gracious Sovereign, and beg humbly to subscribe ourselves, &c., &c.

Richard Holtom
John MacDiarmid
Hugh McLever
Benjamin Turner, his + mark
James R. Clendon
J. W. Bayman
H. Shirley
J. Chapman, *Church Missionary Catechist*
J. Morgan, *ditto*
W. T. Fairburn, *ditto*
Sam. M. Knight *ditto*
The Rev. Alfred N. Brown, *Church Missionary*
J. A. Wilson, *Church ditto Catechist*
James Preece, *ditto*
Edward Clementson
James Farrow
R. Parry
J. A. Macleod
Samuel Jones
P. Tapsell

James Hawkins
Thomas Butler, *son to the Rev. Mr Butler, late Church Missionary*
Gilbert Mair
Robert Davies
Richard Davies, *Church Missionary Catechist*
James Kemp, *ditto*
Henry William, *son of Chairman of Church Missionary Committee*
William Richard Wade, *Church Missionary Catechist*
Charles Baker, *ditto*
John Fairburn, *son of Church Missionary Catechist*
Wm. Powditch
Henry P. Dunman
Dominick Ferari
Wm. Curtis
Henry Beasley, his + mark
George Hawkes

303

Thos. D. Grenville
W. Mullins, his + mark
Thomas Phillips, his + mark
Thomas Burgess, his + mark
The Rev. Nathaniel Turner
  Wesleyan Missionary
The Rev. William Woon *ditto*
The Rev. James Wallis *ditto*
The Rev. John Whitely *ditto*
R. H. Smith
E. Meurant
William Alexander
David Robertson
Thomas Spicer
W. T. Green
The Rev. Henry Williams,
  Chairman of Church
  Missionary Committee
John Wright
A. L. W. Lewinton
William Saunders
George Gage, his + mark
John Fell
John Henry Lewis
H. M. Pilley *Church Missionary*
  Catechist
John Flatt, *ditto*
Samuel Williams, *son of Rev. H.*
  Williams, Chairman of
  Church Missionary Committee
The Rev. William Williams,
  brother of Chairman of
  Church Missionary Committee
H. Boyle
George Hull
William Dodson
W. F. Brown
John Coune
John Fogarty
William Davies, *son of Church*
  Missionary Catechist
John Bedggood
James Davies, *son of Church*

John James, his + mark
James Buller
John Wright
Joseph W. Wright
Robert Hunt
James Reeve
Thomas Kelly
Dennis B. Cochrane
R. W. Nickell
G. F. Russell
H. Chapman
Henry Harrison, his + mark
F. R. Lomerston
James Honey
George Paton
Andrew Reading
Thomas Jones
Charles Darey
John Baker, his + mark
J. W. Cleland
Richard Mariner
M. O. Brien
Francis Bowyer
George Haggey
Robert Augur
John Mawman
William Waters, his + mark
Robert Campbell, his + mark
Alexander Greig
W. Cook
John Dinney, his + mark
William Gardiner
William Greene
Samuel Eggart
H. R. Oakes
Mathew Marriner
John Grant
Henry Button
W. Smith
B. McGurdy
Robert Day
John Shearer
George Gardner

304

Missionary Catechist
G. Clarke, *ditto, and Secretary of the Church Missionary Committee.*
James Kemp, jun., *son of Church Missionary Catechist*
James Stack, *Church Missionary Catechist*
John Skelton
John Bennir
Henry Davies
Thomas Cooper
Robert Lawson
W. H. Curtis
Charles Smith, his + mark
A. J. Ross, M. D.
B. Ashwell, *Church Missionary Catechist*
J. S. Polack
Philip H. King, *son of Church Missionary Catechist*
John Fowler
George Norman
William Young
William Pepplewell
W. Oakes
Thomas J. Bennington
Charles Davis
S. M. D. Monro
H. Monro
W. Monro
Hugh Minshall, his + mark
Thomas Hardman
Michall Harvey
William Smith, his + mark
Benjamin Baker, his + mark
Peter Lynch
Edward Sullivan
Thomas McDonnel, *lieut. R. N.*
Thomas Gales
W. Taylor
Nelson Gravatt

Thomas Wing
Flower Russell
James McNamara
John Fagan
Thomas Graham
W. Smith
Henry Hadder
James Shepherd, *Church Missionary Catechist*
John Edmonds, *Church Missionary Catechist*
Benjamin Nisbet
James N. Shepherd, *son of Church Missionary Catechist*
Peleg Wood
George Clarke, jun *son of Church Missionary Catechist*
Thomas Byan, his + mark
Henry Sonsheil
John Fox, his + mark
Alexander Stephen
Charles Bawn
Philip P. Perry
George Greenway
James Greenway, jun.
John Egerly
Roger K. Bullen
Charles John Cook
Jack Monk
James Lowden
Peter Toohey
Thomas Turner, *Son of the Rev. N. Turner, Wesleyan Missionary*
James Johnson
William Walker
Peter Greenhill
George Coker
Henry Benderson
William Potter
Jno. J. Montefiore
Thomas Florance
Thomas Wheatland, his + mark

James Howland, his + mark
James G. Brane
Richard Fairburn, *son of*
 Church Missionary Catechist
Thomas Johnson
John Best

John King, *Church Missionary*
 Catechist
William Spence King, *son of*
 Church Missionary Catechist.

Appendix 6
THE
KORORARIKA ASSOCIATION,
formed by the undersigned
HOUSEHOLDERS OF KORORARIKA
and its vicinity
TUESDAY, MAY 23, 1838.

This Association has been formed in consequence of the absence of any Magisterial Authority in the Bay of Islands, to frame Laws for the better regulation of matters connected with the welfare of the Inhabitants, both European and Native. The limits of this Association are thus defined:— From Matavy or Brind's Bay, in a straight line across the land to Oneroa, or the Long Sandy Beach, and all the land that is bounded by the coast from the Beach to the Bay.

Resolution 1st:— That in the event of any act of aggression being committed on the Persons or Property of Members of this Society, by the Natives of New Zealand or others, the individuals of this Association shall consider themselves bound to assemble together, (armed, if necessary on being called up to do so), at the dwelling of the person attacked; and if any member shall refuse, he shall be fined Five Pounds sterling; but if the person attacked be at fault, he shall be fined One Pound sterling.

Resolution 2nd:— That no Mariner or Mariners shall be enticed to run away, or to leave any vessel for the purpose of being secreted, nor shall known runaways be received or harboured by any Member, and that if any member shall commit such an offence, he shall pay for each mariner so enticed away, received, secreted, or harboured, a fine of Ten Pounds sterling

Resolution 3rd:— That if any mariner shall absent himself from the vessel to which he belongs, contrary to the Act of William the Fourth for Merchant Seamen, and the Captain of the vessel, or his Officers, make no application to this Association for a space of four clear days after the said Mariner has left the vessel, then such person shall not be considered to be a runaway.

Resolution 4th:— That every Member shall consider himself bound to aid any Commander of a vessel, who may apply for the recovery of runaway sailors, who may be at Kororarika, or in its vicinity, within the prescribed time mentioned in Resolution 3rd., and if any member shall refuse to give such aid, he shall pay a fine of Five Pounds sterling.

Resolution 5th:— That if any person be reported to have committed a robbery on any of the Inhabitants of Kororarika, or in its vicinity, he shall be obliged to appear before at least seven Members of this Association, one of whom shall preside over the proceedings, and they shall examine witnesses in proof of the person's guilt or innocence, and if the evidence goes to prove the guilt of the person so accused, then it shall be necessary for the seven Members to agree unanimously before the accused be pronounced guilty; and if they agree, then the guilty person shall be forwarded to the British Resident to be dealt with as he may think fit, but, if the British Resident refuses to act, then the guilty person shall be punished according to Local Laws, which necessity may compel us to frame.

Resolution 6th:— That if a Member or any other person residing at Kororarika, or in its vicinity, shall receive any property knowing it to have been stolen, and not make report thereof to this Association, he shall be dealt with as a thief would be, according to the foregoing Resolution.

Resolution 7th: That if any boat be landed at Kororarika, for the purpose of business, or, that brings sailors who are on liberty to the house of any of the Members of this society, and the oars and boat be given in charge of the said Member, and such oars and boat be stolen, then all the Members called upon shall exert themselves to the utmost of their power for the recovery of the stolen property and in case of refusing to do so, each shall be fined Five Pounds sterling.

Resolution 8th:— That if any Inhabitant of Kororarika, or its vicinity, refuses to conform to the foregoing Resolutions, he not being a Member of this Society, every Member shall unite to oblige such a person to abide by the Laws, and if any Member refuse, he shall be fined Ten Pounds sterling.

Resolution 9th:— That the Householders or Landholders who may have a house, or houses, or land to let, shall hereafter be obliged to enter into an agreement with their tenant, or tenants, to conform to the foregoing Resolutions, and if necessary, to call on any Members of this Association, to enforce the Laws; and in the event of such landlord neglecting, or refusing to do so, he shall be fined Twenty Pounds sterling, and if any Member shall refuse to give any help in his power to the Landlord for the purpose above named, he shall be fined Ten Pounds sterling.

Resolution 10th:— That if any tenant, or tenants of any Member of this Society or Association shall refuse to pay the rent of the premises he occupies, or will not quit in case of non-payment, it shall be considered right to call in at least five Members to arbitrate the matter, and the aforesaid landlord or tenant, or tenants, shall be bound to abide by their decision.

Resolution 11th:— That this Association shall meet once a month in the house of one of the Members, and the Chairman, Deputy Chairman, and other persons then chosen, shall be the four officers for the ensuing month, to take cognisance of any matter coming under the foregoing Resolutions, and that no Officer shall receive any emoluments for his services.

Resolution 12th:— Should any of the four Officers for the ensuing month be obliged to absent himself, or themselves, and give a satisfactory reason to the Chairman, another Member, or Members, shall be chosen in his or their room for the month, and on the absent Member or Members returning, he or they shall be obliged to serve the time he or they have been absent, in relief of the Member, or Members, taking his or their place; or, if either of the four absent himself *on the day of the meeting,* three to form a quorum, of which the Chairman or Deputy Chairman to be one.

Resolution 13th: That every Member of this Association shall provide himself as soon as possible with a good musket and bayonet, a brace of pistols, a cutlass, and at least thirty rounds of ball cartridge, and that the said arms and ammunition shall be inspected at any time by an Officer appointed for that purpose.

Resolution 14th:— That to form a fund to defray the expenses of this Association, each Member shall pay at the next General Meeting, Ten Shillings, and Two Shillings a month afterwards.

Resolution 15th:— That no person shall be allowed to become a Member of this Association, who may reside out of the limits as before defined, until all these Resolutions have been made and carried, and then, any person so described wishing to join the Society, shall, on application, be proposed at the first General Meeting afterwards, and be ballotted for at the next meeting, or be elected, or rejected, by a show of hands.

(As printed in the 'Bay of Islands Observer', May 26th., 1842.)

Bibliography

Manuscript Sources:
Barthorp, Major M. J., of Jersey, historian of the 58th Regiment. Letter to the author.
Boultbee, John, Journal of. A.T.L.
Chapman, Rev. T., *Letters and Journals.* A.P.L.
Clendon Papers. A.P.L.
Johnson, Dr John, 1840, Colonial Surgeon in New South Wales. A.P.L.
Mair Papers. These were lent to the author in 1944 by the late Gilbert Mair, grandson of the original Gilbert in New Zealand. In that year he advised that other material was in other places, and since then much Mair material has been lodged in the Auckland Public Library. However, in late years, the author has been unable to find, at the library or elsewhere, some of the matter which he quotes, and which he obtained from Mr Mair in 1944. But any that is quoted here may be used with confidence, since the source, and its existence at the time, is in no doubt.
Maning Papers. A.P.L.
Meurant, E., Journal of. A.P.L.
Taonui Manuscript, 1849, A.I.L. This is in Maori, but Mr D. Simmons has done a translation.
Te Rawhiti Block Committee's Minute books. A.I.L., MSS. No. 895, (in the author's opinion).
Thierry, de, C.P.H. 'Historical Narrative of an Attempt to Form a Settlement in New Zealand.' A.P.L.
White, John, Papers. A.P.L. Contains an account of the battle between Heke's and Kawiti's people, and Imperial troops, at Lake Omapere.
Worsfold, Louisa. Letter to the author.

Official Sources: (including Anglican Church Records)
Appendices to the Journals of the House of Representatives. A.P.L.
Busby, J. Dispatch No. 36, British Resident to The New South Wales Government. (Returns of shipping at the Bay of Islands, 1833.) A.N.L.
Chief Surveyor, Auckland, Records of, as below:
Deposited Plans and Deeds Record Plans.
Maori Land Plans
Old Land Claim Files (copies) Originals in National Archives.
Old Land Claim Plan Register.
Old Land Claim Plans.

Survey Office Plans.
District Land Registrar, Auckland, Records of, as below:
Crawford's Index to the Deeds Indexes.
Deeds Indexes
Deeds Registers.
Land Transfer Title Registers.
Wither's Index to the Deeds Indexes.
Gazette Extraordinary, New Zealand, No. 1, C.M.S. Press, Paihia.
A.P.L.
House of Lords, Select Committee of the. Report on the State of the
Islands of New Zealand. B.P.P. No. 680. A.P.L.
Maori Land Court, Tai Tokerau, Minutes of the, Whangarei.
Old Land Claim Files. National Archives, Wellington.
Treaty of Waitangi (facsimiles). Government Printer, 1960.
Turton, H.H.. Deeds of Old Private Land Purchases. Office of the
Chief Surveyor, Auckland.
Waimate Church Registers. Auckland Diocesan Office.

Published Works:
(Place of publication is shown where this is outside New Zealand)
Anderson, J. C. and Petersen, G.C., *The Mair Family*. 1956.
Barton, J. *Earliest New Zealand*. 1927.
Bays, P. *A Narrative of the Wreck of the* Minerva. Cambridge, 1831.
Best, A. D. W. The Journal of (Taylor, N. M. ed) 1966.
Binney, J. *The Legacy of Guilt*. 1968.
Buick, T. L. *New Zealand's First War*. 1926.
Buick, T. L. *The Treaty of Waitangi*. 1914.
Bunbury, T. *Reminiscences of a Veteran*. 3 vols. London, 1861.
Burrows, R. 'Extracts from a Diary Kept ... during Heke's War in
the North in 1845.' 1886.
Colenso, W. *The Signing of the Treaty of Waitangi*. 1890.
Collins, D. *An Account of the English Colony in New South Wales*. 2
vols. London, 1798.
Cook, J., *Captain Cook's Journal* ... etc. (Wharton, W. J. L. ed.)
London, 1892.
Cowan, J. *The New Zealand Wars*. 2 vols. 1955, 1956.
Cowan, J. *A Trader in Cannibal Land*. 1956.
Cruise, R. A. *Journal of a Ten Months Residence in New Zealand*.
London, 1824.
Darwin, C. and Fitz Roy, R. *The Surveying Voyages of H.M.S's.*
Adventure *and* Beagle. 3 vols. London, 1839.
Darwin, C. *Journal of Researchers During the Voyage of H.M.S.*

Beagle (This is volume 3 of the above).

Davidson, J. W. and Scarr, D. *Pacific Island Portraits.* 1970.

Davis, C. O. *The Life and Times of Patuone.* 1876.

Dillon, P. *Narrative and Successful Result of a Voyage ... to Ascer tain the Actual Fate of La Perouse's Expedition ...* 2 Vols. London, 1829.

Dunbabin, T. *Sailing the World's Edge.* London, 1931.

Earl, A., *A Narrative of Nine Months Residence in New Zealand in 1827. 1909.*

Elder, J. R. *Letters and Journals of Samuel Marsden.* 1932.

Elder, J. R. *Marsden's Lieutenants.* 1934.

Encyclopaedia of New Zealand, Government Printer, 3 vols., 1966.

Fitz Roy, R. *Remarks on New Zealand in 1846.* London, 1846.

Glue, W. A. *The History of the Government Printing Office,* 1966.

Hall, T. D. H. *Captain Joseph Nias and the Treaty of Waitangi.* 1938.

Healy, E. T. 'Old Land Claims.' *New Zealand Draughtsmen's Journal,* vol. 1, No. 6, March 1961.

Kelly, L. G., *Journals of the Polynesian Society,* vol. 47.

Kelly, L. G. *Journals of the Polynesian Society,* vol. 49.

Kelly, L. G. *Marion du Fresne at the Bay of Islands,* 1951.

Kent, G., *Company of Heaven.* 1972.

King, M. M. *Port in the North.* 1940.

Lang, J. D. *New Zealand in 1839.* London, 1839; Sydney, 1873.

Lee, I. *The Log-books of the Lady Nelson.* 1915.

McCrae, A. *Journal Kept in New Zealand in 1820.* 1928. A.T.L. Bulletin No. 3.

McLintock, A. H. *Crown Colony Government in' New Zealand.* 1958.

McNab, R. *From Tasman to Marsden.* 1914.

McNab, R. *Historical Records of New Zealand.* 2 vols, 1908, 1914.

McNab, R. *Murihiku and the Southern Islands.* 1907.

McNab, R. *The Old Whaling Days.* 1913.

Markham, E. *New Zealand, or Recollections of it.* (E. H. McCormick ed.) 1963.

Marshall, W. B. *A Personal Narrative of Two Visits to New Zealand in H.M.S.* Alligator *A. D. 1834.* London, 1836.

Martin, S. McD. *New Zealand in a Series of Letters.* London, 1845.

M'Cormick, R. *Voyages of Discovery in the Arctic and Antarctic Seas and Round the World.* 2 vols, London, 1884.

Moore and Barton, *Banking in New Zealand.* 1935.

Nicholas, J. L. *Narrative of a Voyage to New Zealand ...* etc. 2 vols, London, 1817.

Owens, J. M. R. *Prophets in the Wilderness.* 1974.

Pakeha Maori (F. E. Maning). *Old New Zealand.* (Lord Pembroke ed.) London, 1884.

Polack, J. S. *New Zealand, being a Narrative of Travels and Adven tures.* 2 Vols, London, 1838.

Pompallier, J. B. *History of the Catholic Church in Oceania.* 1888.

Ramsden, E. *Busby of Waitangi.* 1942.

Roberton, J. B. W. *Journals of the Polynesian Society,* vol. 78, No. 2.

Robinson, H. *A History of the Post Office in New Zealand.* 1964.

Rogers, L. M. *The Early Journals of Henry Williams.* 1961.

Ross, R. M. *New Zealand's First Capital.* 1946.

Rutherford, J.. *Hone Heke's Rebellion, 1844-1846.* Auckland University, 1947.

Rutherford, J. *The Founding of New Zealand.* 1940.

Savage, J. *New Zealand, Particularly the Bay of Islands ... etc.* London, 1807.

Scholefield, G. H. *Captain William Hobson.* 1934.

Sharp, A. *Duperry's Visit to New Zealand in 1824.* 1971.

Sherrin, R. A. A. and Wallace, J. H.. *Early History of New Zealand.* 1890.

Simmons, D.. *Journals of the Polynesian Society,* vol. 78, No. 1.

Smith, S. P. *Maori Wars of the Nineneenth Century.* 1910.

Smith, S. P. *'The Peopling of the North.' Journals of the Polynesian Society,* supplement to vol. 5.

Sweetman, E. *The Unsigned New Zealand Treaty.* Melbourne, 1939.

Thomson, A. S. *The Story of New Zealand,* 2 vols, London, 1859.

Wards, I. *The Shadow of the Land.* 1968.

Wilkes, C. *Narrative of the United States Exploring Expedition.* U.S., 1845.

Williams, J. B.. Journal of, 1842-1844. (Kenny, R. W. ed.) 1956.

Wilson, E. W. *Land Problems of the New Zealand Settlers in the Forties.* 1935.

Wright, O. *New Zealand, 1826-1827.* 1950.

Wright, O. *The Voyage of the* Astrolabe, 1840. 1955.

Yarborough, A.. *Journals of the Polynesian Society,* vol. 15.

Yarwood, A. T. *Samuel Marsden, the Great Survivor.* 1977.

Yate, W. *An Account of New Zealand,* London, 1835.

Newspapers:

Auckland Times, 18 October 1842; Auckland. A.P.L.

Bay of Islands Advocate. Published in December, January and February, 1842-3, Kororareka. Not referred to. (See Hocken, T. M. *Bibliography of New Zealand Literature,* p.107).

Bay of Islands Observer, January 1842, 2 June 1842, Kororareka. A.P.L.

New Zealand Advertiser and Bay of Islands Gazette, 8 September 1840, 24 September 1840, 1 October 1840, 8 October 1840, 30 December 1840, Kororareka. A.P.L.

Southern Cross, 13 January 1852, Auckland. A.P.L.

Miscellaneous:

Bay of Islands County, Index map of. First sheet, one inch equals one mile. Survey Office, Auckland, September 1888. Printed by Wilson and Horton. Shows the Old Land Claims in the area. (in the author's possession.)

Lee, J. R. Historical Maps of the Bay of Islands. Historic Places Trust, 1970.

New Zealand Temperance Society, Report of the Formation and Establishment of the Paihia, 1836. A.P.L.

Index

Active, brig, 62-7, 73, 80, 89-91, 126, 129, 131, 140, 166
Active, schooner, 164
Adele, 207
Adonis, 38
Ahu-toru, of Tahiti, 19
Akaroa, Frenchat, 183, 233
"Akow" (Kau?), 155
Albion, 43, 53, 60
Alexander, William, 186
Alligator, HMS, 56, 152, 177-8
"Amoongha" (Munga?), 155
Anderson —, 97
Ann, 53, 60-1, 145
Anna Watson, 236
Anne, 94, 155, 160
Antarctic Expedition, McCormick, 186
Argo, 37-8, 60
L'Artemise, 221
Asp, 111
Astrolabe, 232
Atiawa, tribe, 32
Atlanta, 55
Atlantic, 210
Atlas, 242
L'Aube, 233, 247
Auckland, 13, 81, 197, 213, 236-7, 240-1, 247, 259-60, 268
Auckland Provincial Council, 124
Auckland Times, 234
Auha, of Ngapuhi, 25, 32, 35, 151
Auporo, of Waimate, 33
Aupouri, tribe, 31
Australia, 12, 27, 60, 67, 150, 182
Awarua River, 98

Baker, Rev. Charles, 180, 189, 215-16
Banks, J., 17, 28
Banks Peninsula, 208
Barnes, Capt., 61, 66, 72
Bathurst, Earl, 100
Battersby —, 186
The Bay of Islands Advocate, 244
Bay of Islands Observer, 241, 243
Bay of Plenty, 16, 32, 81
Bay of Treachery (Bay of Islands), 24, 148
Bays, Capt. P., 154-8
Beagle, HMS, 153, 179
Bean —, 107
Beckham, Capt., 241, 244, 253-5, 258
Bell, F. D., Land Claims Commissioner, 13, 161, 215, 238
Bennett, Capt. L. L., 209-10
Berry, Alexander, 49-55, 68, 89
"Bethel", 109
Besent, John, 47-8
Bigge, Commissioner, 71, 100
Bickersteth, Rev. E., 173
Biddle, Henry, 192
Birnie, Capt., 42
Black and Green, Messrs, 235
Bligh, Capt. W., Governor, 41, 45-6, 49
Bond —, 192
Bougainville, Capt., 19
Boultbee, John, 124
Bounty, 41
Bounty Island, 60

314

Bourke, Sir R., Governor, 171-3, 175, 177, 182-3, 200-1, 204

Boyd, 11, 25, 32, 43, 52, 54-7, 60, 62-3, 68, 96, 113

Boyle, James, 89

Brampton, 109-14, 129, 131

Brampton Reef, 112, 262, 264

Bream Bay, 65

Brett, Sir Piercy, 15

Brewer, W. V., 212

"Brian Boru", 126

Bridge, Major C., 263-4, 267, 270

Bright, J. F., MRCS, 235

Brilliant, 210

Brind, Capt. W. D., 111, 125, 129, 148, 154-5, 158-9, 247

Brind, Isabella, 247

Brind's Bay, 148

Brisbane, Governor, 132, 173

Britannia, 29, 42-3, 122

British Resident and Residency, 13, 171-7, 192, 200, 229, 270

British Sovereign, HMS, 263

Britomart, HMS, 232-3

Brothers, 42-3, 75, 97

Broughton, Betsy, 53

Bruce, George, 41, 46-7, 57

Buffalo, HMS, 38, 49, 227

Bull, Thomas, 247

Bunbury, Major, 227-8, 230-2, 237

Bunker, Capt. Eber, 28-9, 42, 122

Burr —, 271

Burrows, Rev. R., 257, 259, 263, 268

Busby, James, 13, 148, 162, 164-5, 168-9, 171-9, 181-4, 187, 189, 191-3, 197, 199-203, 208, 210, 214, 217-19, 221-3, 225, 229, 236, 240, 245-6, 249

Busby, Mrs, 175

Butler, Rev. J., 34, 76, 79, 87, 89-99, 104-7, 110, 113-4, 123, 131, 146, 153

Butler, Mrs, 92

Butterworth —, 186

Camden, Lord, 37

Cafler —, 165

Campbell —, 74

Cape Brett (Rakaumangamanga), 13, 15-16, 18-19, 34, 47, 53

Cap Quarre, 19

Cape of Good Hope, 19, 52-3

Carlisle family, 78, 80

Catherine, 74, 94

Catholic chapel, shrine of St. Peter Chanel, 206

Cavalli Islands, 16, 29, 63, 89

Cecile, Capt., 205-7

Ceroni, Capt., 48-50, 55

Chace, Capt. S. R., 42, 53-4, 60, 62

Chalk —, 209-10

Chapman, Rev. T., 178

Chatham Islands, 145, 206, 247

Chisholm, J. M., 186

Church Missionary Society, 12, 58, 60, 62, 66, 78, 87-8, 91, 103-4, 108-9, 129, 134, 137, 139, 141-2, 146, 153, 172, 180, 185, 189, 201-2, 215-6, 272-3

Church Missionary Society's land purchases for Mission families, 215-6

The City of Edinburgh, 49-53, 68, 89, 122, 155

Clarke, Capt., 143

Clarke, George, 112, 139, 142, 146, 152, 184, 215

Clarke —, sealing master, 99-100

Clayton, Capt., 212

Clendon, Capt. J. R., 160, 163-4, 175-6, 181, 184-5, 191, 193, 197, 207, 210-3, 217-8, 225-6, 230-1, 241-6, 266

Clendon Cove, 21, 242

Clendon, Mrs, 261

du Clesmeur, 19-21, 23
Cloudy Bay, 198, 242
Cole —, 186
Colenso, Rev. W., 224-5, 229, 248, 272
Commerce, 42-3, 48-9
Comte de Paris, 208, 233
Conroy, Sawyer, 74
Conway, 155
Convicts, Australia, 27, 42, 67, 72, 91, 128, 143, 160, 169, 185, 195
Cook, William, 124, 128, 165
Cook, Bert, 124
Cook, Lieut. James, RN, 11, 13, 15-20, 26-7, 32, 122
Cook's Strait, 200, 243
Cooper —, 165
Cooper and Levery, 127
Coquille, 112, 115
Coromandel, 38, 97, 98, 99
Cossack, 113
Cretan, 76
Crozet, Capt., 22-24
Cruise, Capt., RA., 83, 96, 123
Cunningham —, 186
Customs, HM, 166, 176, 231, 241, 250, 254, 267

Daedelus, HMS, 28-9, 63
Dalrymple, Capt., 46
Daphne, HMS, 267
Darling, Governor, 86, 115, 168, 173
Darwin, Charles, 162, 179
Davis, C.O., 81
Davis, Miss, 137
Davis, Rev. R., 146, 152, 153, 157, 215, 257
Davis, Thomas, 53
Day, Robert, 124, 165, 192
Dean, Capt. E., 156-158
Declaration of Independence of NZ, 182-4

Despard, Lieut. Col. Henry, 264-70
Diana, 55, 73
Dillon, Capt. Peter, 62, 111, 119, 122, 124-7, 139, 166, 183
Dix, Capt., 113
Dolphin, 259
Doubtless Bay, 17-18, 20, 28
Downie, Capt., 97
Doyle, Edward, 201
Dragon, 114-5, 131, 135
Dromedary, HM Storeship, 72, 82-3, 92-103, 123
Duke of Marlborough Hotel, 126
Duke, Capt. R., 111, 113, 126, 128, 139, 143-4, 154, 186
Dunbabbin, Thomas, 85
Duperrey, Capt., 40, 112, 115, 124
Durham, Earl of, 192
D'Urville, Capt. Dumont, 95, 145, 166

Eagar, G. A. and Co., 234
Earle, Augustus, 71, 82-3, 90, 119, 127-8, 141, 143, 186
East Cape, 81
East India Company, 27, 122, 200
East Indies, 27, 47
Echo, 93
Edgar, Charlotte, 42-3
Edmonds, John, 215
Edney —, 186
Egmont, Mount, 19
Elphinstone, 268
Eliza, 48
Elizabeth, 43, 150, 156, 158, 160
Emily, 125
English Bay, 235
Endeavour, 15-18
England, Maori visitors to, 40, 60, 98, 103
Enterprize, 177
d'Entrecasteau, Capt., 126

Erie, 176
Evans —, 196
Ewels —, 97
Experiment, 56

Fairburn, W. T., 107, 143, 146, 216
Fairfowl, Dr, 71, 100
La Favorite, 166-7
Favourite, HMS, 232, 247
Ferret, 37, 39
Fiji, 50
Firearms, trade in, 12, 29, 72, 81-4, 93, 104-5, 117-18, 166
Fishing-net, Maori, 18
Fitz Roy, Capt. R., 153, 179-80, 249-51, 254-5, 257, 260-1, 264, 267-8, 271
Fitzsimmons —, 186
Fitzwilliam, Lord, 40
Flag of NZ, 177-9
Flagstaff on Maiki Hill, 254-8, 271
Flax trade, 27-8, 56-7, 127, 165-6, 193-4
Florance —, 218
Flying Fish, 259
Flying Fish, USS, 232
Fop —, 76
Fortitude, 193, 243
Foveaux, Lieut. Gov., 49
Foveaux Strait, 85
France, 24
Frederick, 60-1
French in New Zealand, 166-7, 182-3, 191, 197, 200-8, 221, 232
du Fresne, Capt. M., 11, 18-29, 34, 37, 47, 89, 95, 115, 122, 148, 167

"Gambier", river, 90
Gardiner, Capt., 144
Gateau, Capt., 206
Gazette Extraordinary, 234
General Gates, 72, 87, 95, 99
General Wellesley, 46

George, *see* Te Aara
George III, King, 60, 104
Gipps, Sir G. Governor, 214, 218-21, 227, 230, 235, 237-8, 254
Girl's War, 34, 154-60, 173, 178, 252
Glatton, 243
Glory, 145
"Gloucester", town of, 87, 148
Goderich, Lord, 168, 171-2
Godfrey and Richmond, Land Claim Commissioners, 237-8
Gordon family, 80
Goulding, James, 201
Graham, Capt., 74
Grand Sachem, 48
Gray, A., 165, 186
Great Southern continent, 15, 19
Greenway, G., 160, 164, 175, 194, 198
Grey, Capt. Geo., Governor, 238, 253, 267-72
Grimwood, T., 206

Hadfield, Rev. O., 272
Hagerty, Catherine, 42
Hakiro, of Ngapuhi, 21
Hall, W., 35, 60-3, 67, 73-5, 78, 80, 104, 108, 110, 129-30
Hall, Mrs, 63, 67, 74, 148
Hamlin, Mr J., 146, 152
Hannibal, 209-10
Hansen, Capt., 63, 80, 91, 126, 160, 189
Hansen, Mrs, 67
Hansen (son of Capt.), 65
Hanson, Lieut., 28, 89
Hapu, 31
Haratua, of Ngapuhi, 252, 266, 270
Harriet, 143
Harrington, 48
Harris —, 186
Harwood, Capt., 143
Hasselberg, Capt., 55

317

Haumere, of Ngapuhi, 270
Hauraki, of Hokianga, 263
Hauraki Gulf, 26, 56, 81, 124, 127, 136
Hautungia, of Ngapuhi, 270
Hawaii, 181
Hawaiki, 26
Hawke's Bay, 183
Hazard, HMS, 254-9, 265
Hector, Cornthwaite, 212, 258-9
Heke, Hone, 13, 32, 37, 175, 204, 225, 250-72
Heke's War, 229, 252-71
Helensville, 97-8
Hengi, of western Bay of Islands, 156-7
Herald, 129, 146, 162
Herald, HMS, 221, 226, 232
Herd, Capt., 108, 126-7, 139
Herd's Point, 127
Heroine, 205, 207
Heta te Haara, of Ngapuhi, 252
Hihi-o-tote, of Ngatiwhatua, 135
Hikitene, of Ngapuhi, 270
Hikurangi, *see* Tautoro
Hikutu, *hapu,* 32, 109, 263
Hinaki, of Panmure, 104
Hingston —, 255, 261
Hinuata, of Ngatirehia, 32
Hobbs, Rev., 109, 134, 137, 147, 273
Hobson, Capt. William, 13, 164, 172, 184, 200, 211, 214, 218-34, 237-8, 241, 244, 248-50
Hobson Hotel, 235
Hobson, Mrs, 227
Hokianga, 16, 22, 25, 32-3, 57, 84, 87-9, 95-103, 113, 127, 129, 137-42, 147, 151, 157, 181-2, 192-3, 199, 203-5, 226, 229
Hokianga, Additional British Resident at, 181-2, 192
Hokianga, Ship-building at, 127, 147, 177

Home, Sir Everard, 264
Hongi, Hare (Hongi Hika's son), 136
Hongi Hika, of Ngapuhi, 12, 25, 32-4, 42, 54, 56, 61-4, 67, 73, 79, 81-9, 95, 98, 104-7, 110-15, 123, 130, 134-142, 151, 252-3
Hookey —, 186
Horeke (Deptford), 127, 147, 177, 193
Hou, of Panmure, 145
Houpa, of the Thames, 65, 81
Hull —, 186
Hulme, Lieut. Col., 254, 261-3
Human heads, preserved, trade in, 85
Hunahuna, battle, 139
Hunt, Capt., 72
Huru, of Te Rawhiti, 28, 29, 63, 89

Imogene, HMS, 172
Independence, later *Tokerau,* 94, 243
India, 27, 47, 200
India, 155, 160
Indian, 94
Indispensible, 43
Inspector, 43, 48, 55
Integrity, 233
Iwi, 31

Jameson, Dr, 234
Jean Bart, 206-7, 247
Jefferson, 61, 66, 72
Johnson, Dr John, Colonial Surgeon, 222, 227-9, 246
Johnson, John, 125-6, 128, 186
Johnston, M. G., 186
Jones, Capt. L., 72

Kaeo, 53-4, 96, 109, 134, 137-8, 140
Kahu-unuunu, a chief, 32
Kahuwera, pa, 95, 123, 155

Kaiapoi, 173
Kaihiki, 32, 103, 109
Kaikohe, 25, 32-4, 73, 90, 135, 140, 147, 151, 199, 252, 254, 257, 266
Kaingaroa, of Ngapuhi, 33, 65, 73
Kaipara, 88, 97-9, 134-5, 139, 168
Kaipatiki, 263, 271
Kaitaia, 146, 228
Kaiteke (or Kemara, or Tareha), of Ngapuhi, 21, 33-4, 110, 135, 223, 225
Kaitoke, of Whangaroa, 48-50
Kaiwaka, 98, 136
Kao, of Hokianga, 253
Kapotai, of Waikare, 252, 263
Kapotai, tribe, 31, 165
Karere, 146
Karetu, 269
Karuhi, of Rangihoua, 111
Kauri gum trade, 128, 162, 193, 212, 260
Kawakawa River, 45, 50, 62, 64-6, 68, 74, 95, 107, 123, 157-8, 160, 163-4, 177, 179, 185, 192, 262, 268-9
Kawhia, 81
Kawiti, Te Ruki, of Ngapuhi, 13, 225, 229, 251-71
Kelly, L., author, 22, 24-5
Kelly, mate of *Venus,* 42
Kemara, *see* Kaiteke
Kemp, J., 107, 142, 146, 215, 253
Kendall, Mrs, 67
Kendall, Rev. T., 61-3, 66-9, 73, 75-80, 88-93, 100-15, 123-4, 134, 144, 146, 182, 199, 203
Kent, Capt., 93, 99
Ker, Capt., 99
Kerikeri, 17, 32-5, 56, 62, 64-5, 73, 87, 91, 97, 100, 105-7, 128, 137-8, 147-8, 152, 189-90, 195, 262-4
Kerikeri, Butler's house at, 146, 153
Kerikeri, mission station, 12, 89, 92, 108, 110, 150, 153
Kerikeri River, 67, 90, 93, 262, 264
Kerikeri, stone store at, 153
Kihi, of Ngapuhi, 228, 247
King George, 53, 72
Kingi, Hori, of Ngapuhi, 270
King, John, 60-1, 63, 67, 73, 75, 88, 96, 151, 190, 215-6, 223
King, Mrs, 63, 66-7, 75
King, Philip Gidley, 27-9, 37-8, 41, 43, 45, 55, 122
King, Thomas Holloway, 66
Kingston, Capt., 55
Kite, of Hokianga, 192, 247
Kiwikiwi, of Ngatimanu, 95, 142, 155-9, 178
Kokouri, of Ngapuhi, 270
Kororareka, 12-14, 34, 45, 50, 57, 62, 66, 91, 94-5, 109, 113, 118-19, 122-8, 141-4, 148, 153-5, 160, 163-6, 177-9, 185-6, 189, 195-9, 204-6, 212-13, 221-2, 228, 230-1, 234-5, 241, 243-7, 253-64, 267, 271
Kororareka Association, 132, 208-9, 222, 235, 241
Kororareka Land Company, 212-3, 236
Kororareka, Town survey, 244
Korokoro, of Ngare Raumati, 34, 48, 62-3, 77, 83, 88-9, 94-5, 123
Kororipo, pa, 33-4, 56, 64, 105
Kotahi, of Ngare Raumati, 27
Kuao, of Ngapuhi, 270

Lady Nelson, 41-2, 46, 56, 91
Lambert, Capt., 177
Lancashire —, 42
Land Claims Commission, 185, 204, 235-8, 246
Land Claims Ordinance, 238
Land Claims Settlement Act, 238
Land Speculation, 214, 217-18, 237-40

Lang, Rev. J. D., 119, 161, 180, 186, 196-7, 212, 216
Langlois, Capt. J., 207-8
Laplace, Capt., 167-8
Lauriston Bay, 18
Lavaud, Capt., 233
Lee, Professor, 79, 103
Leigh, John, 124
Leigh, Mrs, 135
Leigh, Rev. S., 109, 134
Leith, William, 45-7, 56-7, 165
Lewington, Mrs, 261
Lewington, W. J., 236
Long Beach, see Oneroa
Lord —, 253
Luminary, 242

Maanu, see Rewa
McCormick, R., 186
McCrae, Ensign, 71, 82, 100, 105
McCurdy, Hugh, 124, 165
McDiarmid —, 186
McDonnell, Lieut. T., 181-2, 192, 204
McKay, Donald, 186
McLean, John, 186
McNab, R., 193
Macquarie, Gov. L., 46, 49, 59, 63, 66, 92
Mahurehure, *hapu,* 141-2
Maiki Hill, 254, 257-9, 271
Maioha, S., 21
Mair, Gilbert, 128-9, 146, 162-5, 174-5, 184, 193, 208, 213, 217, 231, 236, 240-6, 249, 261
Maketu, of Ngapuhi, 247-8
Manawaora Bay, 18, 21, 88, 95
Manawaora River, 68
Mangakahia River, 98, 135, 189
Mangamuka, 138-9
Mangawhai, 135
Mangonui land purchase, 267
Mangonui Inlet (or River), 17, 32-3,

38-40, 57, 77, 103, 109, 151, 168
Mangungu, mission station, 147
Maning, F. E., 84-5
Manukau Harbour, 88, 99
Maori language, 68-9, 75, 79, 102-3
Maoris as seamen, 37, 70, 83, 126, 131
Maori wars, tribal, 42, 81, 83, 118
Maratea, of Whangaroa, 139
Marianne, 144
Markham, E, 120-1, 153, 179
Marquis de Castries, 19-20, 23-4
"Marquis of Waimate", see Titore Takiri
Marsden Cross, Oihi, 78
Marsden, Martha, 199
Marsden, Rev. S., 12, 37, 40-1, 47, 54-76, 79, 80-1, 85-117, 127-31, 135, 144, 150-1, 155, 158-9, 166, 171, 173, 185, 198-200, 215, 273
"Marsden Vale", (Paihia), 110, 148
Marshall, W. B., 119, 152, 165, 174, 177-8, 180, 184
Maru, of Ngapuhi, 270
Mary Anne, 113, 122
Mascarin, 19-20, 22, 24
Matangi, of Hokianga, 168
Matapo, of Whangaroa, 139
Matara, of Ngatirehia, 38, 49, 51
Mataraua, 33-4
Matauri Bay, 16-17, 54, 63, 140
Matauwhi Bay, 62, 109-10, 114-15, 123-5, 144, 148, 159, 186, 235, 254, 257-8
Matengaha (Matingaro), of Bay of Islands, 52-3
Mathew, Felton, (Acting Surveyor), 219, 221, 229-31, 237, 244
Matilda, 122, 259
Matthew, John, 186
Matuku, of Ngapuhi, 136
Mauinaina, pa, 106
Maungakawakawa, 264

Maungaturoto, 90, 147
Mauritius (Ile de France), 19-20
Mawhi Kairangi, 259
Mayhew, William, 213, 242, 244-5, 250, 256, 271
Mercury, 126, 130, 139
Milne, Capt. R., 271
Minerva, 154
Missionary land purchases, 215-6, 271
Moehanga, of Bream Bay, 40-1, 65
Moetara, of Hokianga, 136, 168
Moewaka, daughter of Rewa, 155, 159
Moka, of Hokianga, 32-3, 67, 135-6
Moka, brother of Hongi, 98
Moka (Kaingamataa), of Ngapuhi, 151
Montefiore, J. I., 186
Moore, Capt., 112, 114, 131
Moore, settler, 186
Mokoia (Panmure), 81, 98, 104, 106-7
Moremonui, 98, 135-6, 140
"Morgan McMarragh", 126
Morley, Anne, 53
Morris, Capt., 55
Motu-Arohia (Roberton Is.) 17, 20, 247
Motuapo, 41
Motukawa, 29
Motukiekie, 20
Motu Tara, 62
Motu Wai (Red Island), 52-3
Moturoa, 67, 93, 159
Motukokako, 15
Moturua, 18, 20-2, 24, 34
"Mt Isabel", 204
Muriwai, of Hokianga, 90, 103, 142, 204
"Murtoch O'Brien", 126
Murupaenga, of Ngatiwhatua, 98, 136
Mutunga, of Ngatirehia, 32

Nanto-Bordelaise Company, 183, 208, 233
Ne, of Hokianga, 16
Nene (Tamati Waaka), of Hokianga, 16, 33, 136, 168, 184, 204, 225, 252-6, 260-71
New South Wales, 27, 29, 46, 59, 67, 72, 140, 172-4, 195, 199, 201, 211, 218, 227, 236, 251
New South Wales New Zealand Company, 47, 75
New Zealand Advertiser and Bay of Islands Gazette, 213, 230, 233-5
New Zealand Banking Company, 128, 213, 242-6
New Zealand, claimed for France, 24
New Zealand Company of 1839, 192, 214, 218, 233
New Zealander, brigantine, 177
New Zealander, whaler, 103
New Zealand Government Gazette, 234, 245
Ngaitawake, *hapu,* 33-4, 151
Ngahuruhuru, of Whangaroa, 138
Ngaitahuhu, tribe, 31
Ngai-te-Rangi, tribe, 42
Ngapuhi, tribe, 12, 16-17, 22, 25, 31-5, 45, 50, 56-7, 65, 73-4, 81, 83, 88, 104, 106-7, 110, 123, 135, 140, 151, 157, 217, 229, 252-3, 267
Ngaraa, of Whangaroa, 39
Ngare Raumati, tribe, 21-2, 31, 33-5, 124
Ngatiawa, tribe, 16, 31-2
Ngatihine, *hapu* of Ngapuhi, 22, 255
Ngatihineira, *hapu,* 151
Ngatikahu, tribe, 31-2
Ngatikorokoro, tribe, of

321

Hokianga, 45
Ngatikura, *hapu,* 151
Ngatikuta, *hapu,* 151
Ngatimanu, tribe, 31, 33-4, 50, 81, 95, 124, 128, 141, 155-7, 160, 192
Ngatimaru, tribe, 35, 104, 106, 124
Ngatimiru, *hapu,* 32-3, 35, 151
Ngati-Paoa, tribe, 81, 104, 106
Ngatiporou, tribe, 42
Ngatipou, tribe, 31-2, 35, 73, 135-6, 138, 151, 253
Ngatirahiri, *hapu,* 32-4, 252
Ngatirangi, *hapu,* 263
Ngatirehia, sub-tribe, 31-2, 35, 73
Ngatitautahi, *hapu,* 33
Ngati Toa, tribe, 106
Ngatiuru, tribe, 21, 31-2, 53, 135-8
Ngatiwai, tribe, 21, 31, 33-4
Ngatiwhatua, tribe, 31, 134-6, 141
Ngaungau, pa, 151
Ngawha, *see also* Ohaeawai, 90
Ngunguru, 165, 236, 242
Nias, Capt. J., 226-7, 232
Nicholas, J. L., 41, 56, 62-5, 67-8, 82, 103
Noa, of Kawakawa, 192
Norfolk Island, 28-9, 38, 49, 61, 122, 143-4
North Cape, 18-19, 29, 130
North Star, HMS, 260-2, 268

O'Connor —, 175
Ohaeawai, 90-1, 147, 190, 252
Ohaeawai, pa, 263-6
Oihi, 33, 39, 41, 64, 65-8, 96, 99, 129
Oihi, mission station, 12, 74-5, 78-82, 108, 110, 130, 146, 150-1
Okaihau, 260, 262
Okiato, *see also* Russell, 160, 163-4, 185, 201, 211, 226, 231, 268
Okura River, 90
Okuratope, pa, 33, 65, 151
Old Bay Road, 147

Old Land Claims, 13, 212
Omapere, lake, 33, 65, 136, 259, 262-4
Omata, 164, 201
Oneroa, 258
One Tree Point (Opua) 148
Onewhero (Red Beach), 262
Oporehu, 139
Opua, port of, 14, 95, 148, 160, 177, 195, 235, 273
Orari (Craig's Point), 165
Orokawa Bay, 11, 22-3
Oromahoe, 252
Orsmond, J. D., 215-16
Oruru, 134
Otamatea River, 136
Otangaroa, 138
Otuihu, pa, 157-60, 178, 184-6, 195, 198-9, 261-2, 269
Owairaka (Mt Albert), 99

Paeroa, pa, 22, 24
Pahangahanga, pa, 151
Paihia, 124, 129, 139, 147-8, 157, 159, 189, 195, 234-5
Paihia, mission station, 12, 14, 34, 85, 90, 109-10, 127-8, 146-7, 150, 153-4, 162, 165, 229
Pakaraka, 190, 228, 252, 259
Pakinga, pa, 25, 140
Panakareao, Nopera, of Kaitaia, 184, 228, 267-8
Panaki, 29
Parakao, 189
Parker, Capt., 55, 73, 76
Paroa, 34, 47, 57, 62, 74, 77, 88-9, 94-5, 99, 123, 156, 158-9, 198, 256
Parramatta, 37, 47
Parramatta, NSW, 39
"Pater Noster Valley", 109, 123
Pattison, Capt., 49, 52-3, 55
Patuone, of Hokianga, brother of Nene, 16, 90, 103, 136, 138, 140-2,

168, 184, 204, 225, 252, 268

Pegasus, 48

Pehi, daughter of Hongi Hika, 155-6, 159

Penantipodes Islands, 42

Pene Taui, of Ngapuhi, 252, 263, 265, 270

La Perouse, Capt., 122, 126

Perseverance, 55

Petitions of 1831 and 1837, 187, 190-1

"Phelim O'Rourke", 126

Philippines, 27, 48

Phillip, A., Governor, 27-8

Philpotts, Lieut., 258-9, 266

Phoenix, 48, 73, 76

Pi, of Waima, 142

Piercy Island, 15, 18

Pikiorei, of Tangitu, 21-2

Piner, J., 186

Pinia, pa, 137

Pipiroa Bay, 231

Piraunui, 263

Pirongia, 107

Poaka, of Hokianga, 253

Pohoriki, of Whangaroa, 29

Point Pocock, 13, 16, 18, 148

Polack, J. S., 30, 71, 84, 123, 163, 166-7, 172, 175, 179-80, 183, 186, 191, 196-9, 217-8, 231, 257

Pomare II, or Whetoi, of Ngatimanu, 95, 109, 123, 142, 145, 156-60, 178, 184-5, 197-9, 252, 261-2, 265, 269

Pomare Nui, of Ngatimanu, 62, 85, 95, 107, 123, 125, 136, 141-2, 144

Pompallier, Rt. Rev. J.B., 179, 205-6, 221, 223, 225, 233, 250, 272

Pororua, of Ngapuhi (at Mangonui), 267

Porpoise, 232

Port Dalrymple, 42

Port Jackson (Sydney), 27-8, 38-9, 41-3, 47-9, 52, 59, 61-2, 67-8, 76, 85, 87, 99, 122-3, 127, 132, 143, 167

Port Marion, 20

Port Pegasus, 124

'Port Te Pouna', 40

Post Office, 163, 232, 241

Pouerua, 90

Powditch, William, 163, 175, 246, 249

Poyner —, 186

Pratt, Rev. J., 92

Prince of Denmark, 85-6

Prince of Wales, 150

Prince Regent, 95, 99

Printing and publishing, *see also* individual newspapers, 150, 153, 241

Providence, 108

Puckey —, 89, 146

Puhi-moana-ariki, eponymous ancestor of Ngapuhi, 31

Puketi, 138

Puketi Forest, 89

Puketohunoa, pa, 269

Puketona, 33-5, 90, 174-5, 190, 228

Puketotara River, 89, 147

Pumuka, of Kawakawa, 258

Pungaere, 138

Pupuke, 138, 140

Purakau, Hokianga, Catholic mission station, 206

Putahi, 263

Pyramus, 199

Queen Charlotte Sound, 26

Rahiri, of Kaikohe and Hokianga, 31-2

Rahiri, settlement, 204

Raiatea, 204

Rainbow, HMS, 144-5, 150

Raine and Ramsay, 127

Rakaumangamanga (Cape Brett),
13, 15
Rangiahua, 203
Rangihoua, 32, 39, 60-1, 65-6, 76,
82, 89, 97, 134
Rangihoua Bay, 39, 73
Rangihoua, pa, 39, 64, 111
Rarawa, tribe, 31, 267
Rattlesnake, 200-1
Rawene, 127
Rawhi, of Ngapuhi, 21-2
Rawhiti, *see* Te Rawhiti
Ray, Capt., 206-7
Razeline Reef, 20
Rebecca Sims, 206-7
Red Beach, *see* Onewhero
Research, 126, 128
Repa, a chief, 268
Reti, of Ngapuhi, 174-5
Rewa, of Ngapuhi, 33-4, 87, 106,
114, 142, 145, 151, 155-7, 160, 167,
225, 231, 247, 252
Rewharewha, *see* Ururoa
Richmond, 209
Richmond (and Godfrey), 237-8
Riggs, Capt., 72, 95
Ringa, Maria, 110, 144
Ririwha (Stephenson's Island), 48
Ritchie —, 175
Roberton, Capt. J., 247
Roberton Island, *see* Motu-
Arohia
Roberton, Mrs E., 247
Robertson, Capt., RN, 257-8
Rogers —, 175
Rongo, Hariata, Hongi's daugh-
ter, 252
Roroa, tribe, 138
Rosanna, 127, 139
Rose —, 186
Ross, Dr, 165, 186
Ross, Sir James Clark, 247
Rotorua, 107

Roux, Lieut., 20-4
Royal Hotel, 235
Royal Sovereign, 111, 155-6, 160,
264
Ruapapaku Is., 193
Ruapekapeka, 13, 260, 268-70
Ruatara, of Ngatirehia, 32, 35, 37,
54, 60-7, 73, 82, 150
Ruhe, of Ngapuhi, 247
'Rum Rebellion', 49
Russell, 14, 128, 148, 160, 208, 230-
7, 241, 244-5, 251, 256, 268
Russell, George, 196
Russell, Lord John, 231

St. Jean Baptiste, 18
St. Louis, USS, 259
Saint Patrick, 115
Salamander, 122
Samuel, 145
Santa Anna, 60
Saracen, 99
Sarah, 113
Savage, Benjamin, 209
Savage, Dr John, 39-40, 65, 98
Schmidt, G. E., 245
Sealing, 27, 42-3, 60, 70, 72, 165-6
Shah Hormuzear, 28
Shand —, 186
Shaw Savill and Albion shipping
line, 178
Shepherd, James, 99-100, 146, 215
Shortland, Willoughby, Acting-
Governor, 226, 228, 246, 249-50
Sinclair, Andrew, Col. Sec., 244,
256
Sir George Murray, 177
Sisters, 126, 139, 143-4, 154
Skinner, Capt., 95-6
Slains Castle, 261-2, 267-8
Slains Castle Rock, 262
Smith, H. G., 250, 256, 271
Smith, John, 217

Smith, S. P., author, 21, 139
Solander, D. C., 17
South America, 53, 115
Southern Cross, 50
Speke, 55, 104
Spicer, T., 186, 197, 246
Spikeman, W., 146
Spence, Capt., 93
Stack, Rev., 134, 137, 273
Stanley, Capt. Owen, 232-3
Star, 48, 52
Stephenson, S., 175, 243
Steward —, 196
Stewart, Capt. W., 50, 124
Stewart's Island, 50, 124, 128, 165
Stivers, Capt., 90
Stockwell, R., 67
de Surville, Capt., 17, 18, 20, 26
Swindells, Capt., 145
Sydney, *see* also Port Jackson, 28, 38, 45, 47, 49, 53-4, 60, 62, 66, 72, 75, 83, 90, 100, 104, 124, 129, 131, 144, 165-6, 193-4, 200-1, 214, 234
Sydney Gazette, 227

Tahapango, of Whangaroa, 32, 136
Tahapirau, of Hokianga, 16
Taheke, 90, 147
Tahiti (Society Islands), 15, 19, 172, 181
Taiamai, 90-1, 97, 147, 252
Taipa, 33
Taiwhanga, of Kaikohe, 136
Takou, 33, 249
Tamaki, 81
Tamati Waaka Nene, *see* Nene
Tangiteroria, 98
Tangitu, pa, 21
Tangiwhare, sister of Turikatuku, 32, 136
Taonui, Makoare, of Hokianga, 32, 90, 168, 184, 252, 260, 262, 264, 268-9

Tapeka, 148
Tapeka Point (Point of Currents), 20, 33
Tapsell, Philip, 111, 144
Tapua, of Hokianga, 16, 33
Tapuaeharuru (Mawhe), pa, 33, 136, 259
Tara, of Ngatimanu, 47-54, 62, 64, 67
Taranaki, 16, 32, 81
Taratara, pa, 138
Tarawaua, 204
Tareha, *see* Kaiteke
Tareha, of Te Tii, 33, 151, 159
Tari, sister of Nene and Patuone, 138
Tasman, Capt. A. J., 15, 19
Tasmania, 42, 47, 62, 72, 128, 195
Taumarere, 107, 269
Taumata tungutu, pa, 151
Taura, son of Kawiti, 263
Taura-tumara, of Hokianga, 17, 32
Tauranga, 97, 111, 129, 183
Tautoro (Hikurangi), 140, 157, 252, 265, 268-9
Tawhai, of Hokianga, 184, 252, 268
Tawkainga, 235
Taylor, Rev. Richard, 216, 223, 272
Te Aara, of Whangaroa, 52, 54, 63, 96, 135, 137
Te Ahuahu, 90, 252, 263-5
Te Atuahaere, of Ngapuhi, 168
Te Awa, of Ngapuhi, 270
Te Haara, of Ngapuhi, 168, 270
Te Hapuku, of Hawke's Bay, 184
Te Harotu, canoe, 16
Te Hinaki, of Ngati-Paoa, 81, 106, 145
Te Homai, canoe, 16
Te Horeta, of Thames, 104
Te Hotete, of Kaikohe, 32-3, 35, 65, 88, 151
Te Hue, cove, 23

Te-Ika-a-Ranga-Nui, 98, 135
Te Kahika, pa, at Lake Omapere, 263
Te Karae, *see* Totara Point
Te Kemara, *see* Kaiteke
Te Koki, of Ngatirehia, 32, 68, 110, 142, 157
Te Kuri (Tacoury), of Manawaora, 21-2, 24
Te Morenga, of Ngapuhi, 42, 67, 81, 98, 136, 159, 168
Temperance Society, 180-1, 191
Te Nana, of Ngapuhi, 151, 198
Te Ngaire, 140
Te Pahi, of Ngatirehia, 12, 25, 31-2, 37-57, 60-1, 67-8, 73, 78, 89
Te Pahi's Island, 39, 41, 55-6
Te Pohui, pa, 96
Te Puhi, of Ngatiuru, 25, 39, 52, 63, 96, 135, 137-8
Te Puna, 32, 38-9, 42-50, 55-6, 62, 64, 66, 76-7, 96, 150-1, 177, 189, 192, 195
Te Puna, mission station, 12, 126, 150-1
Te Pure, Hare, of Ngapuhi, 270
Te Rauparaha, of Kawhia, 106, 173
Te Rawhiti, 28-9, 33-5, 57, 123, 142, 157
Te Ripi, of Ngapuhi, 168
Te Rore, 107, 123, 136
Te Taniwha, of Hauraki Gulf, 26
Te Tihi, of Hokianga, 253
Te Tii Mangonui, 33
Te Tii Waitangi, 252
Te Toke, mission station, 147
Te Totara, pa (Hauraki Gulf), 106
Te Tikitiki, canoe, 16
Te Tumuaki, canoe, 16
Te Wahapu, 128, 162-3, 201, 243, 250, 256, 270-1
Te Wera Hauraki, of Ngapuhi, 135
Te Wherowhero, Potatau, 184, 261

Thames (Hauraki Gulf), 18, 41, 65-6, 75, 83, 97, 99, 106-7, 200
de Thierry, Baron C.P.H., 103, 119, 182-3, 203-4
Thomas, Yves, 23
Thompson, Capt., 52-6, 80, 131
Thomson, Dr A. S., 71, 195
'Tiarrah', of Ngatirehia, 39
Tigris, 121
Tiki, of Ngatimanu, 141
Timber trade (spars, plank, etc.), 27, 29, 45, 51-4, 65, 93-100, 127, 147, 165-6, 185, 193-4, 212, 236, 273
Tiraha, wife of W. Cook, 165
Tirarau, of Mangakahia, 136, 184
Titoki, 189
Titore Takiri, of Waimate (The Marquis of Waimate), 33-4, 85, 126, 142, 145, 151, 156-60, 168, 174, 197-9
Tohua, of Ngapuhi, 270
Tokerau, 243
Toko, of Ngapuhi, 35
Toretore ("Nobby") Is., 163
Tory, 218
Totara Point, Hokianga, 205-6
Toward Castle, 154
Trapp —, 186
Treaty of Waitangi, 13, 94, 184, 222-9, 250
Treaty of Waitangi, Maori dissatisfaction with, 228-9, 248, 252, 256-7
Treaty, unsigned, for Sovereignty of New Zealand, 214
Trial, 74
Tucker, William, 85
Tuhi (or Katikati, or Tupaea), 123
Tuhikura, of Ngatirehia, 32
Tukerehu, of Ngapuhi, 270
Tuki, of Doubtless Bay, 28-9, 63
Tungaroa, of Kaihiki, 108-9

Tupe, of Ngatimanu, 50-4, 67
Turikatuku, of Ngatirehia (wife of Hongi Hika), 32, 136
Turi-o-Kana, of Oihi (Kana), 32, 65, 67
Turner, Benjamin, 124, 163, 165, 186, 196-7, 246
Turner, Mrs, 135, 137
Turner, Rev., 109, 134, 137
Tuwhera, of Hokianga, 16

United States Consulate, 207, 210-11, 225-6, 234, 242, 255
United States Exploring Expedition, 185, 232
United Tribes of New Zealand, The, 184
Upokorau Stream, 138
Uriti, 257
Uru Mihi, wife of Kiwikiwi, 155-7
Urupukapuka, 20
Ururoa, of Whangaroa, 33, 155-9
Urutuki, enemy of Moehanga, 41
Utakura, 260, 271

Vancouver, Capt., 28, 122
Vanikoro, 126
Vansittart, 72
Venus, 38, 42-3, 50, 65, 81
Victoria, 256, 259
"Victoria" (town), 148, 218, 230
Vincennes, 232

Wade, Rev. W., 134, 137
Waetford, C., 245, 250, 261, 271
Wahineiti, *hapu*, 32, 35, 151
Wai, of Ngapuhi, 223
Waihoanga Stream, 89, 138, 147
Waihou River (Thames), 97
Waihou Valley (Hokianga), 89, 100, 138, 147, 204, 260
Waikare River, 65-6, 68, 107, 158, 160, 164-5, 185, 198, 263
Waikato, district, 107, 136, 141
Waikato, of Hikutu, Ngapuhi, etc., 103-6, 192
Waima, 141-2, 147, 199, 264
Waimate, 22, 25, 33-5, 65, 69, 73, 85, 97, 135, 140, 150-1, 168, 189-90, 195, 199, 226, 252, 254-5, 257, 265-7
Waimate Mission Station, 152-3, 162, 265
Waiomio, 259, 262-3, 267-8
Waioruhe River, 90, 147
Waipahihi, of Ngatimanu, 124
Waipao, bay, 20, 24
Waipapa, 100, 147
Wairoa River, 98
Waitangi, 20, 32, 34-5, 73-4, 78, 109, 147-8, 165, 174, 177, 182-4, 189, 257
Waitangi, British Residency, 13-14, 222
Waitangi River, 90, 147, 152
Waitapu, sister of Hongi, 98, 135
Waitemata, 35, 40, 56, 88, 97-9, 226, 229, 233
Waiwhariki, 104, 106
Walker, Capt., 55, 131
Waraki, of Waitangi, 32, 35, 73-4
Warren, 242
Watkins —, 177
Webster, William, 214
Weller, E. and G., 214
Wellington, 143
Wellington (Port Nicholson), 81, 84, 107, 218
Wellman —, Police Magistrate, 237, 244
Wentworth, W. C., 214
Wesleyan Methodist Mission, Hokianga, 147, 190, 272-3
Wesleyan Methodist Mission, Whangaroa, 93, 109, 134-5, 137,

139, 147
"Wesleydale" (Kaeo), 134, 137
Westminister, 222, 227
Westmoreland, 104
Whakaaria, of Ngapuhi, 32, 151
Whakarongo, sister of Auha and
  Whakaaria, 151
Whakataha, pa, 151-2
Whale Rock, 18, 20
Whaling and Whalers, 27-9, 32, 37,
  43, 58, 61, 70, 72, 76, 93-4, 113,
  120-3, 129, 131, 145-8, 176-81, 195,
  197, 203, 207, 210-11, 240, 242, 273
Whananaki, 192
Whangamumu, whaling station,
  124
Whangarei, 42, 88, 98, 106, 134,
  236, 242
Whangaroa, 11, 16, 21, 25, 29, 31,
  33-4, 39, 48-57, 65, 81, 83, 92-6,
  99-100, 109, 130, 134-9, 143, 146,
  168, 190, 246
Whangaruru, 98
Wharepaepae, 140
Wharepoaka, of Rangihoua, 111,
  150, 155
Wharerahi (Wharenui), of Nga-
  puhi, 33, 138, 142, 151, 168
Whareumu, of Ngatimanu, 33-4,
  95, 98, 111, 113, 123, 135, 141-2, 144
Whatitiri, 264
Whe, of Ngapuhi, 270
Wheeler, W. J., 244
Whirinaki, 17, 32, 263

Whitaker, F., 245
White, John, 21, 25
White, W., 130, 134
Whitely, Rev., 273
Wilkes, Commdr, C., USN, 119,
  185, 225
Wilkinson, Capt., 48, 52
William IV, 167, 172, 174, 184, 187
William and Ann, 28, 122
William Hamilton, 209
Williams, J. B., US Consul, 242,
  243, 250
Williams, Rev. H., 79, 93-4, 105,
  109-10, 117-19, 129, 138, 142, 146,
  153-4, 157, 162-3, 171, 181, 184,
  201, 210, 215-19, 221, 223-4, 228,
  246, 253, 256-7, 259-62, 264, 266,
  271-3
Williams, Rev. W., 146, 189, 192,
  272
Willson, Capt., 111
Wilson, William, 235, 246
Wiwiki, Cape, *see* Point Pocock
Woodford, 155, 160
Woon, Rev. W., 273
Worsfold, Mrs Louisa, 194
Wright, Capt. John, 163-4, 175,
  201, 255, 261
Wright, Mrs, 261

Yate, Rev. W., 85, 150-3, 162, 168,
  172, 186, 199

Zebra, HMS, 168

328